Cement Eclipses

Small interventions in the big city

ISBN 978-0-9559121-8-4

The information and images in this book are based on are materials supplied to the publisher by the contributors. While every effort has been made to ensure it's accuracy, Pro-actif Communications does not under any circumstances accept responsibility for any errors or omissions.

A catalogue record for this book is available from the British Library.

First published in Great Britain in 2011 by Carpet Bombing Culture
Cameron House, 42 Swinburne Road, Darlington, Co Durham DL3 7TD
email: books@carpetbombingculture.co.uk

Isaac Cordal 2011

www.carpetbombingculture.co.uk

Little Grey Men Against the Machine

"Aunque emocionarse parece hoy algo anacrónico, hay una tristeza que precede a la melancolía, y esta, a su vez, puede ser el fondo sobre el que se despliega cierta tendencia al pesimismo que no dejó de existir en la tardomodernidad."

"Even though to get emotional these days seems a bit anachronistic, there is a sadness that preceeds melancholy, and that, in its place can be the foundation upon which the tendency toward pessimism in late modernity can be displaced."

So says Vanesa Diaz Otero in her 2009 essay on Isaac Cordal *"El Fracaso de la Persona o Los Muchachos del Cemento"*. And basically she means that a little bit of sadness can be the doorway into a more proactive place. When we let the sadness in we allow ourselves to feel something rather than disconnect our emotions with blank pessimism. The sadness can then be the foundation of something positive.

Yes, the little scenes in Cement Eclipses are somewhat poignant but they do not invite you to weep passively for lost worlds you never knew. They are there to provide a one handed clap to shake you from your reveries and plug you back in to the world.

Boredom is political! And Isaac´s men in grey are an act of defiance against that boredom plain and simple. They respond to the commodification of time by refusing to move. Ford said 'Time is Money!' and although nobody ever really said 'yes' nobody ever quite said ´no' loud enough either.

Otero draws illuminating parallels between the 1973 children´s literature classic 'Momo - Or the Strange Story of the Time Thieves and the Child who Brought the Stolen Time Back to the People' and the Cement Eclipses.

The story (by Michael Ende, Author of classic kids flick ´The Never Ending Story´) describes how an idyllic city is ruined by shadowy men in grey who convince people that they must save time and gradually all the joy of life is sucked away by this process as people stop doing anything 'inessential' such as play. Sound familiar to your own life?

So Cordal's men in grey are a little message of hope in spite of their forlorn appearance and they are there to remind you that pessimism is not common sense, it´s just pessimism.

So make sure you do something inessential today. Go on, the grey men don´t want you to.

Are you afraid of them...?

PUBLIC SWIMMING POOL
LONDON
2009

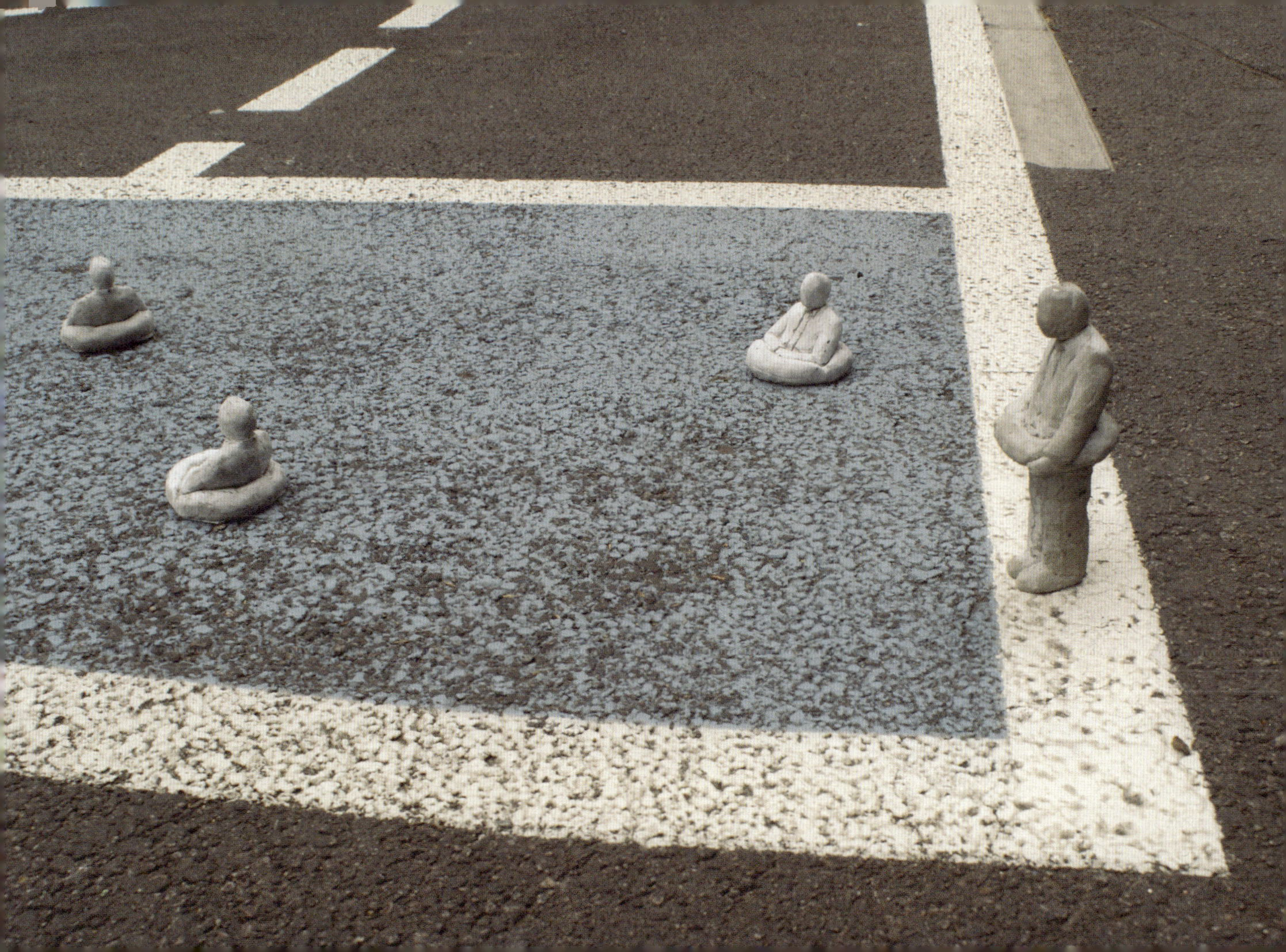

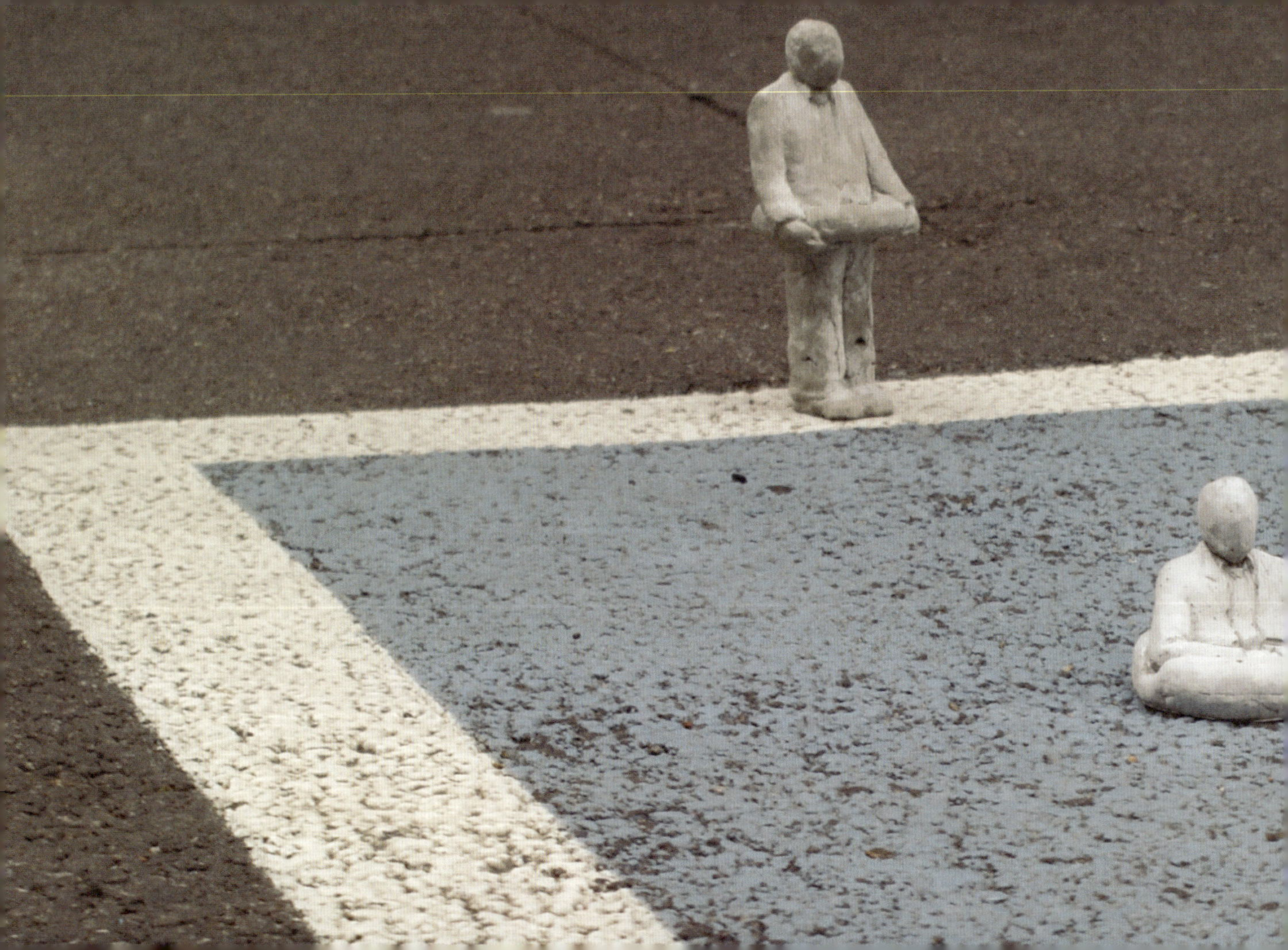

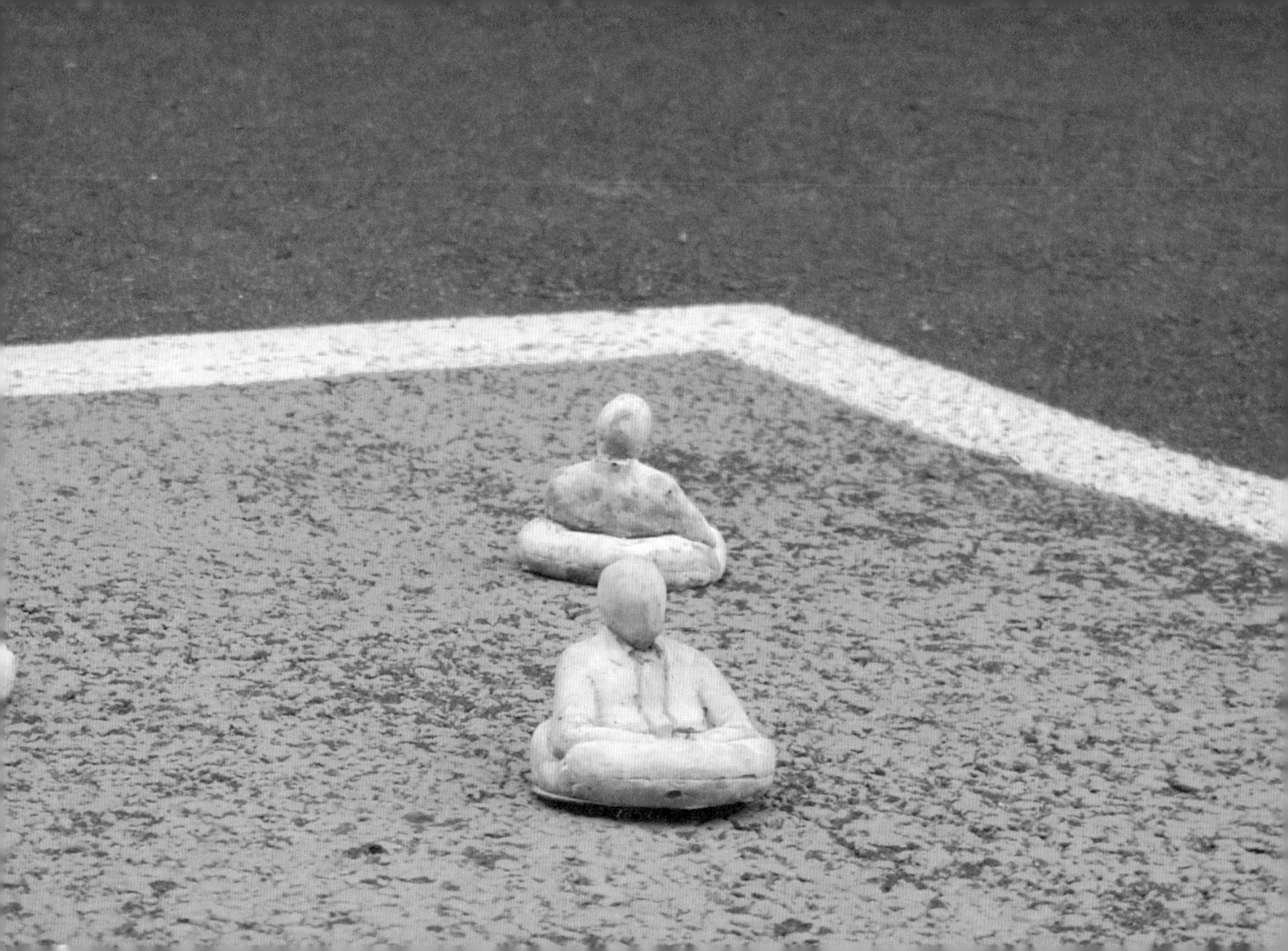

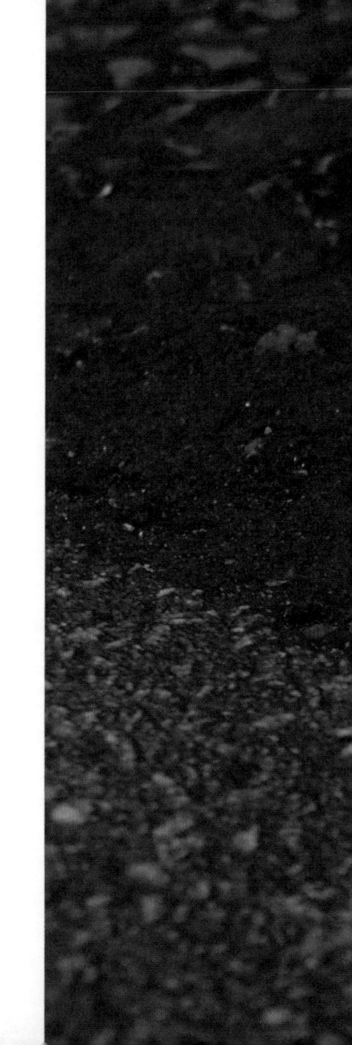

SLOWLY SINKING
LONDON
2010

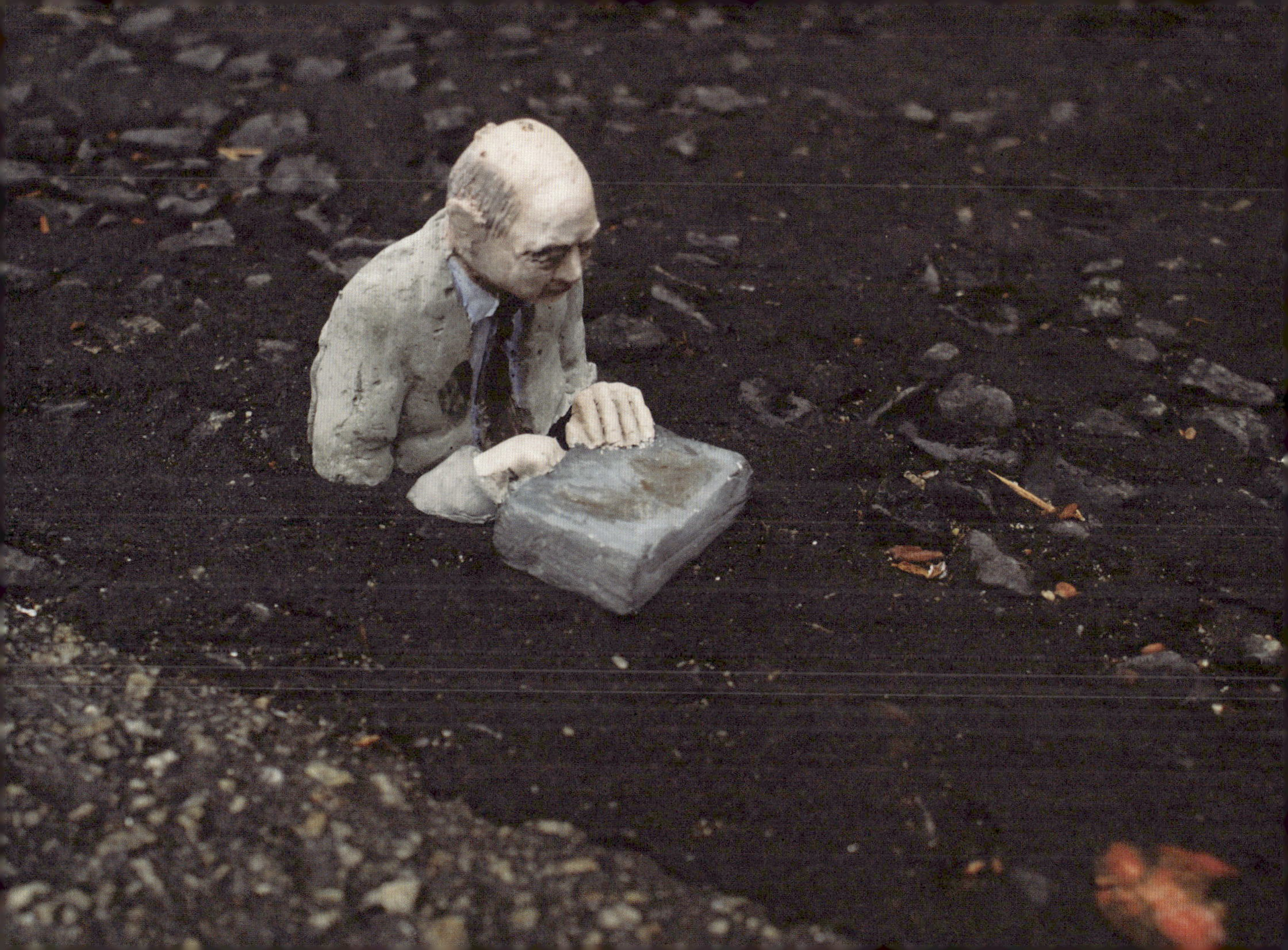

SUMMER SPONSORED BY BP
LONDON
2010

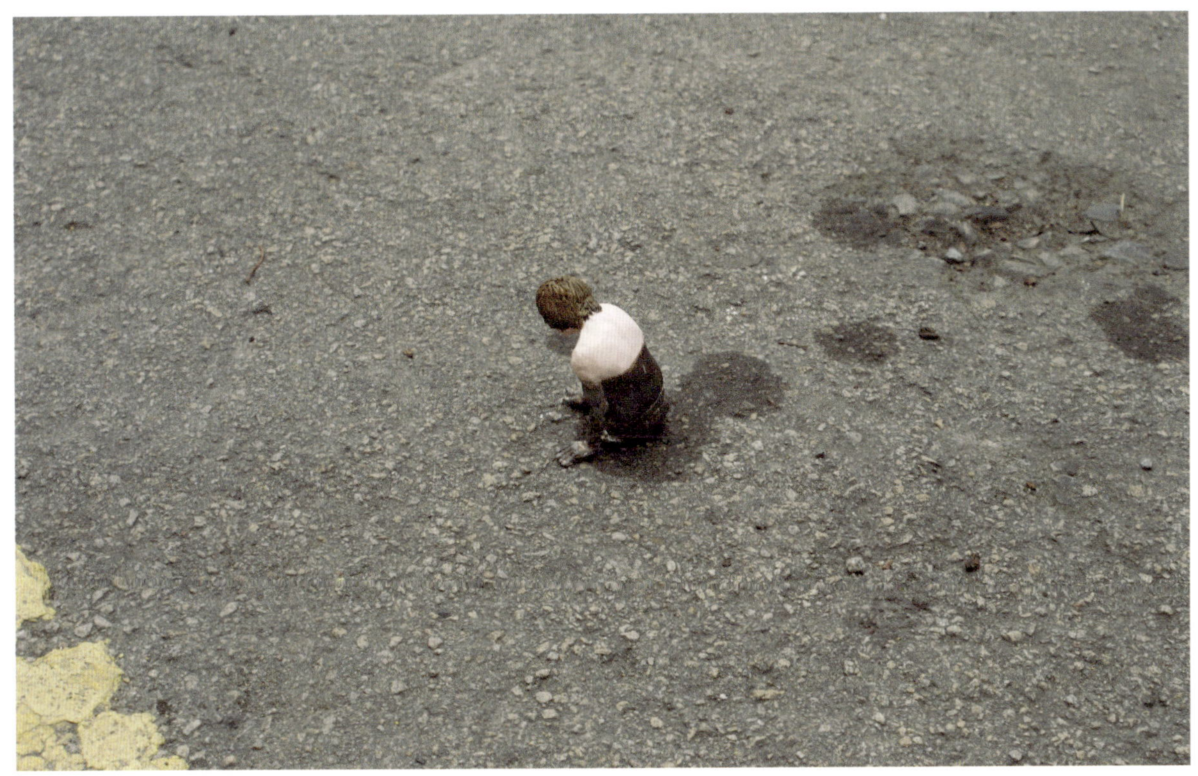

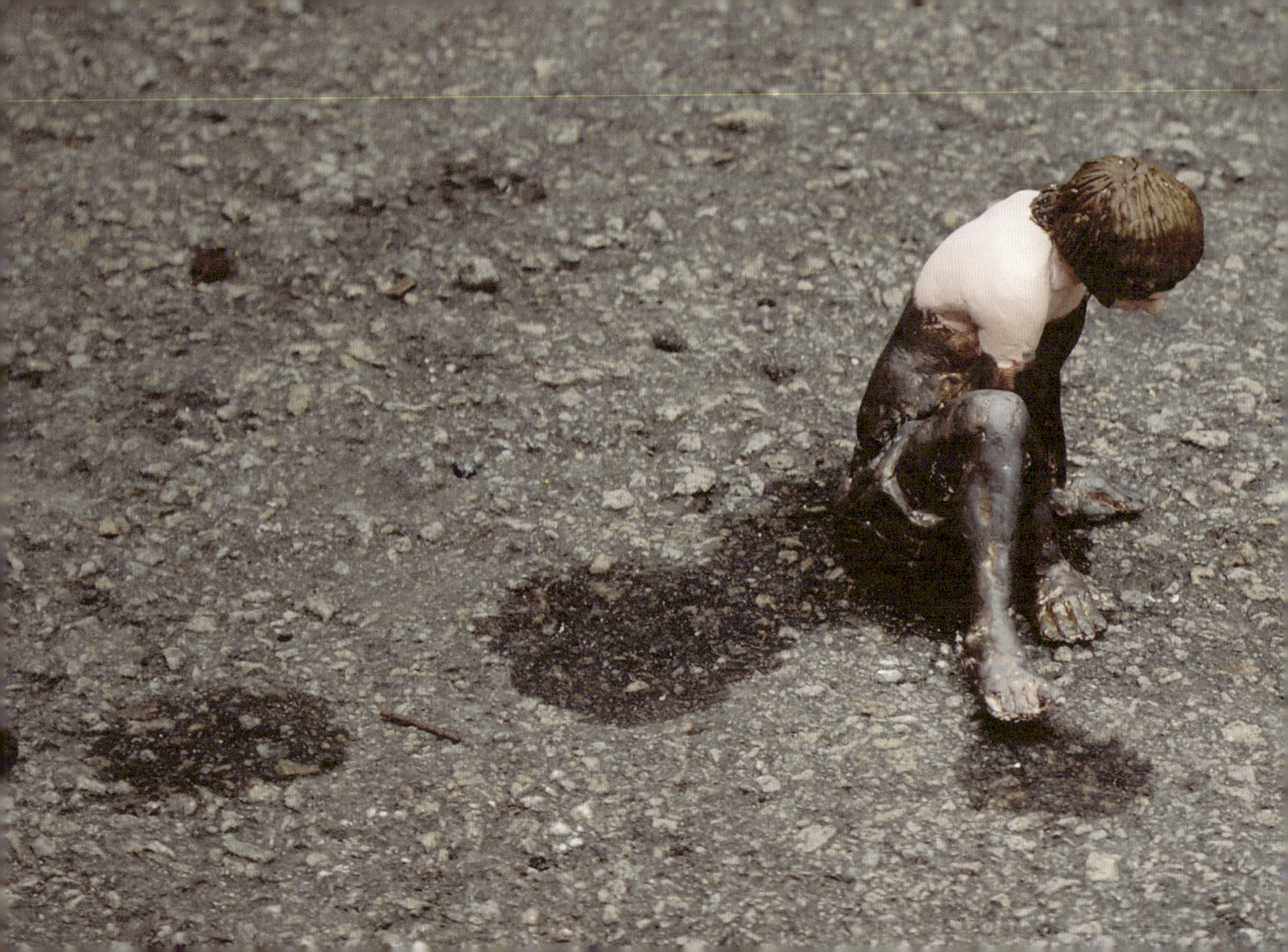

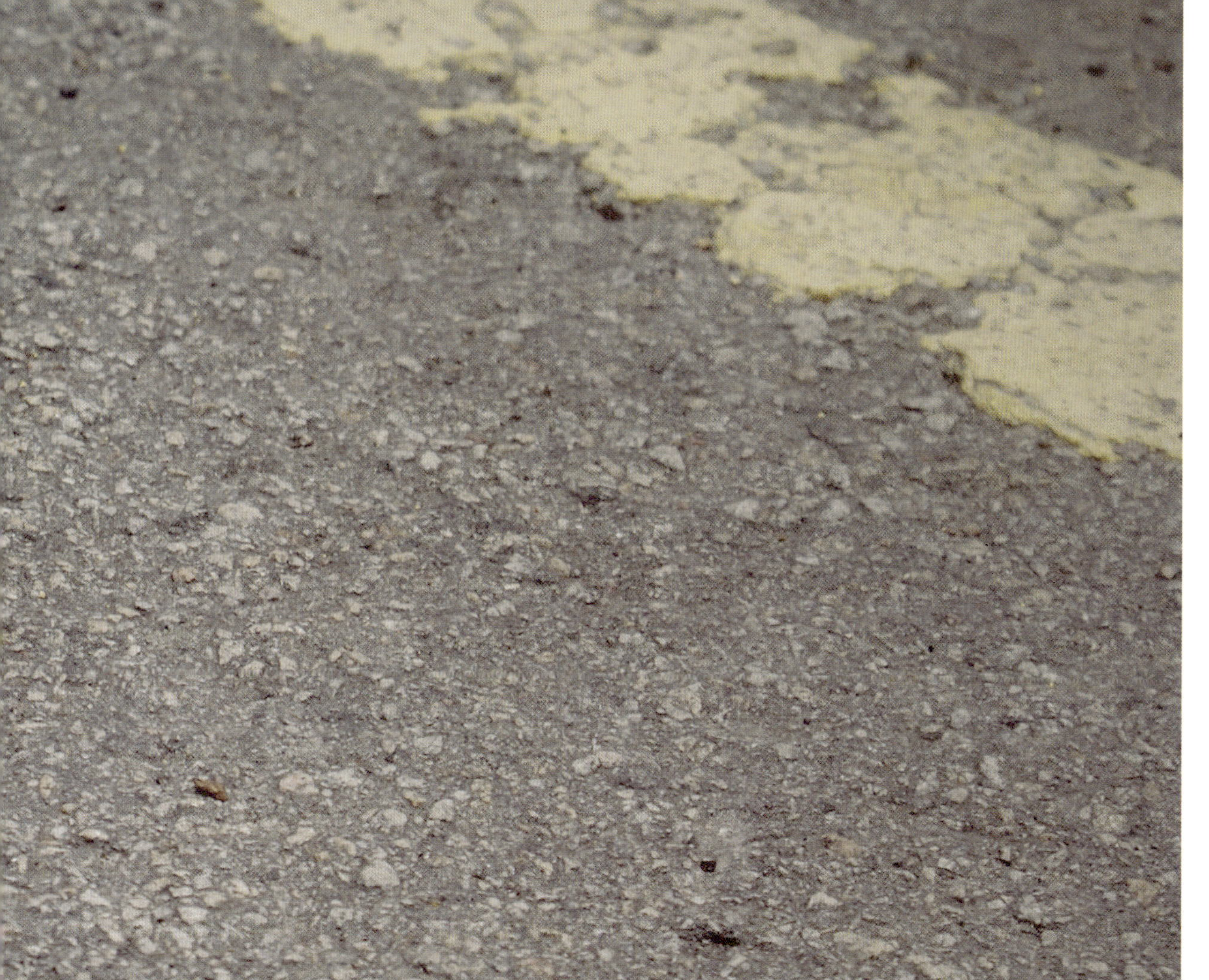

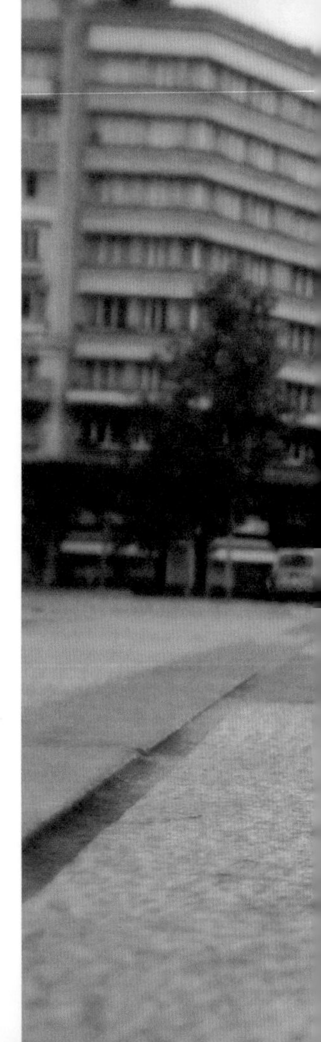

SWINE FLU INFECTED AREA
BRUSSELS
2010

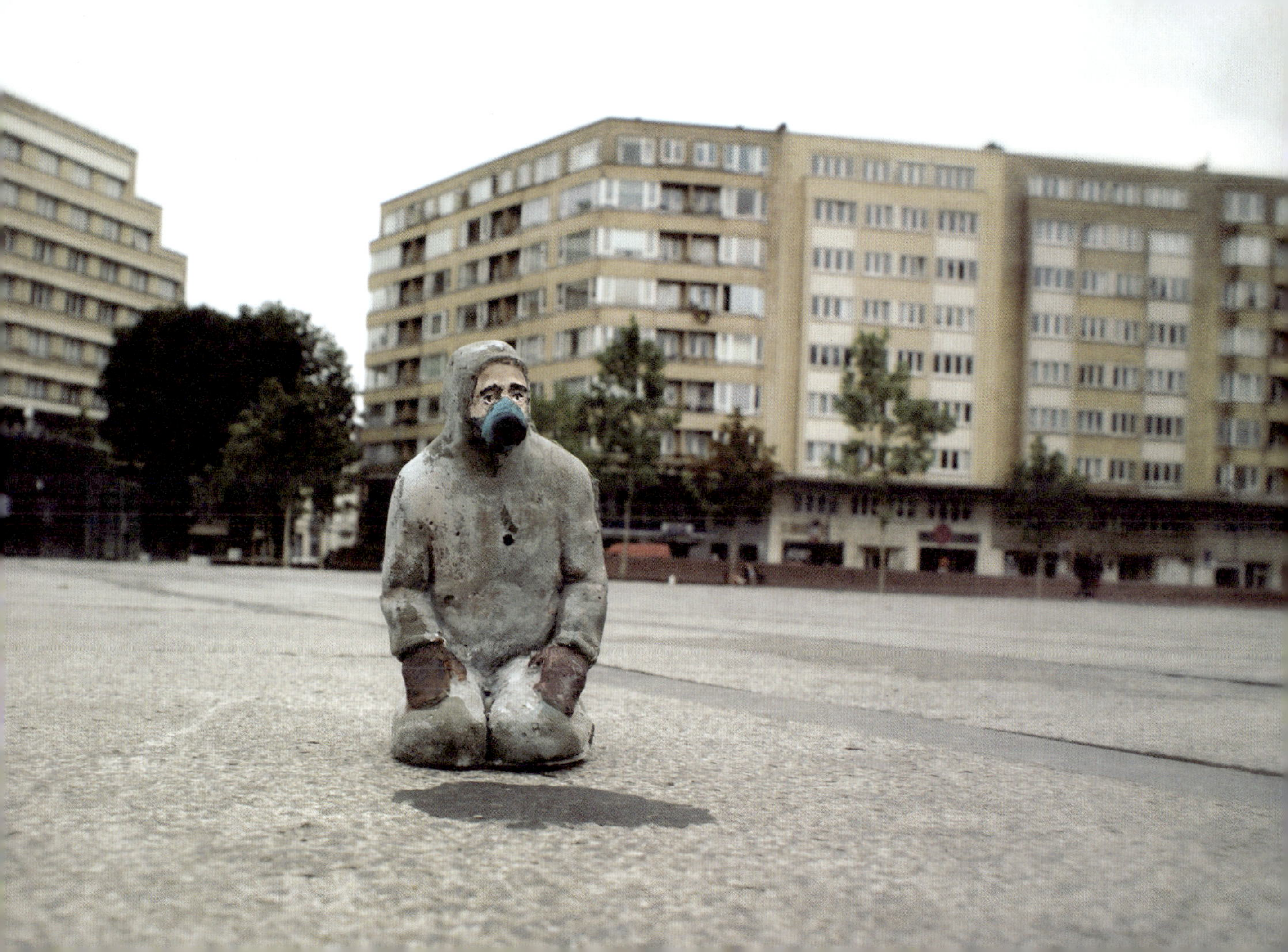

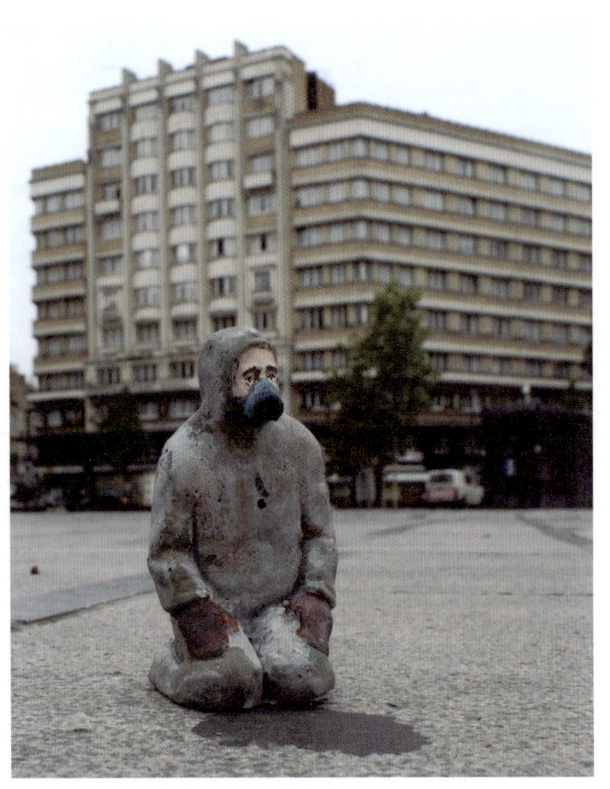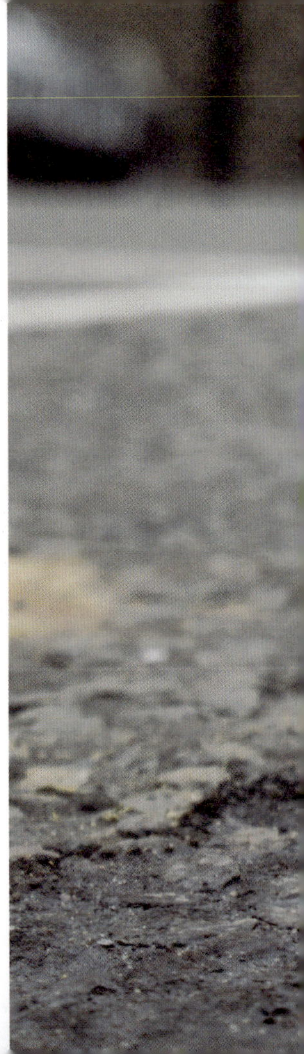

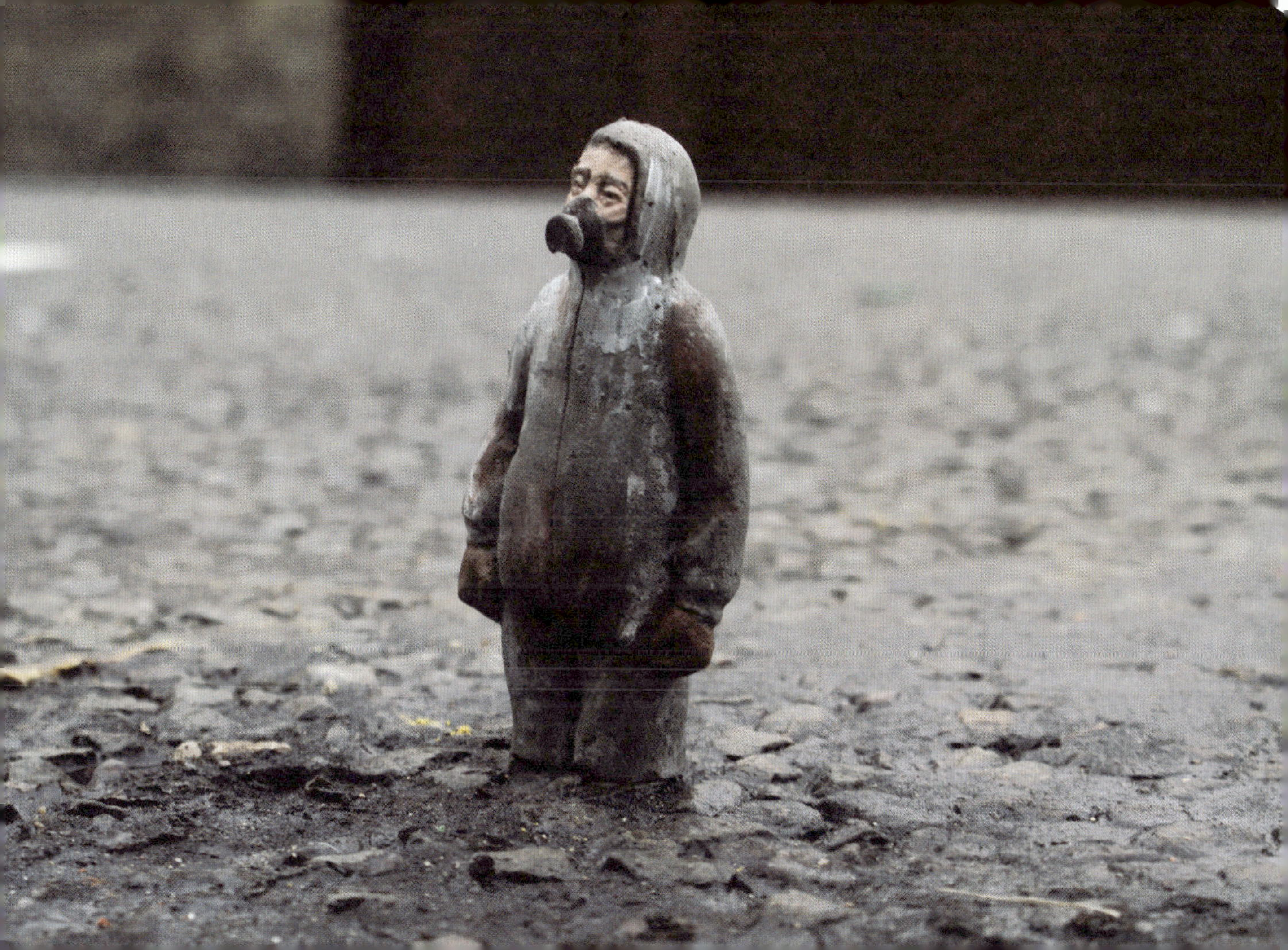

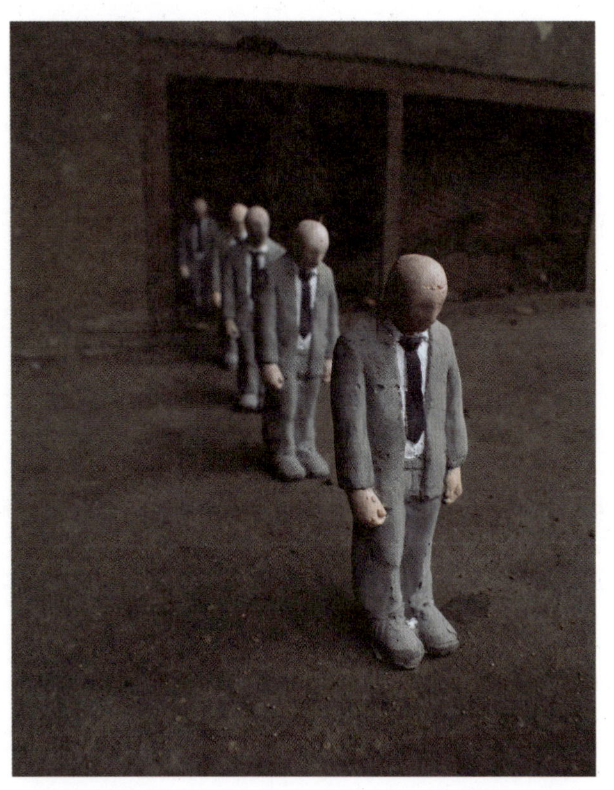

FOLLOW THE LEADER
BRUSSELS
2010

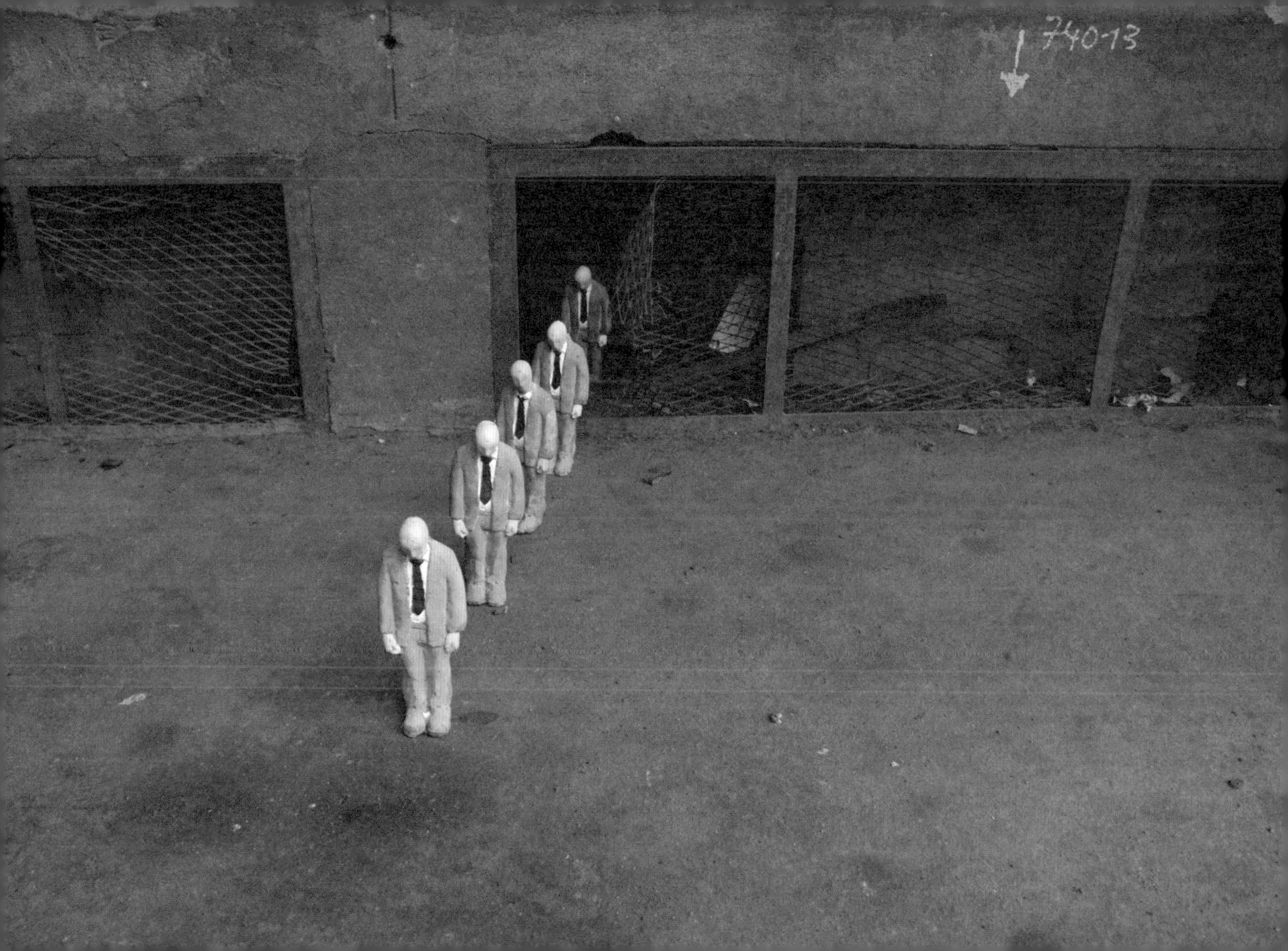
74013

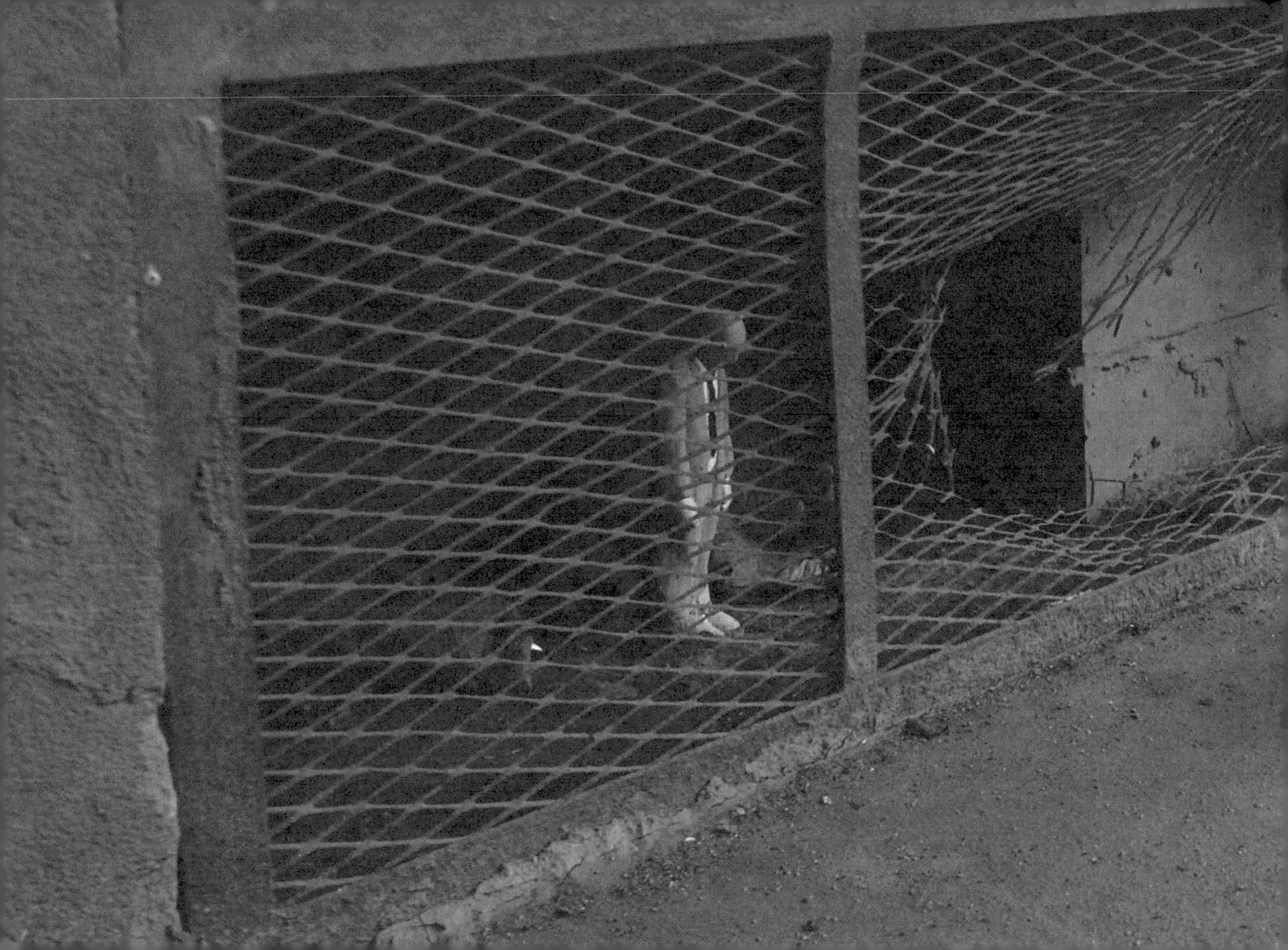

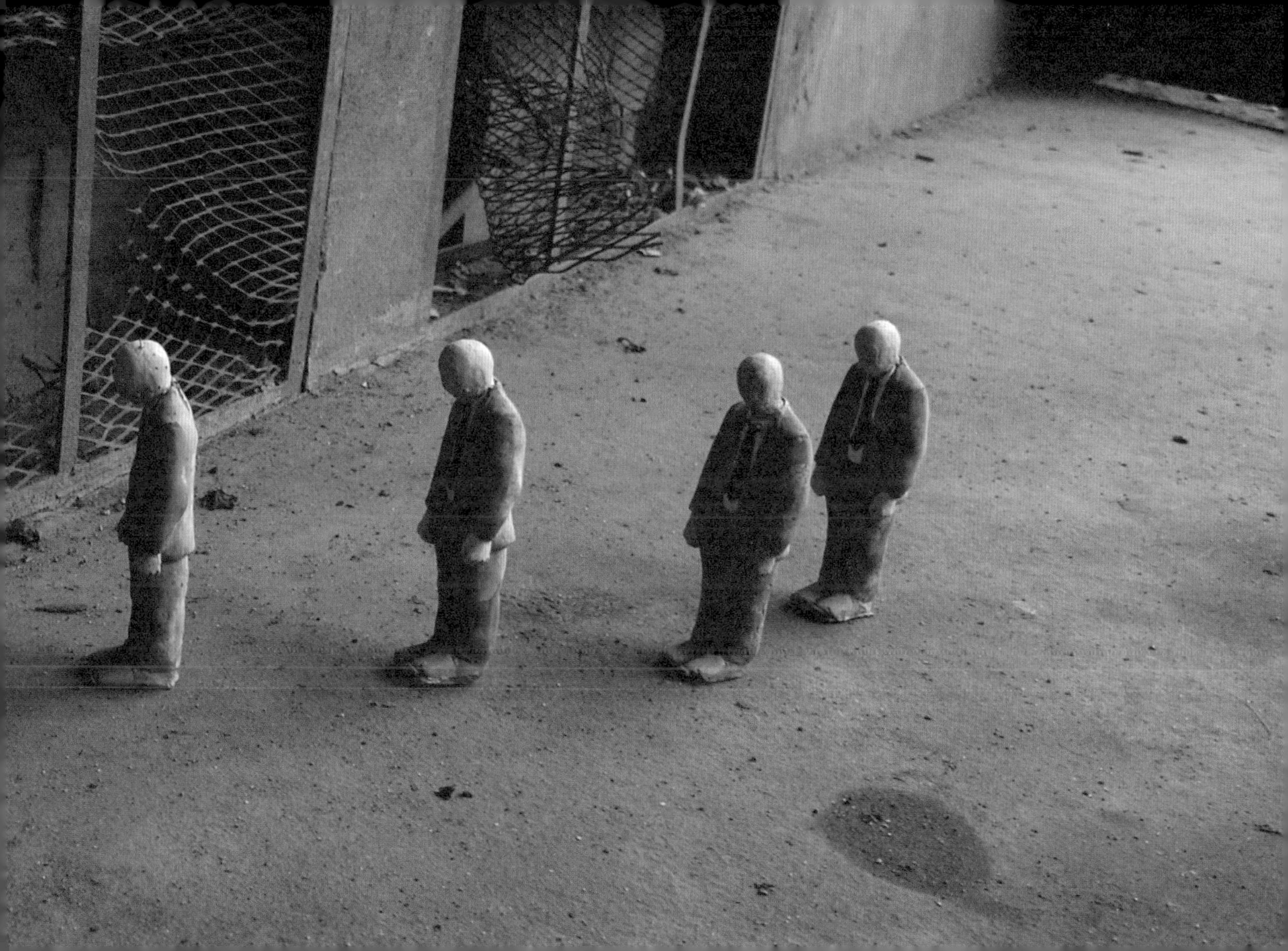

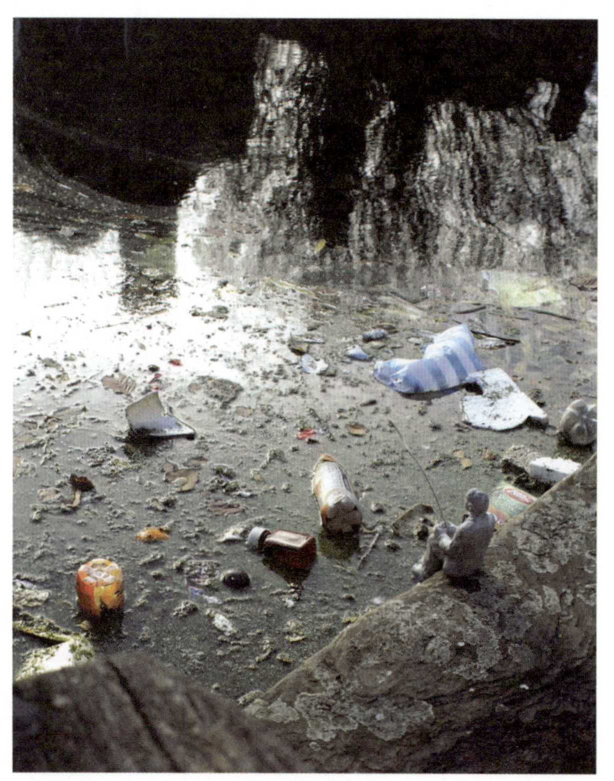

HOXE NON HAI NADA
LONDON
2009

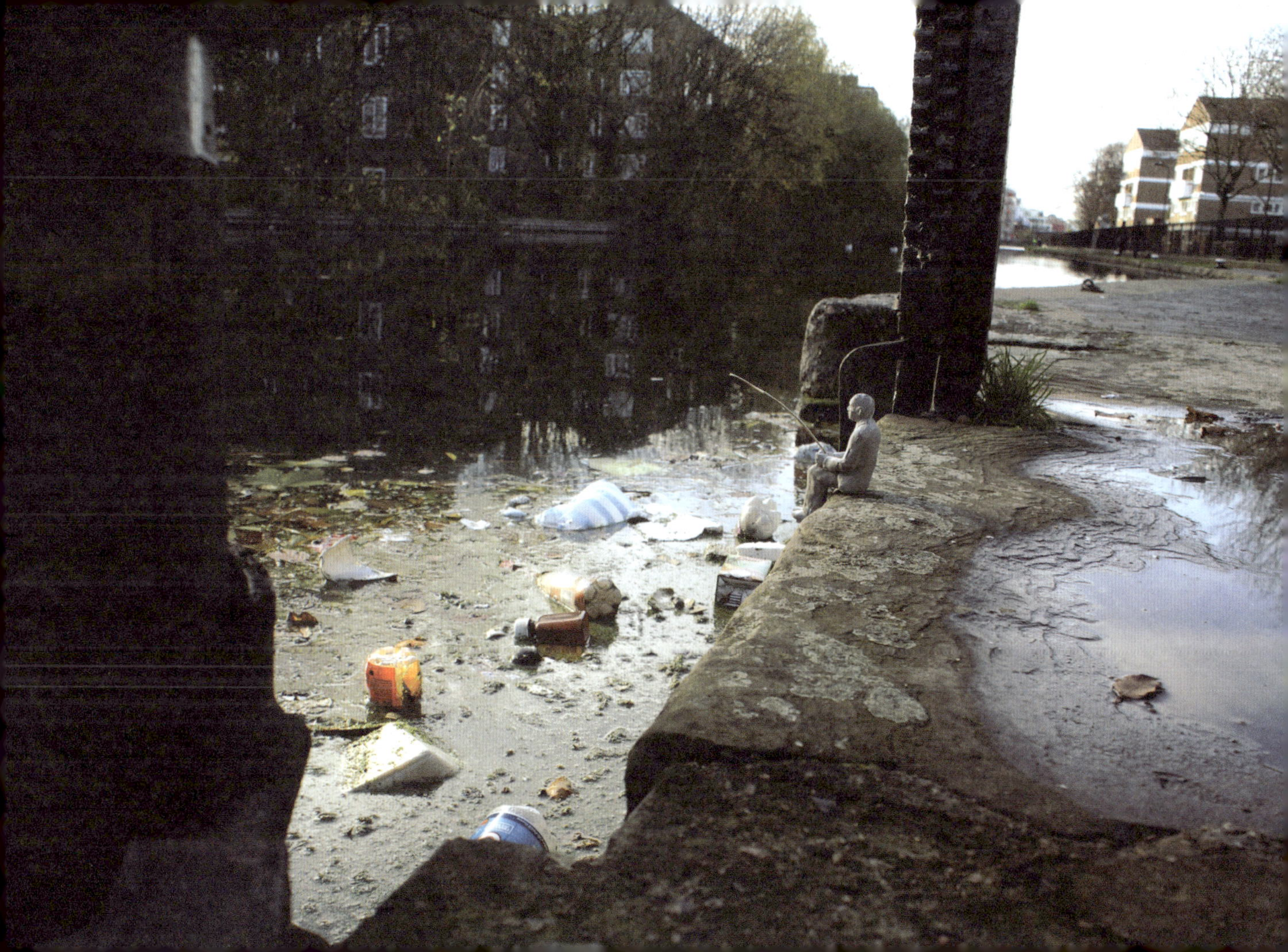

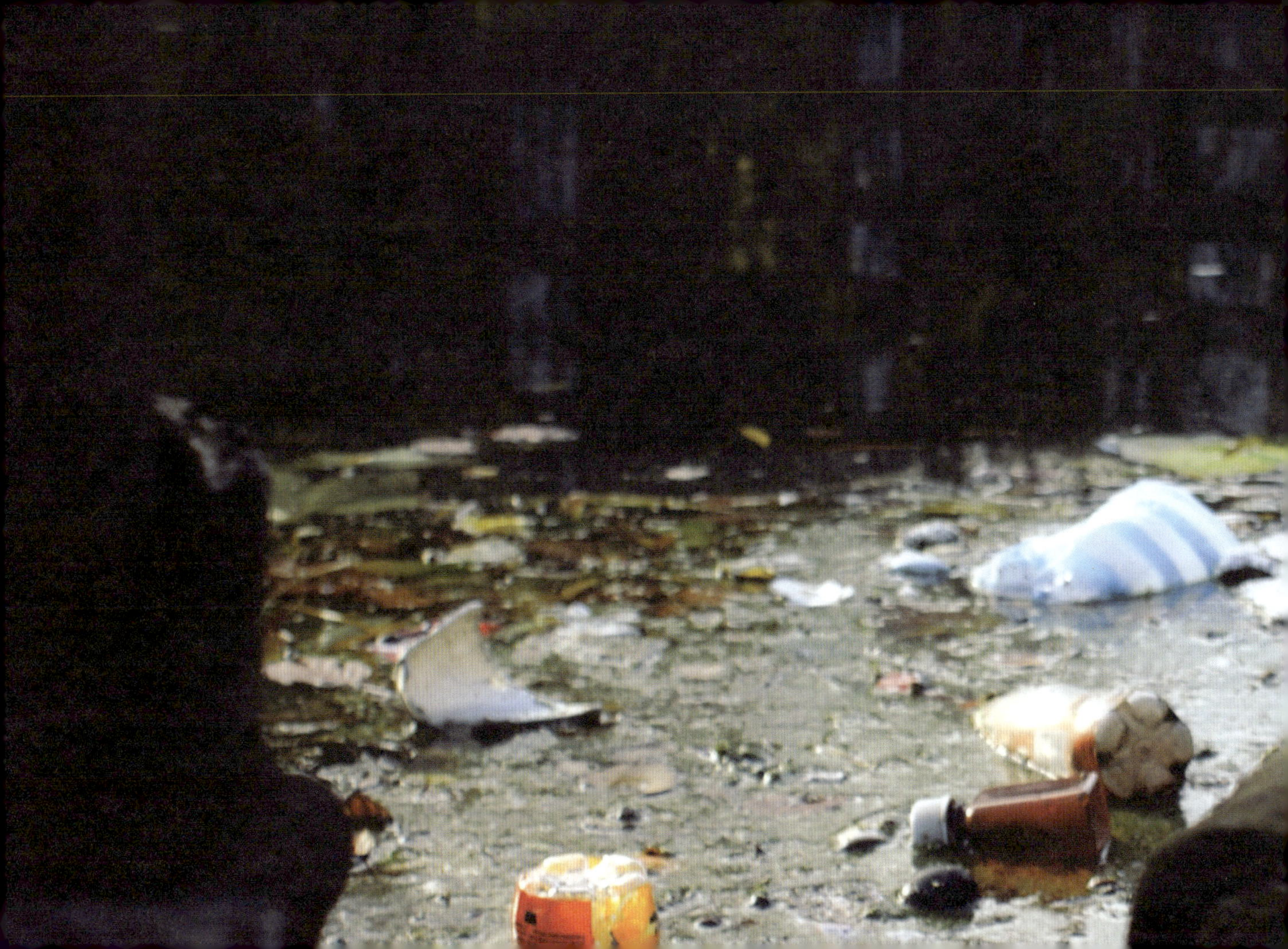

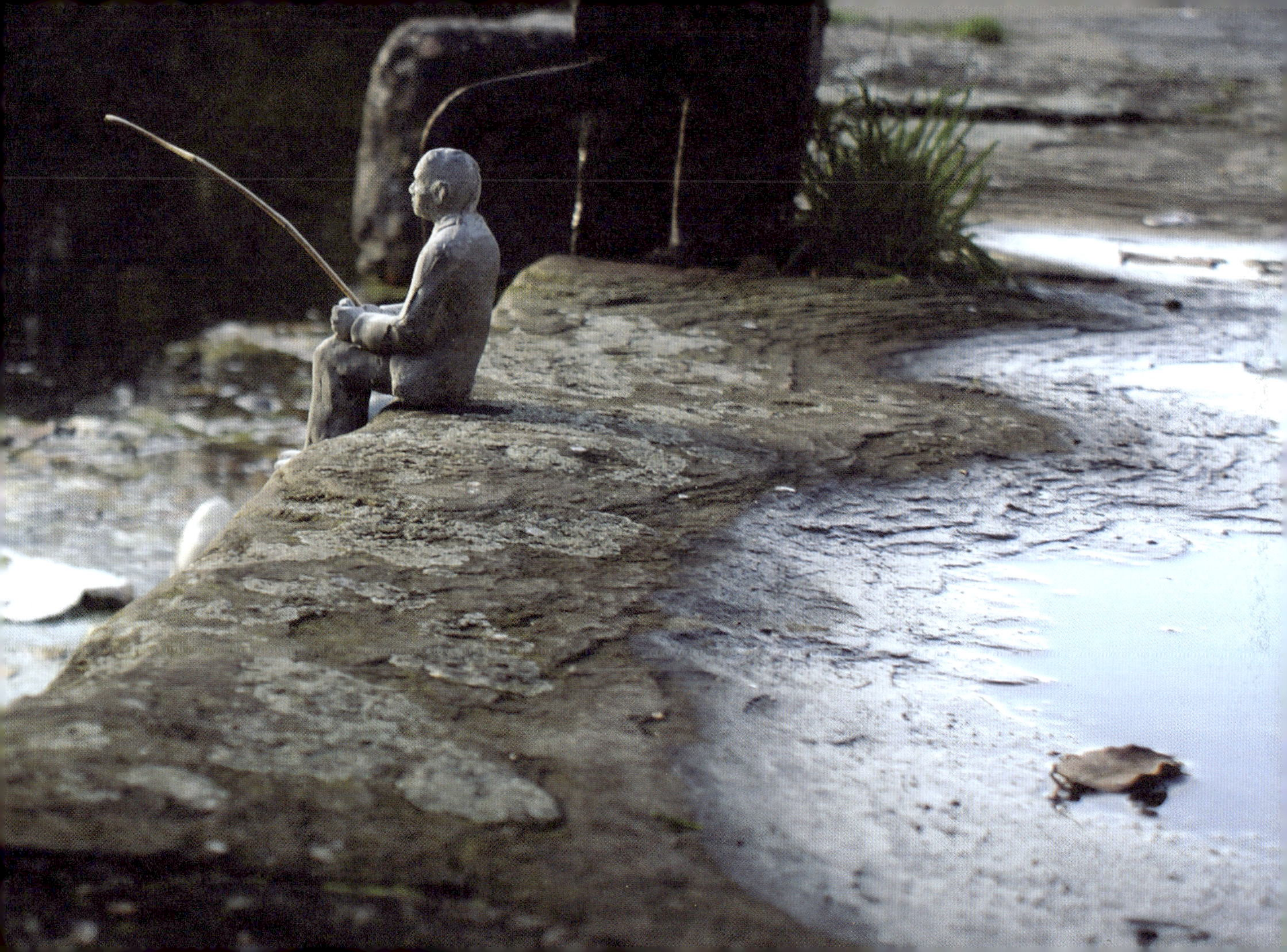

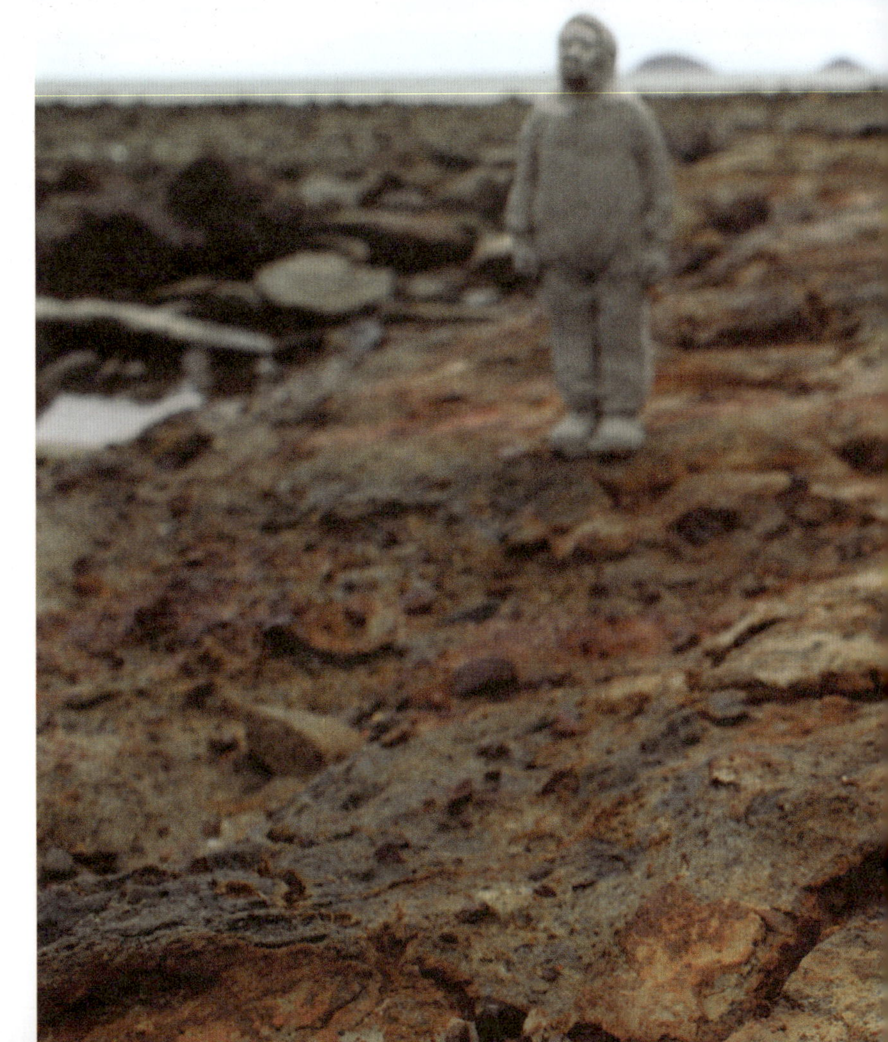

MARTE
BRETAGNE, FRANCE
2010

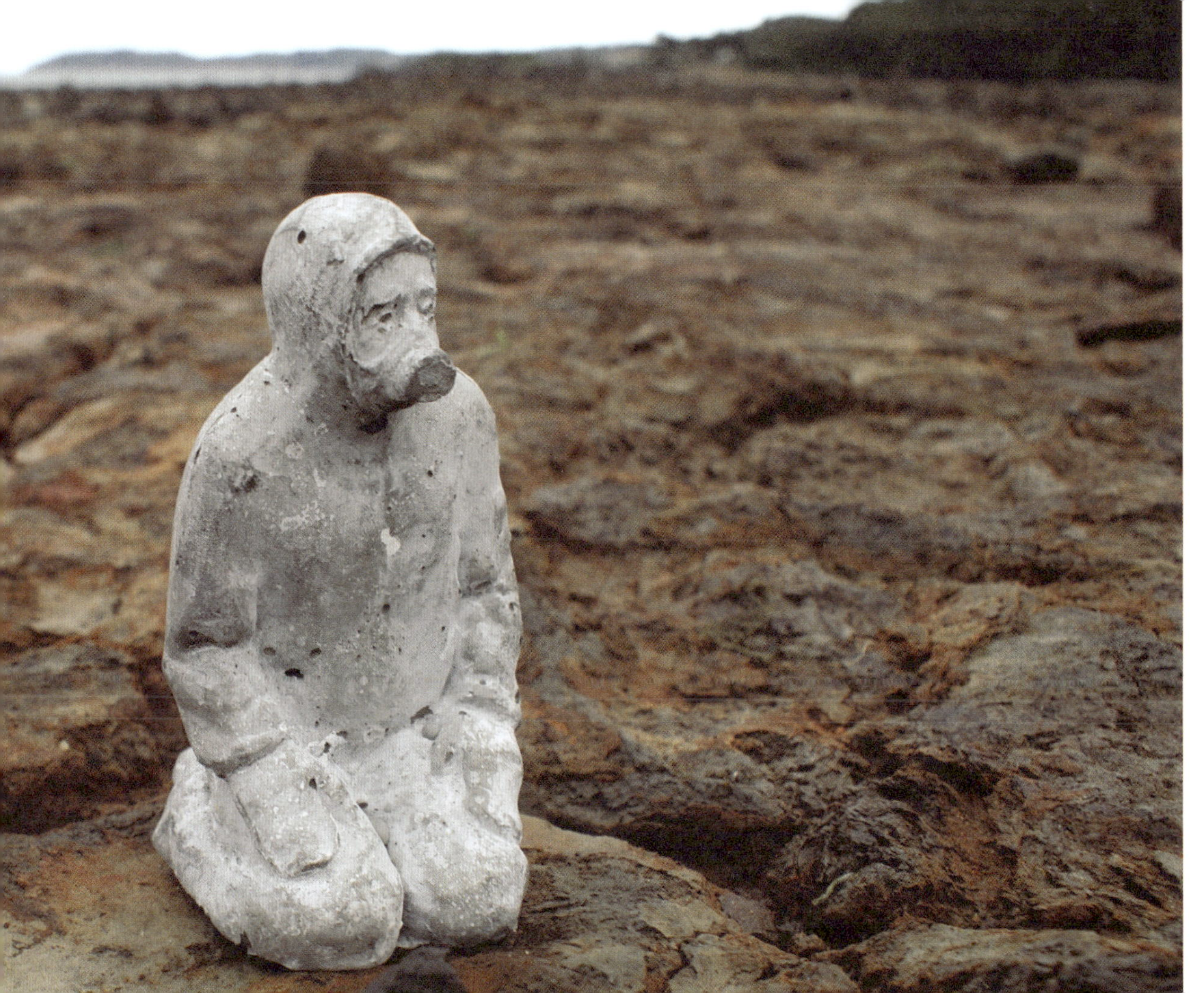

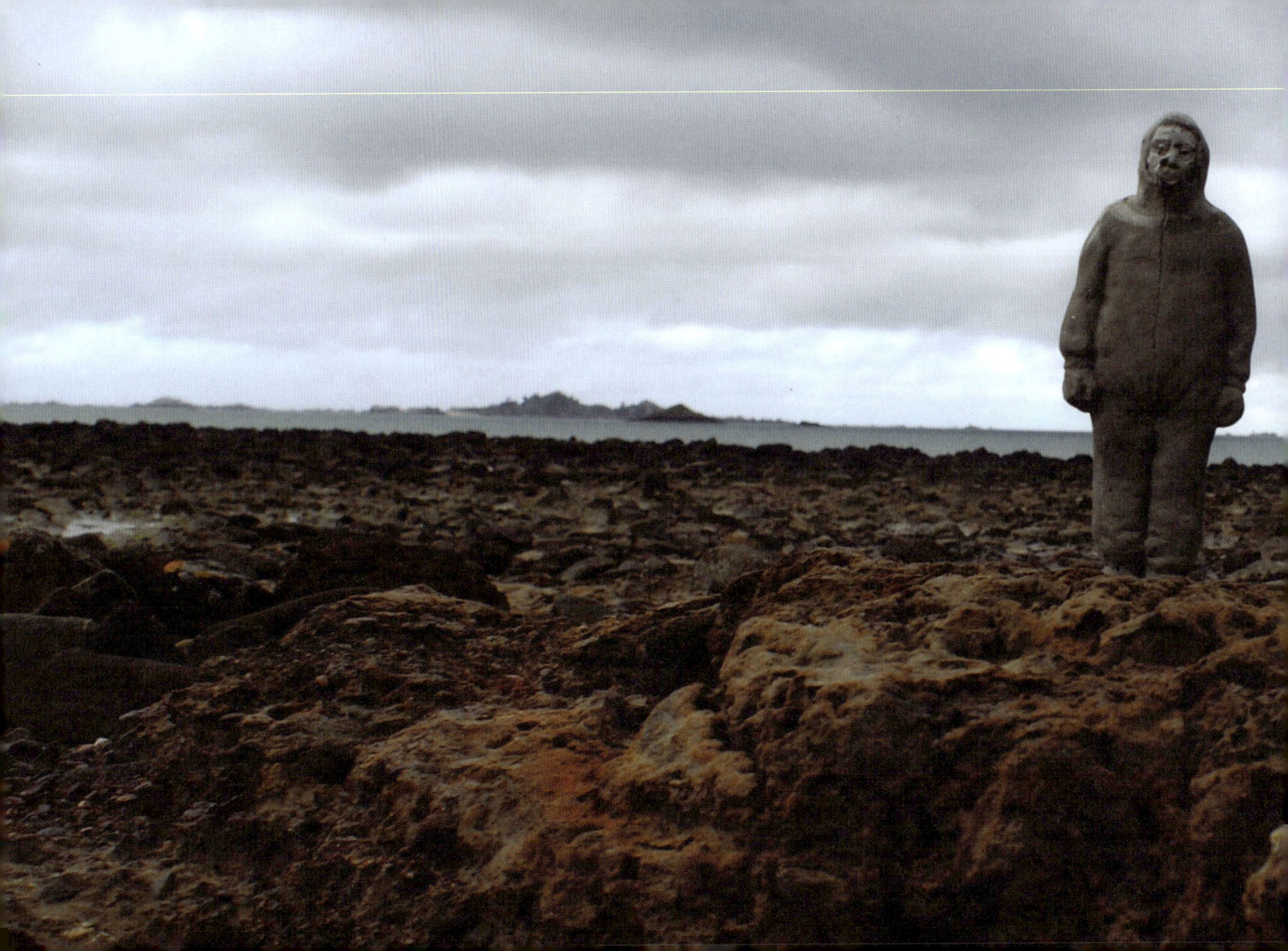

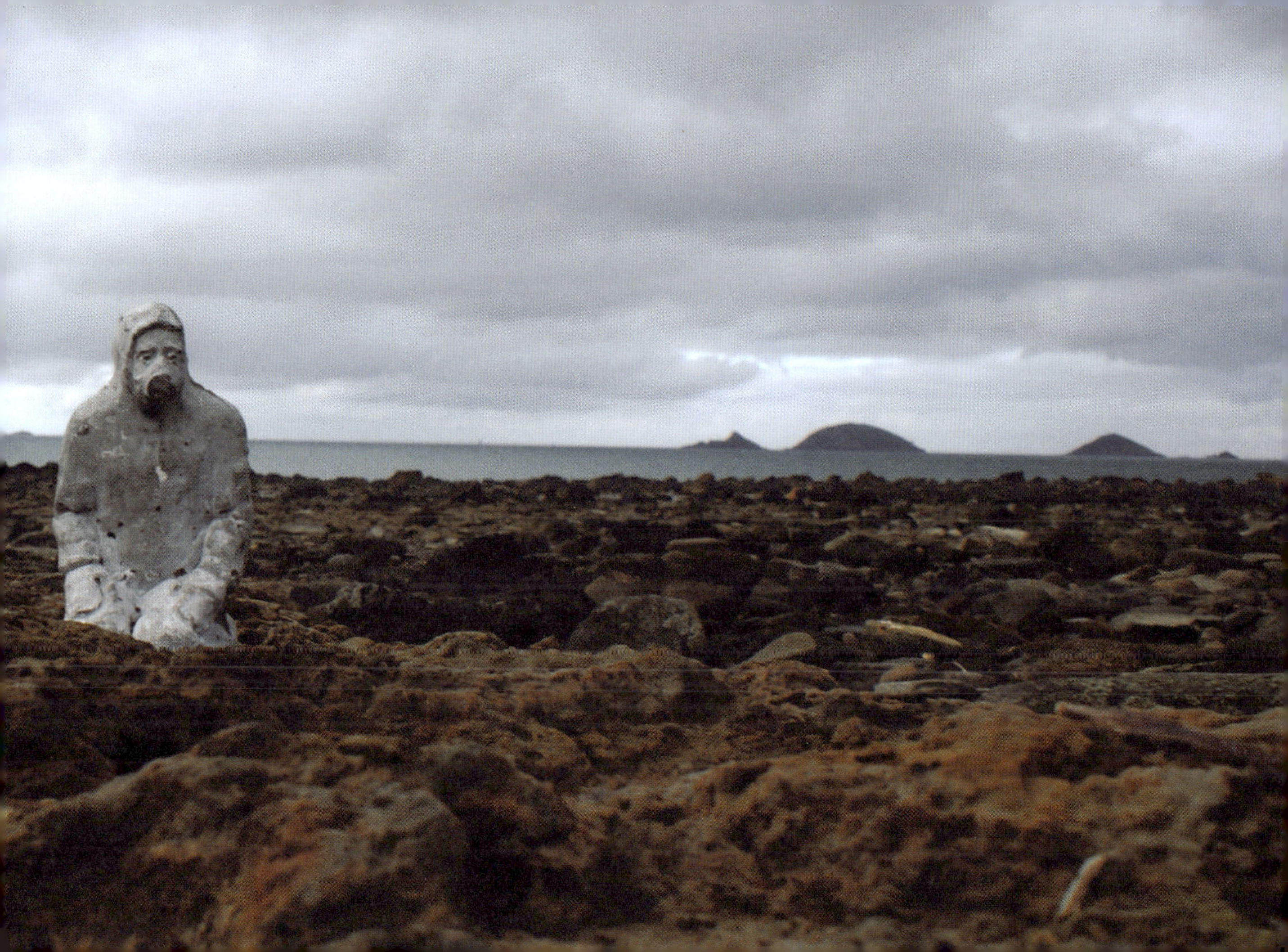

RIVER
LONDON
2010

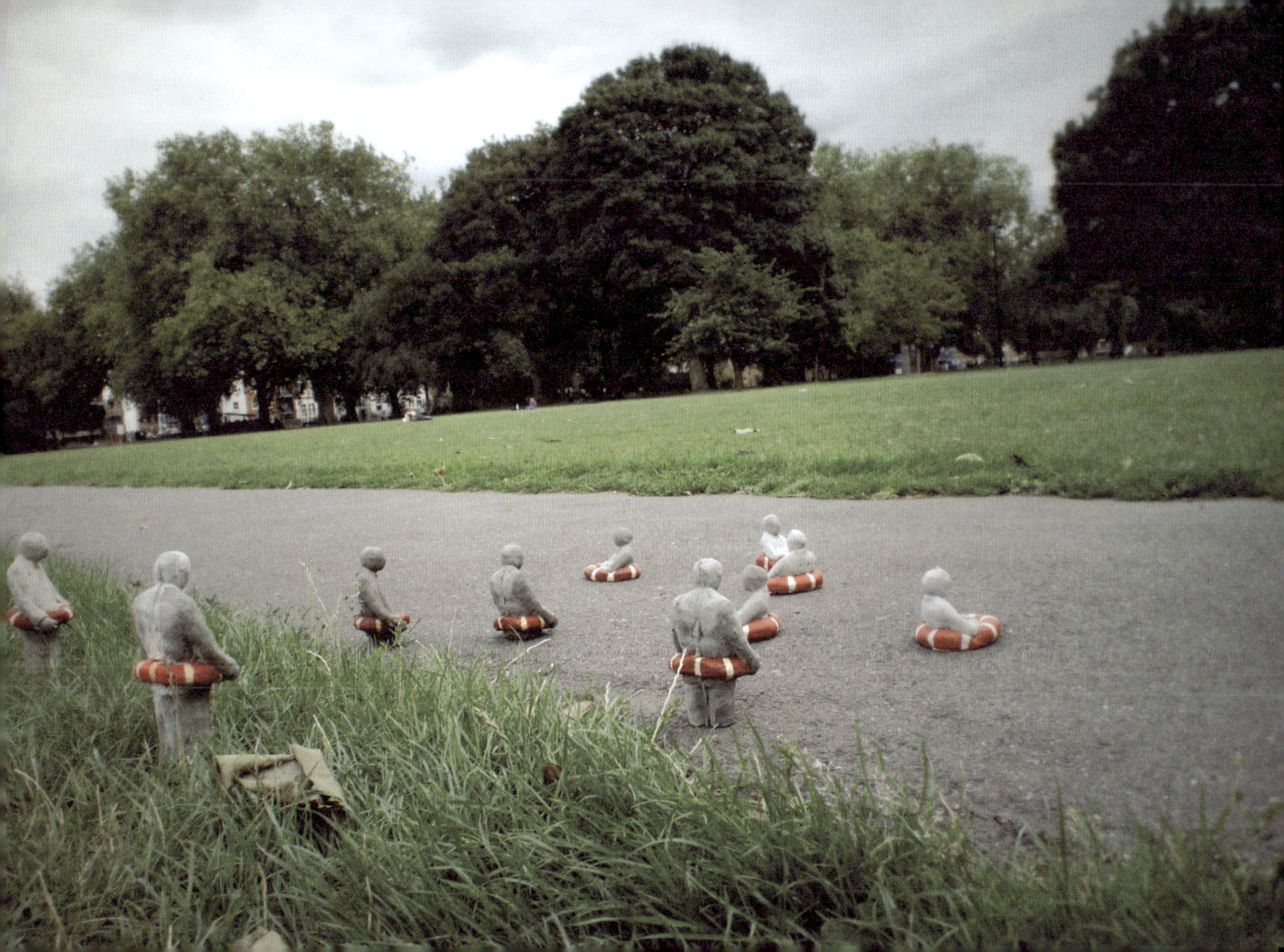

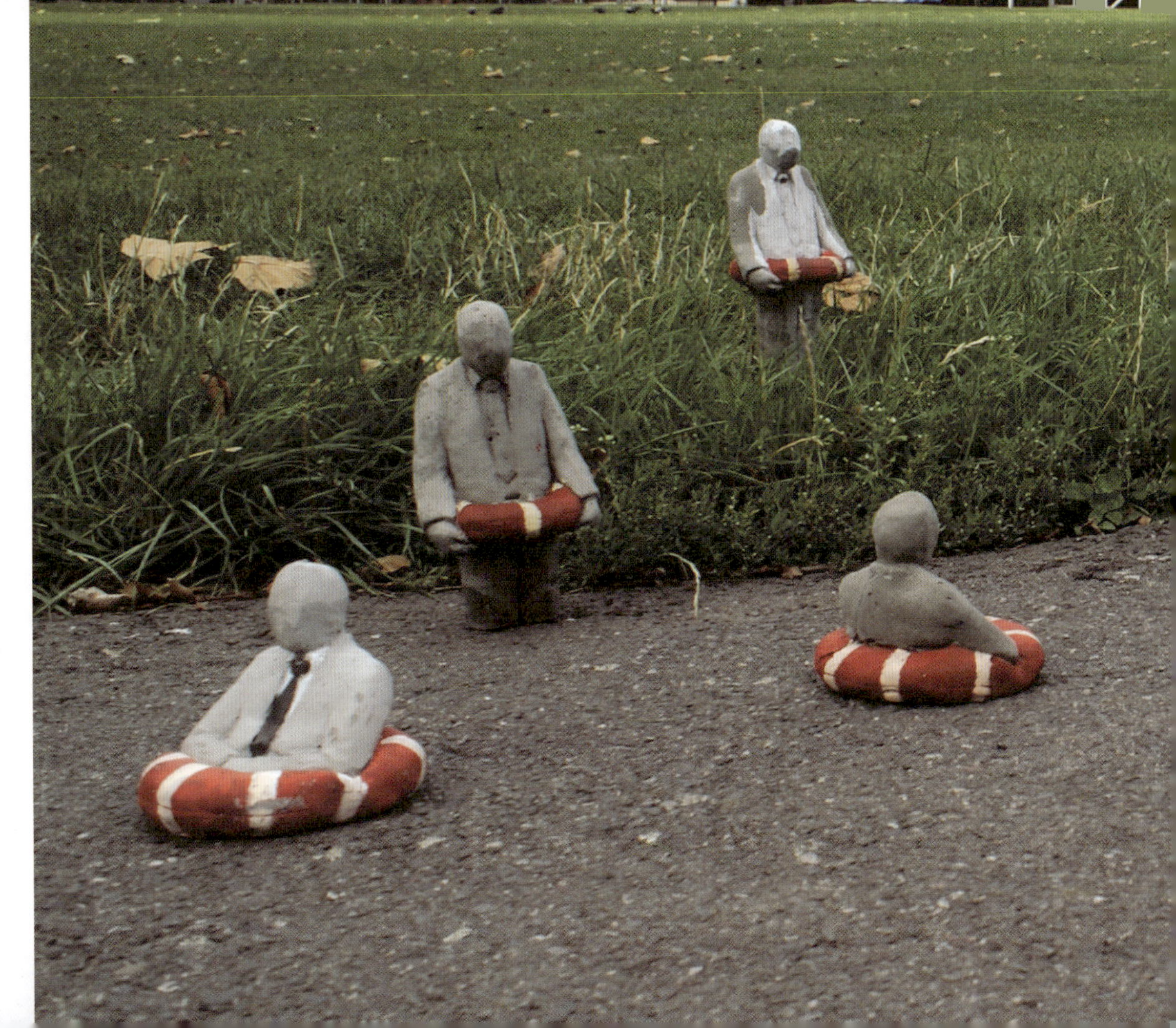

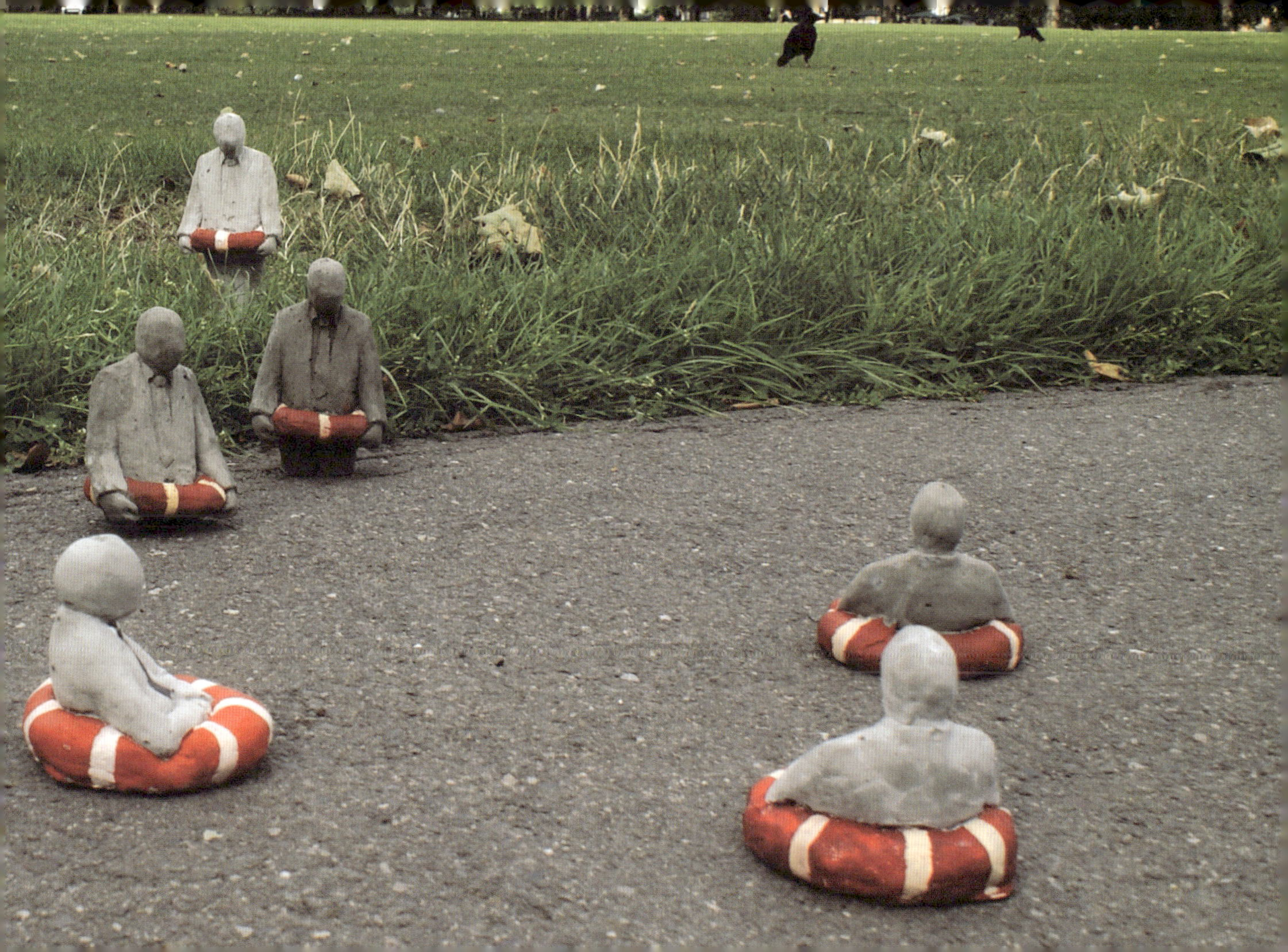

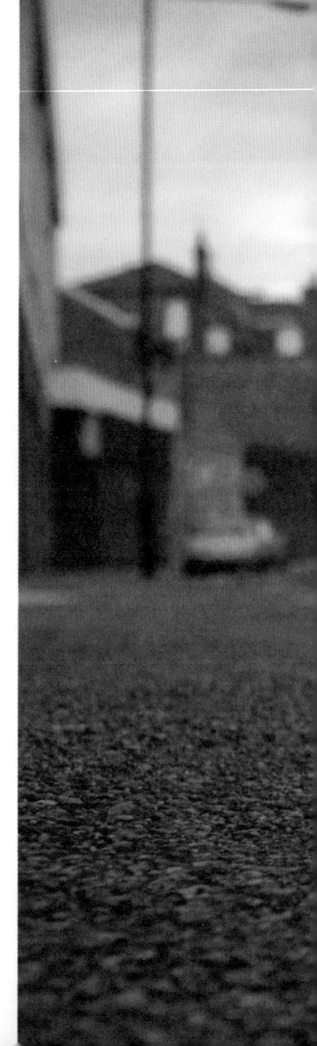

LOVERS
LONDON
2010

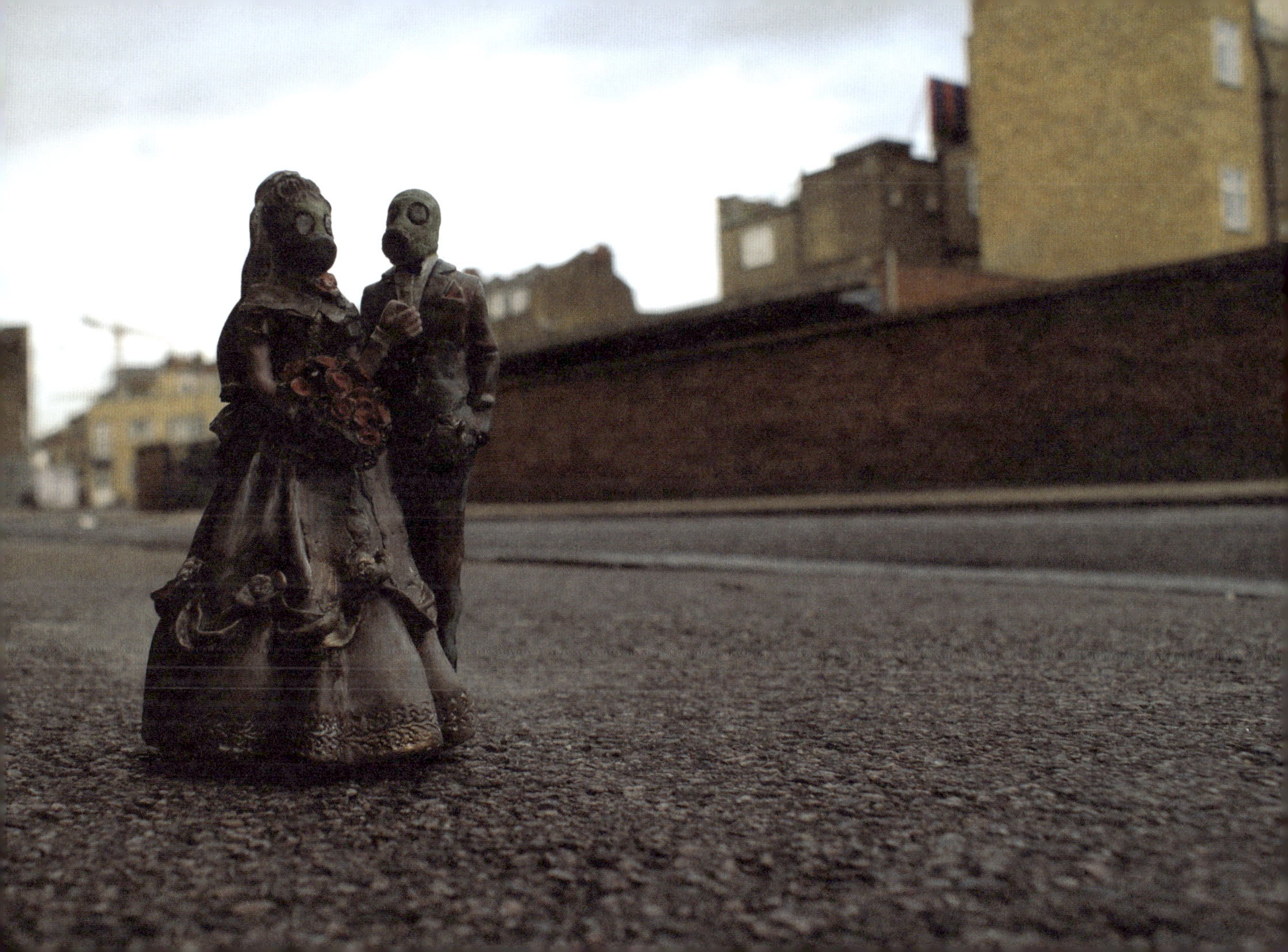

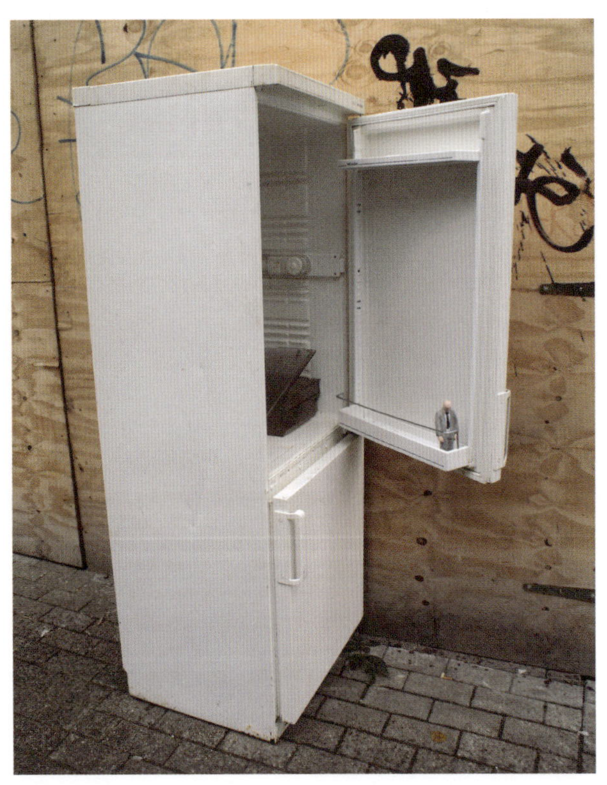

EMPTY FRIDGE
BRUSSELS
2010

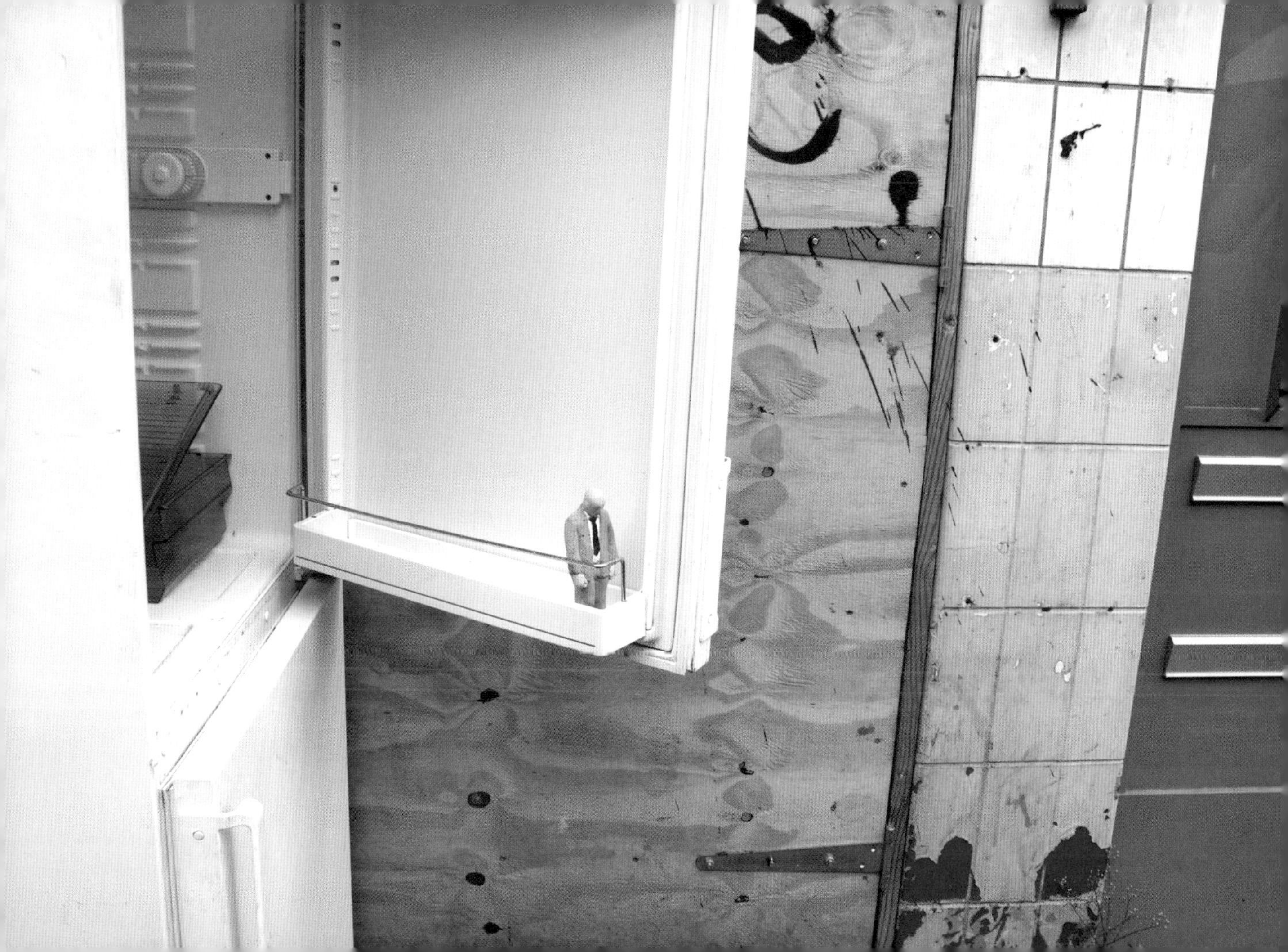

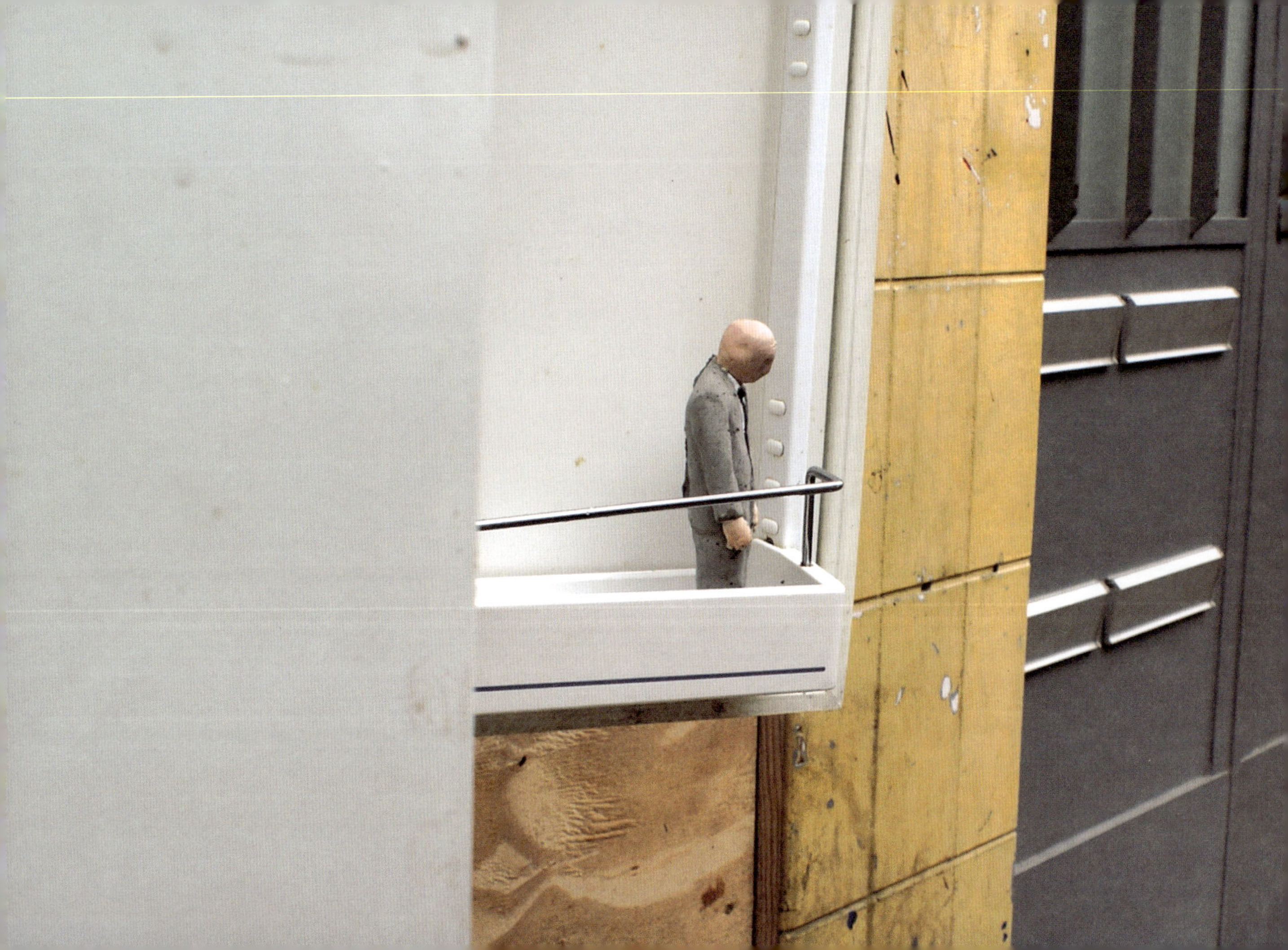

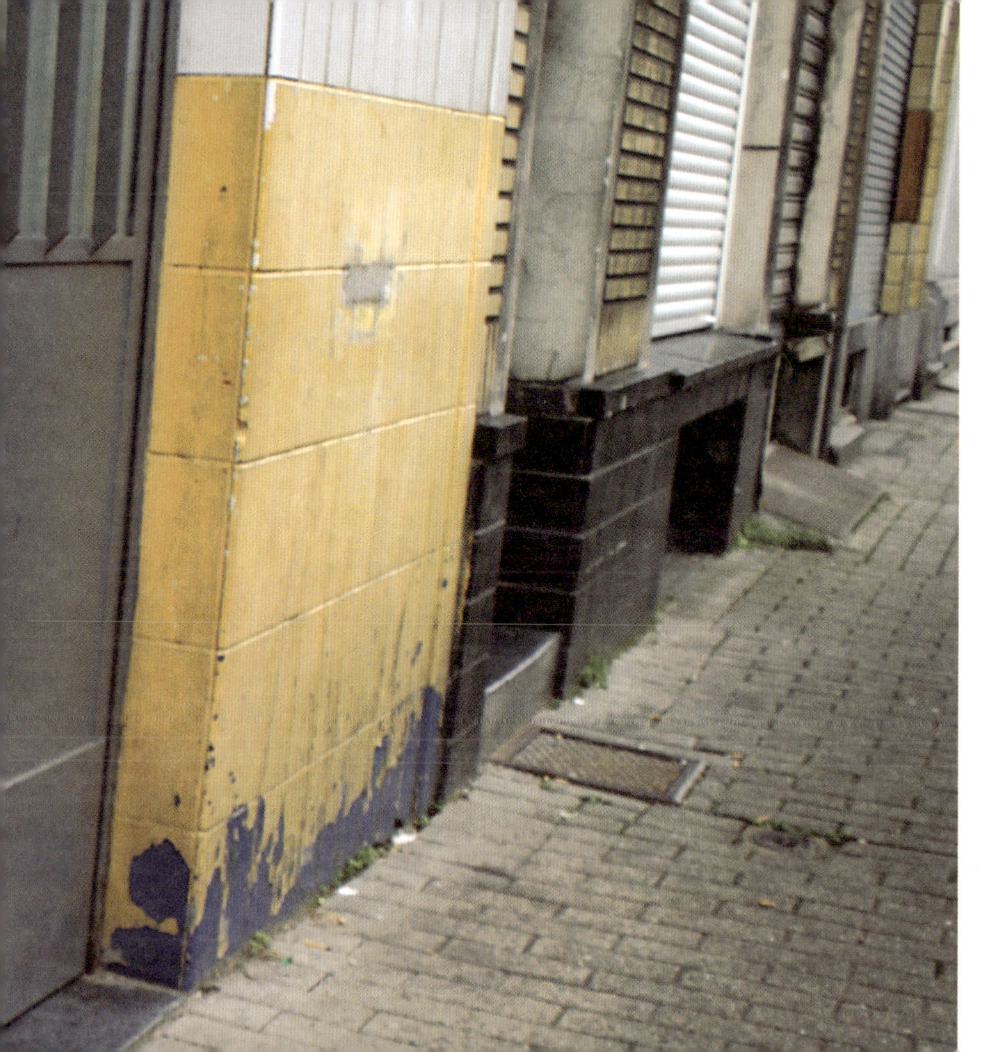

PLAYGROUND
LONDON
2010

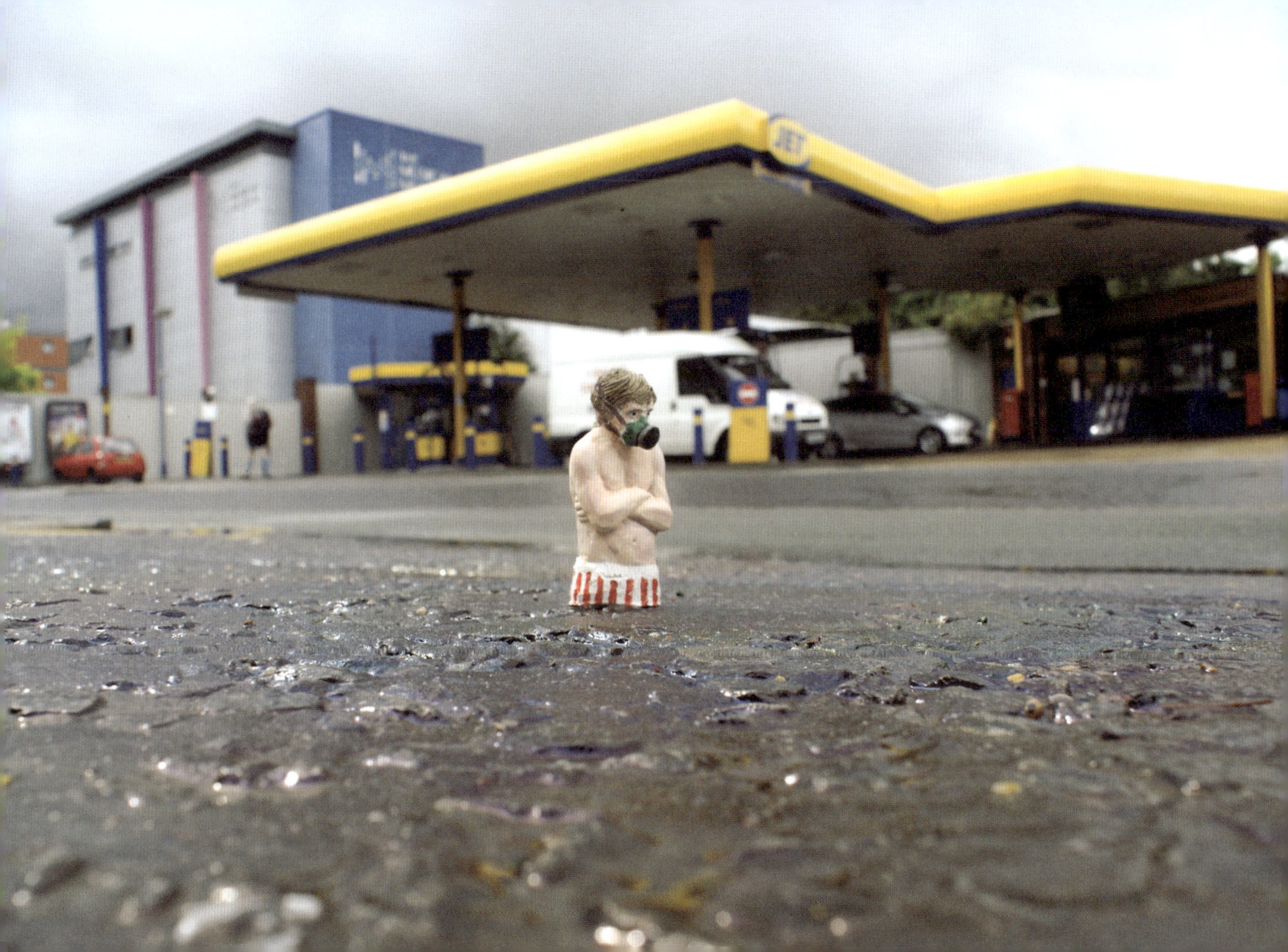

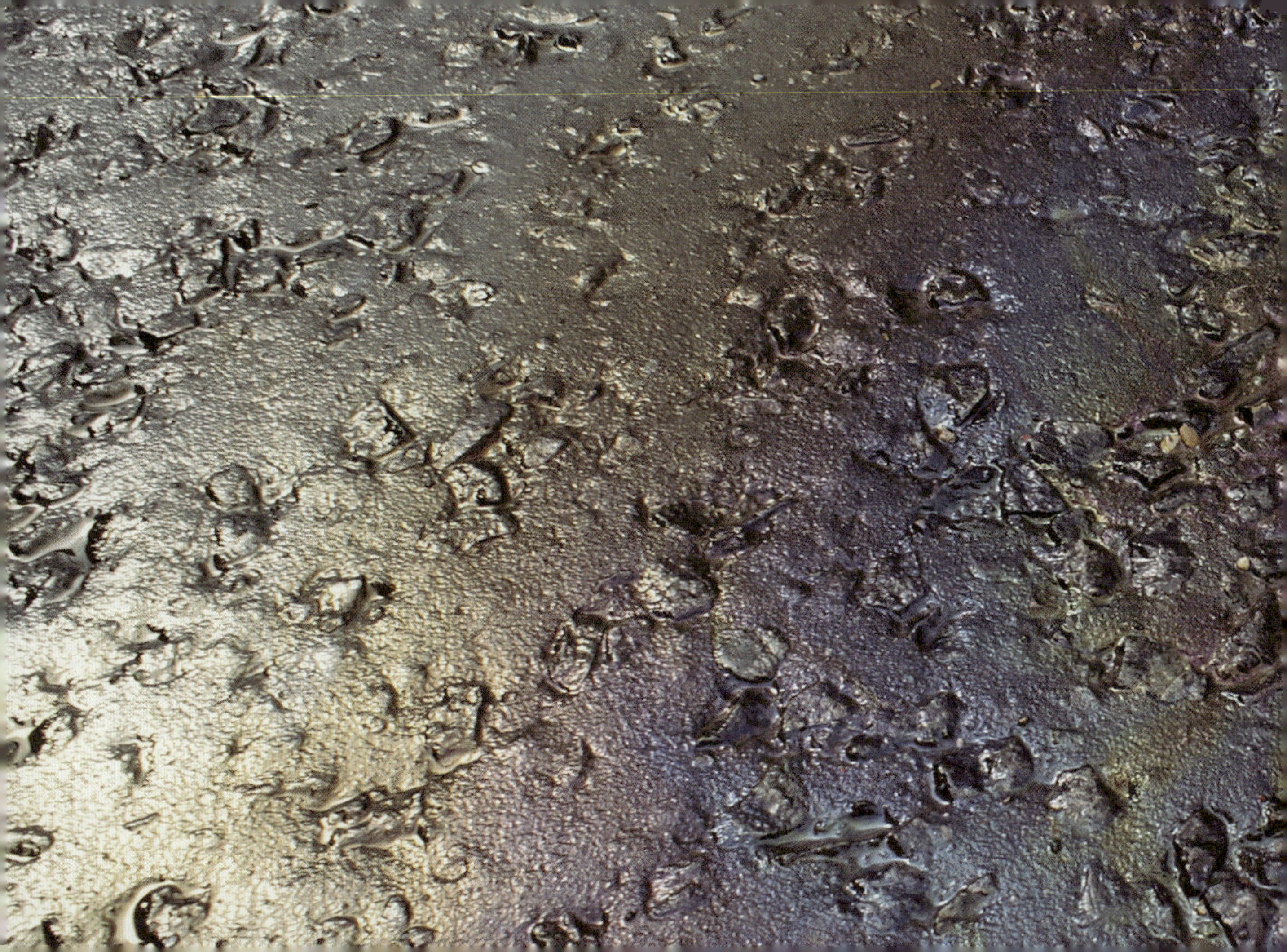

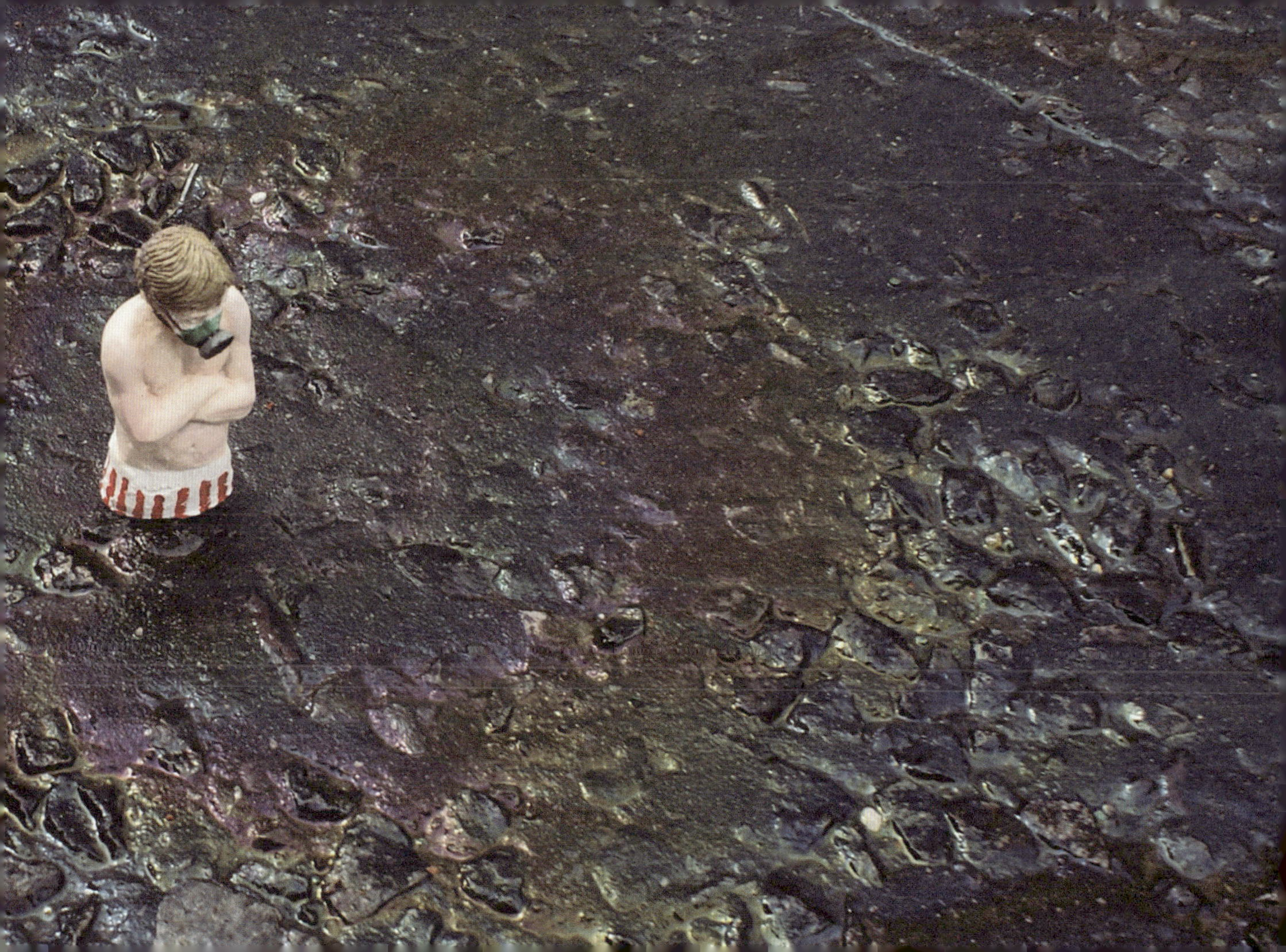

FOLLOW THE LEADER
LONDON
2010

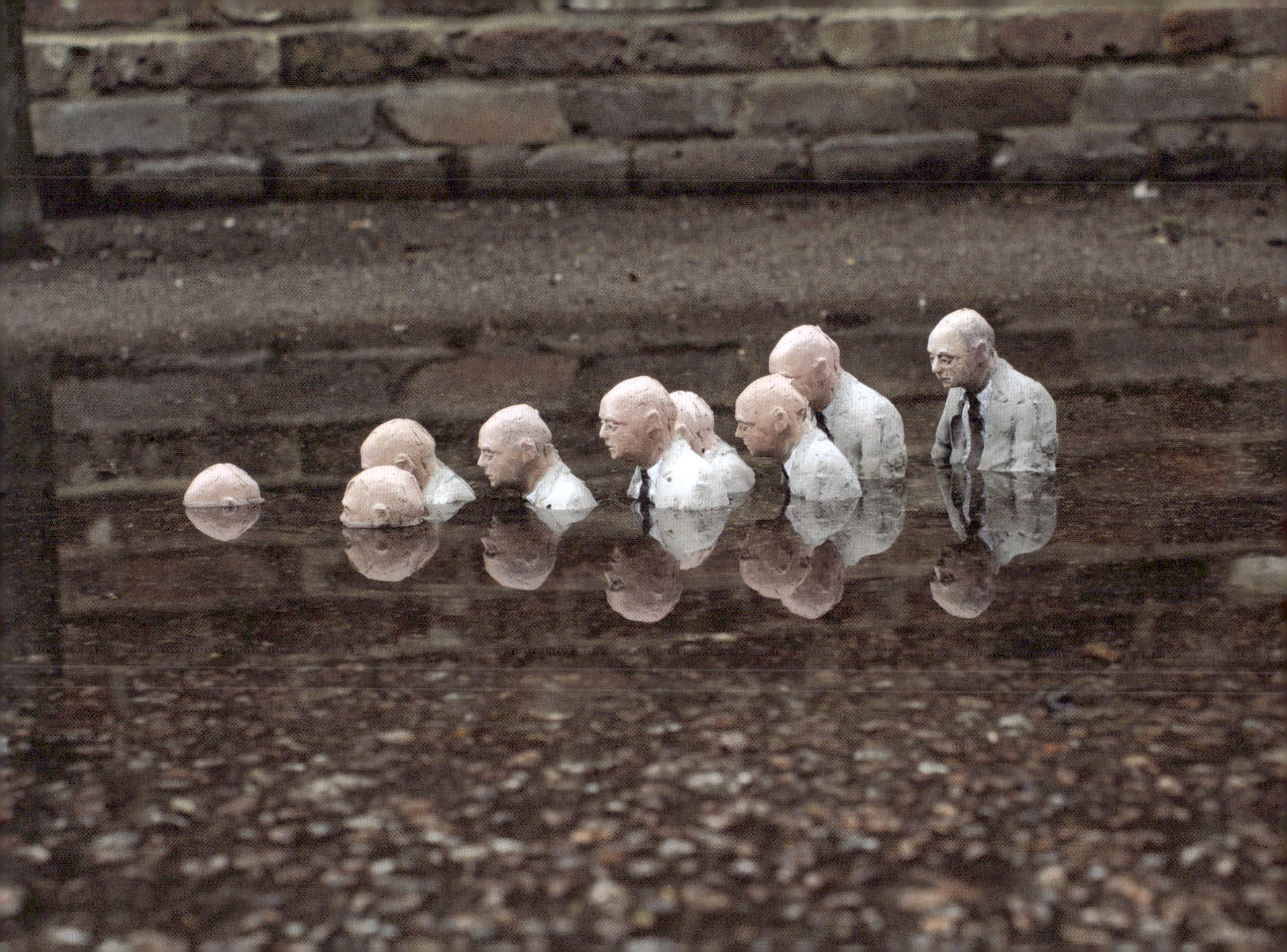

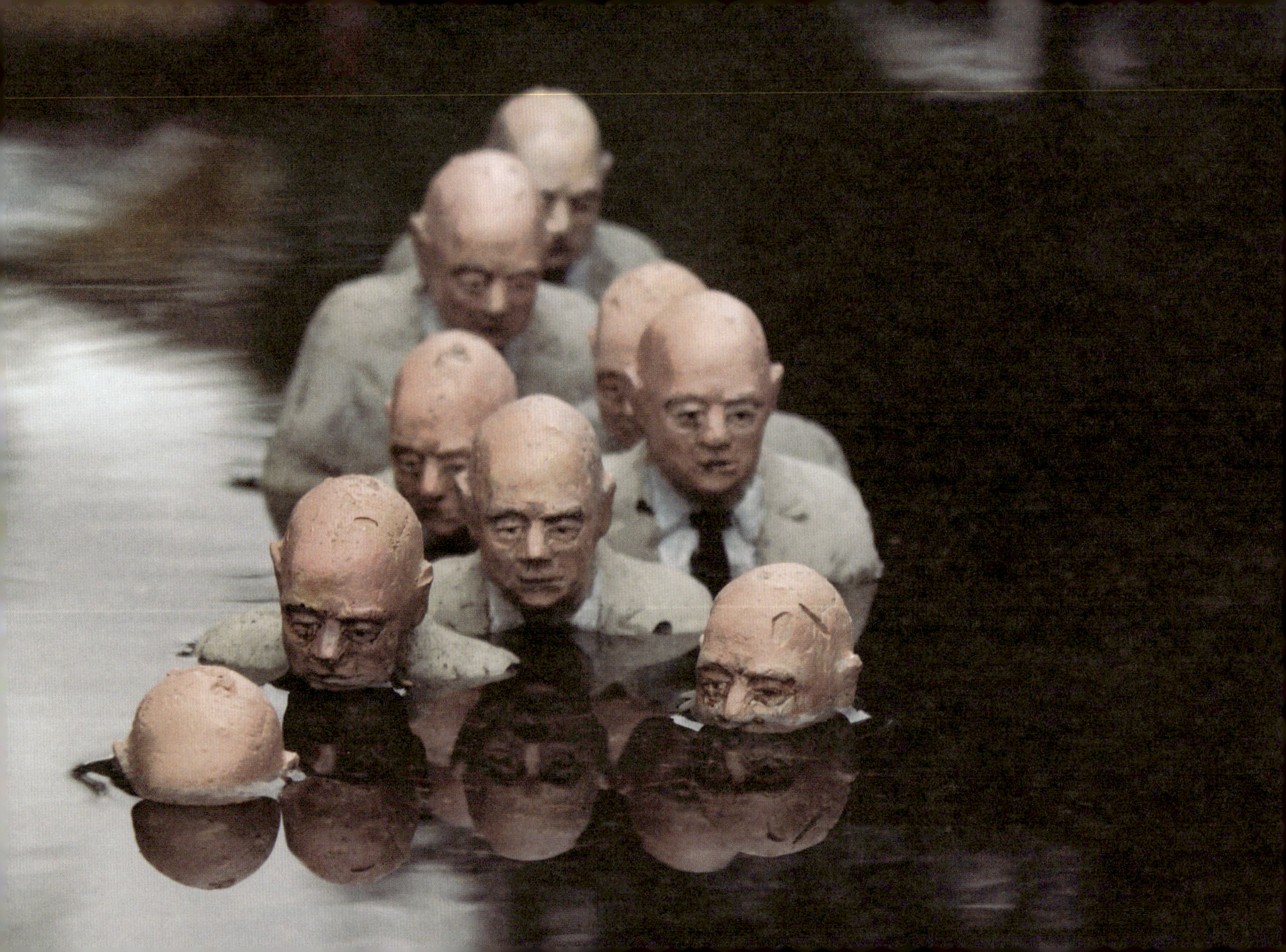

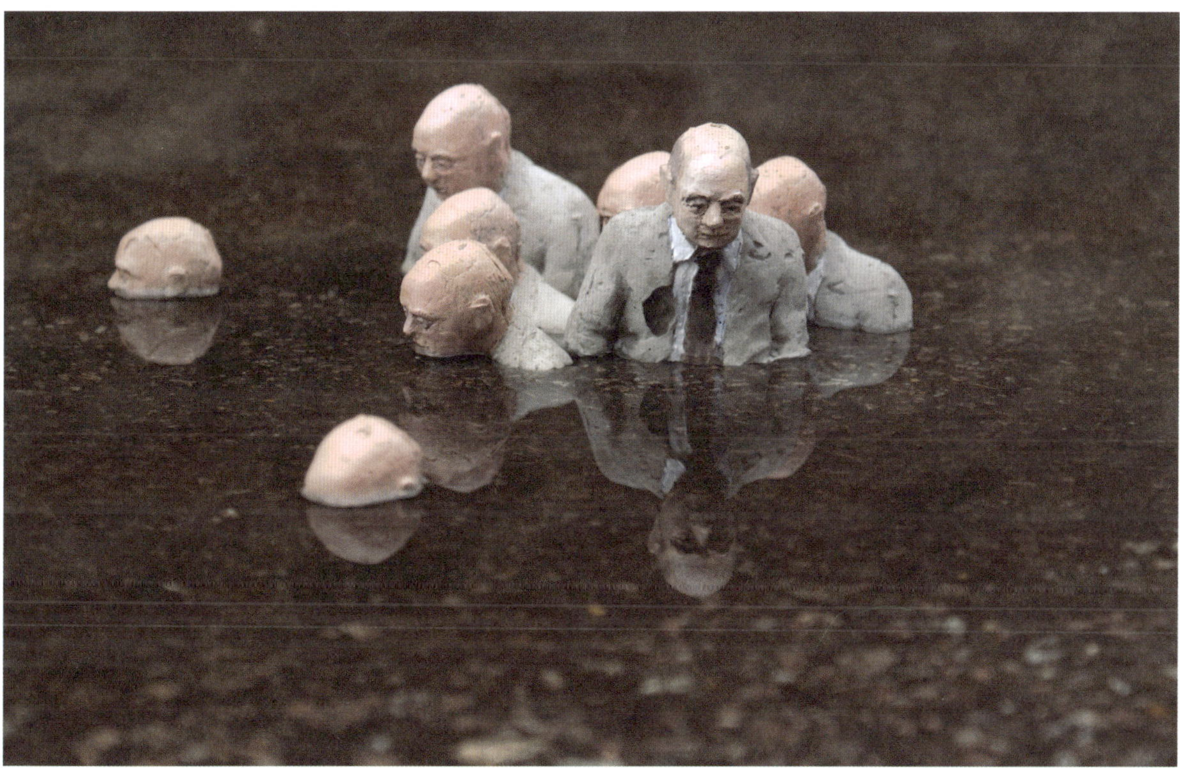

THE TENANT
LONDON
2010

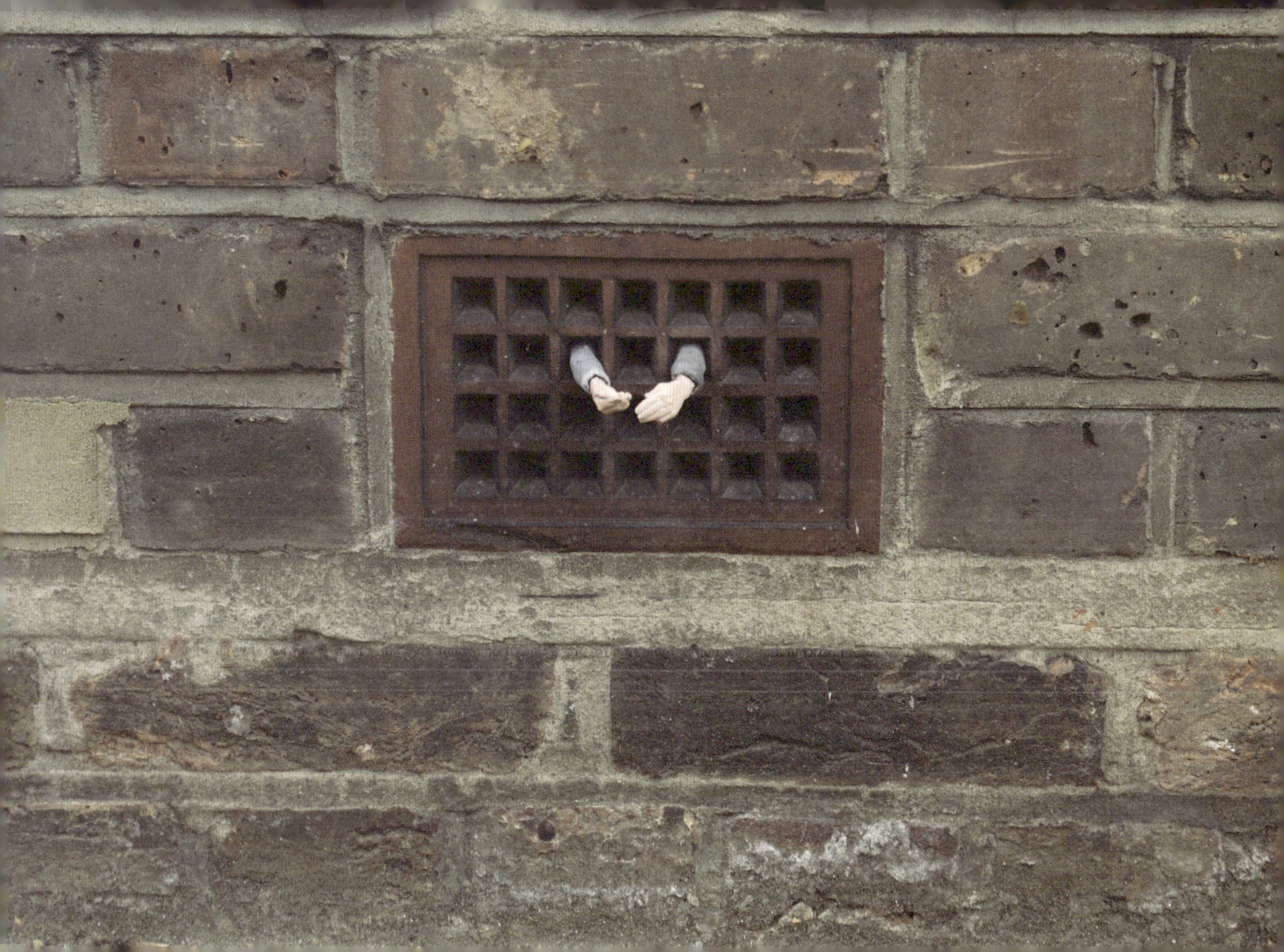

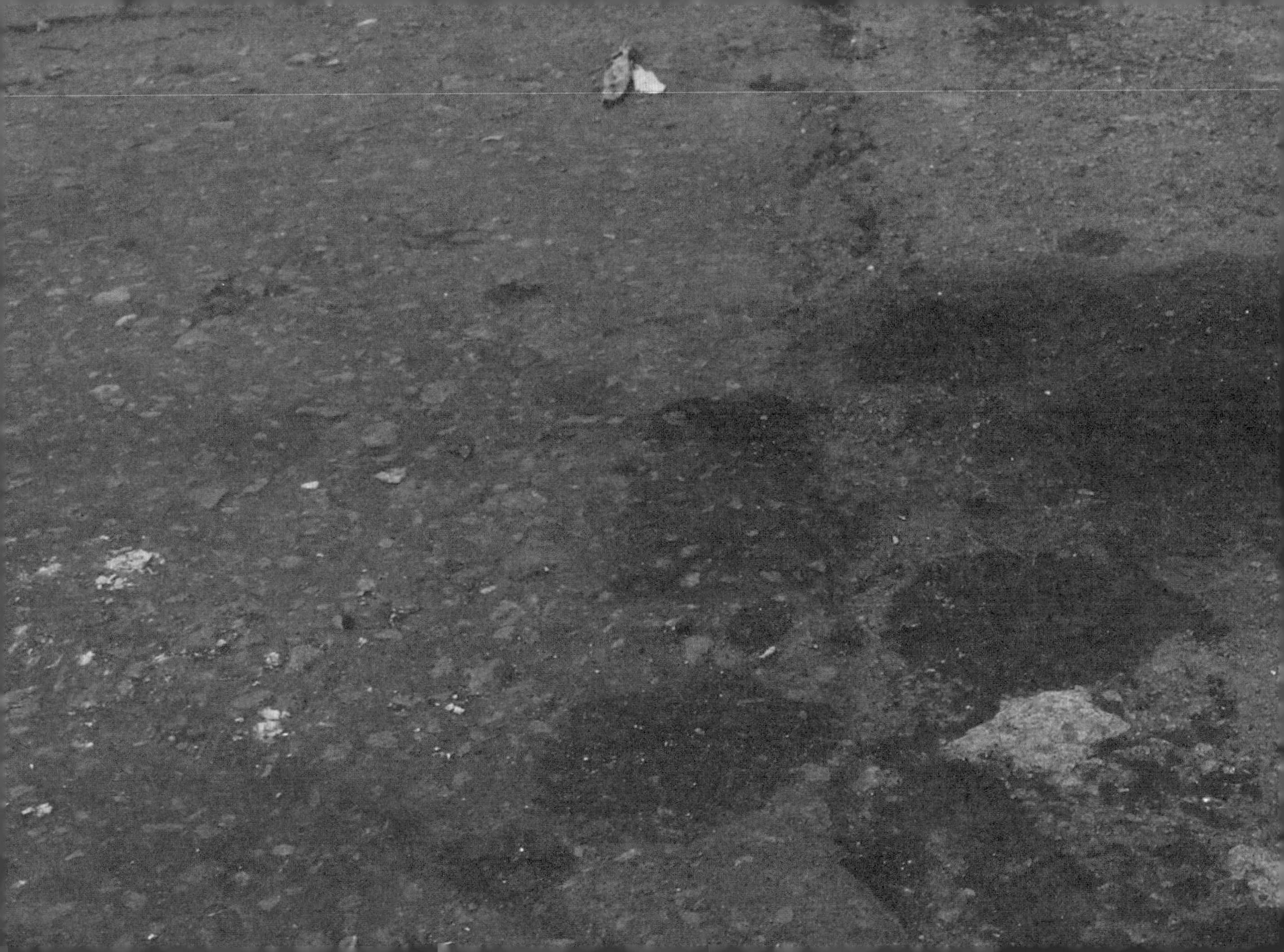

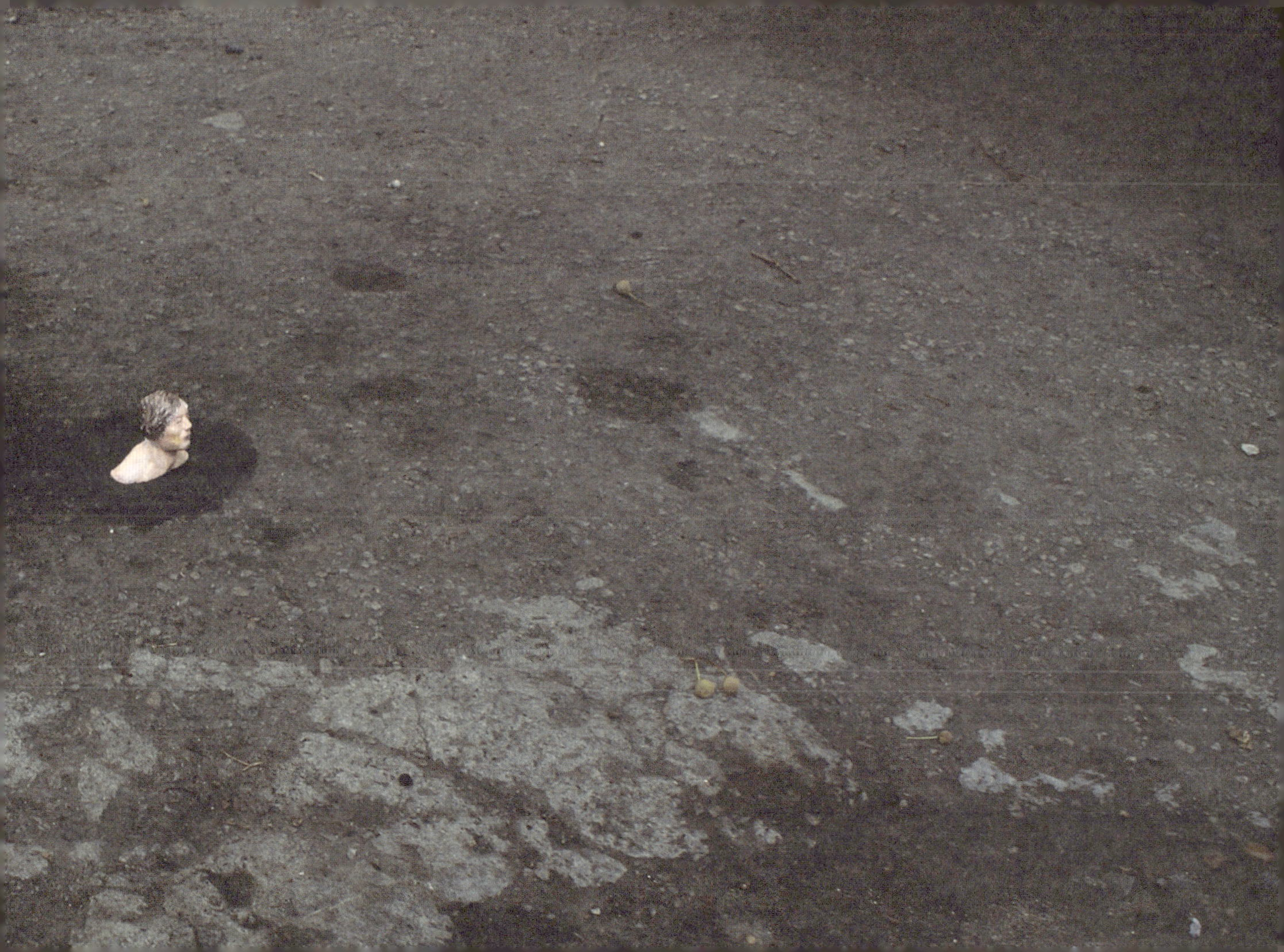

ANOTHER PUBLIC SWIMMING POOL
LONDON
2010

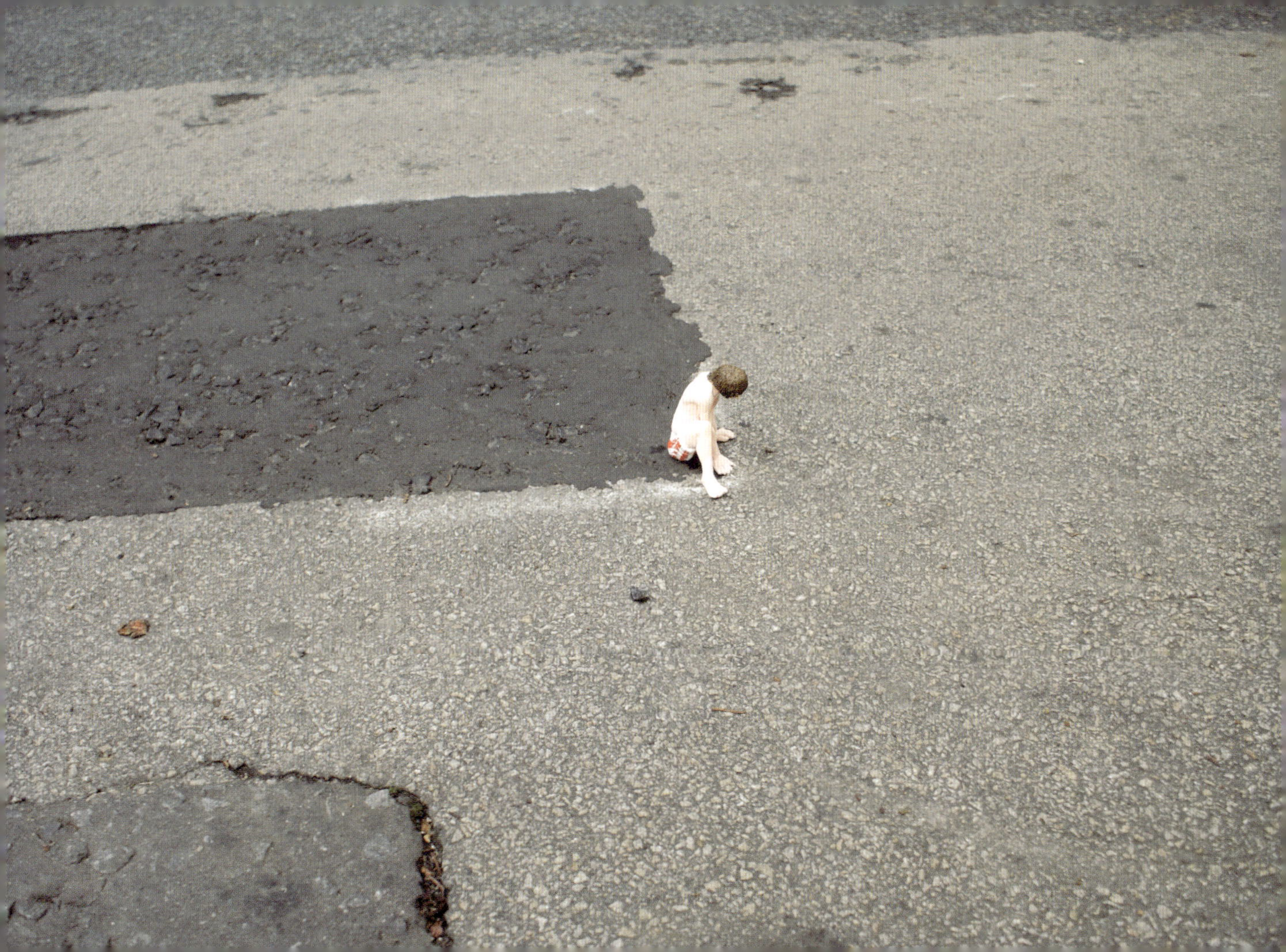

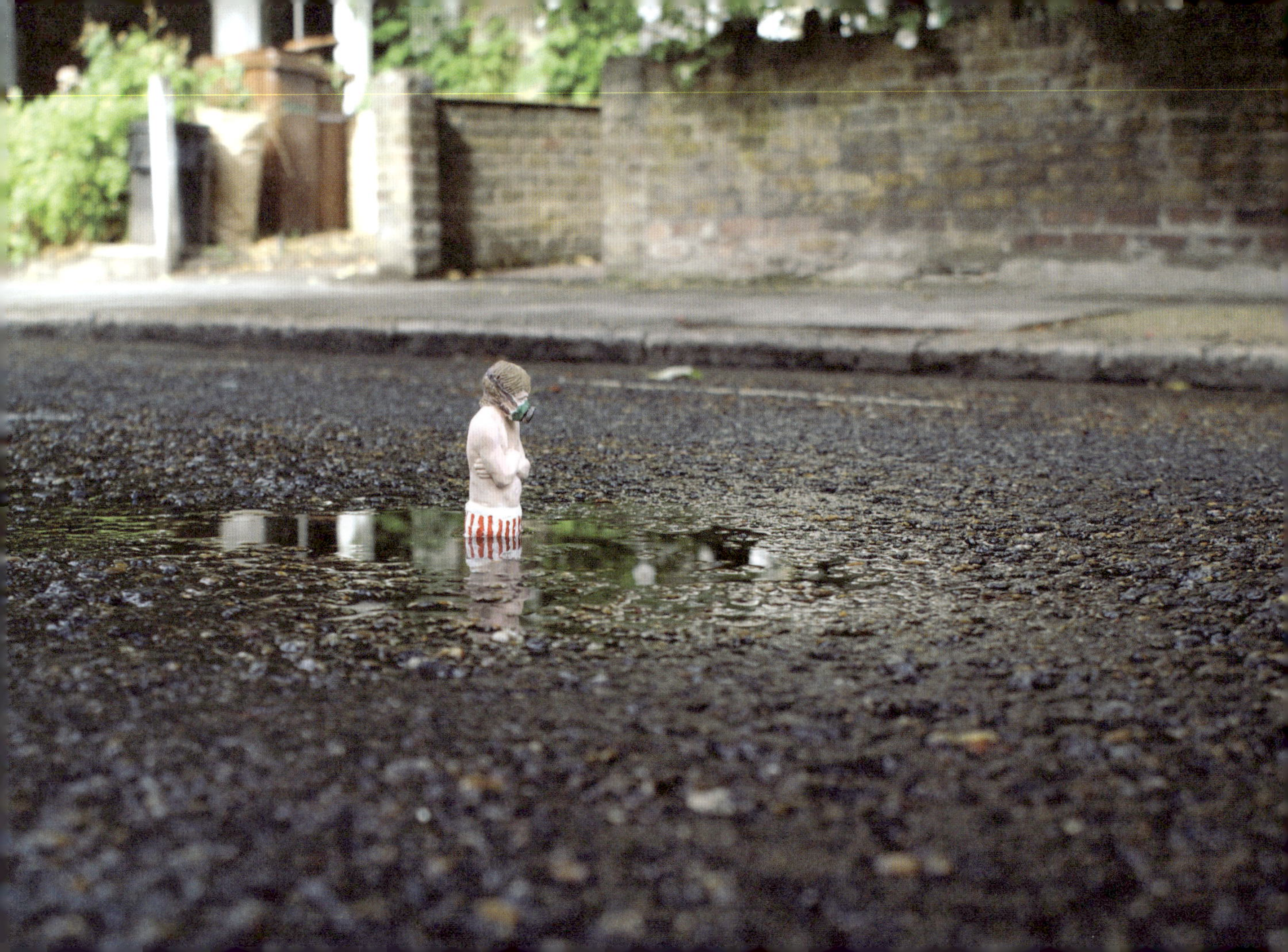

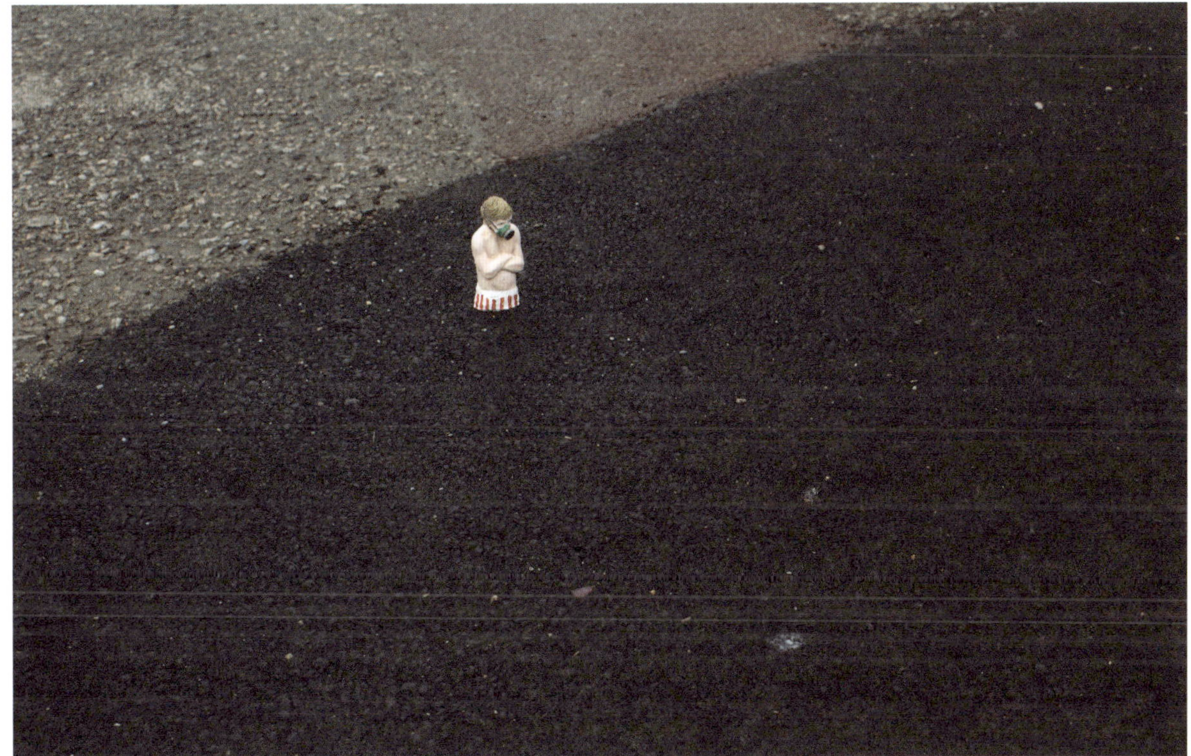

ADDICT
LONDON-BRUSSELS-PONTEVEDRA
2010

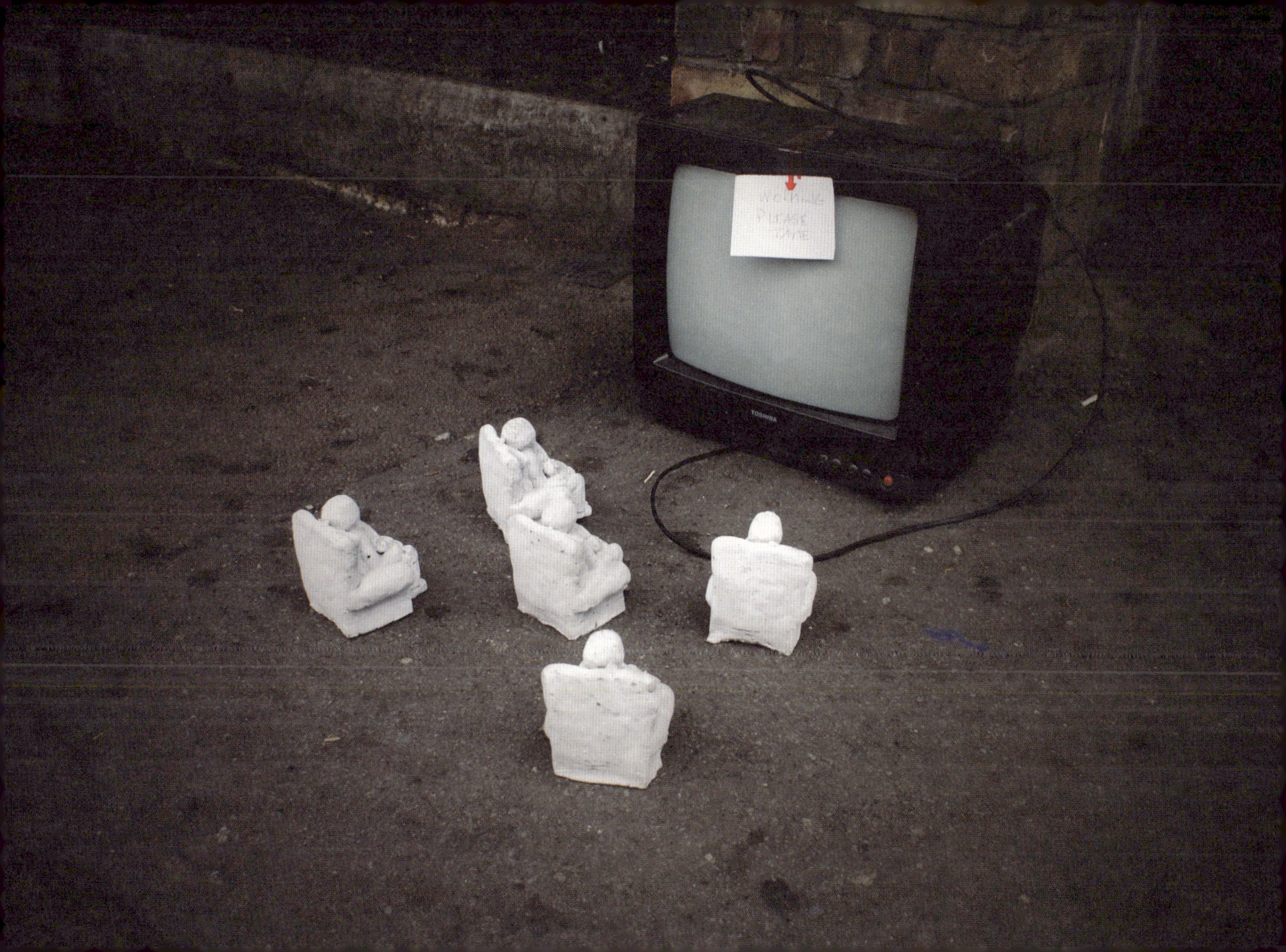
WORKING
PLEASE
WAIT
TOSHIBA

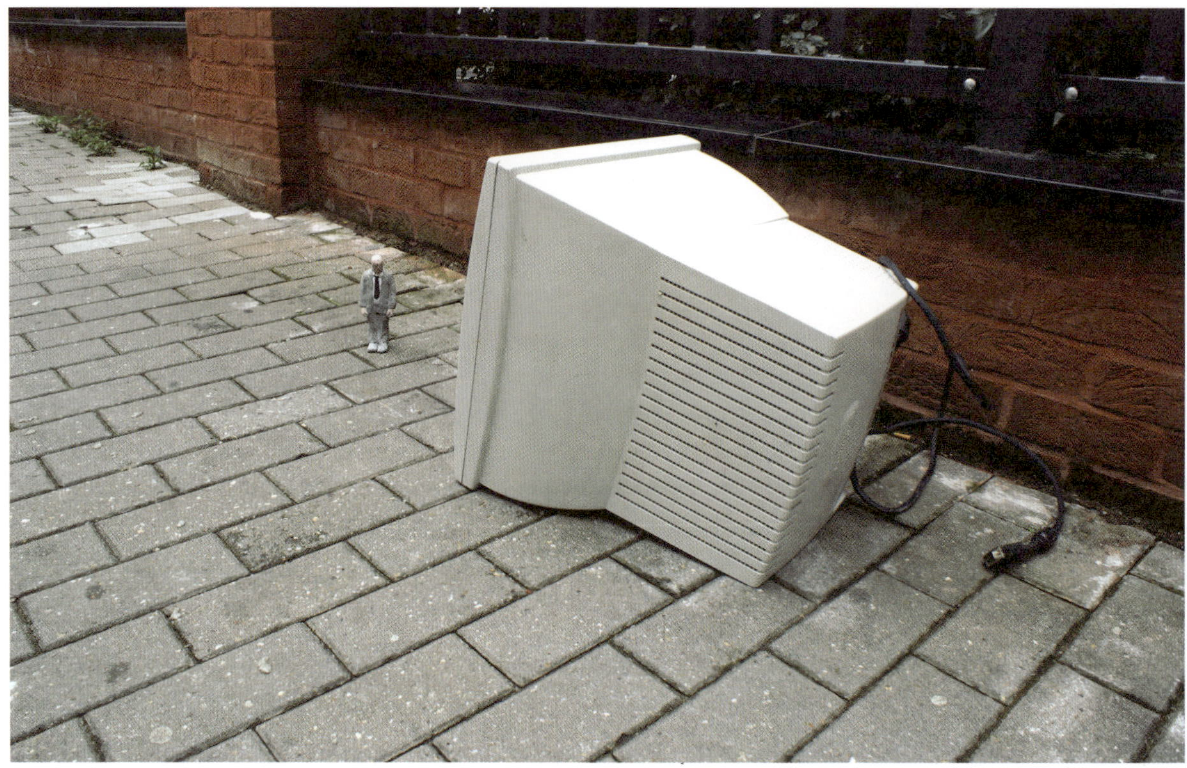

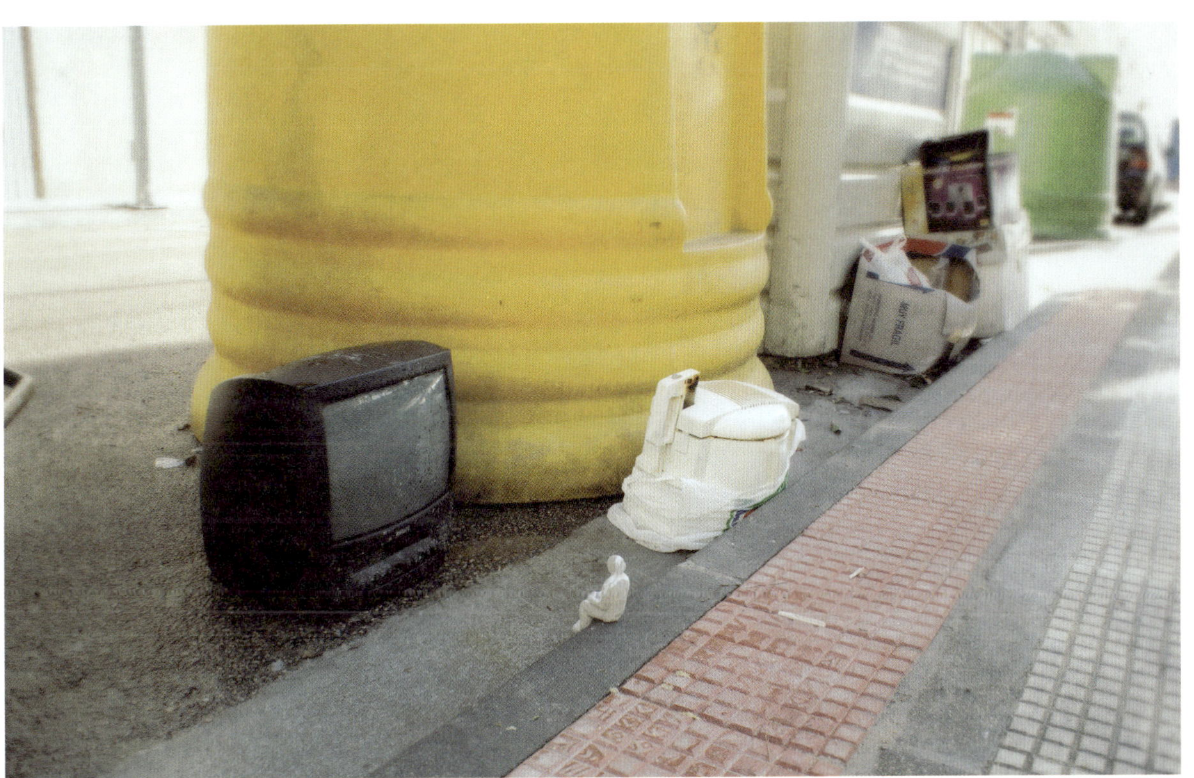

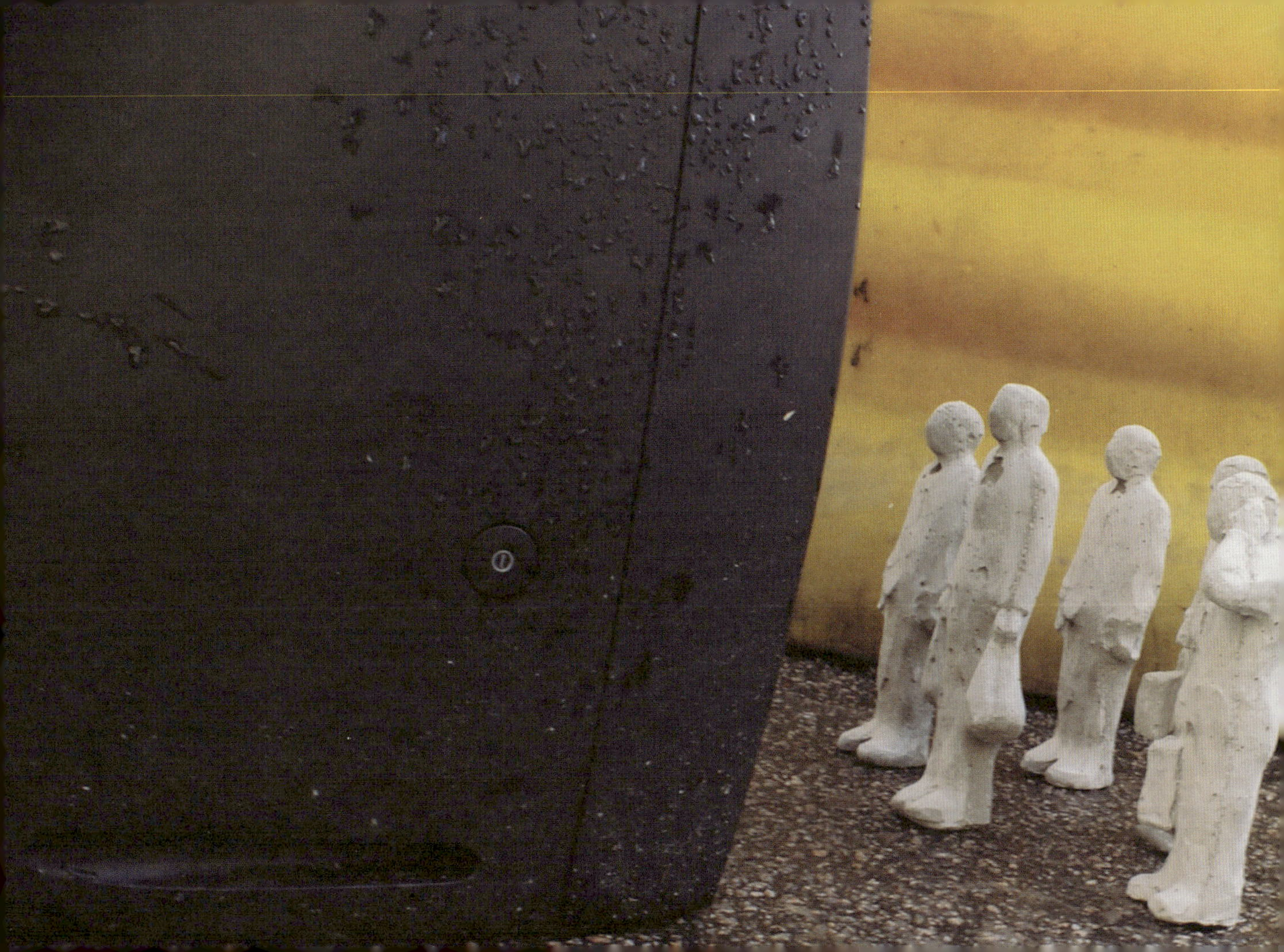

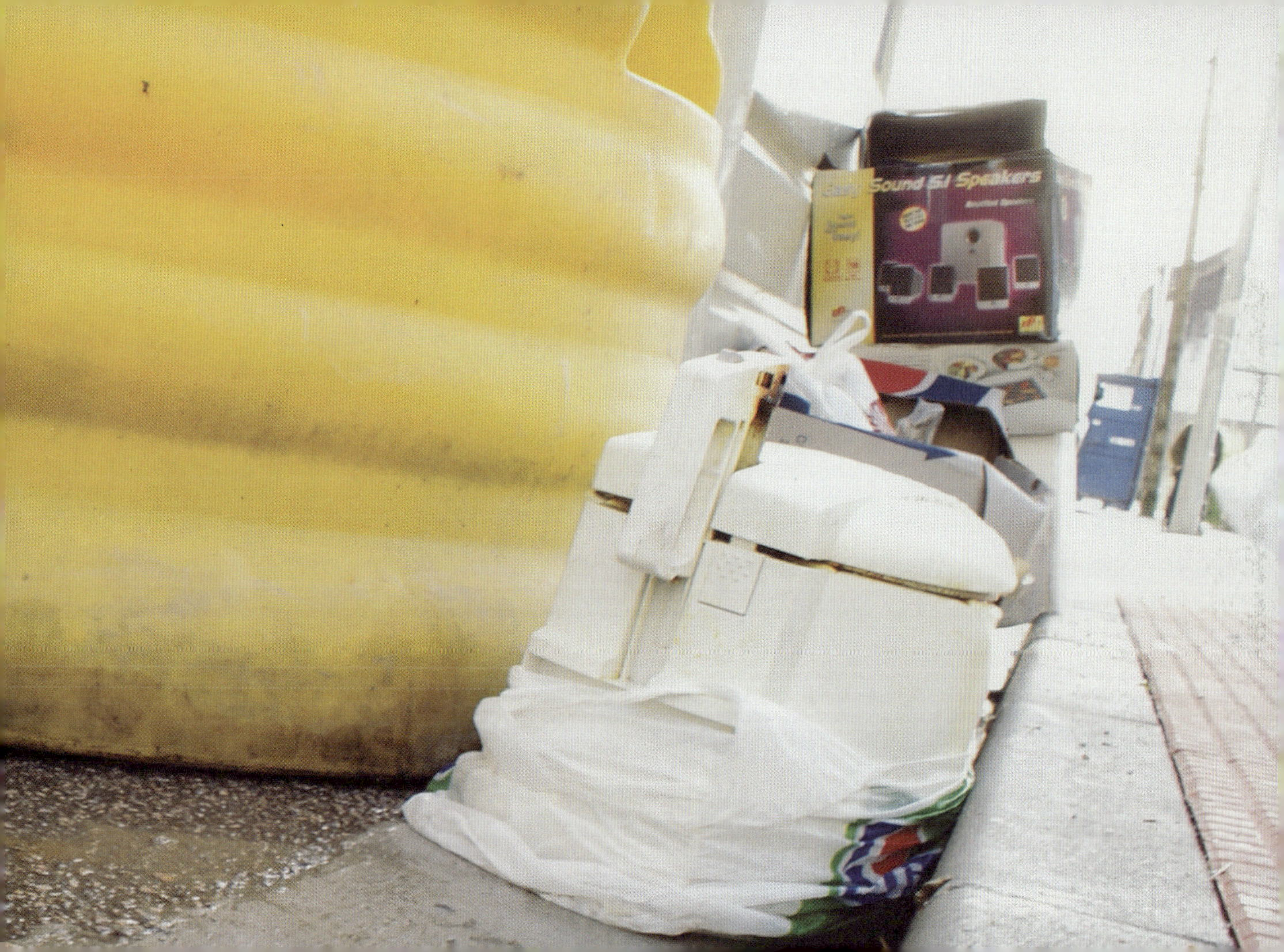

Sound 5.1 Speakers

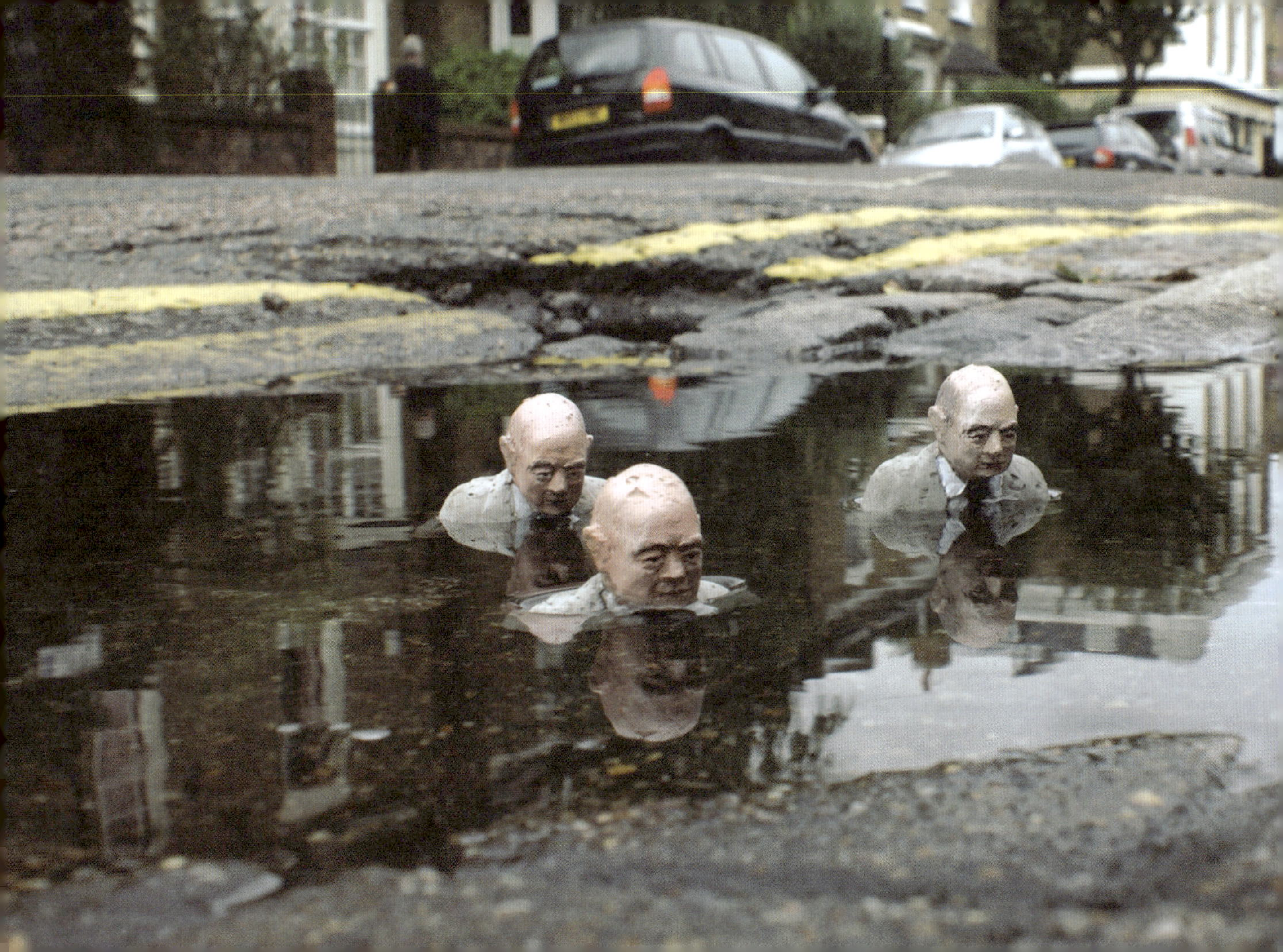

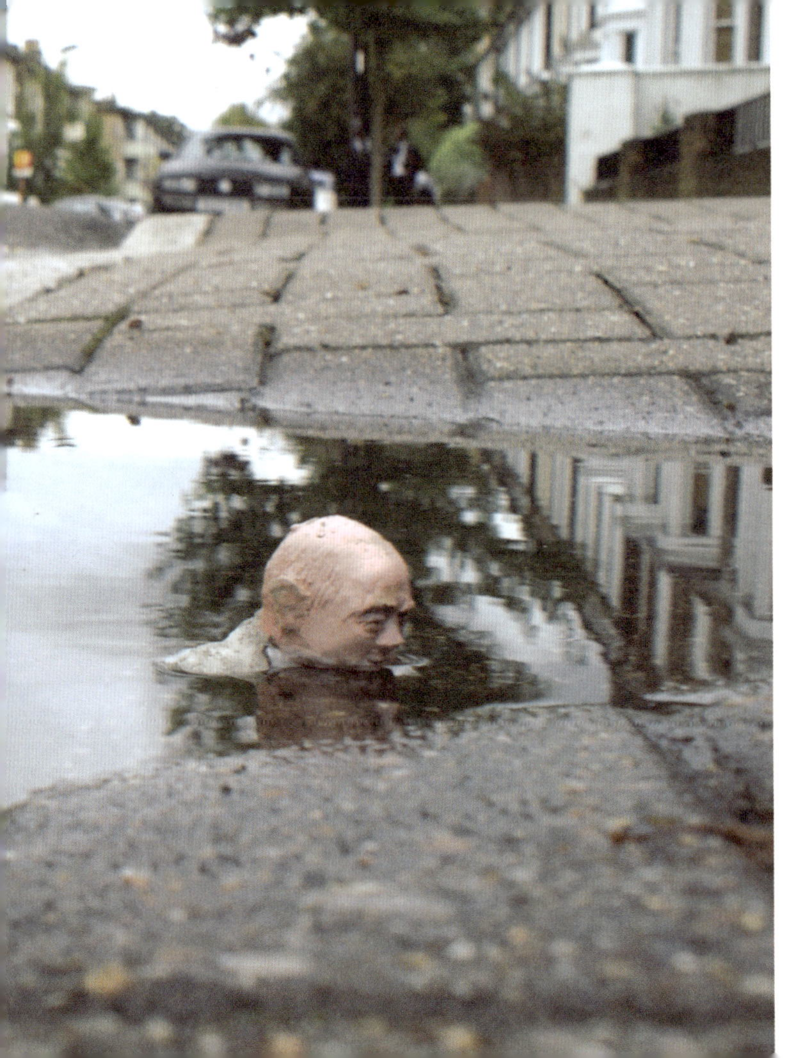

EMIGRANTS
LONDON
2010

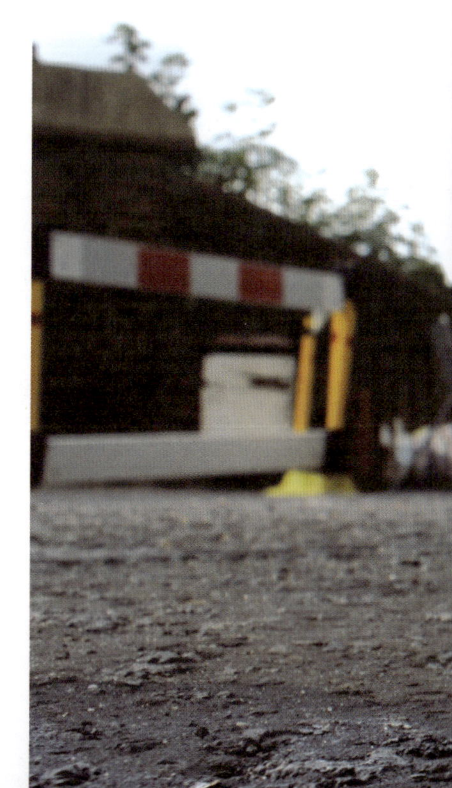

BP SPLASHED US
LONDON
2010

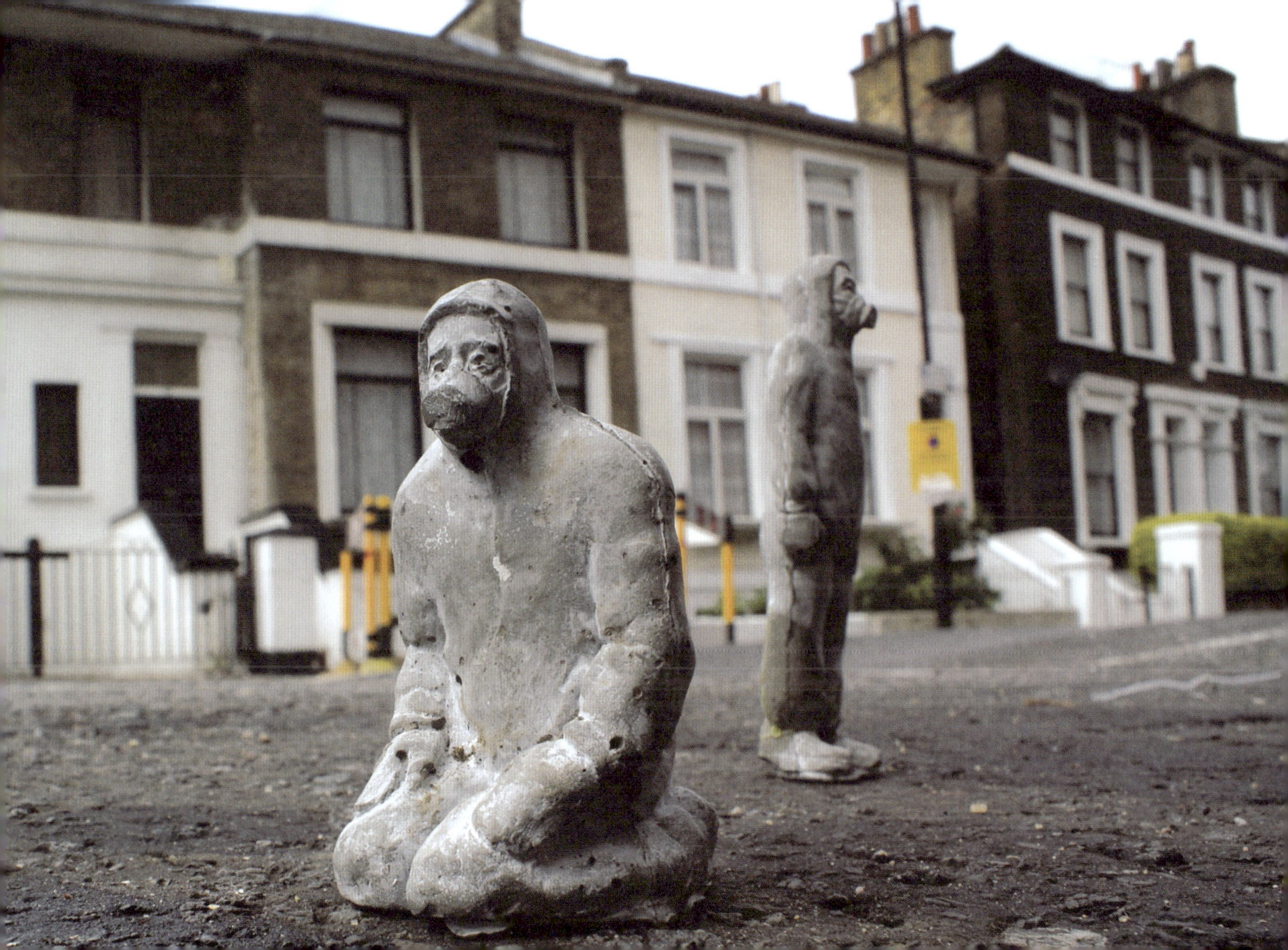

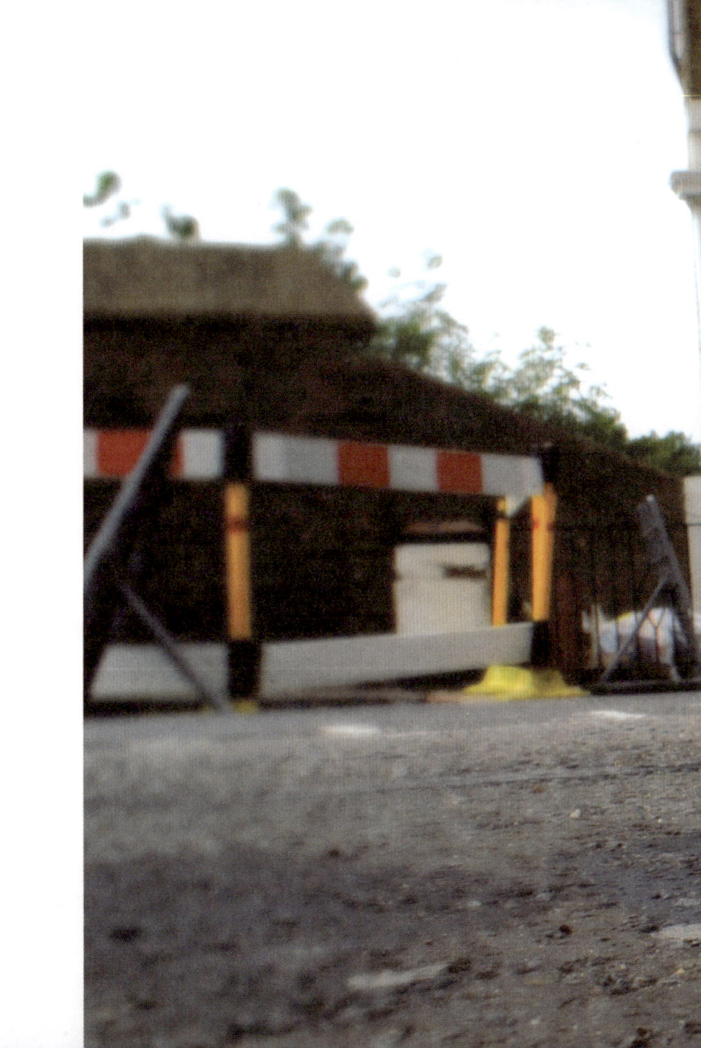

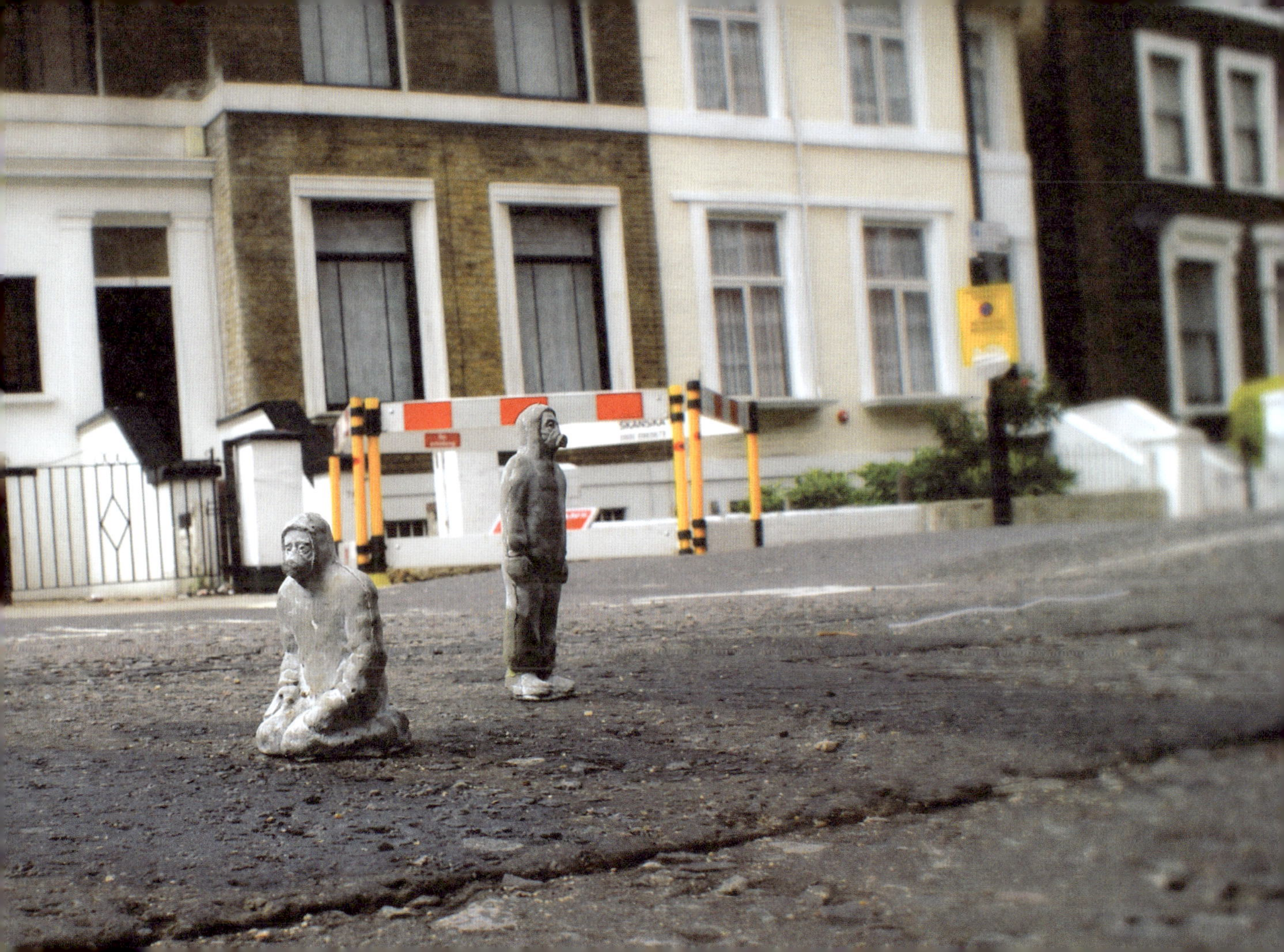

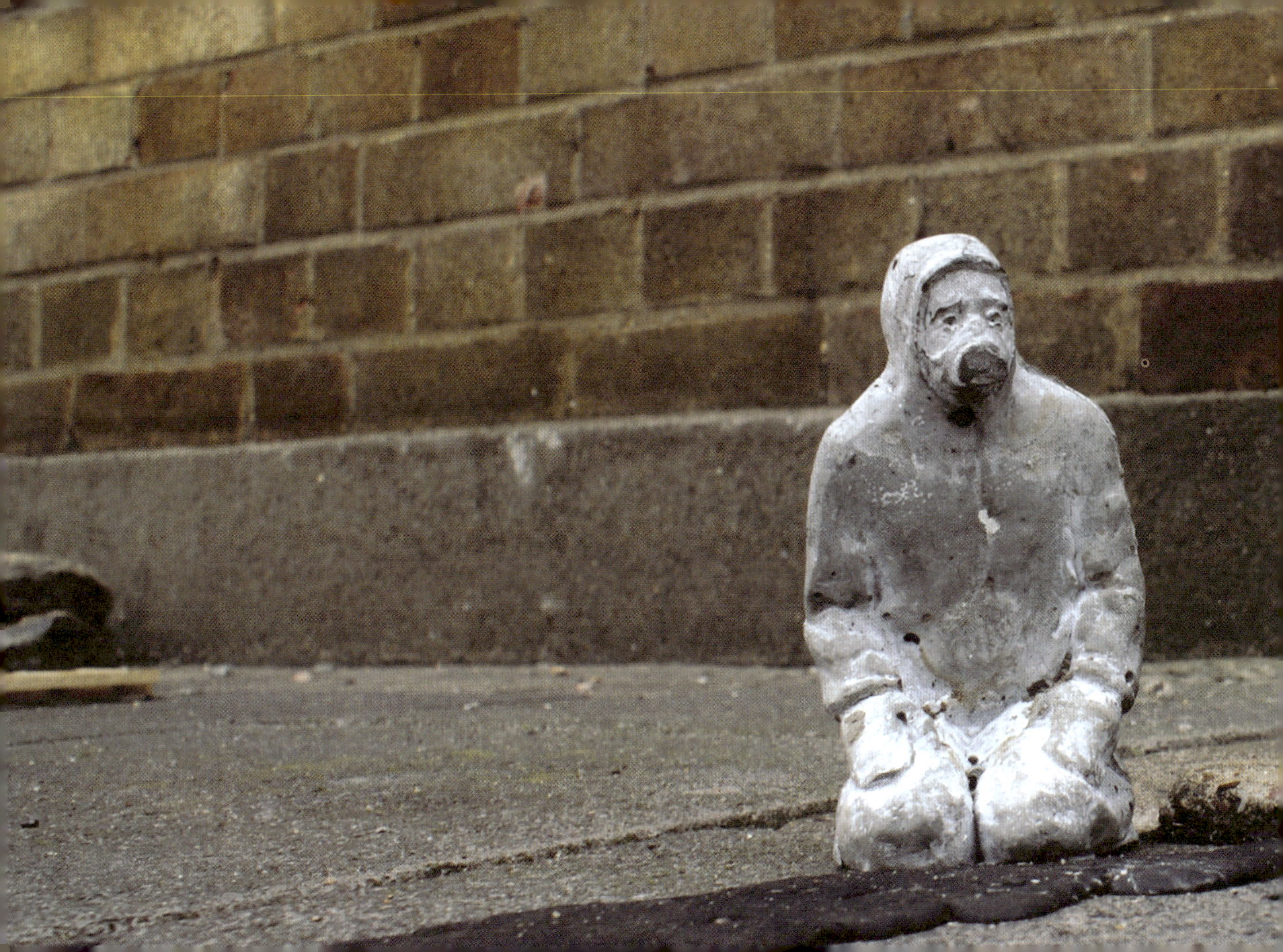

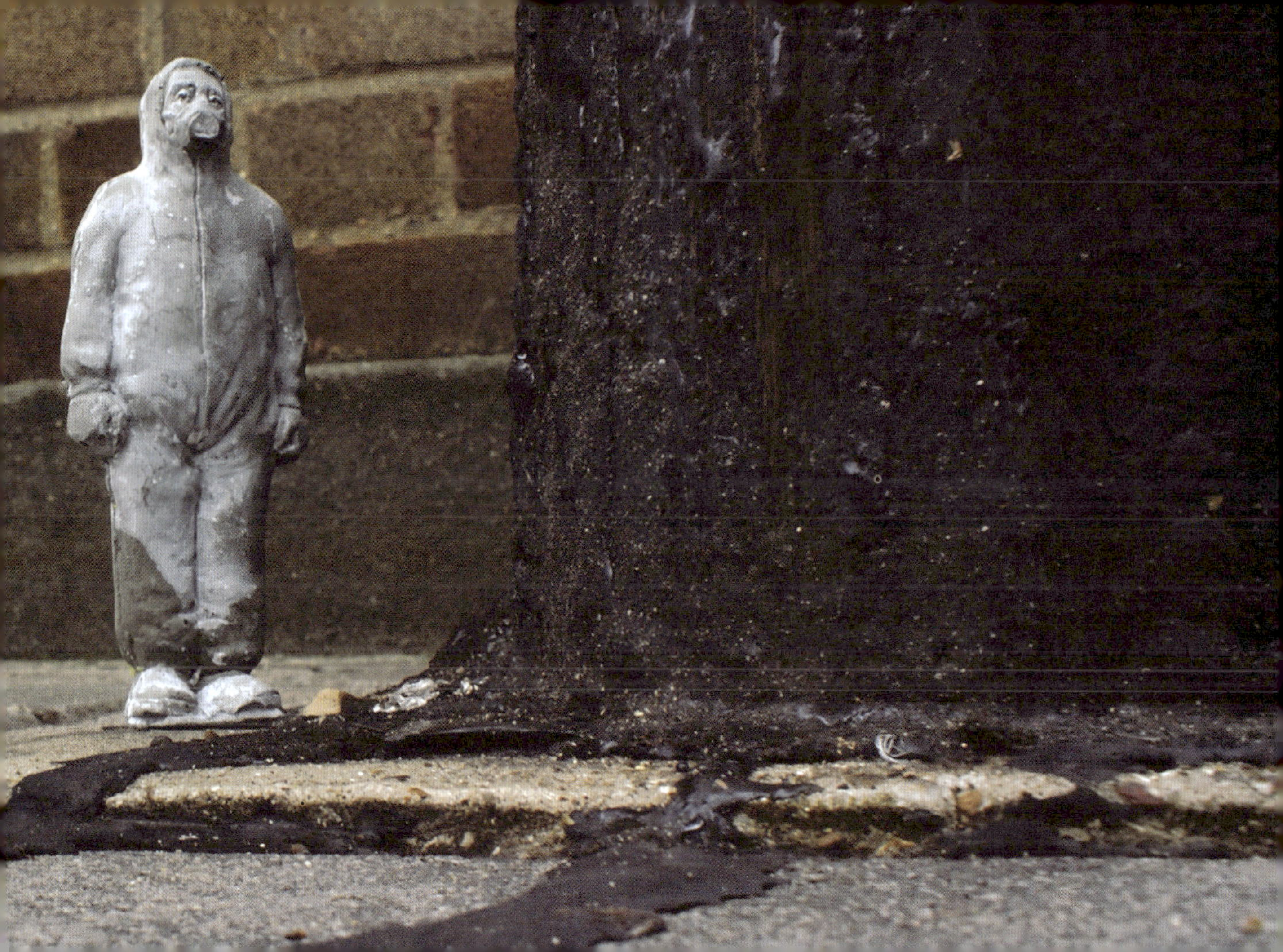

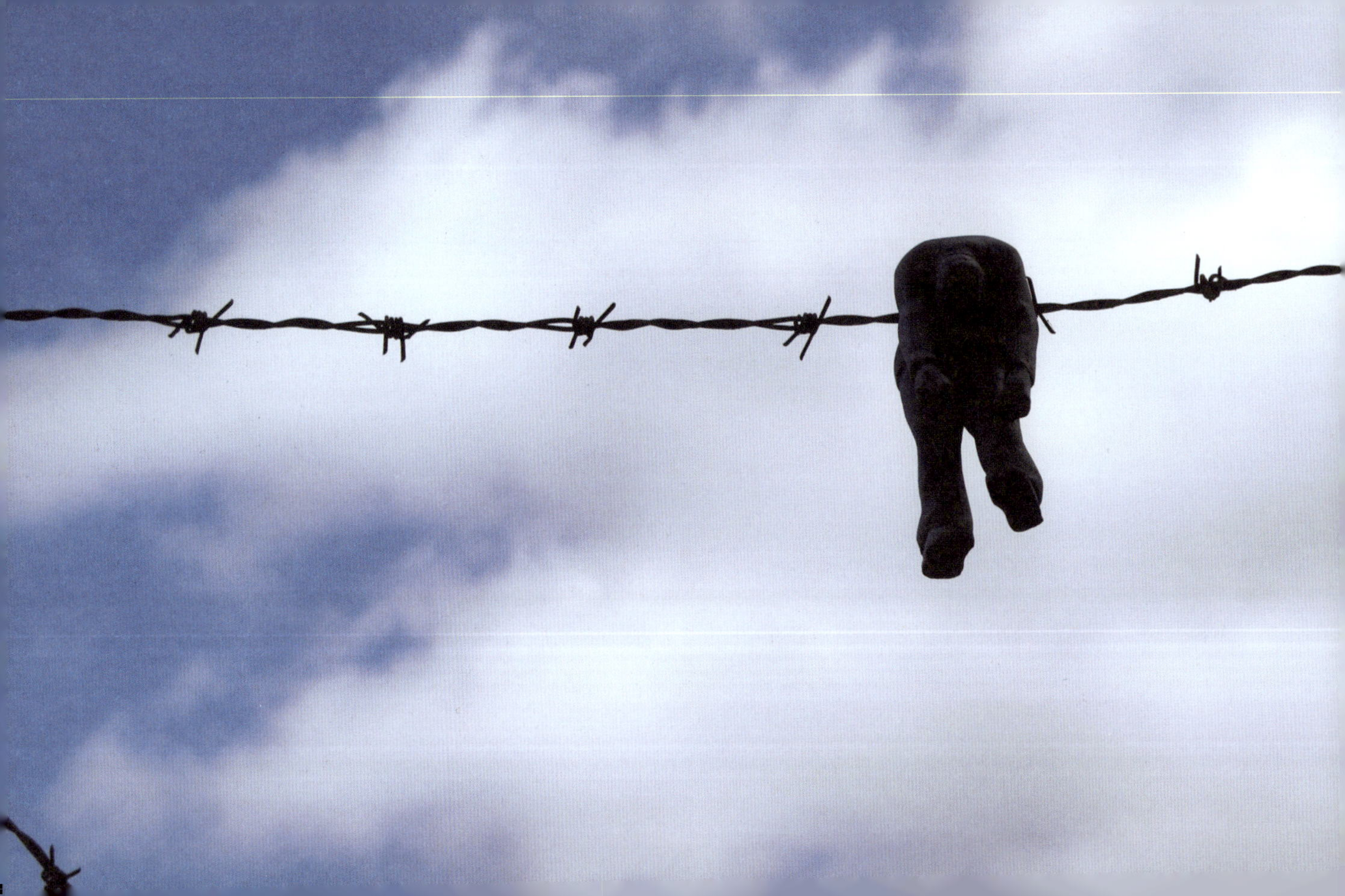

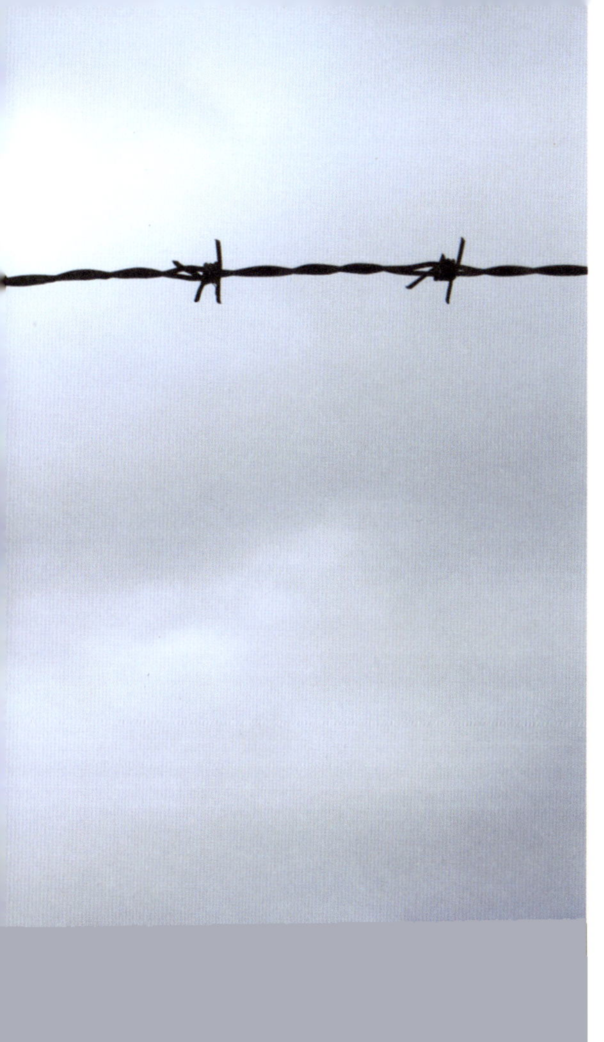

BORDER
LONDON
2010

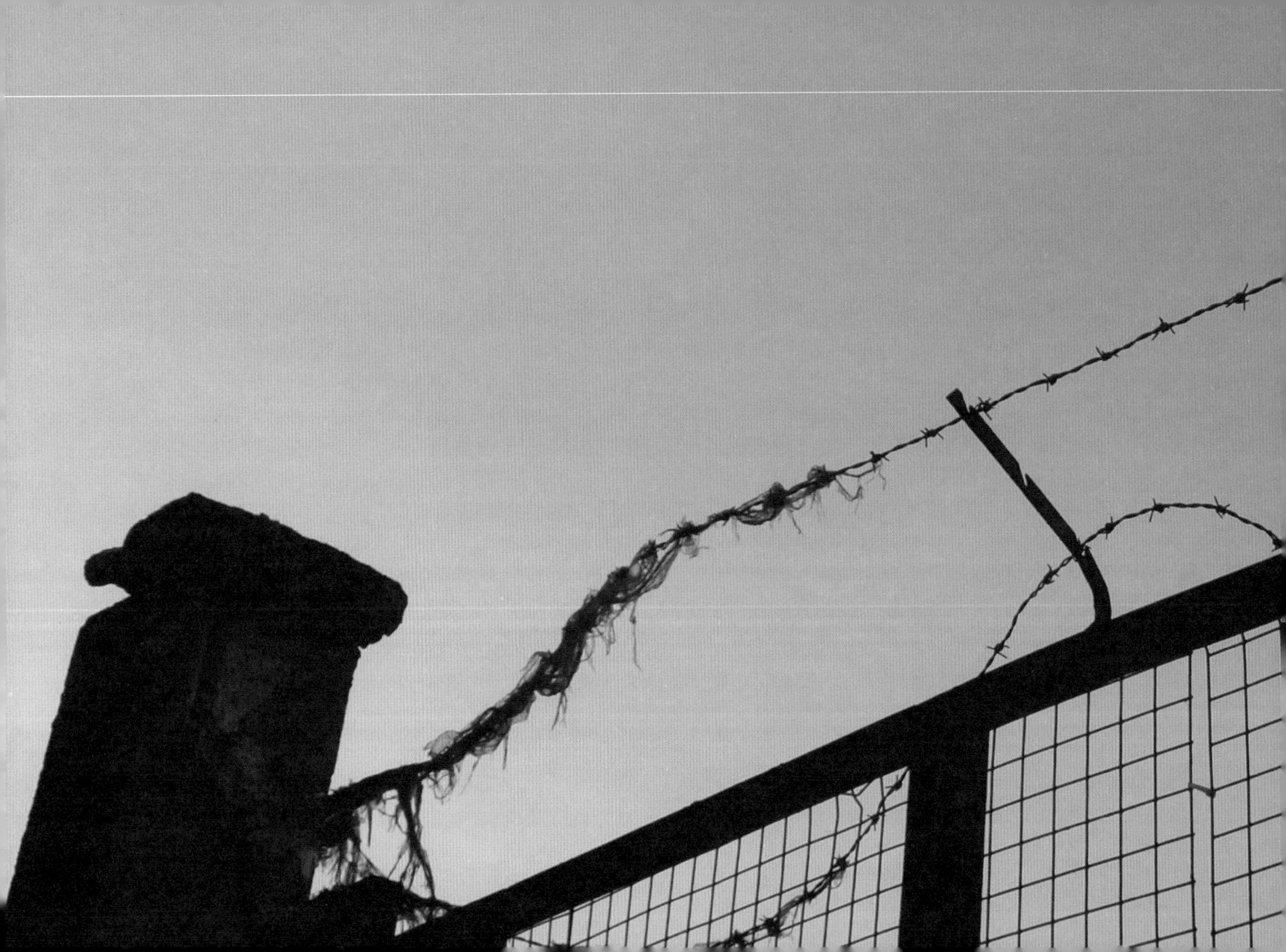

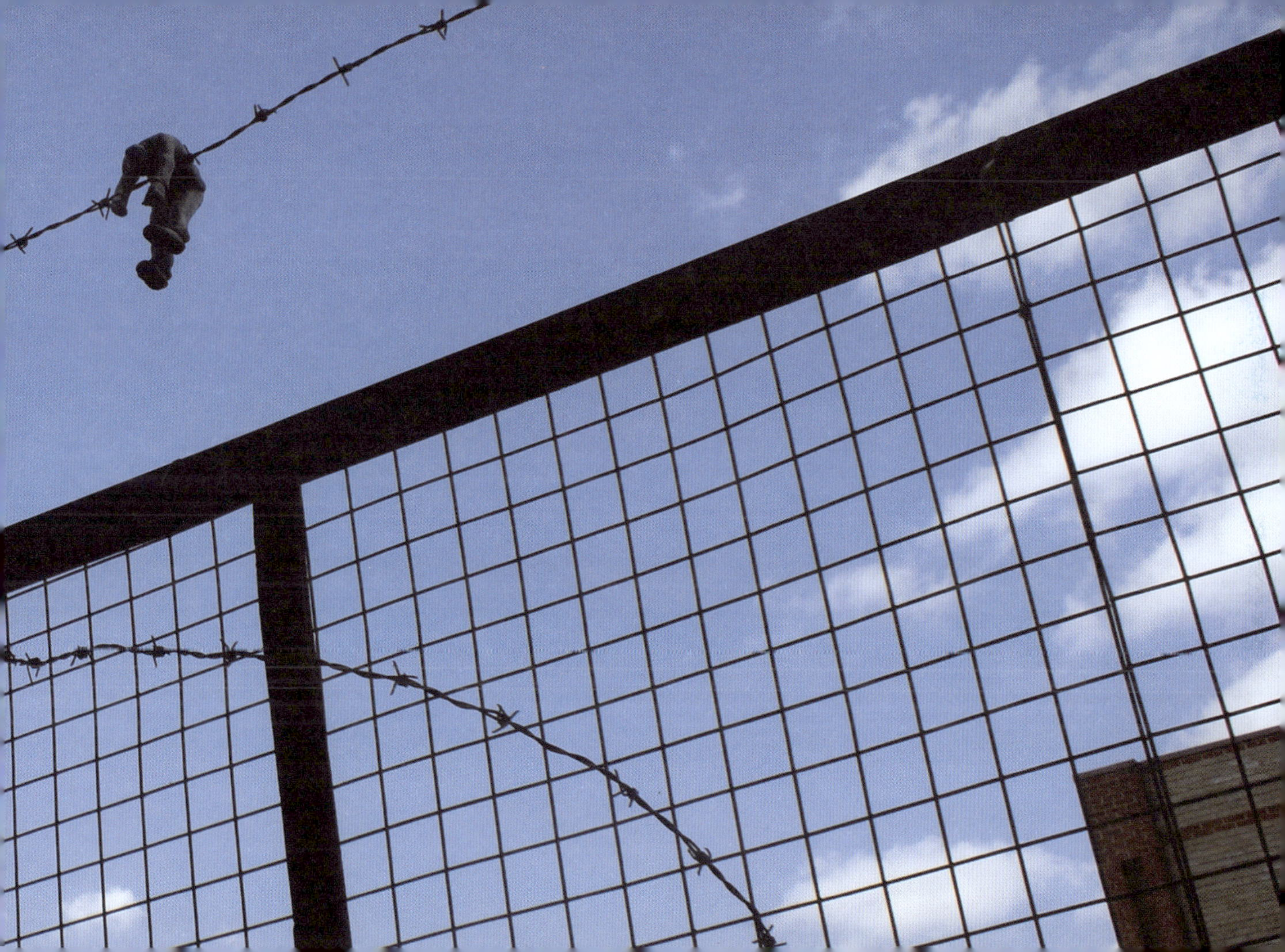

BOWLING FOR CAMBERWELL
LONDON
2009

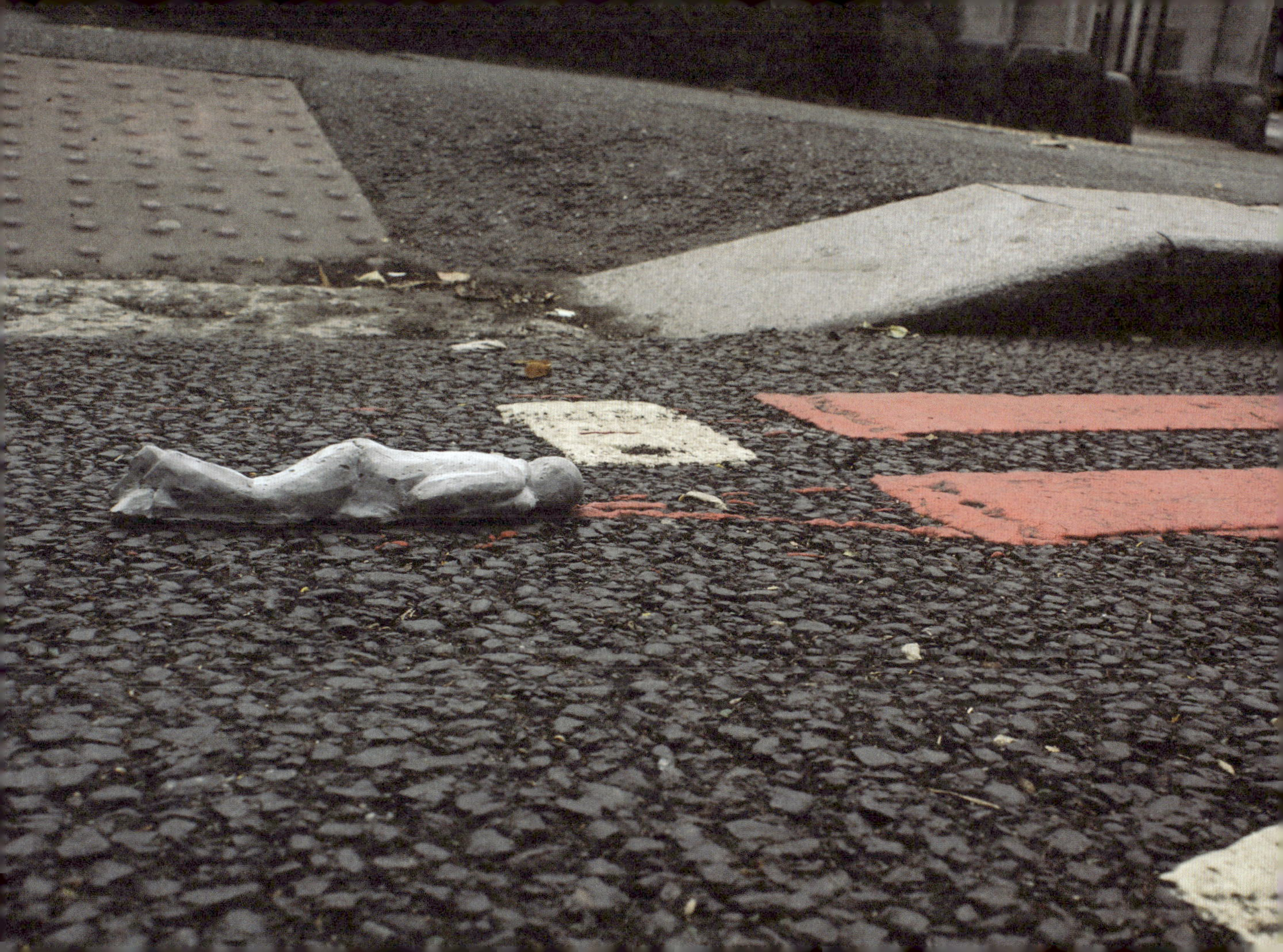

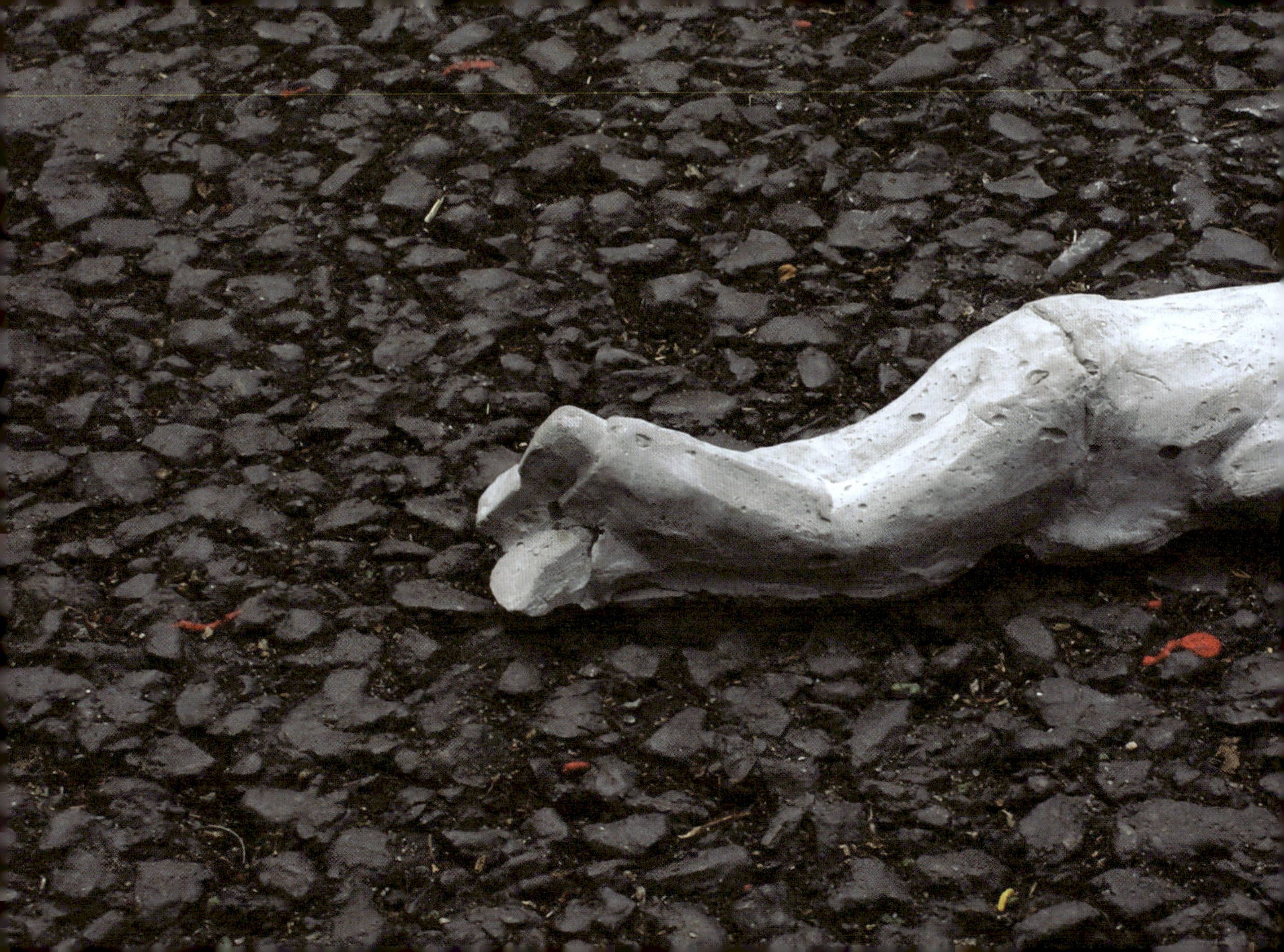

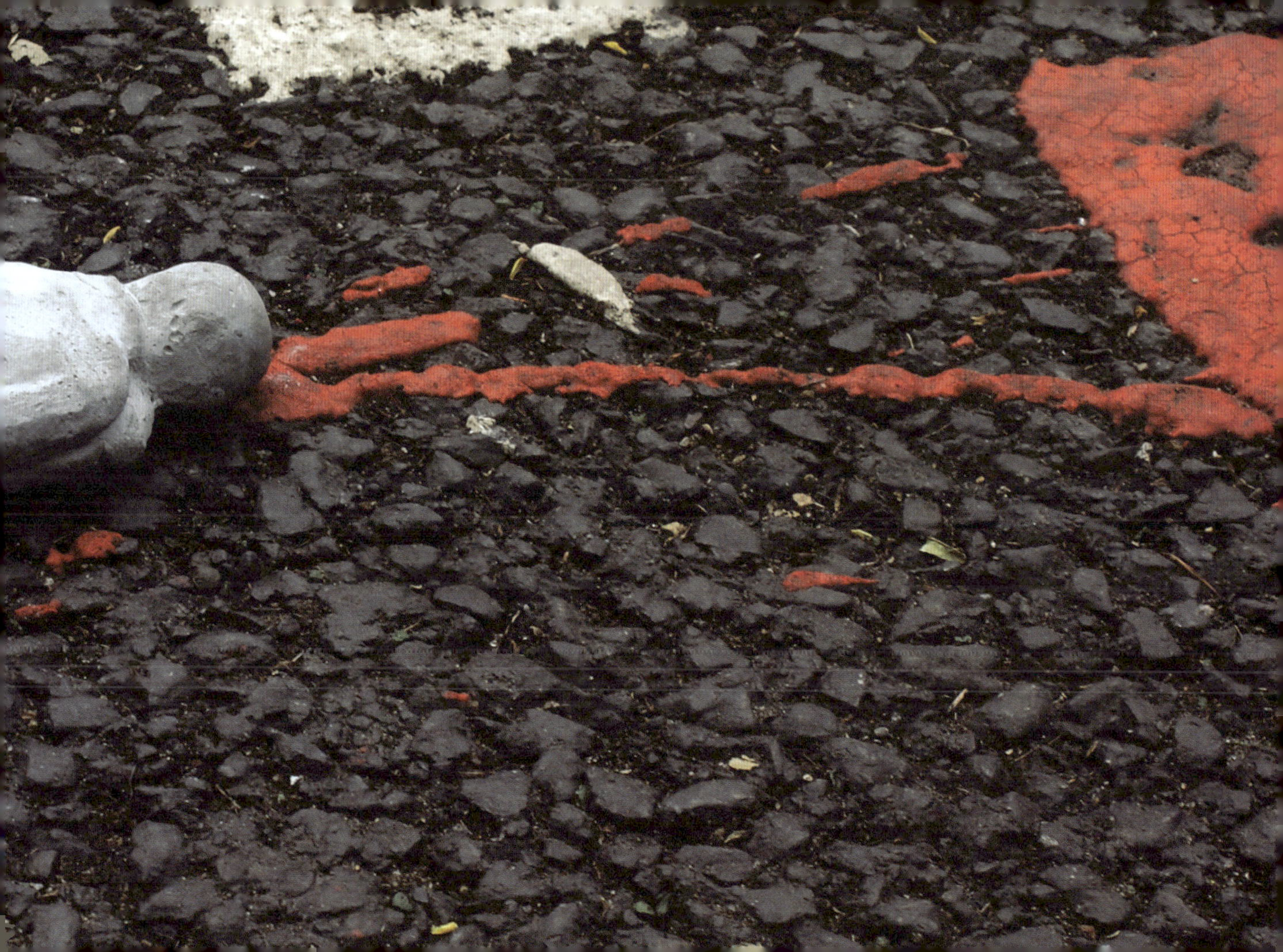

A NOMAD ISLAND
LONDON
2010

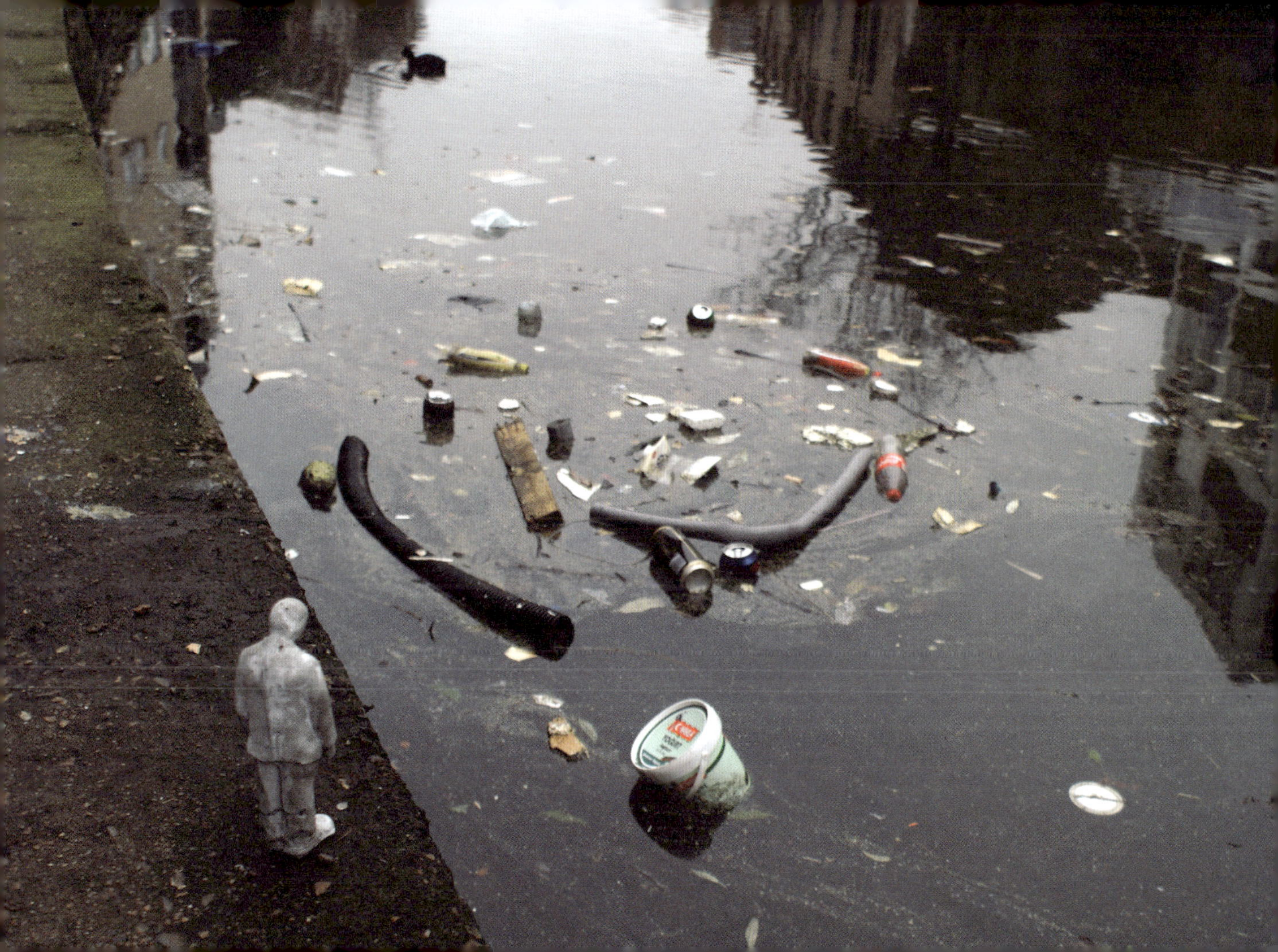

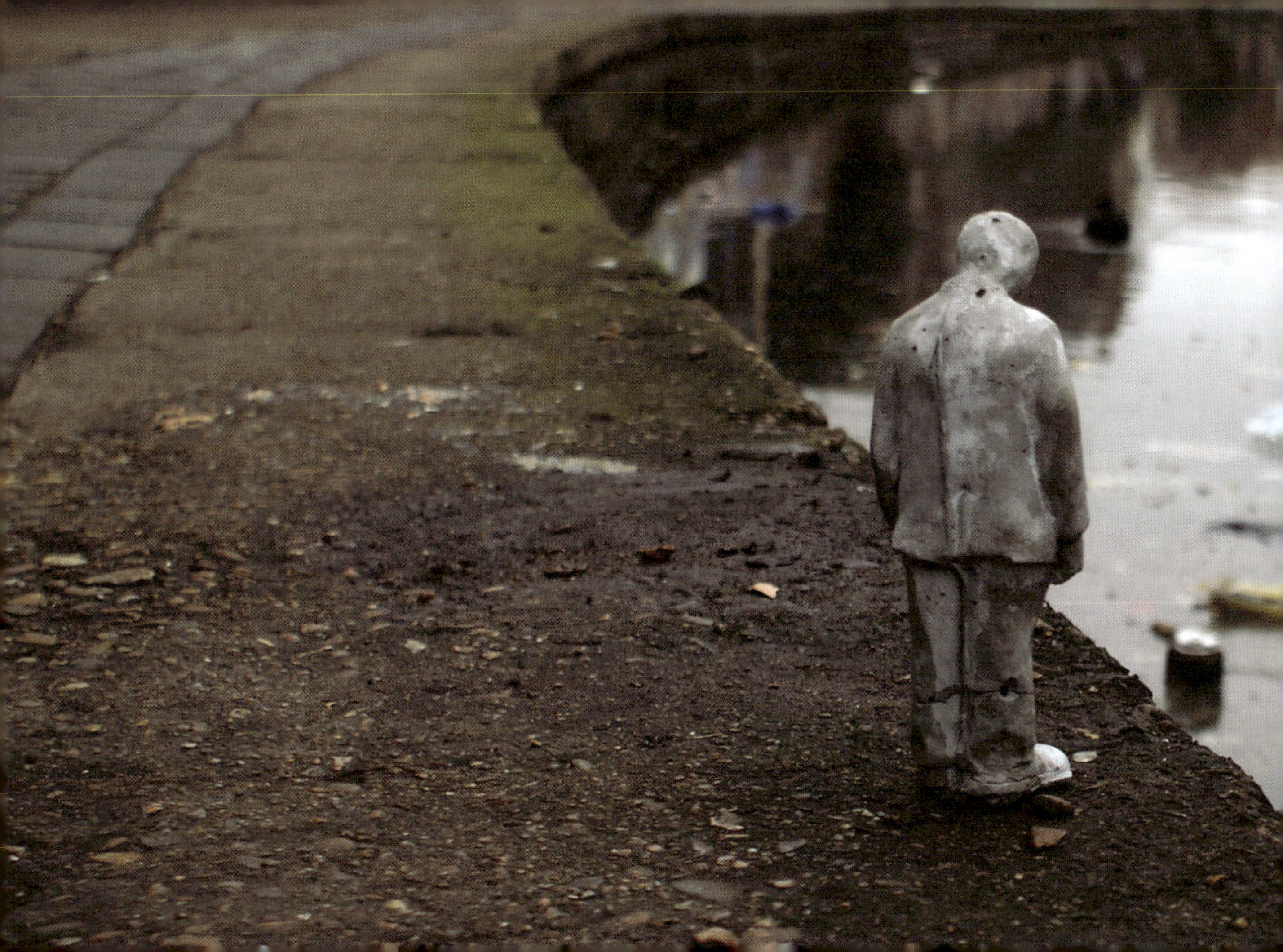

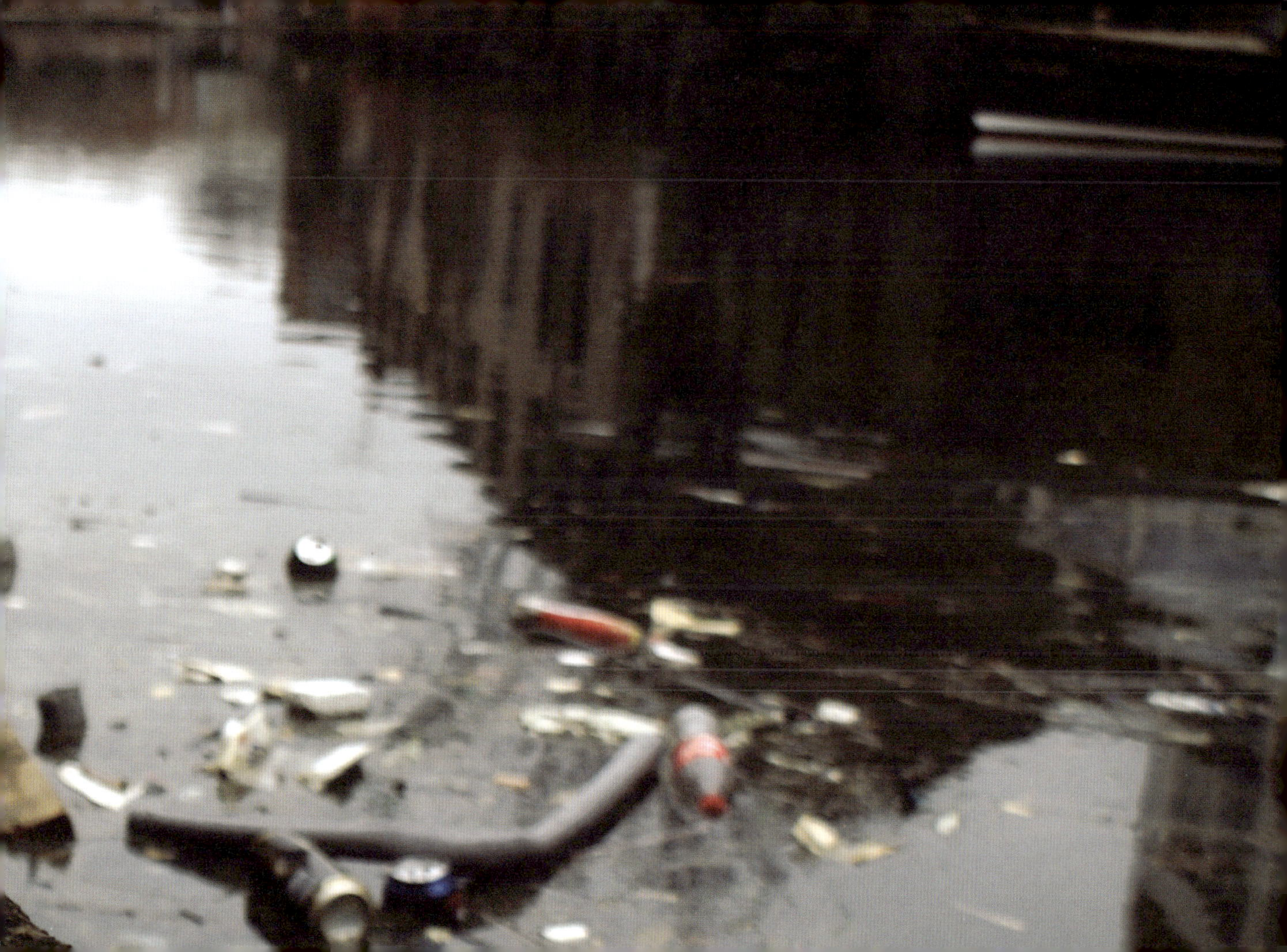

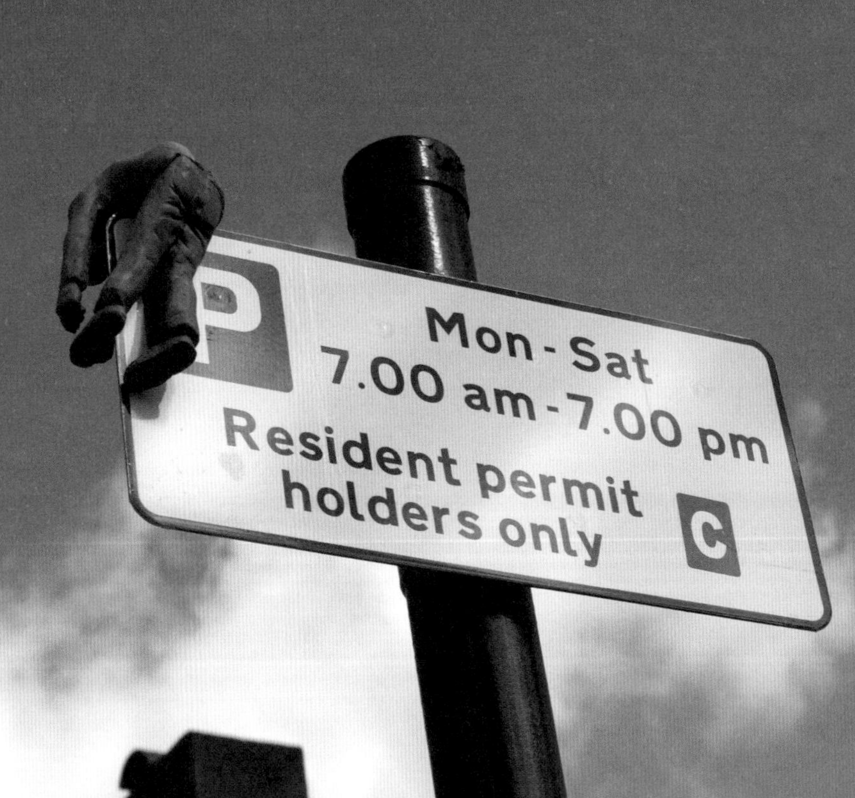

P
Mon - Sat
7.00 am - 7.00 pm
Resident permit
holders only
C

RESIDENT
LONDON
2010

SLEEPWALKER
LONDON
2009

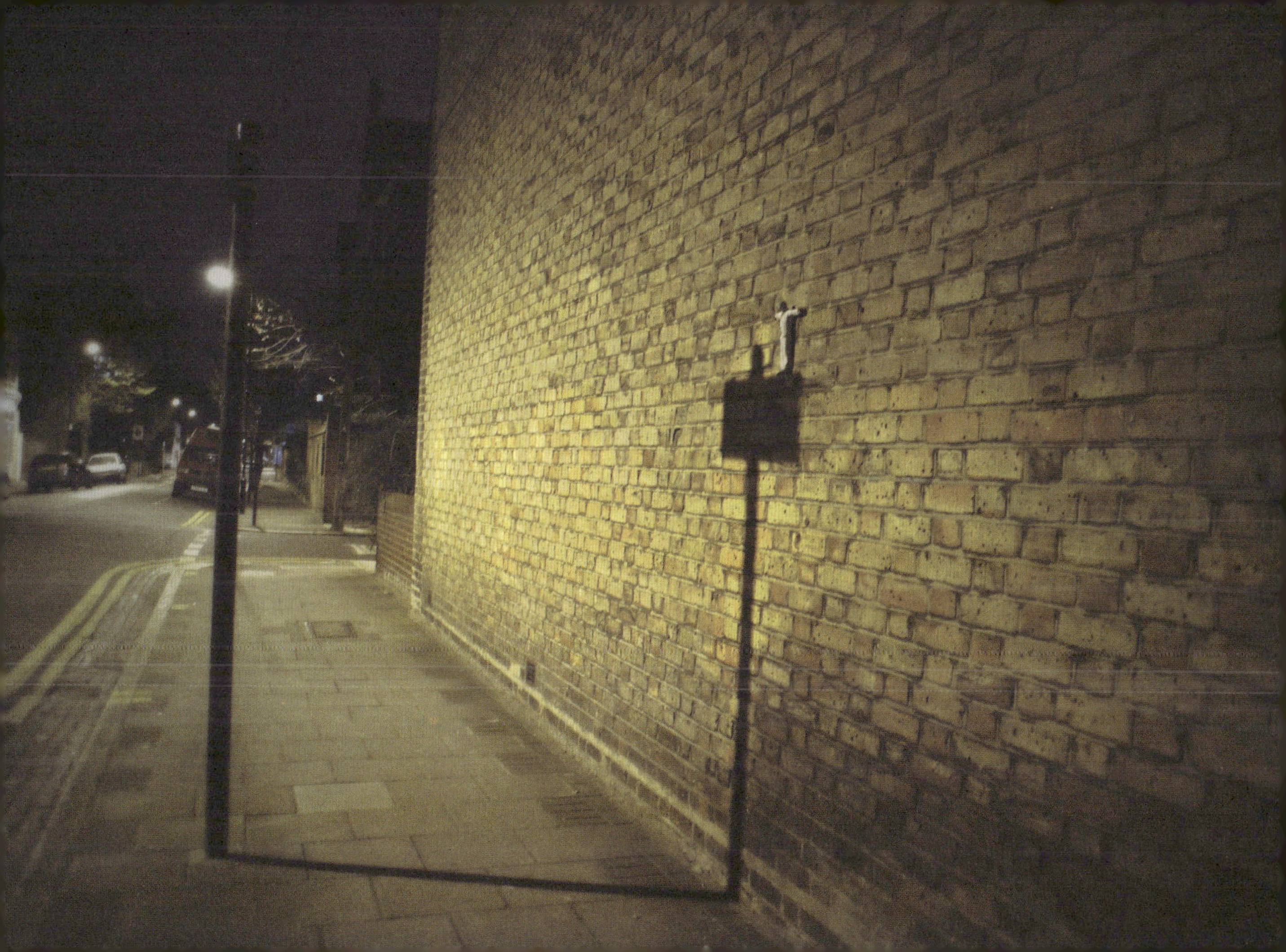

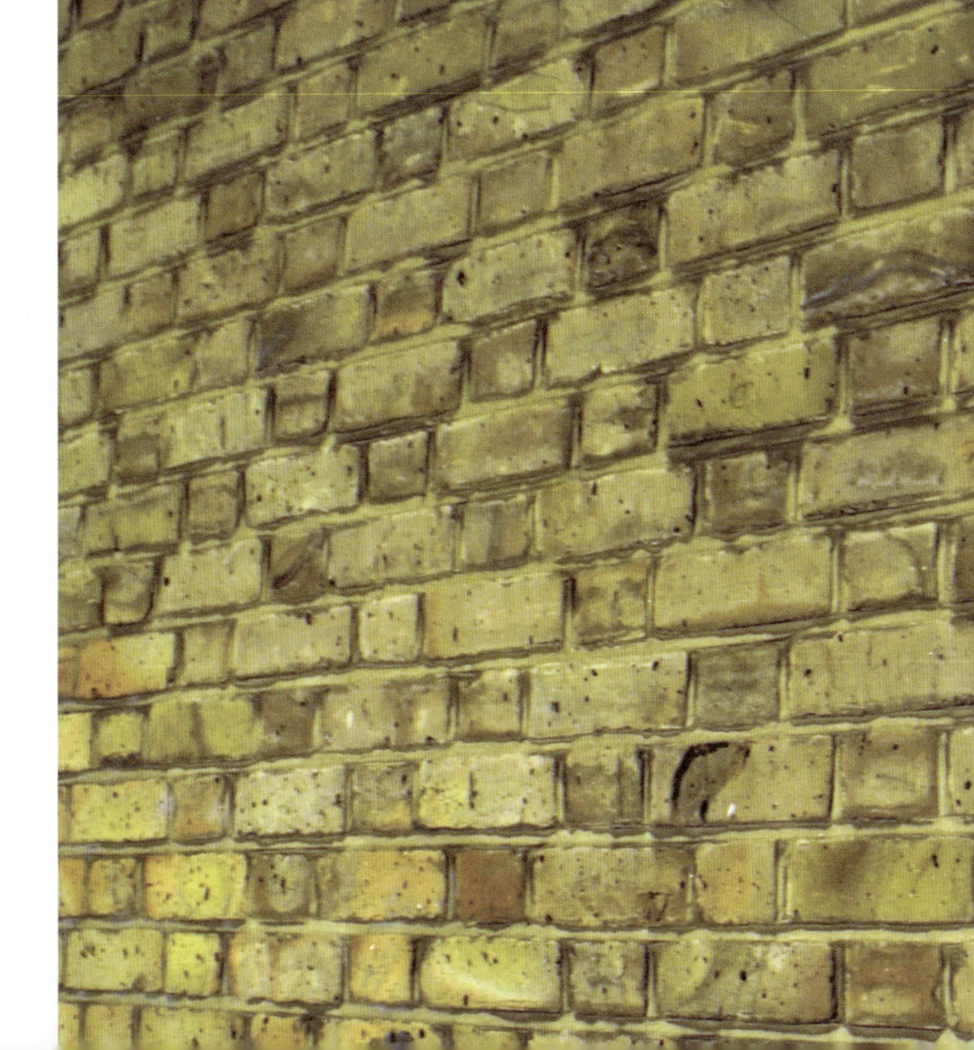

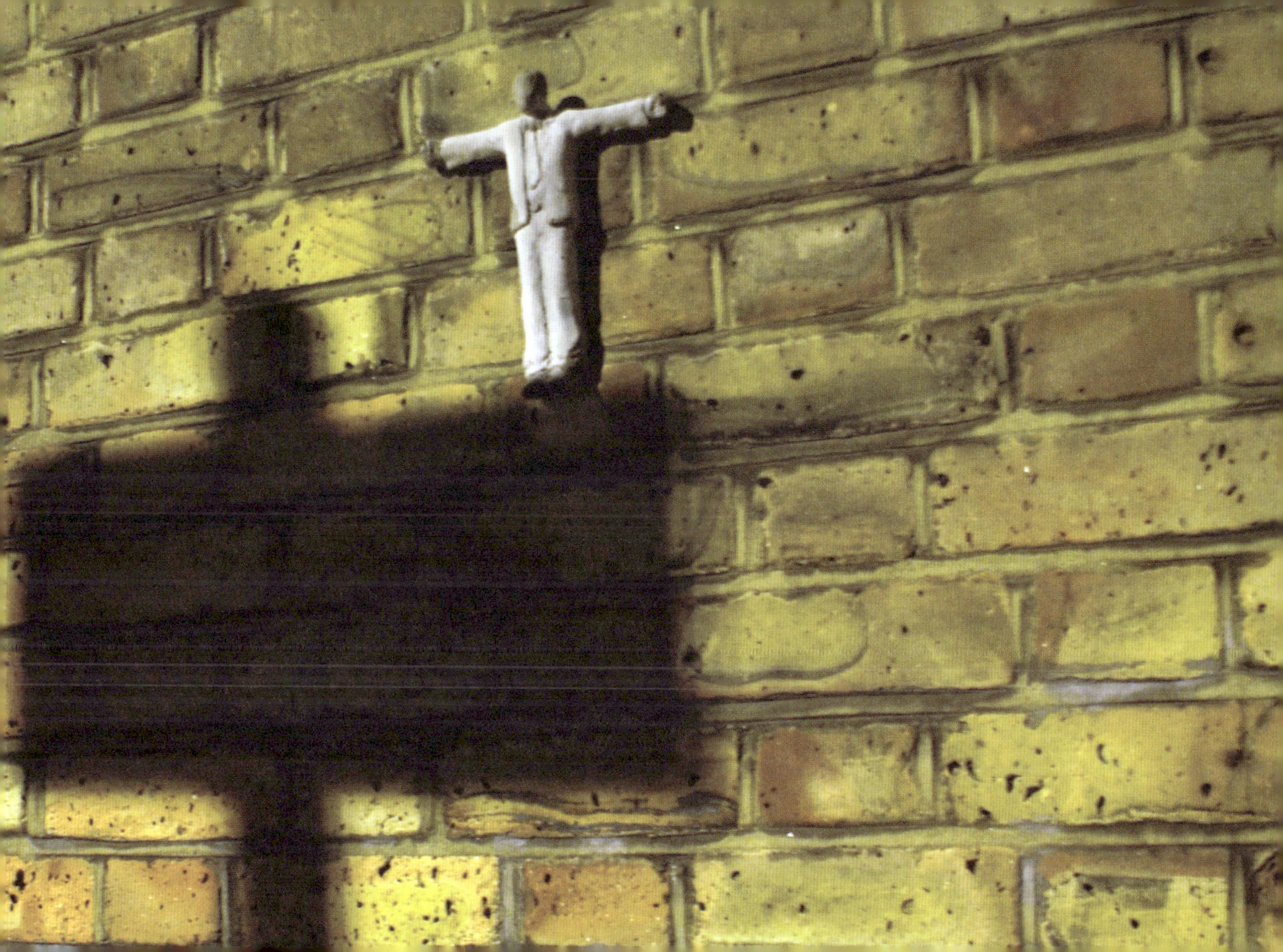

HOMELESS
BRUSSELS
2010

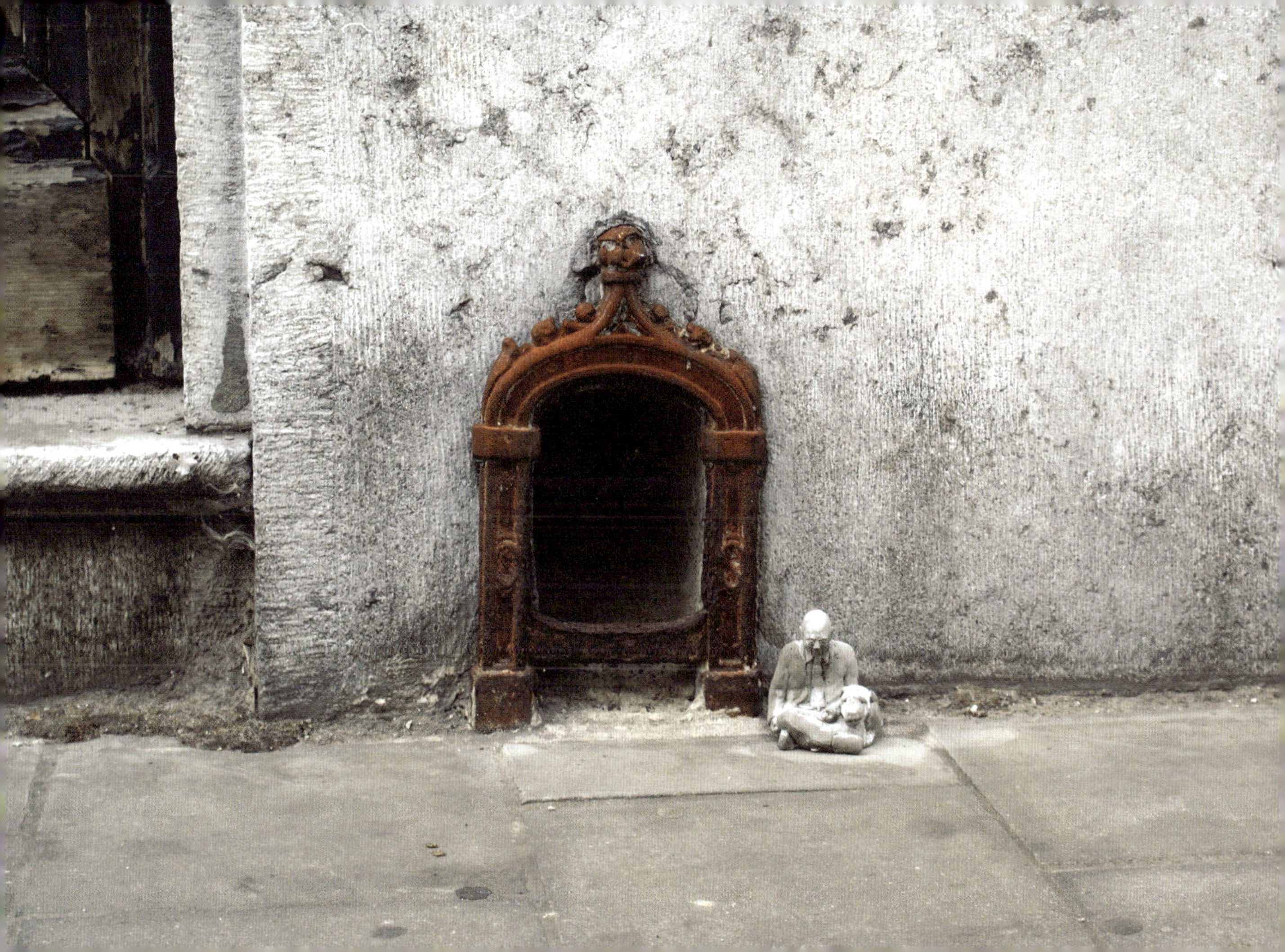

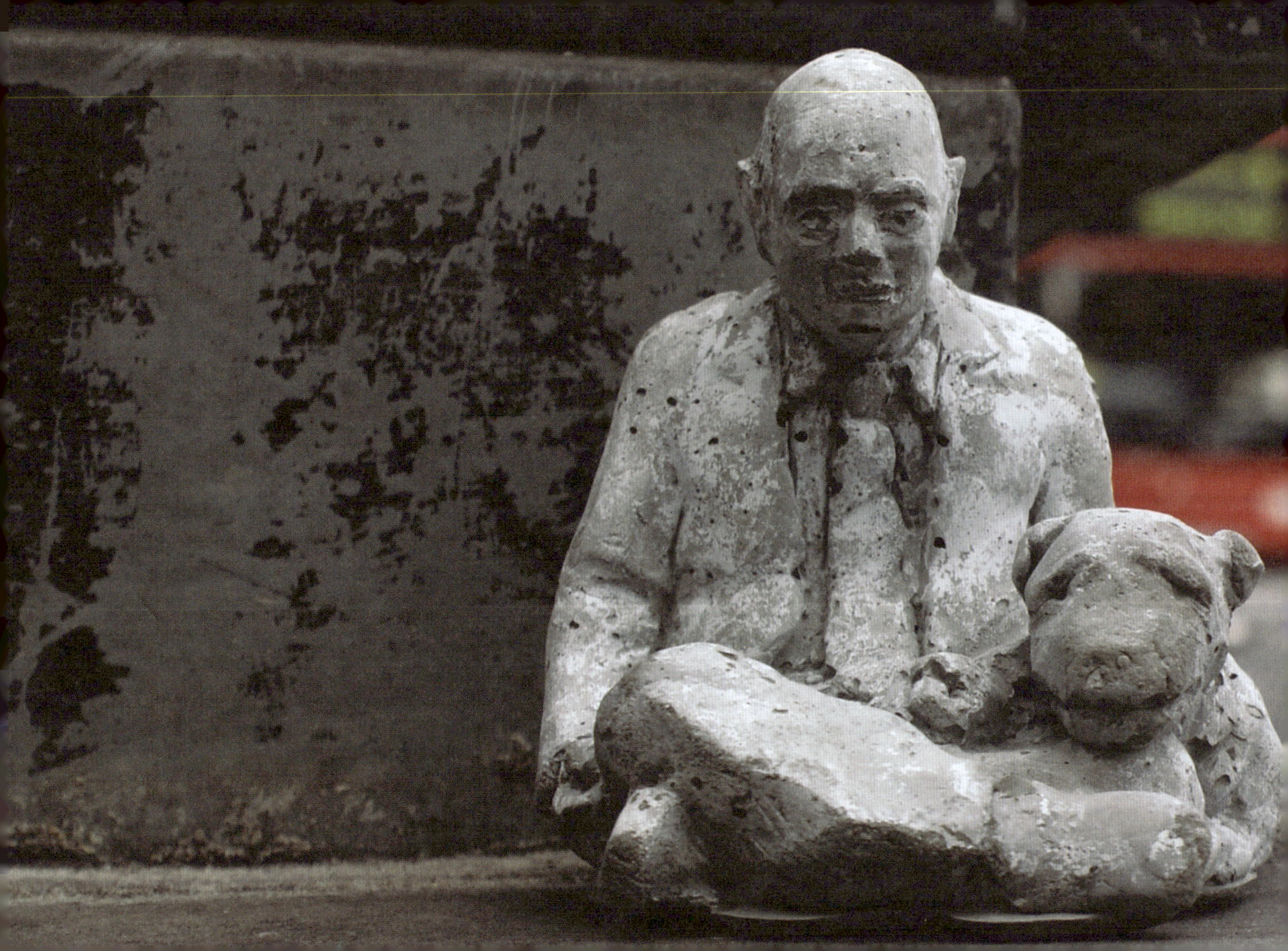

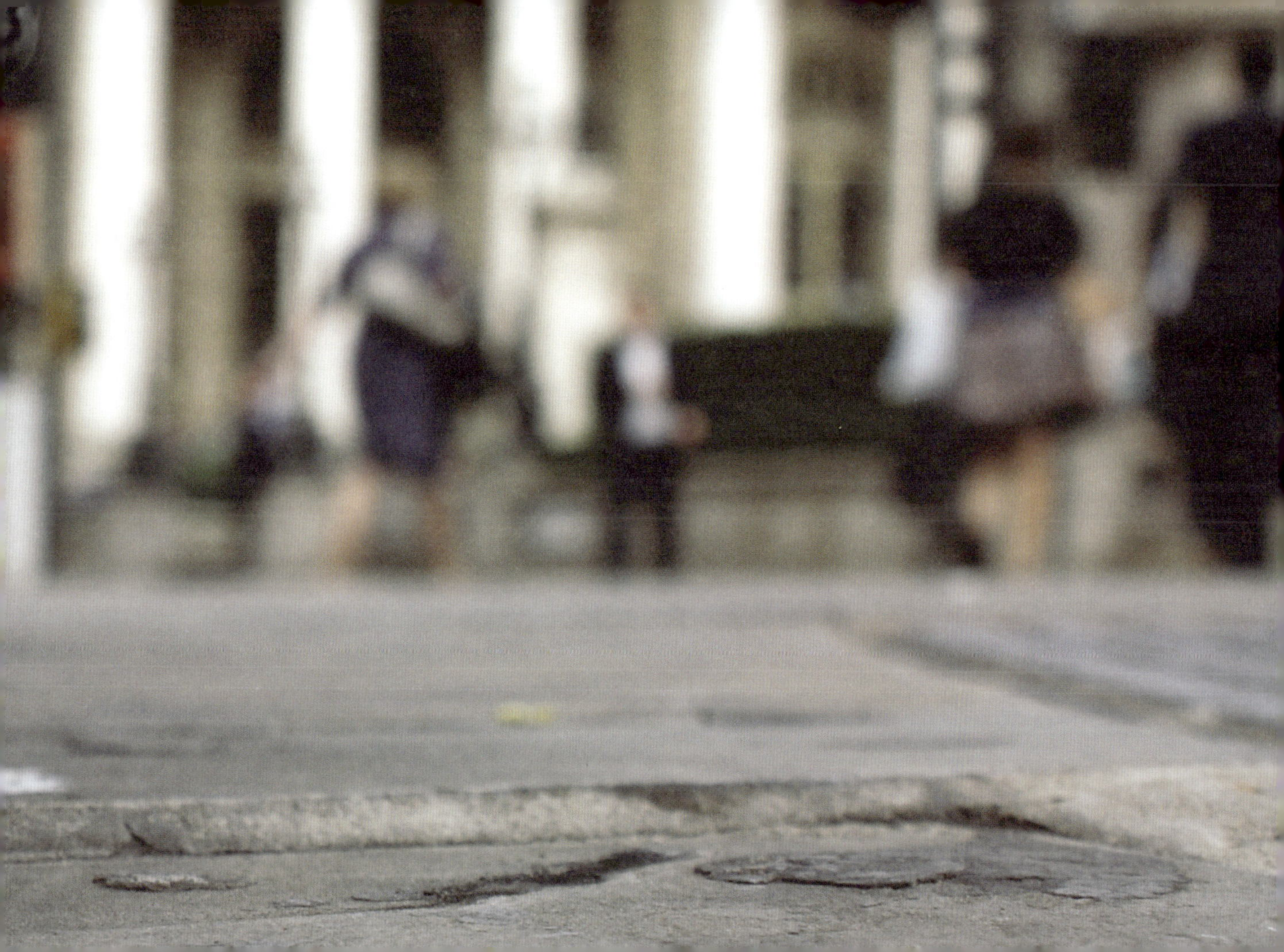

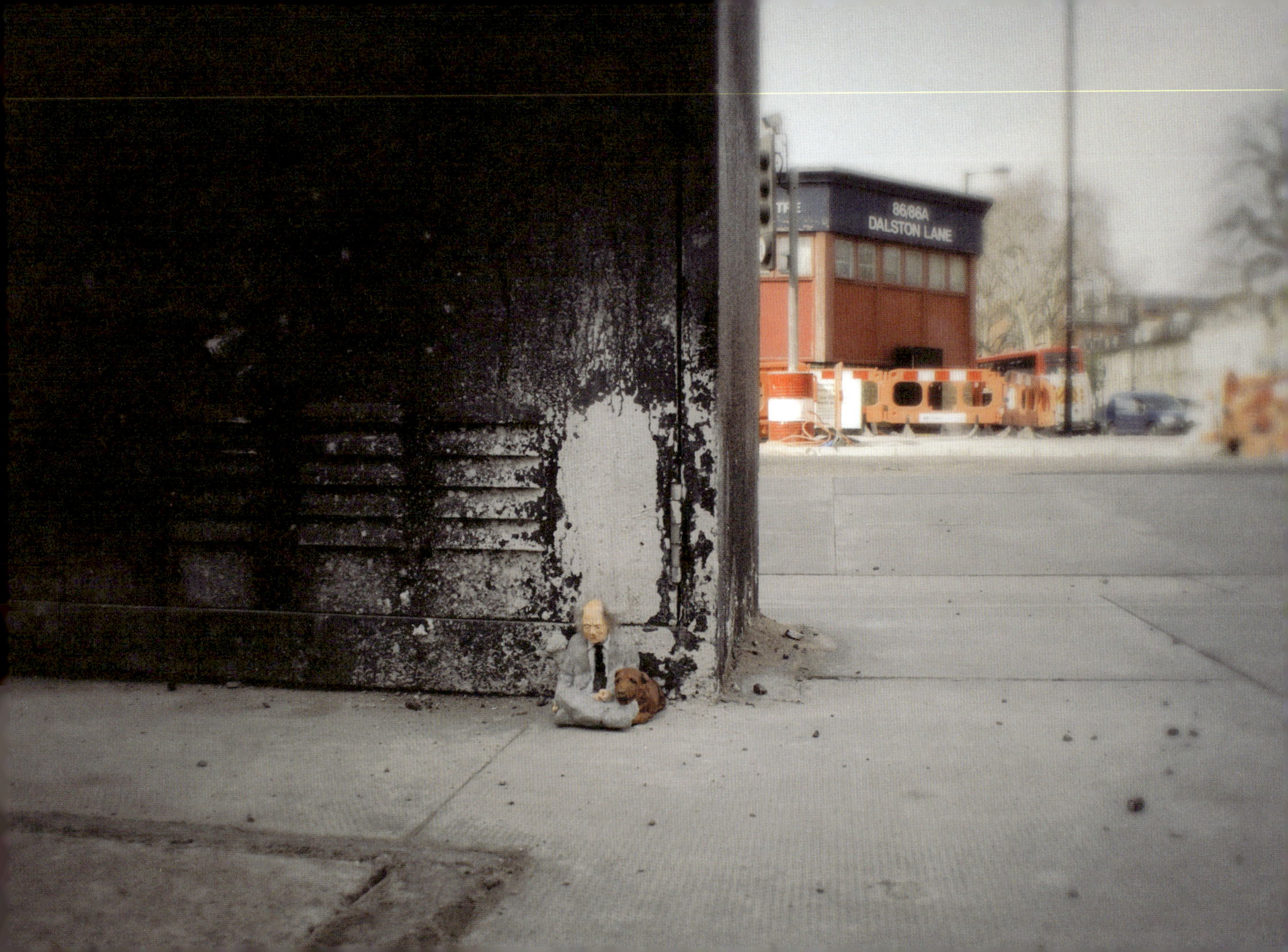
86/86A
DALSTON LANE

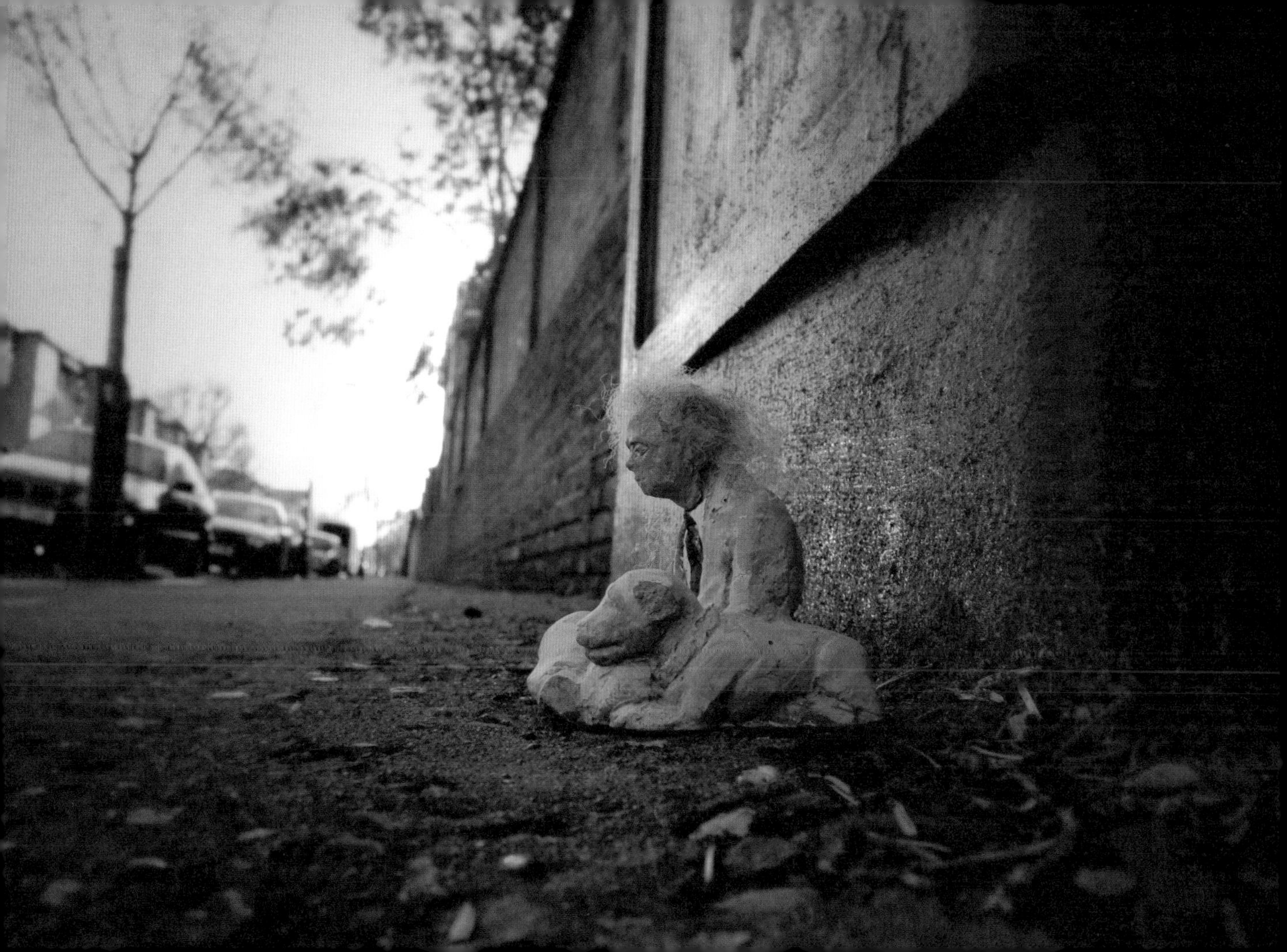

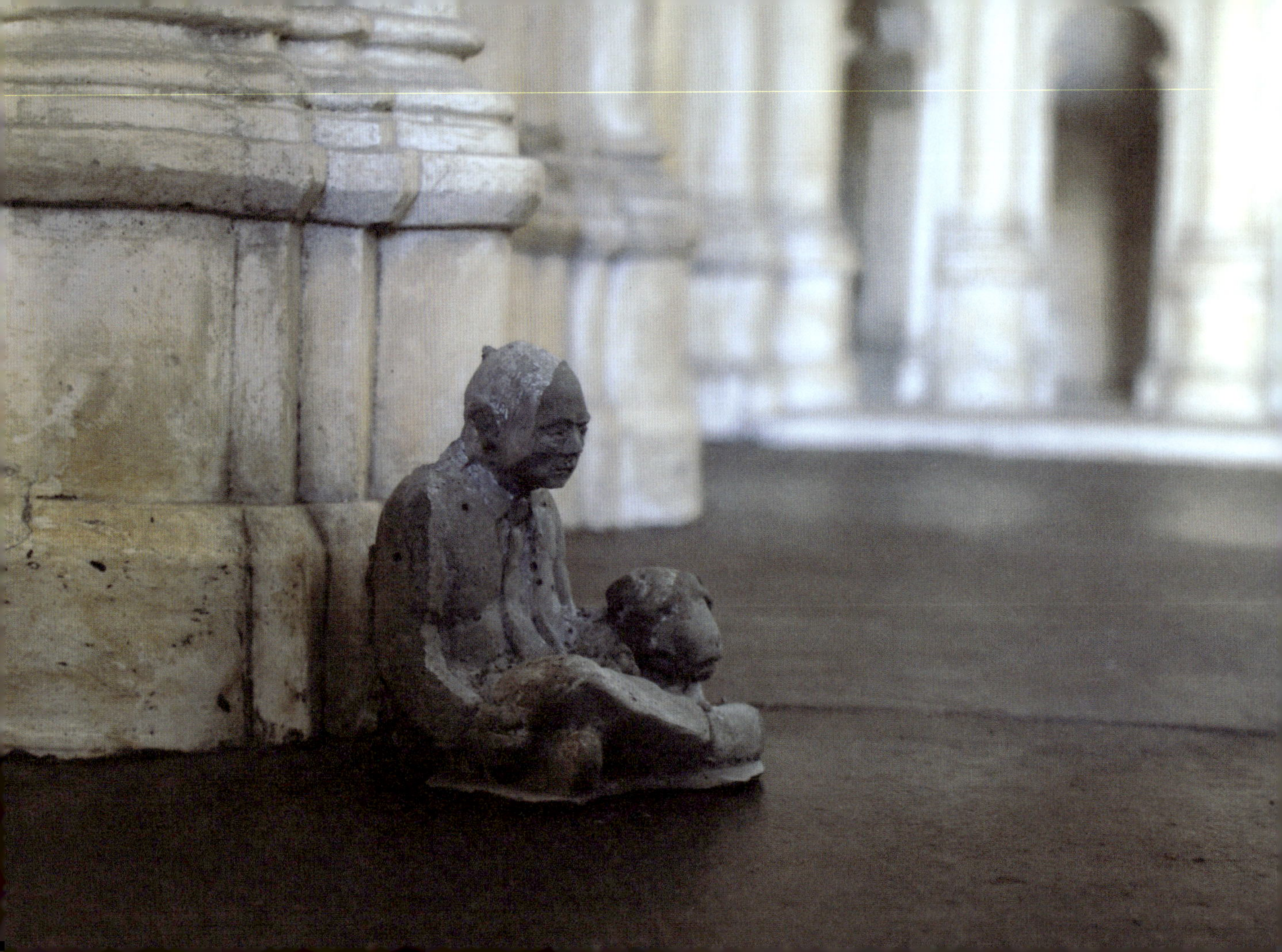

THE LAKE
BRUSSELS
2009

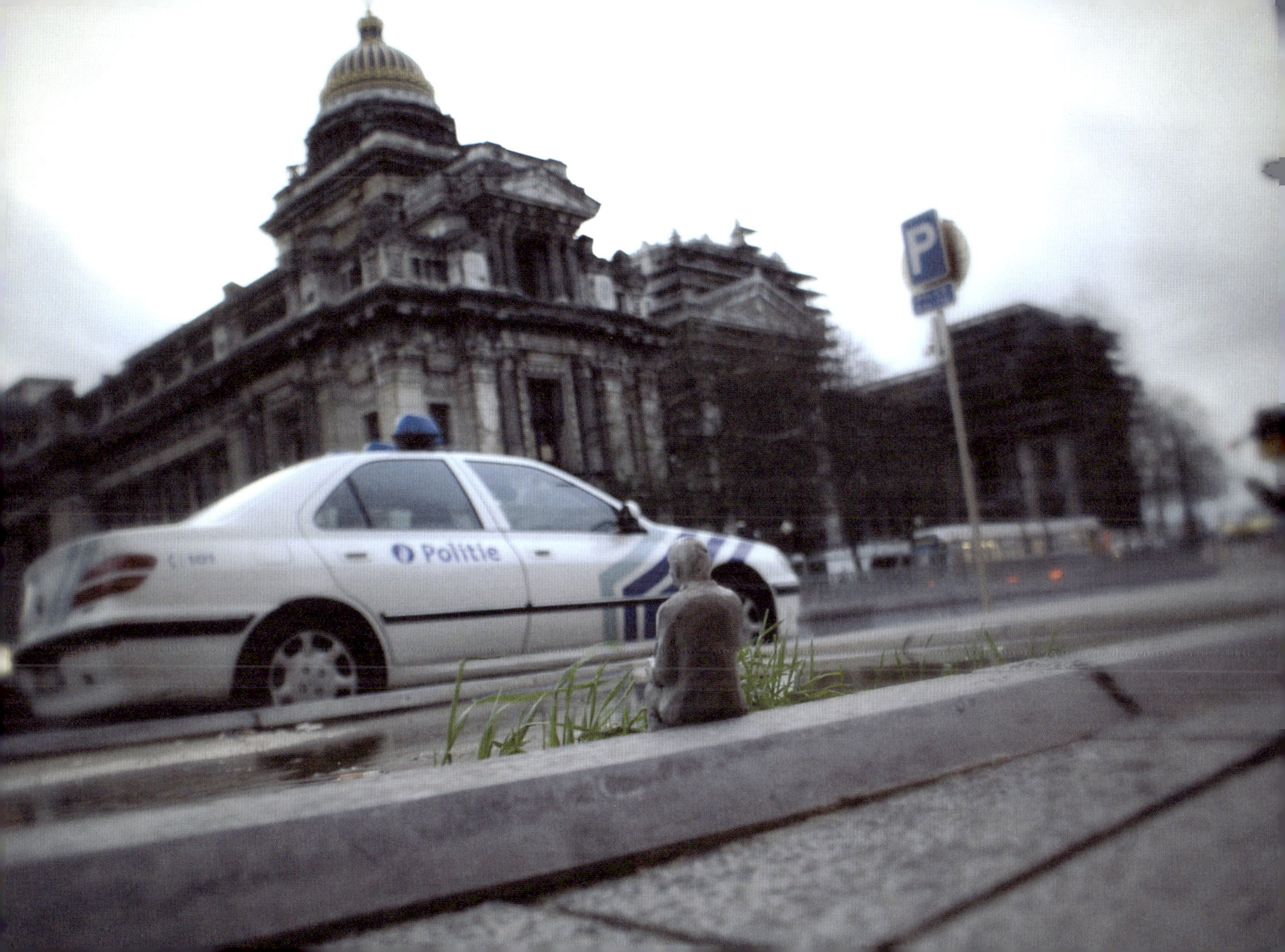

Politie
P

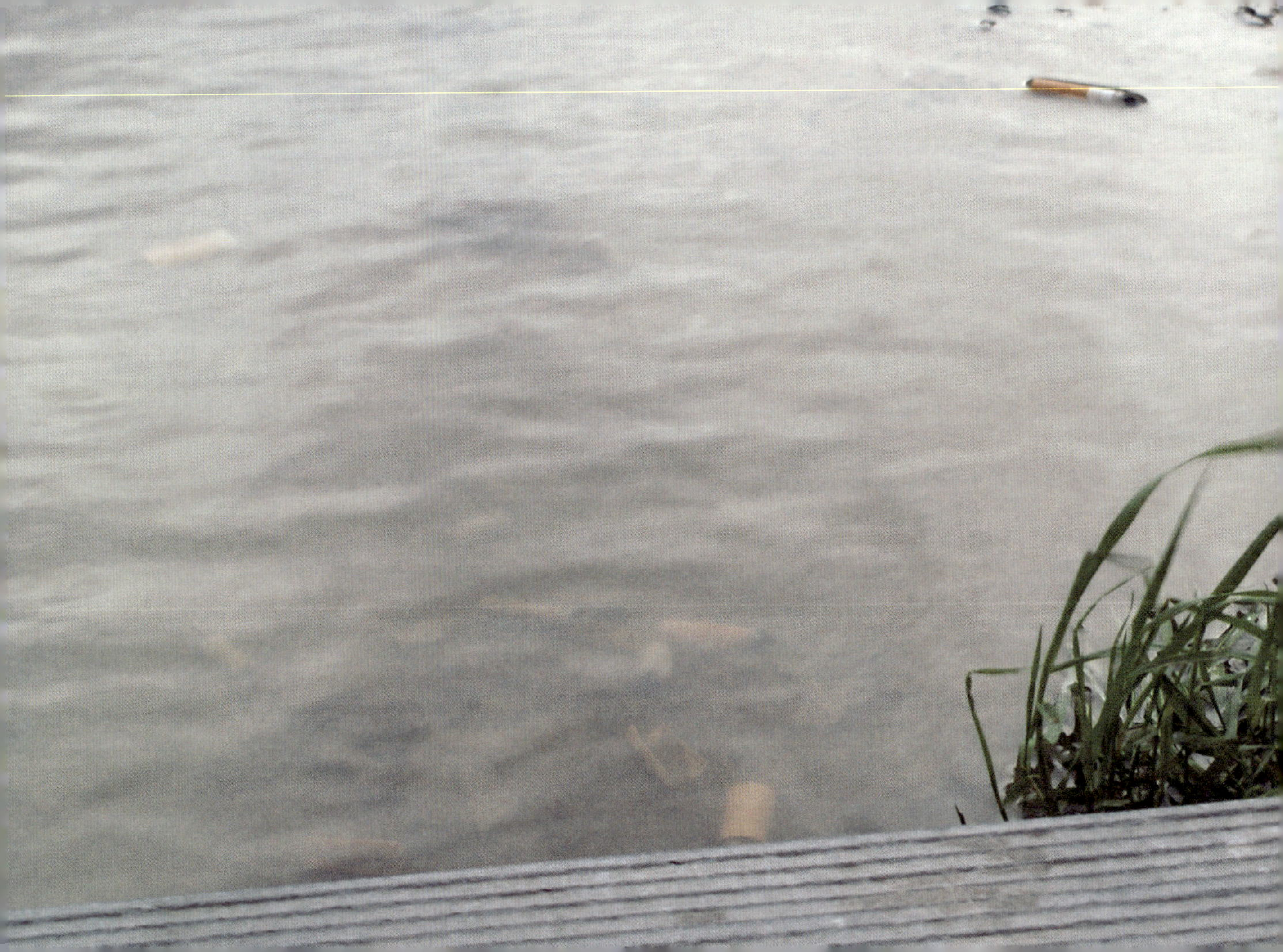

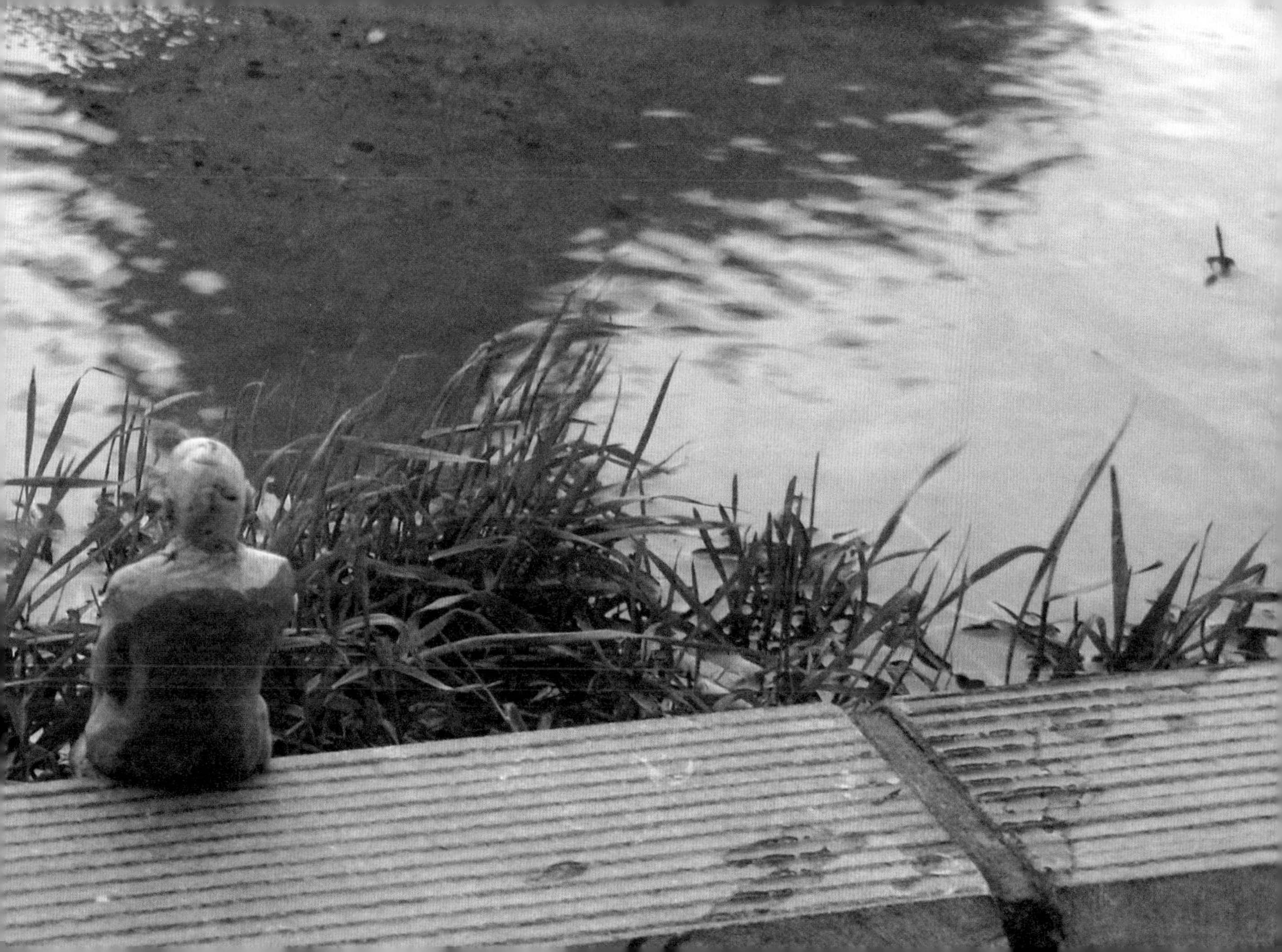

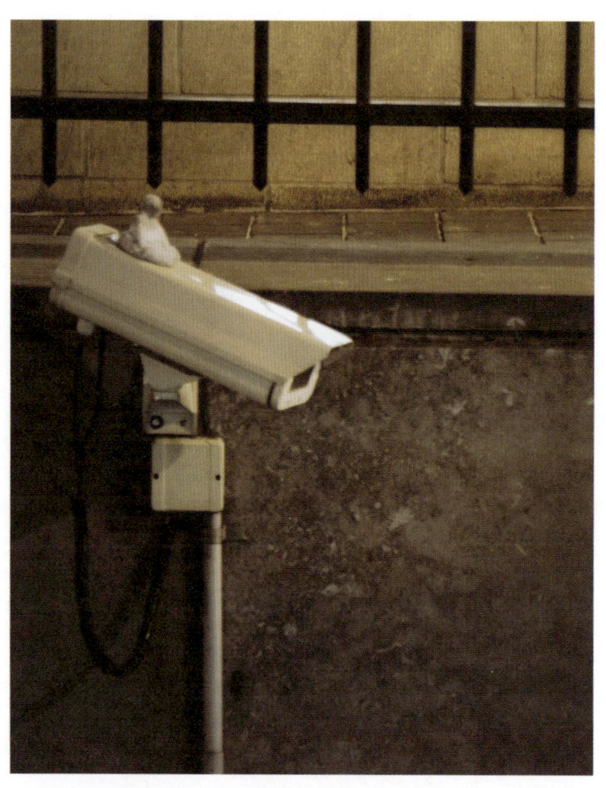

CCTV PARASITE
BRUSSELS
2009

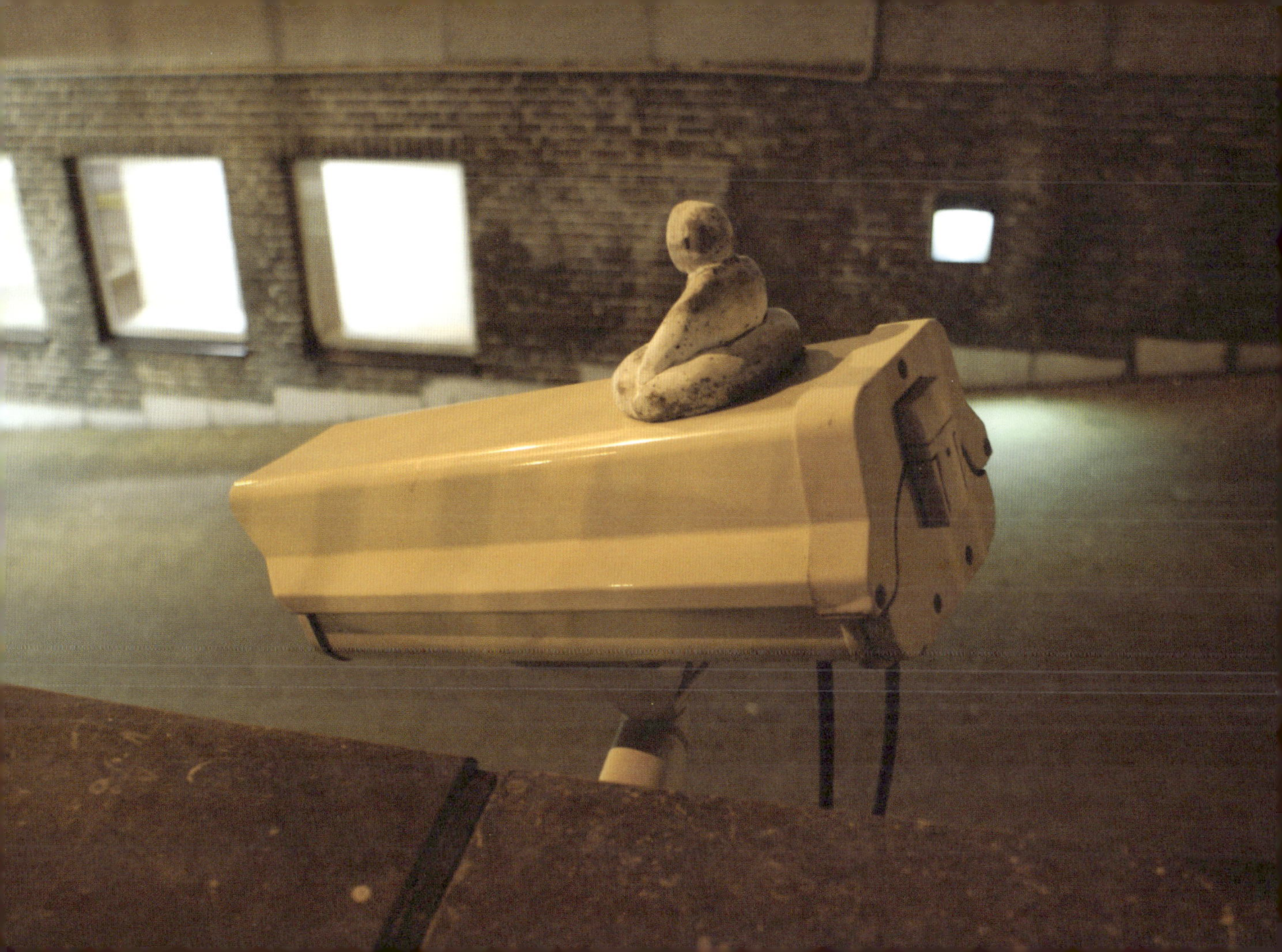

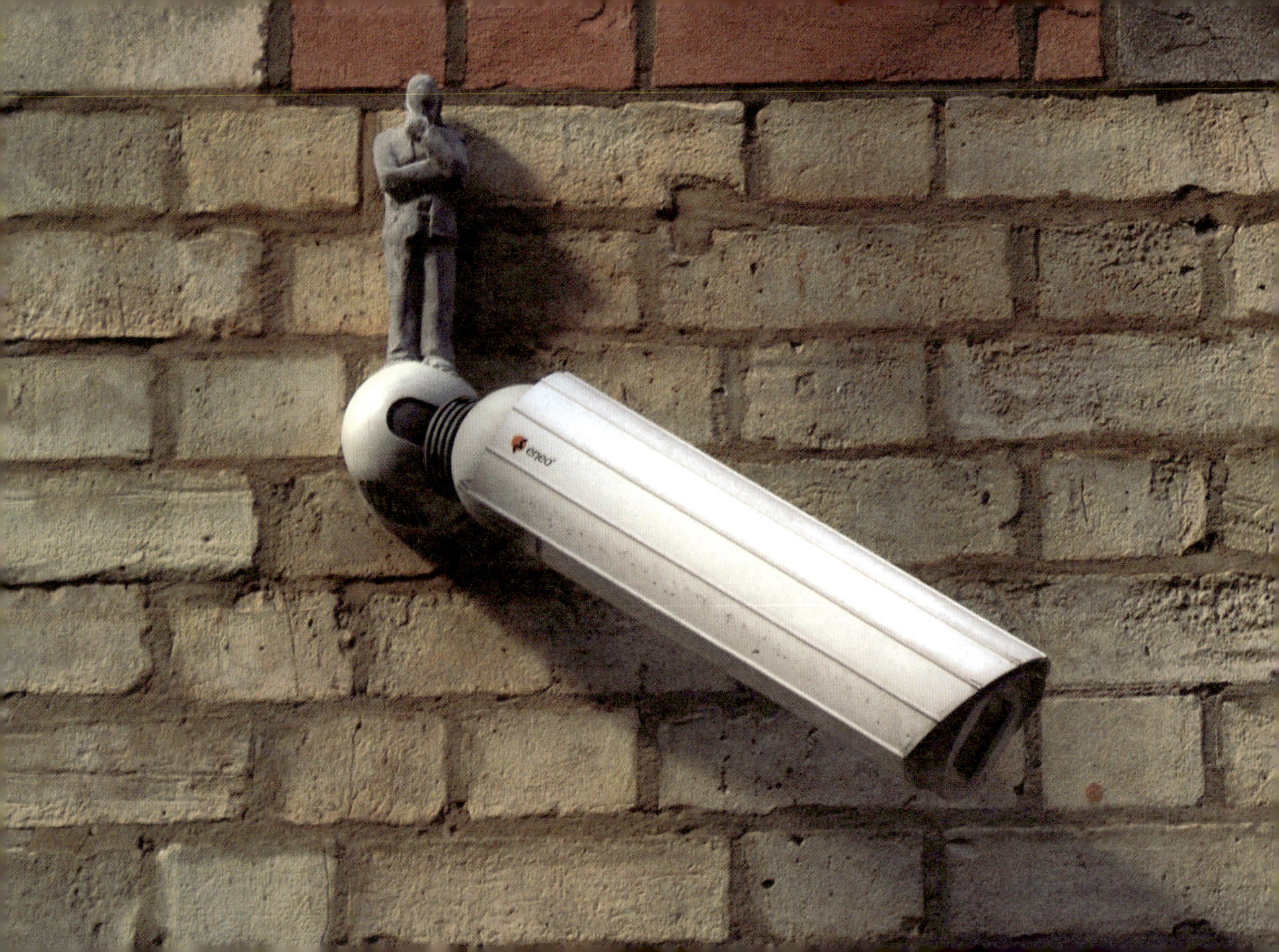
eneo

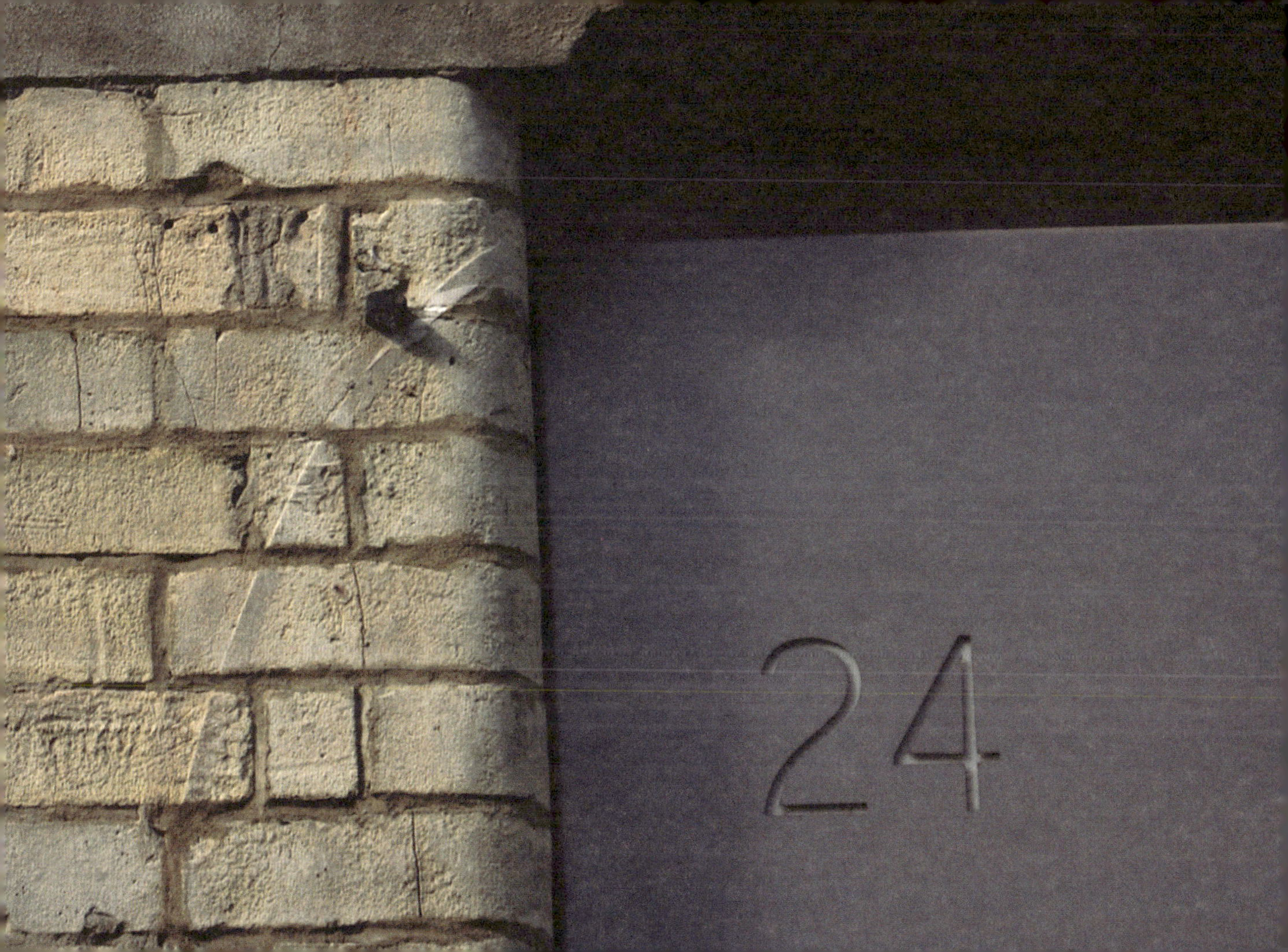
24

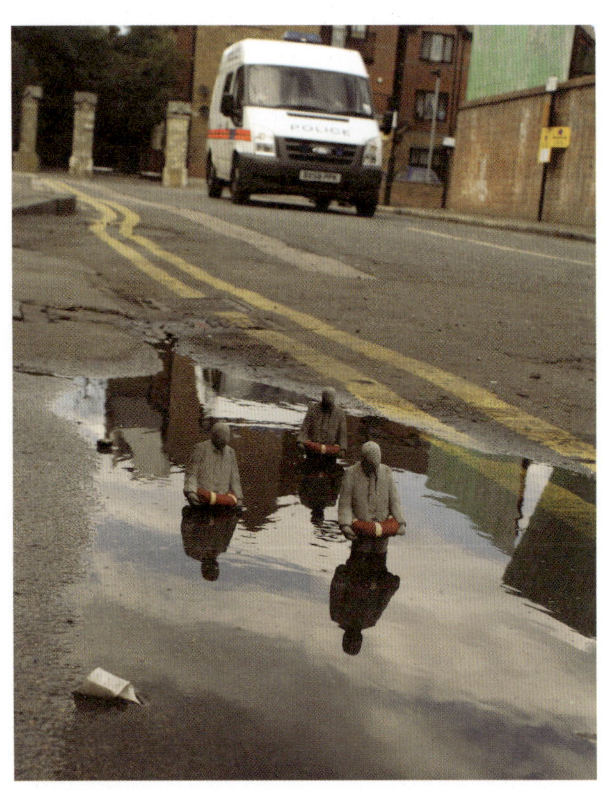

CLIMATE CHANGE EXPEDITION
LONDON
2009-10

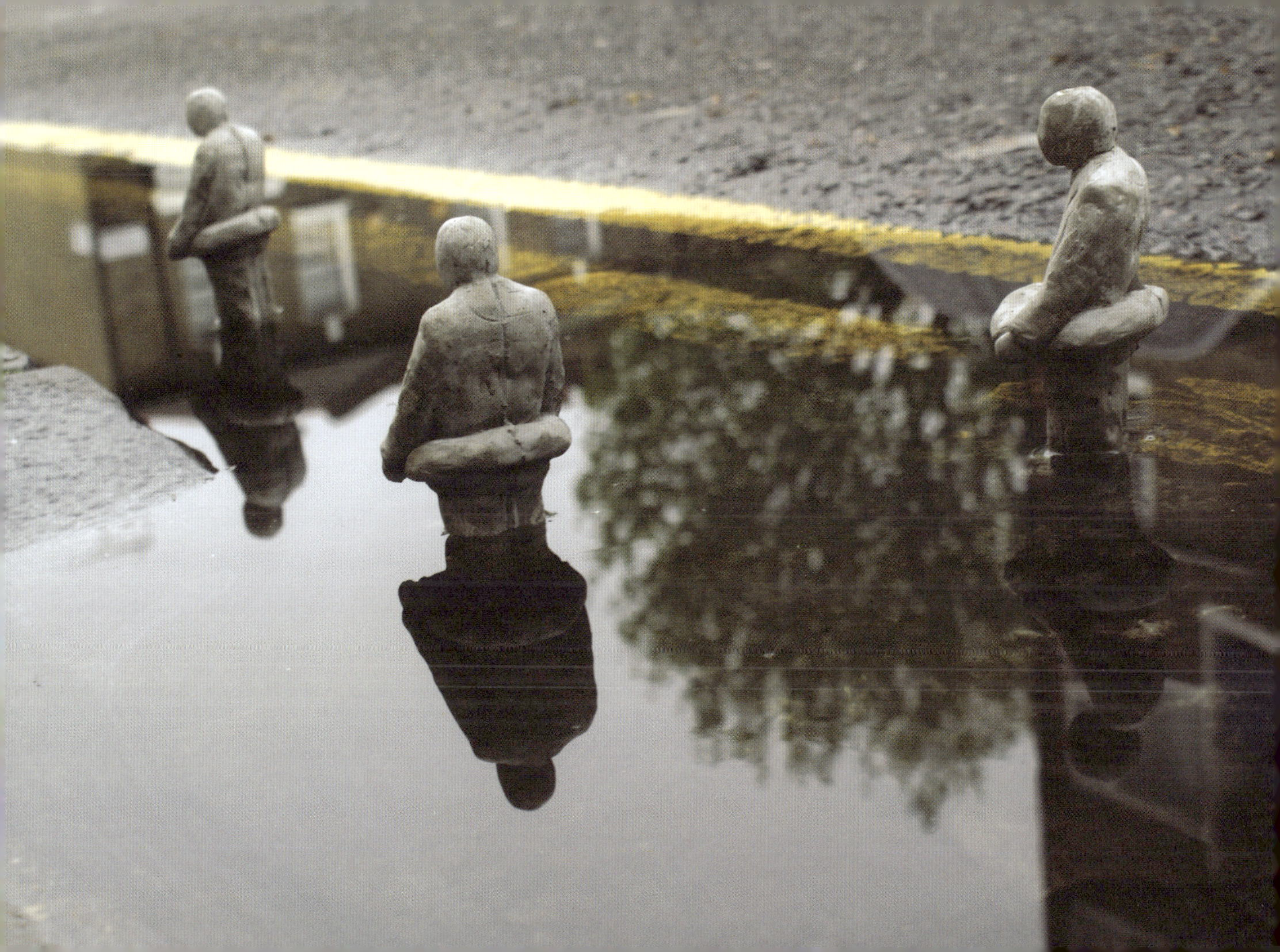

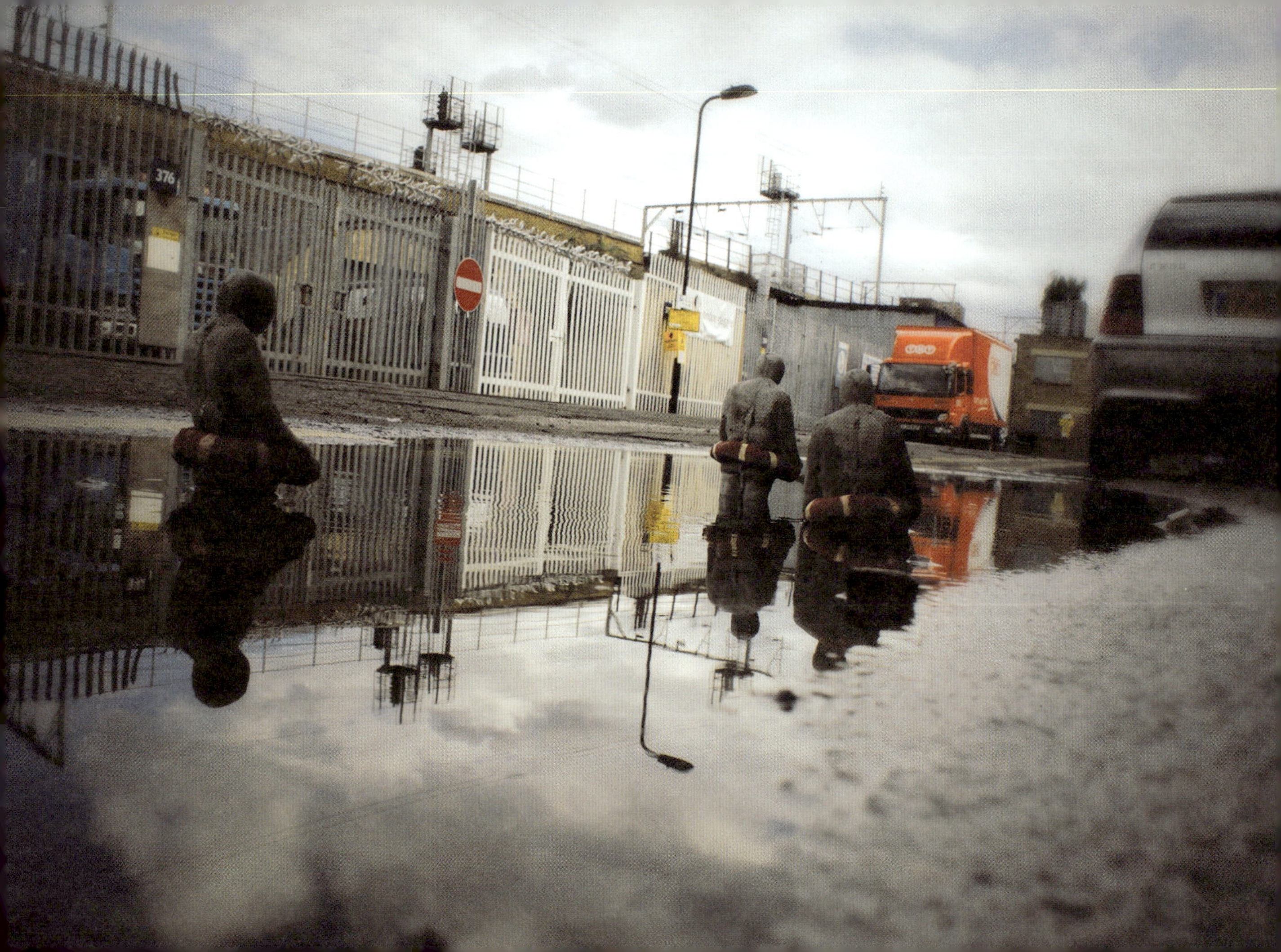

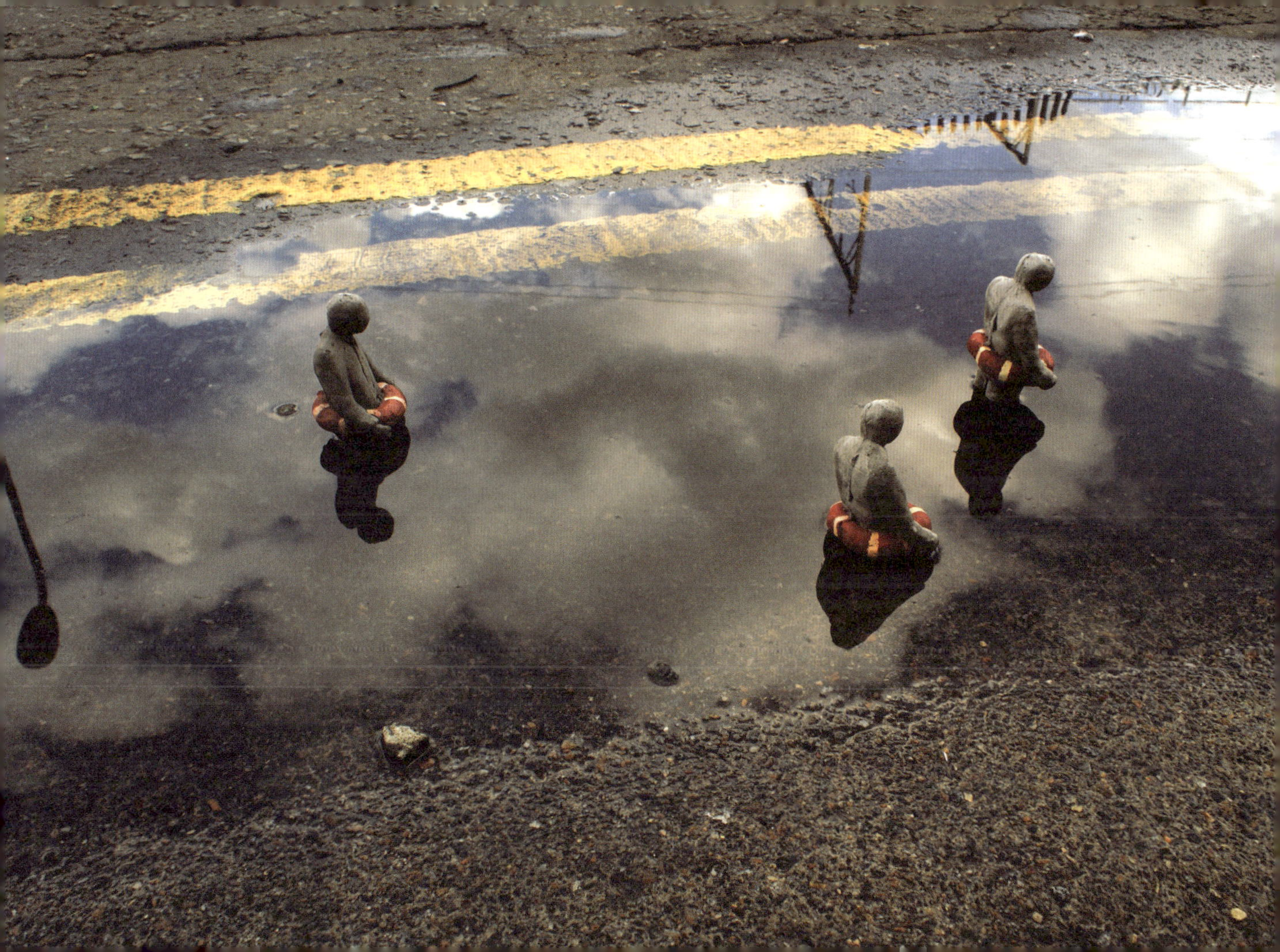

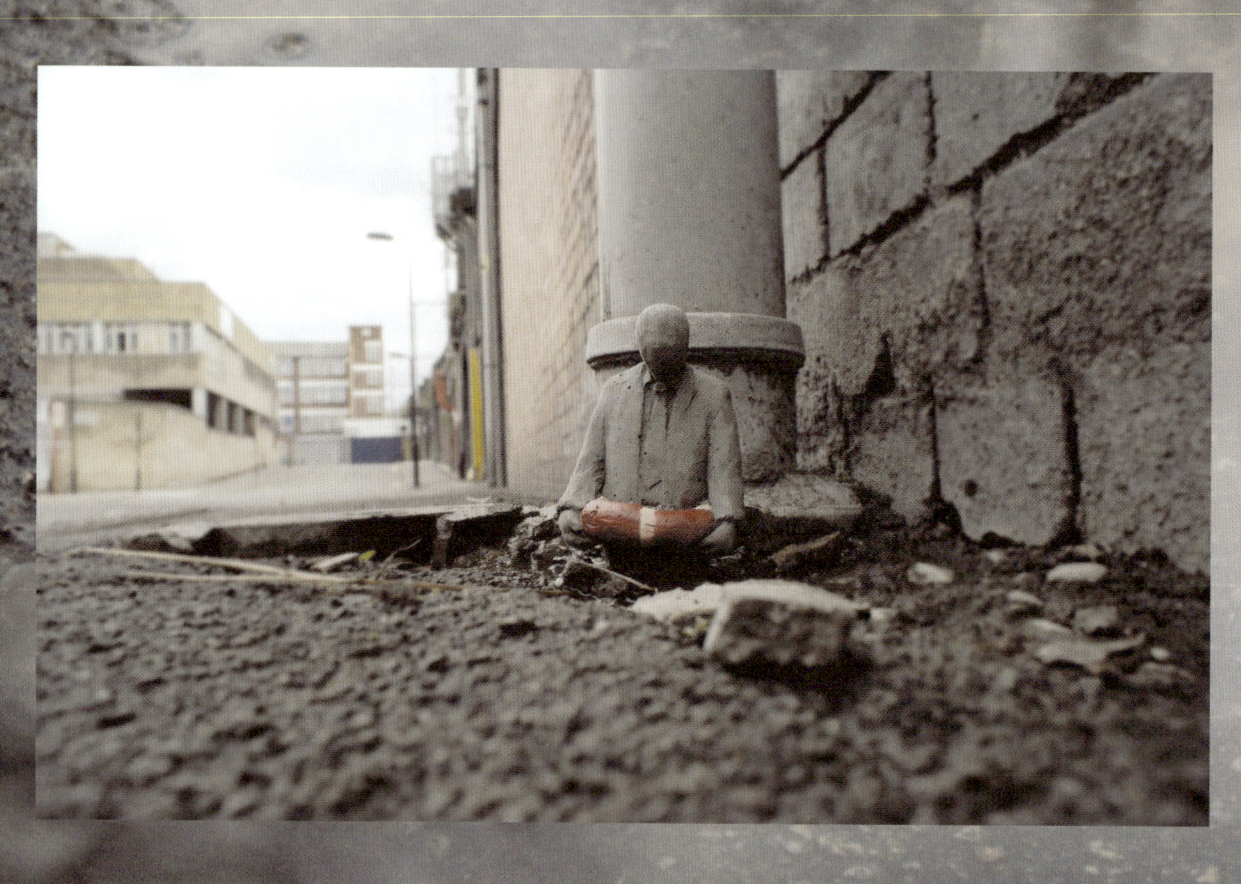

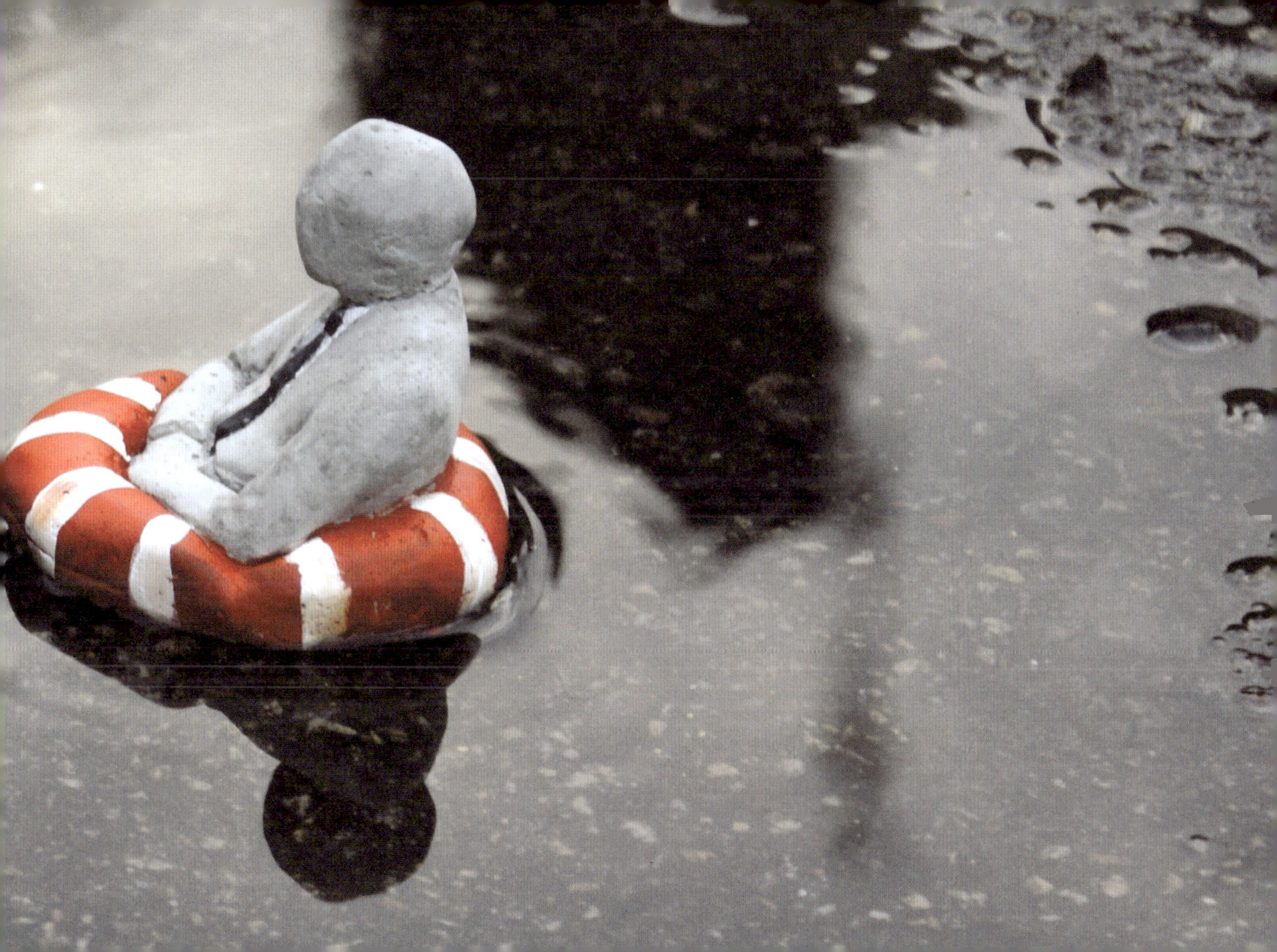

MAN ON RED PAINT STAIN
BARCELONA
2009

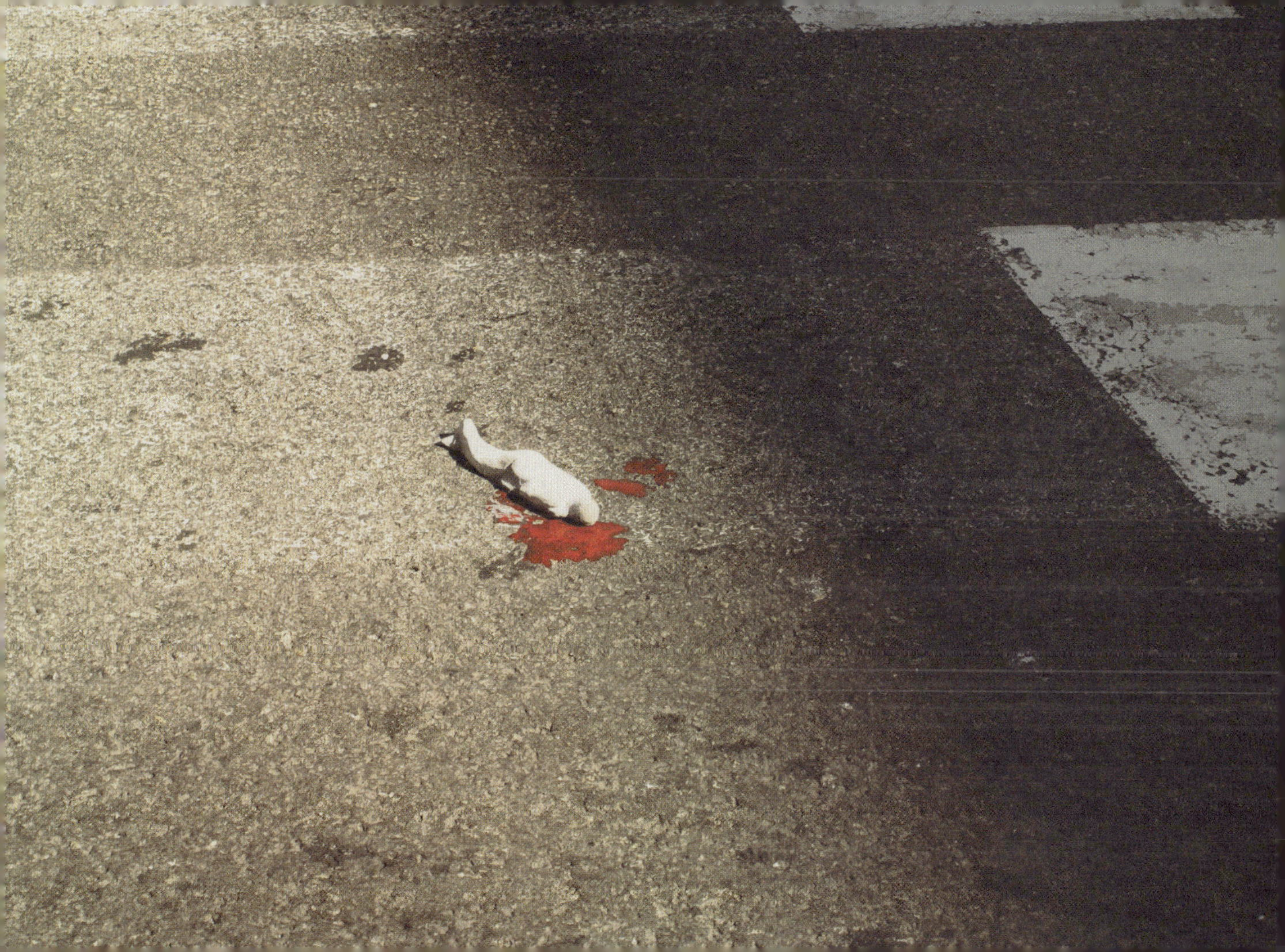

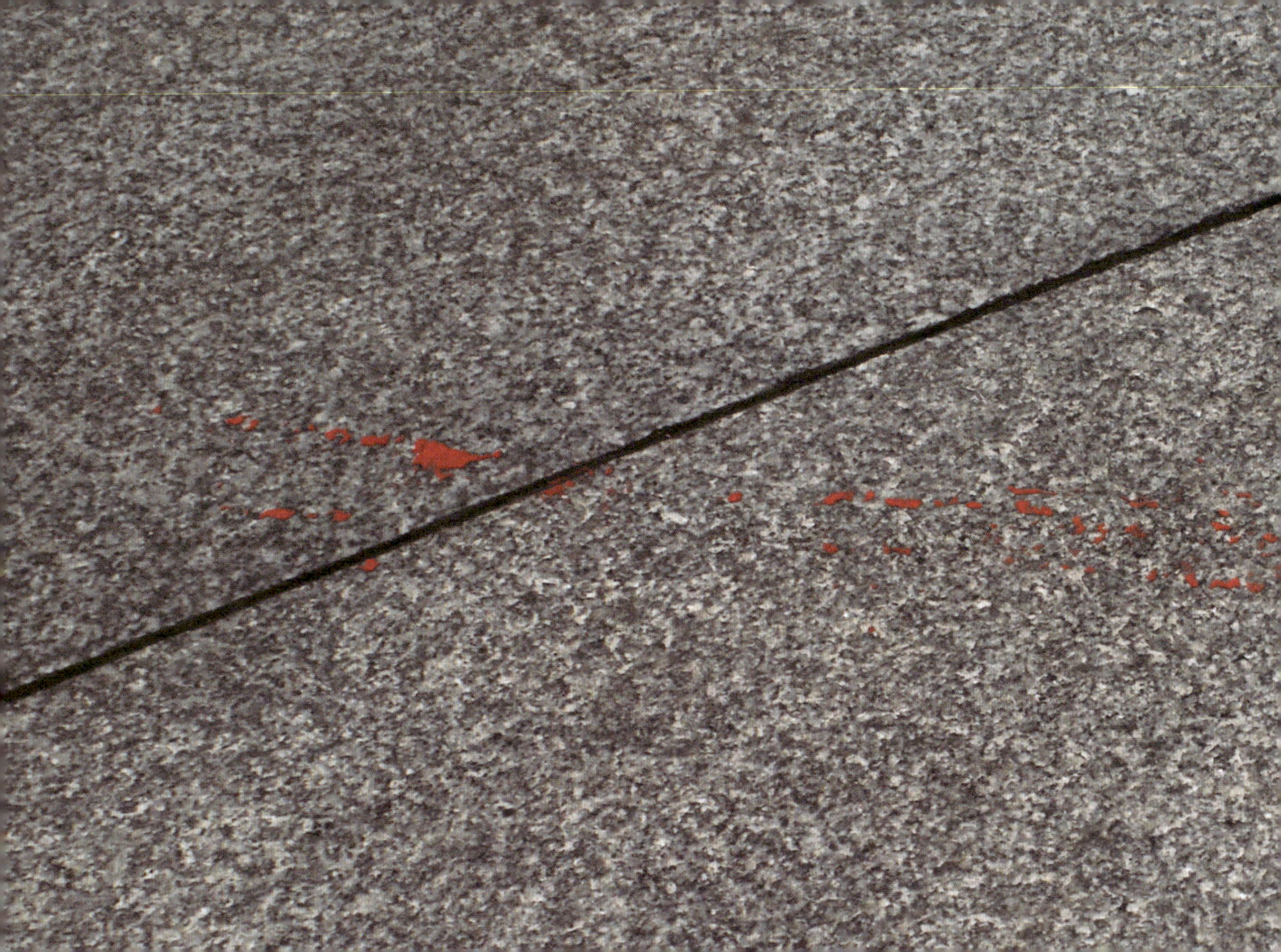

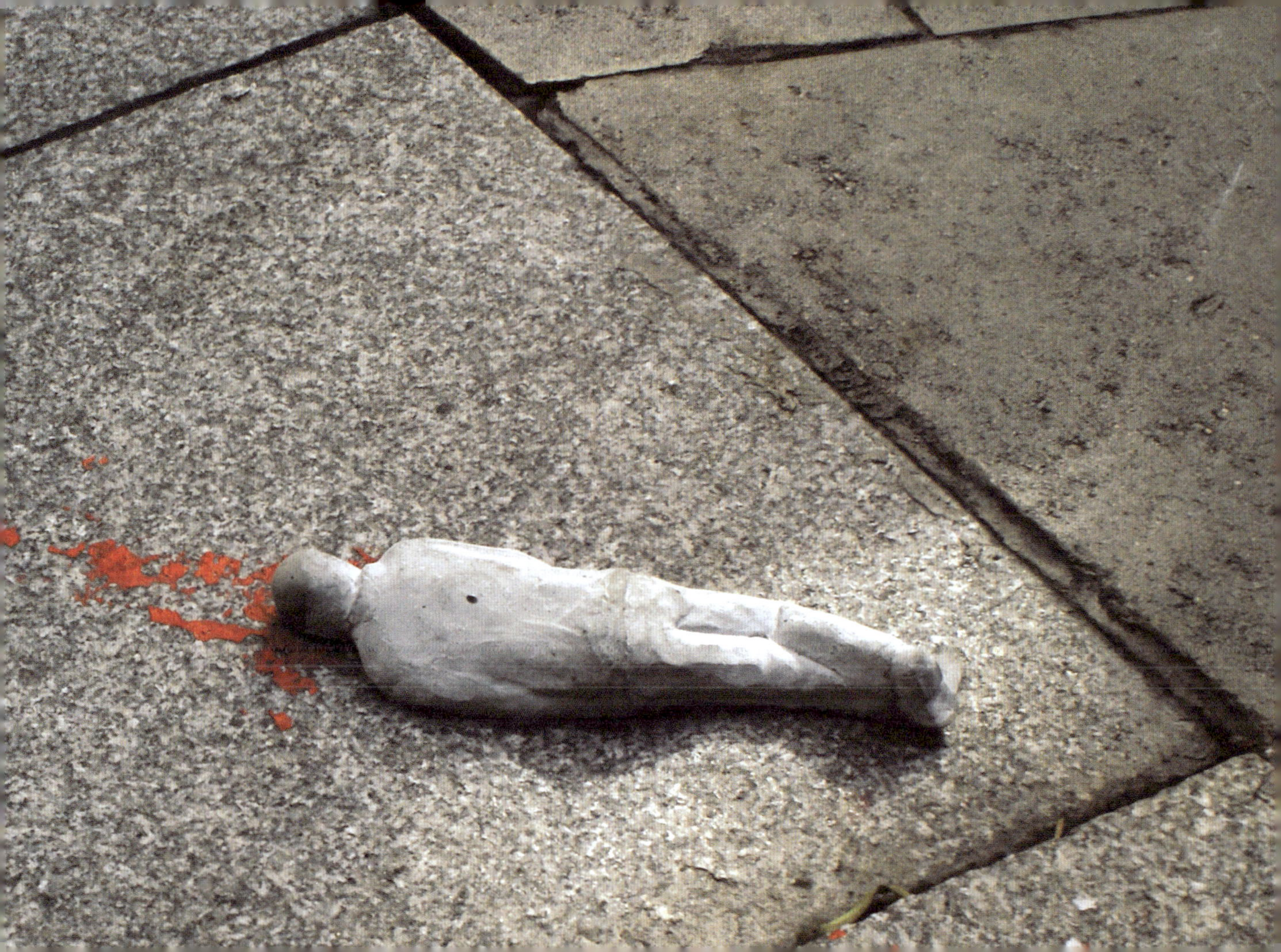

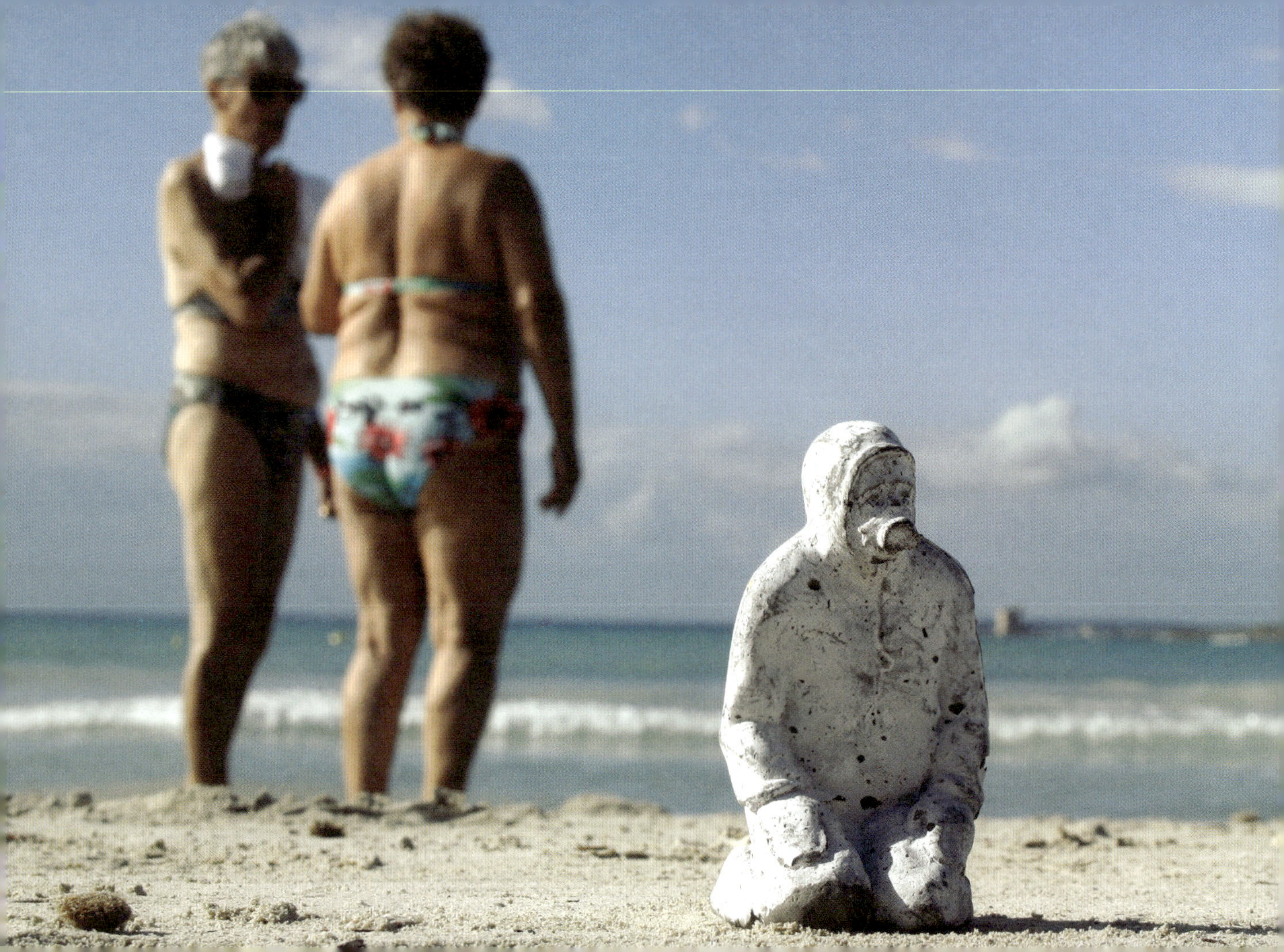

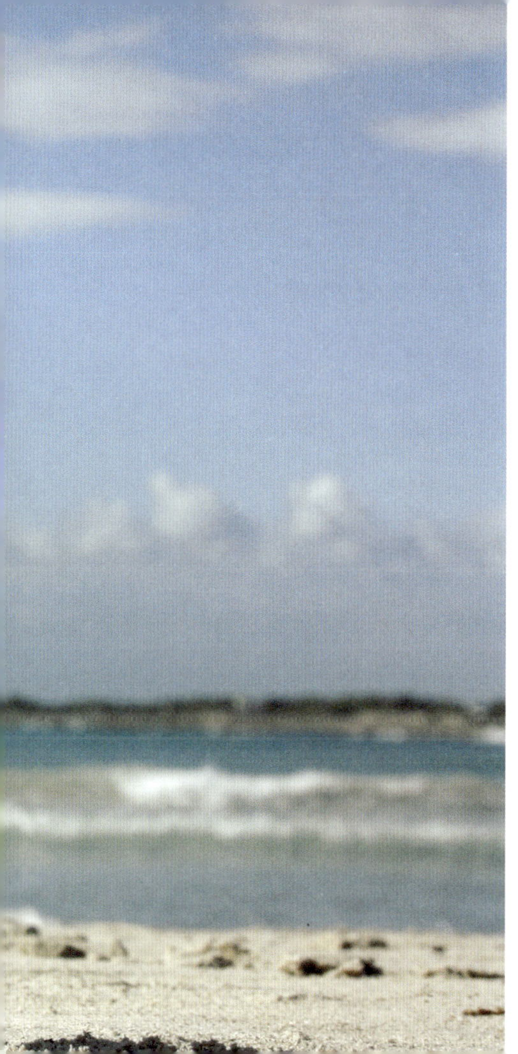

LAND OF THE GIANTS
ITALY
2010

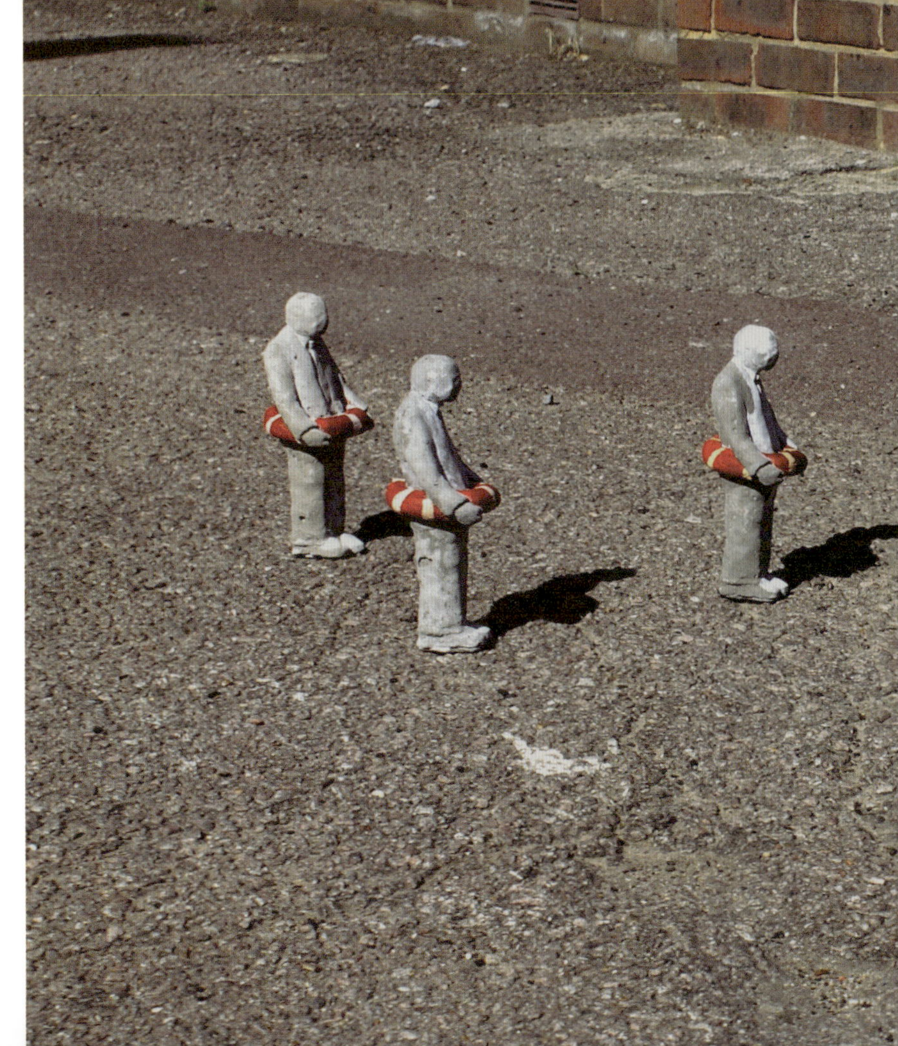

AUGUST
LONDON
2010

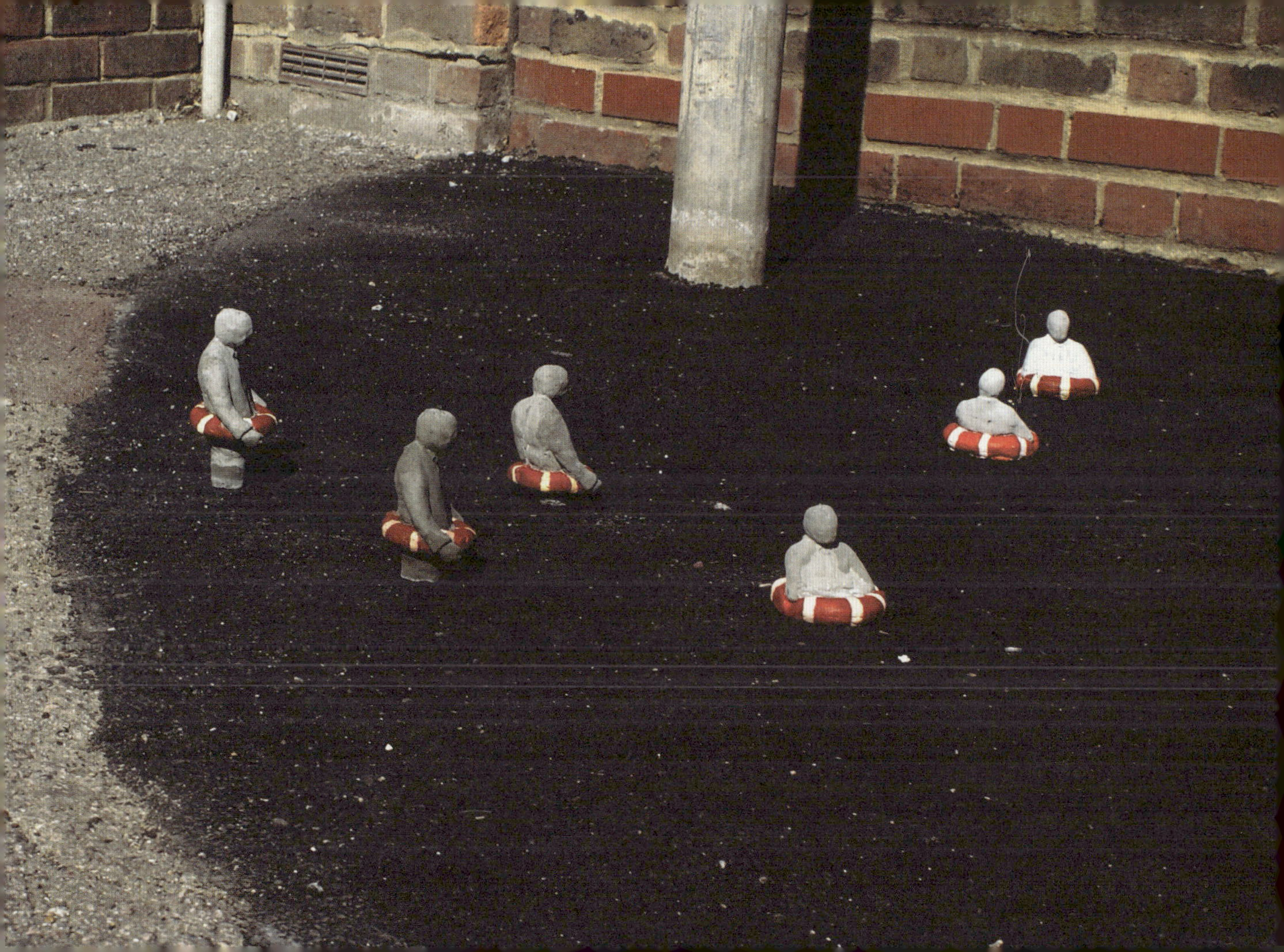

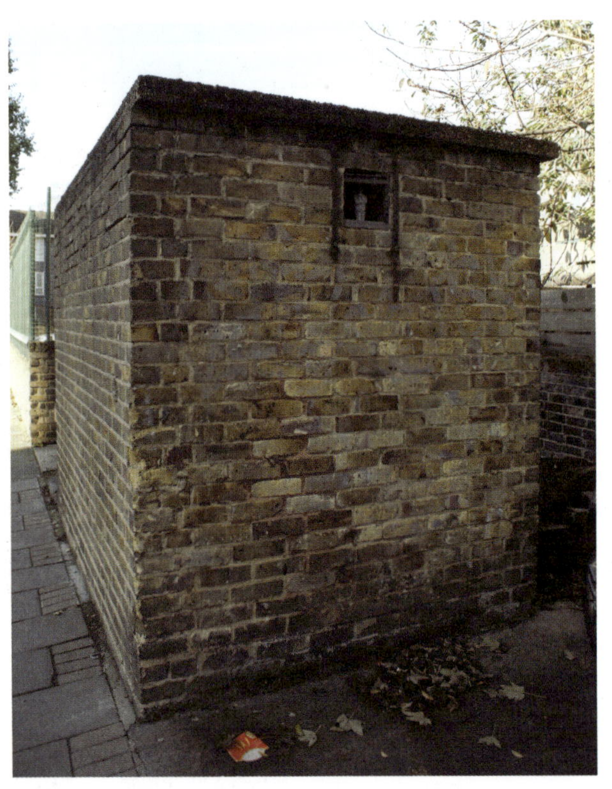

THE LONELY NEIGHBOUR
LONDON
2009

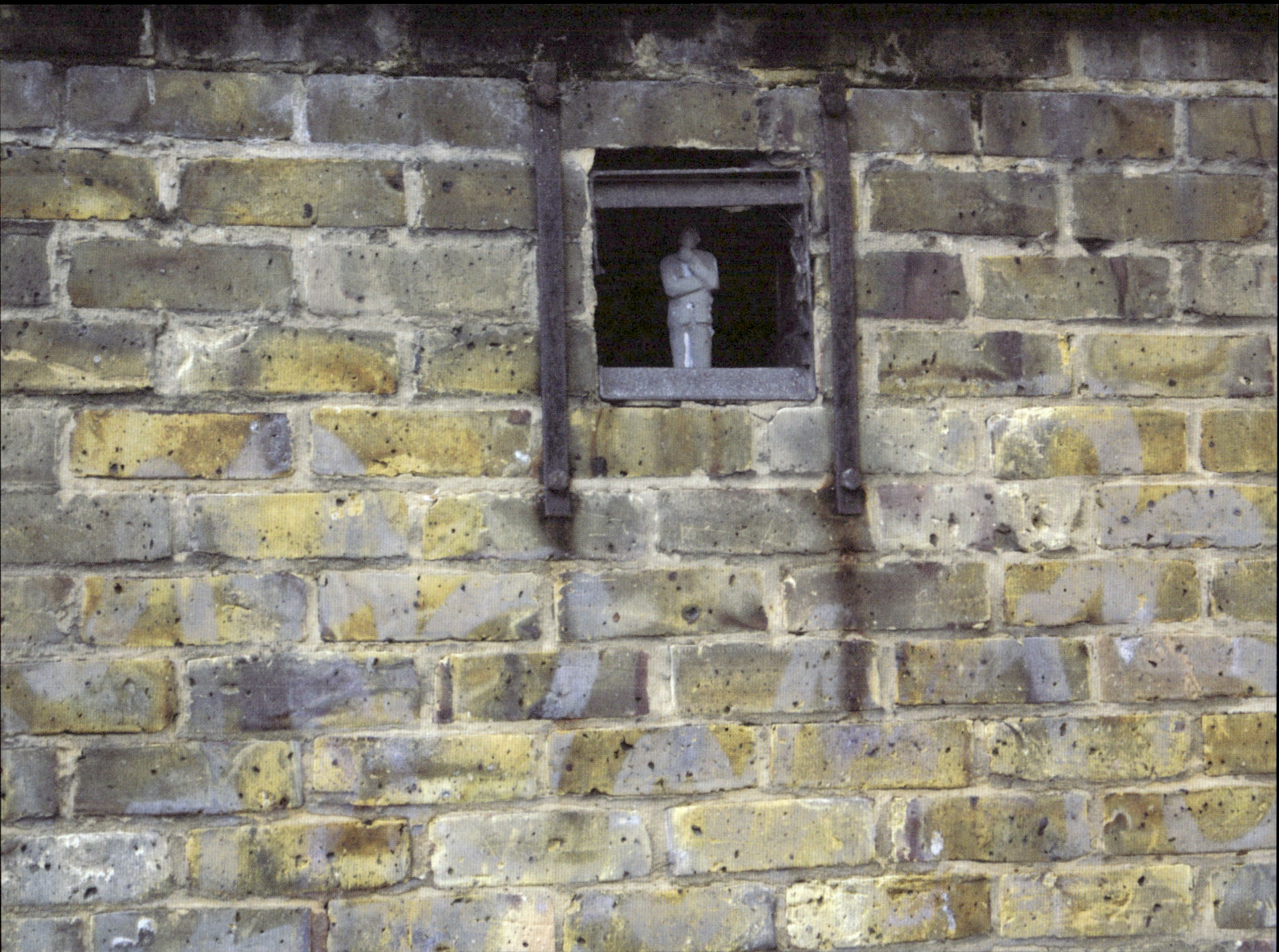

CEMENT THRONE
PONTEVEDRA, GALICIA
2009

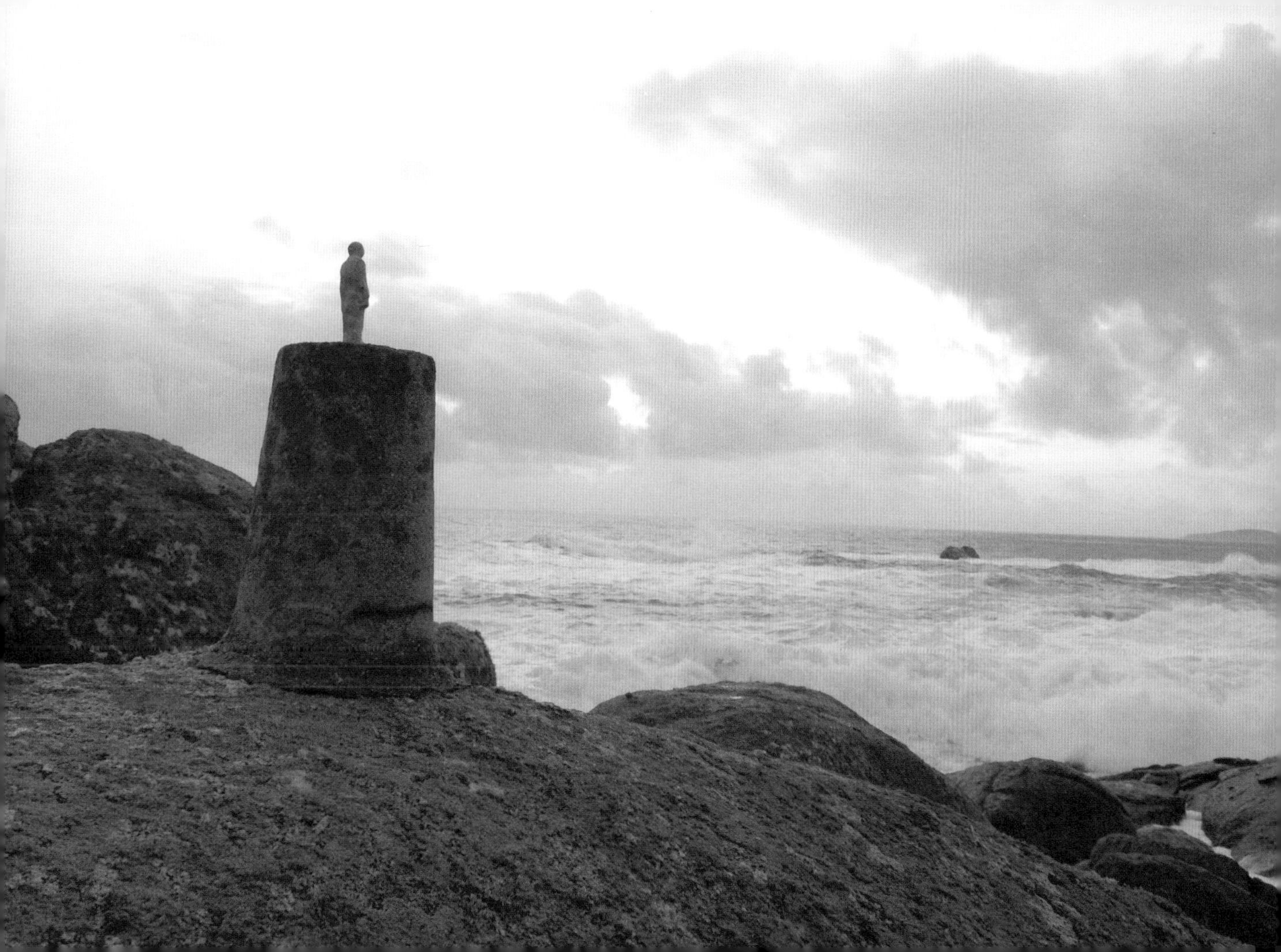

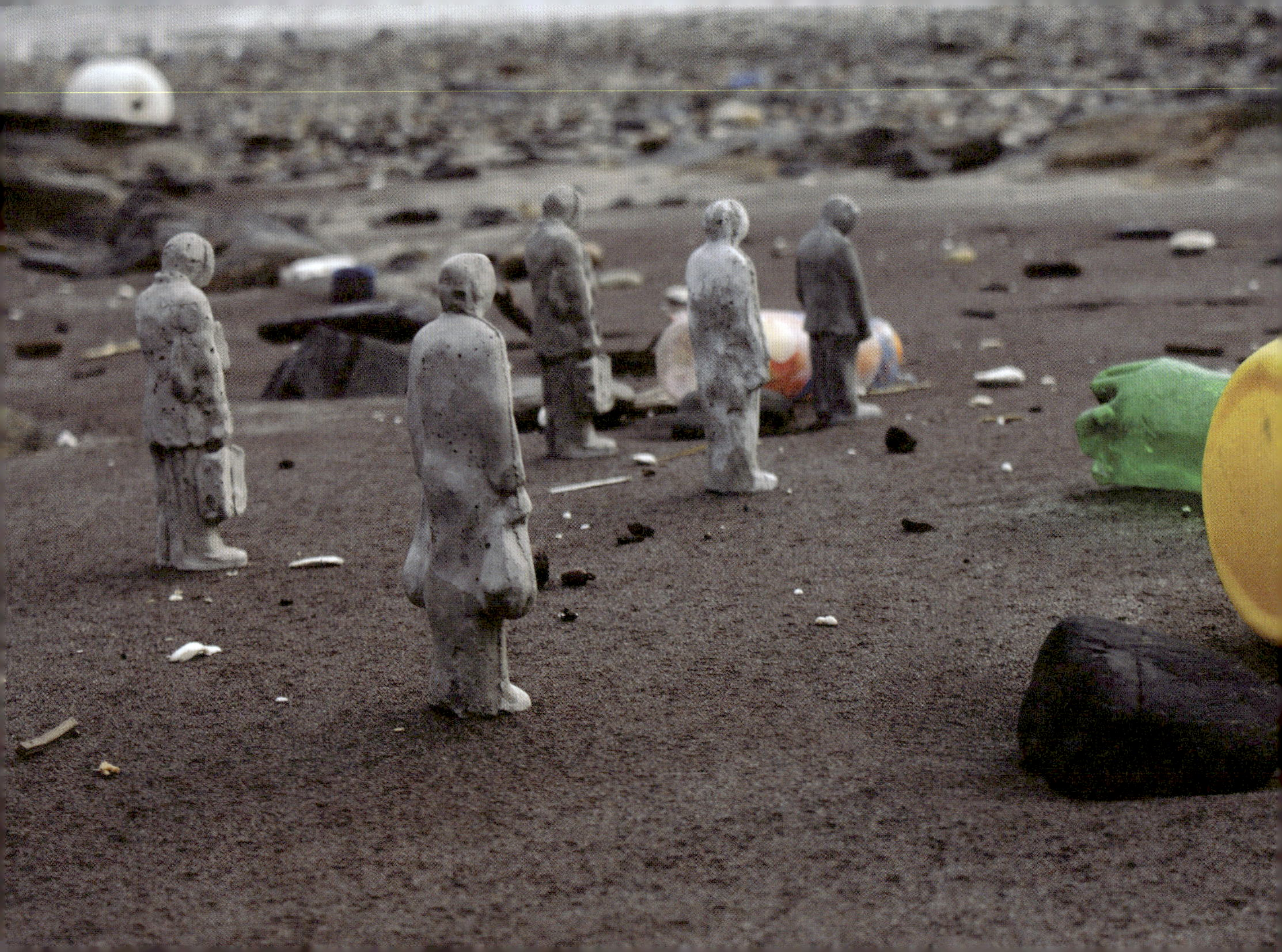

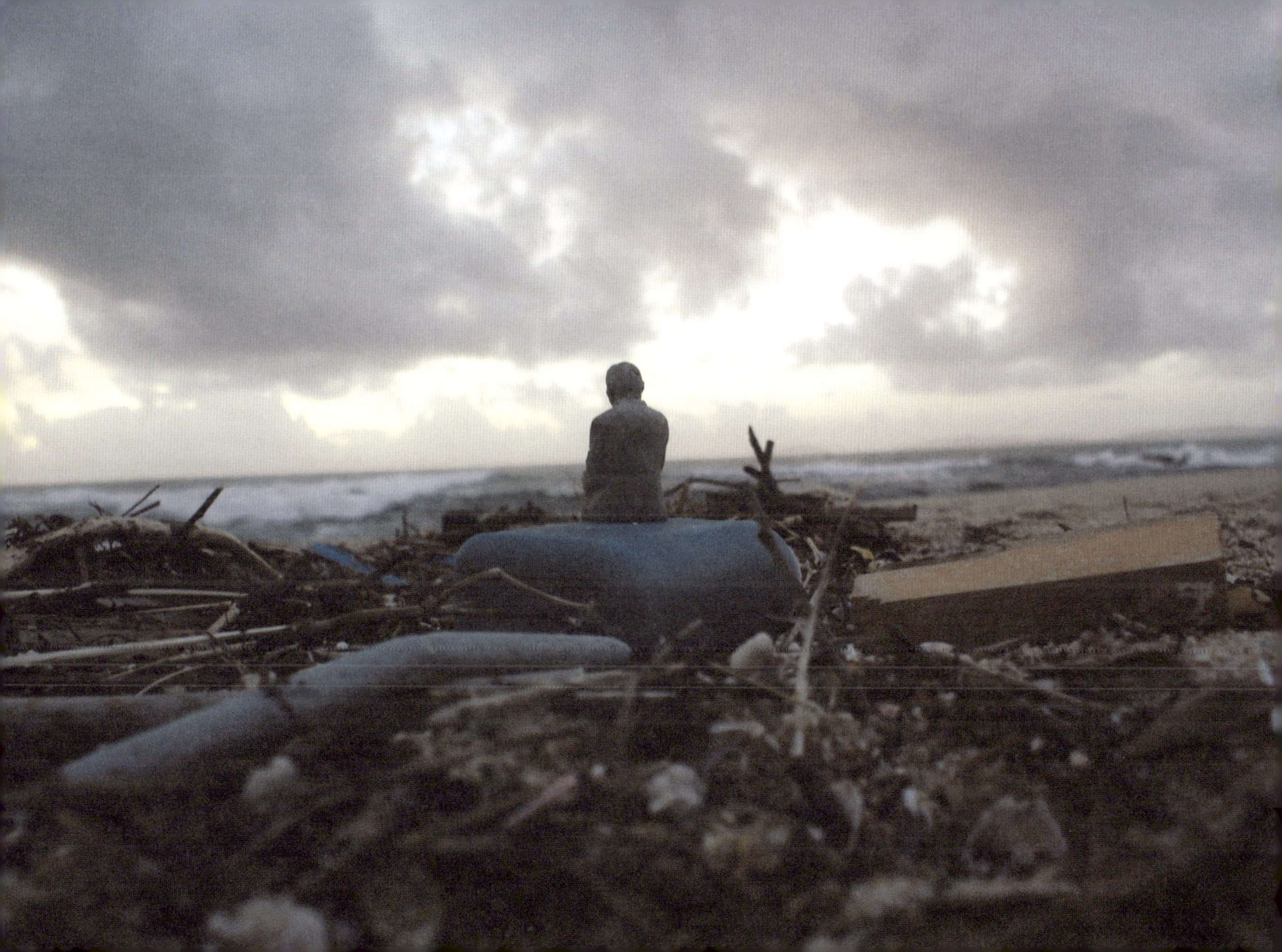

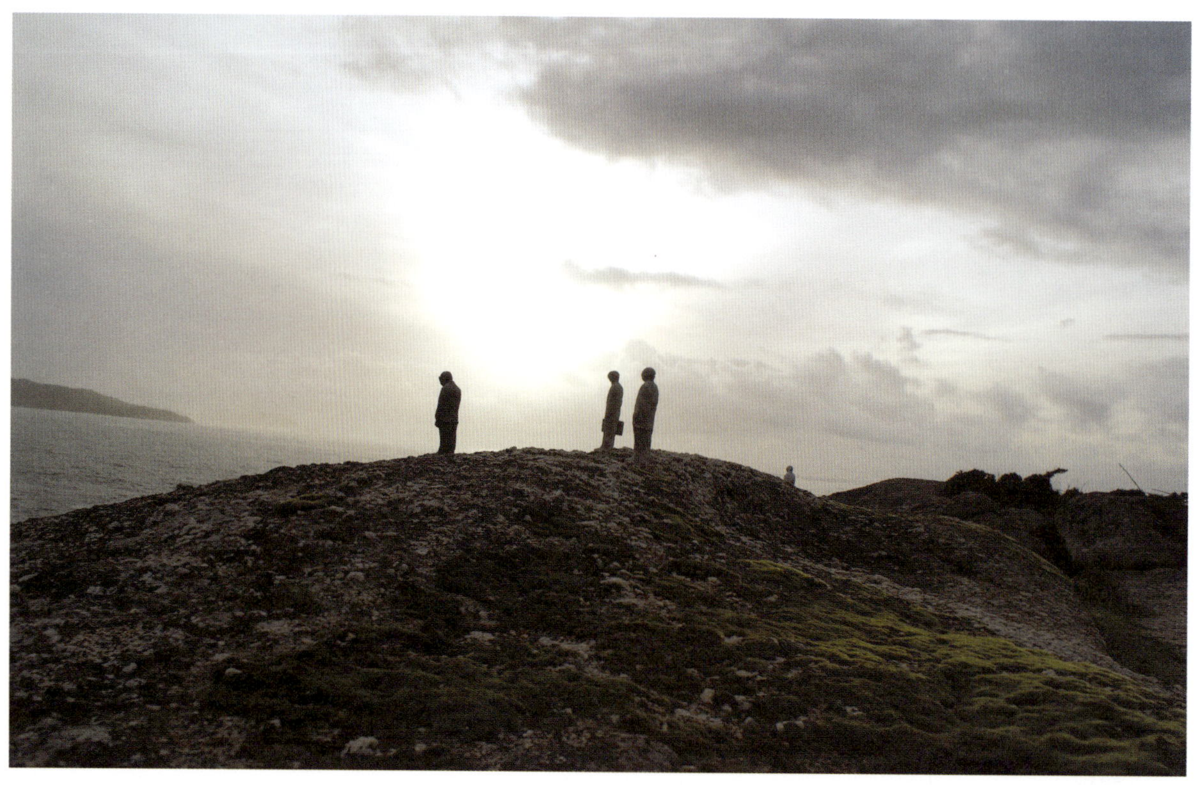

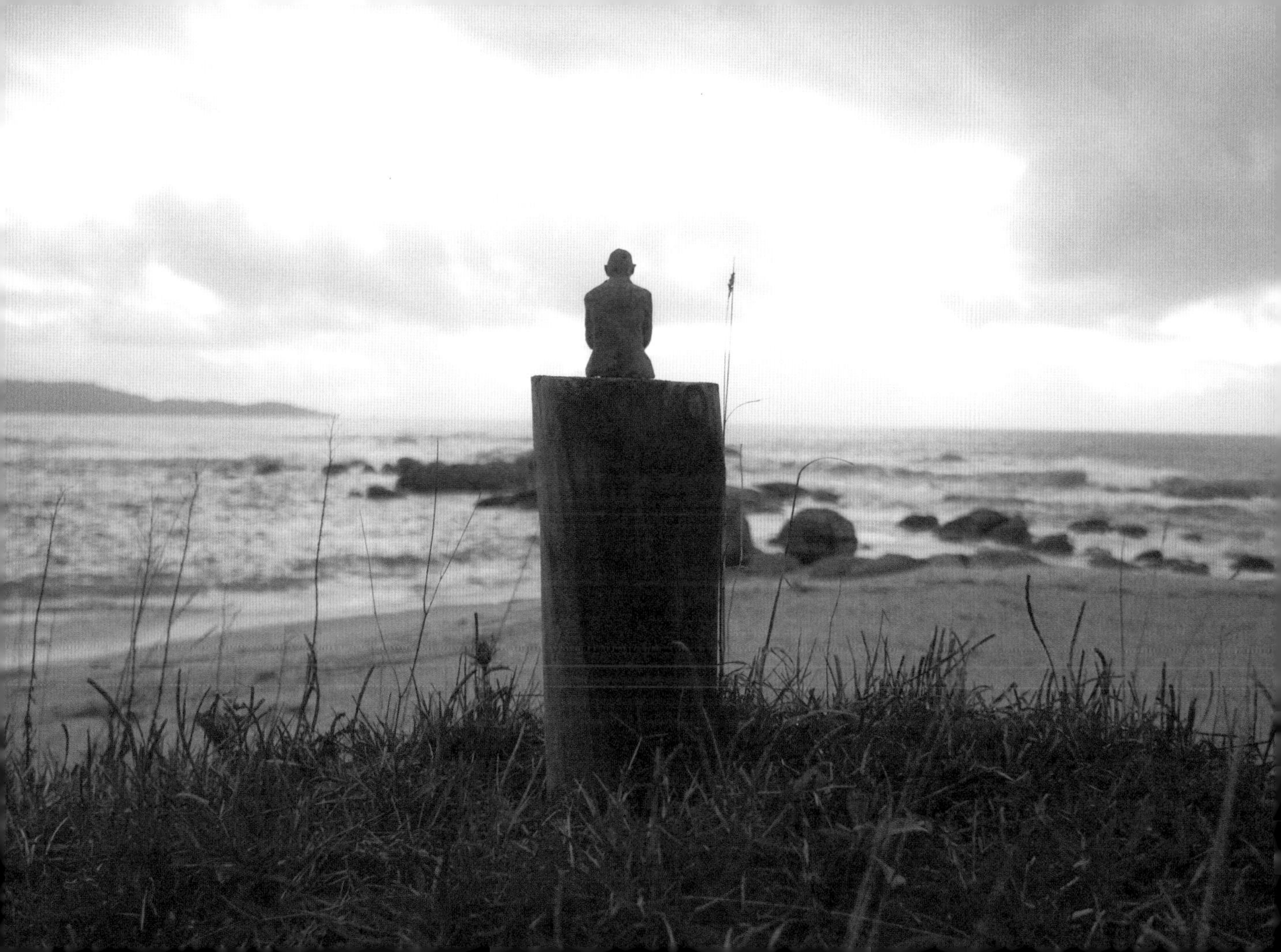

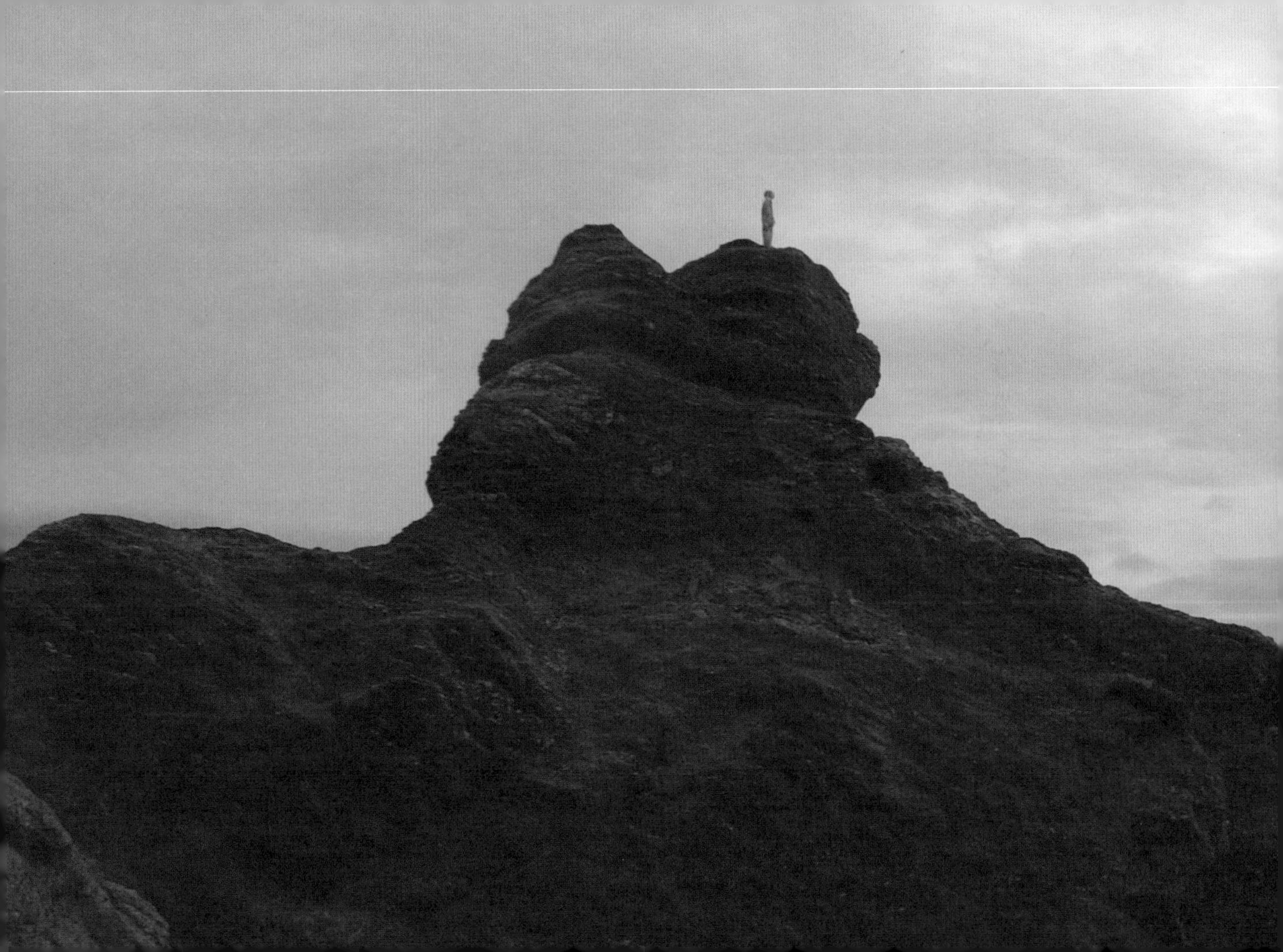

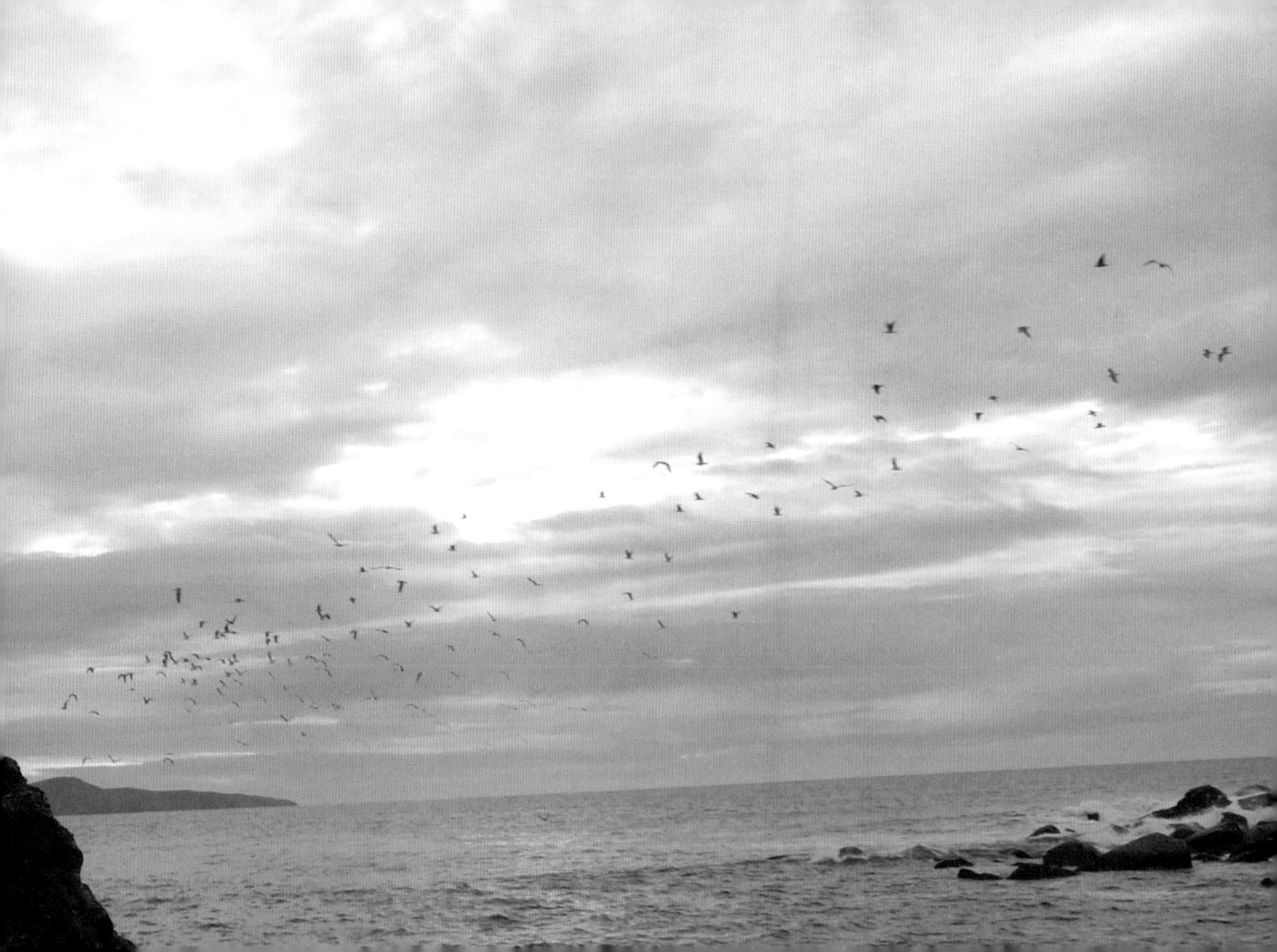

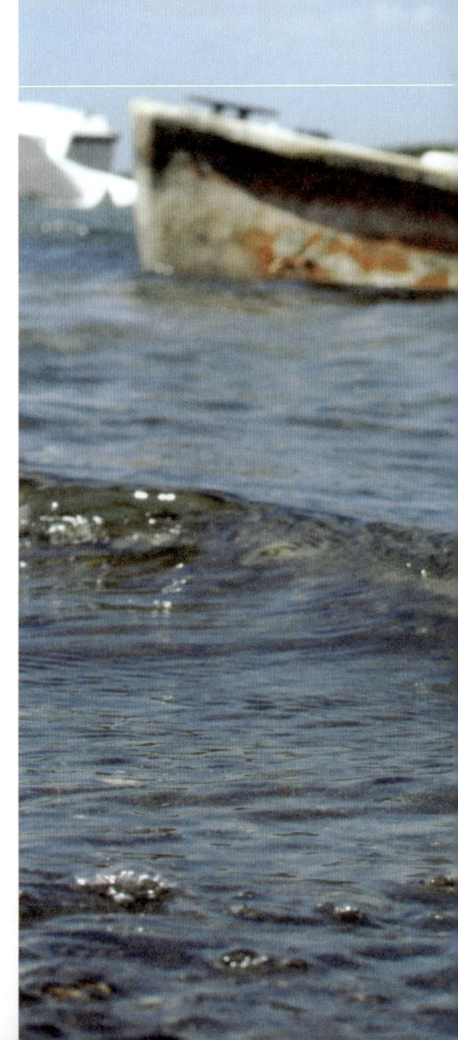

LEAVING A SINKING SHIP
ITALY
2010

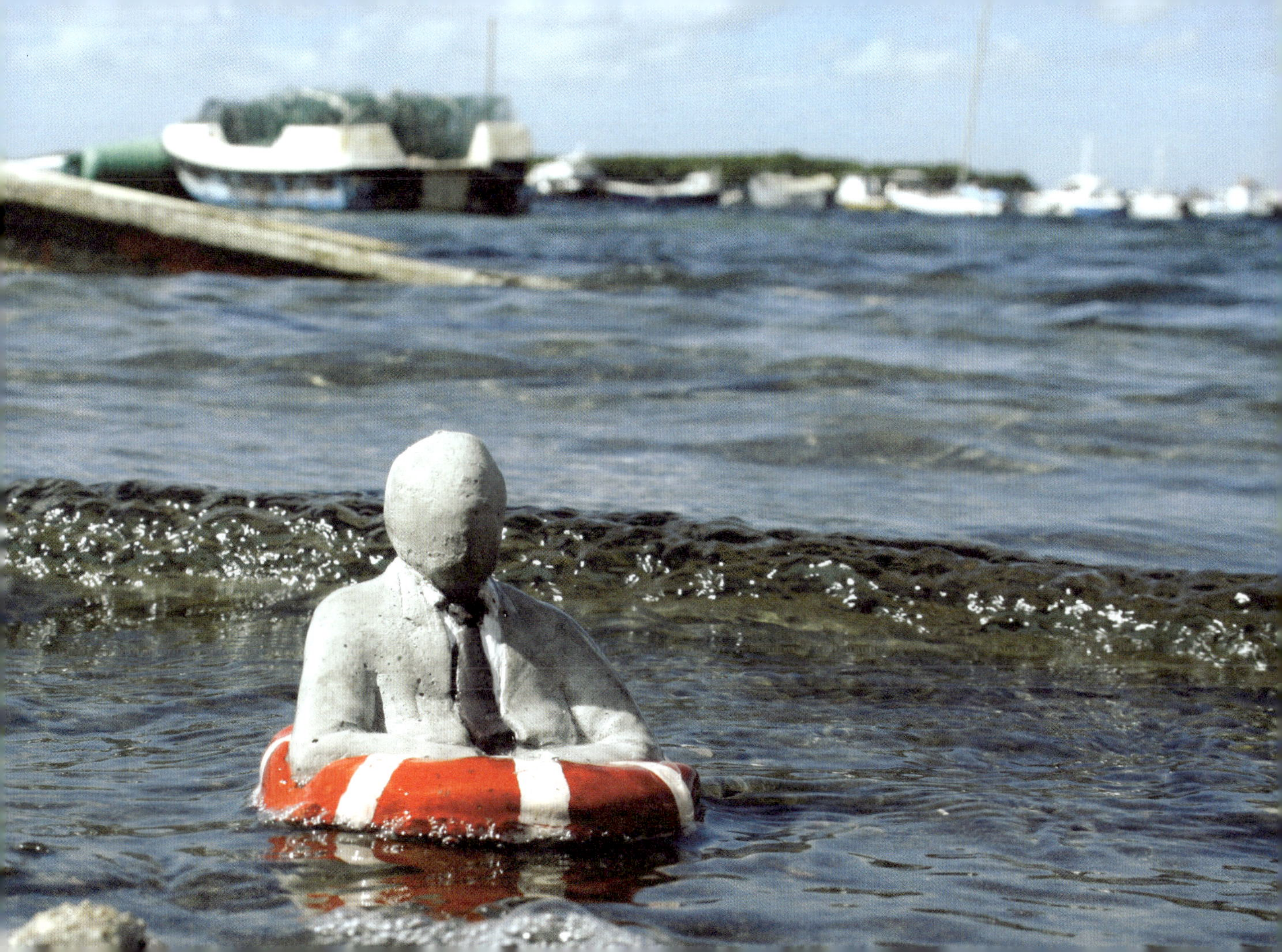

IN RUINS
LONDON
2009

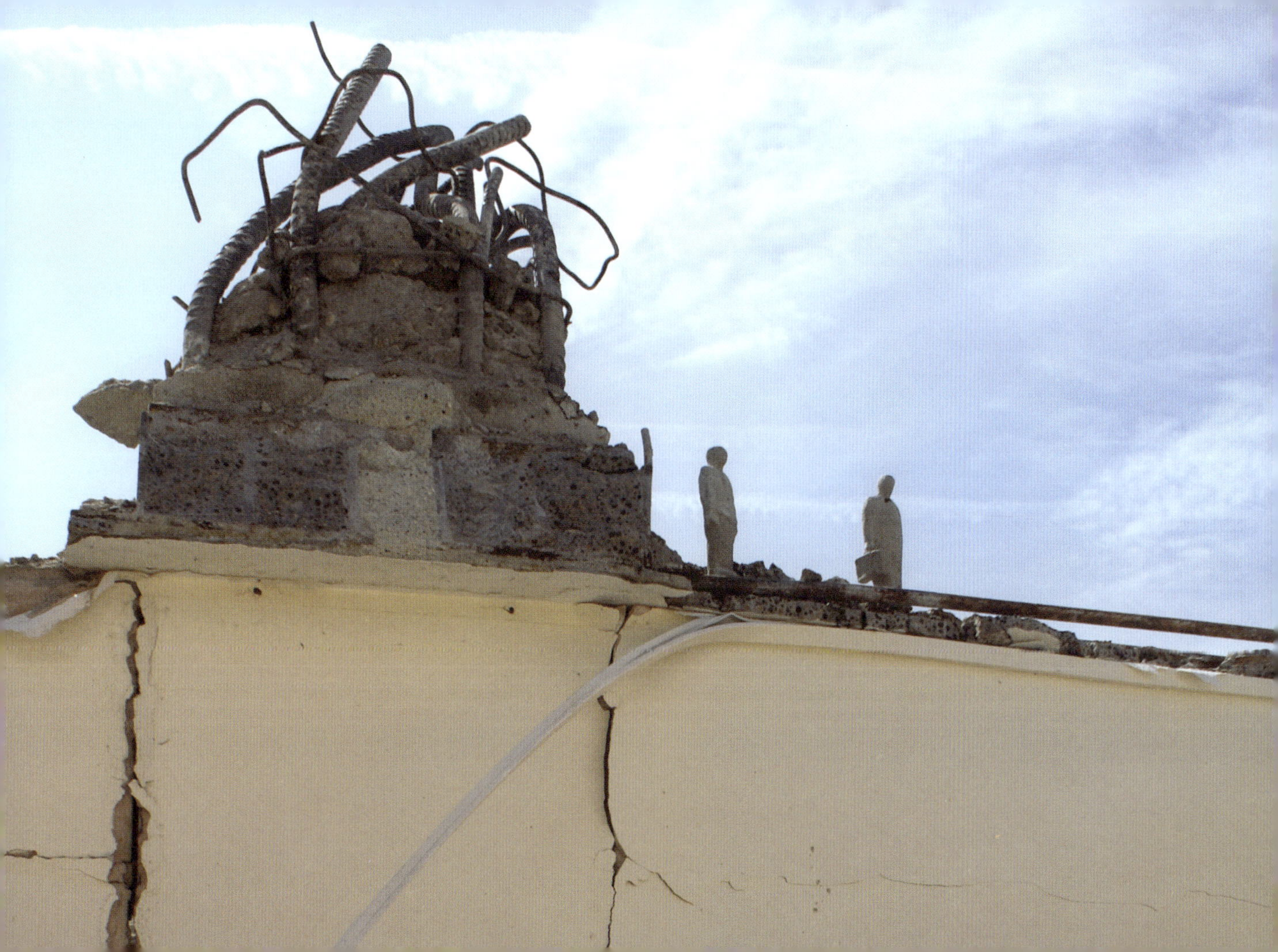

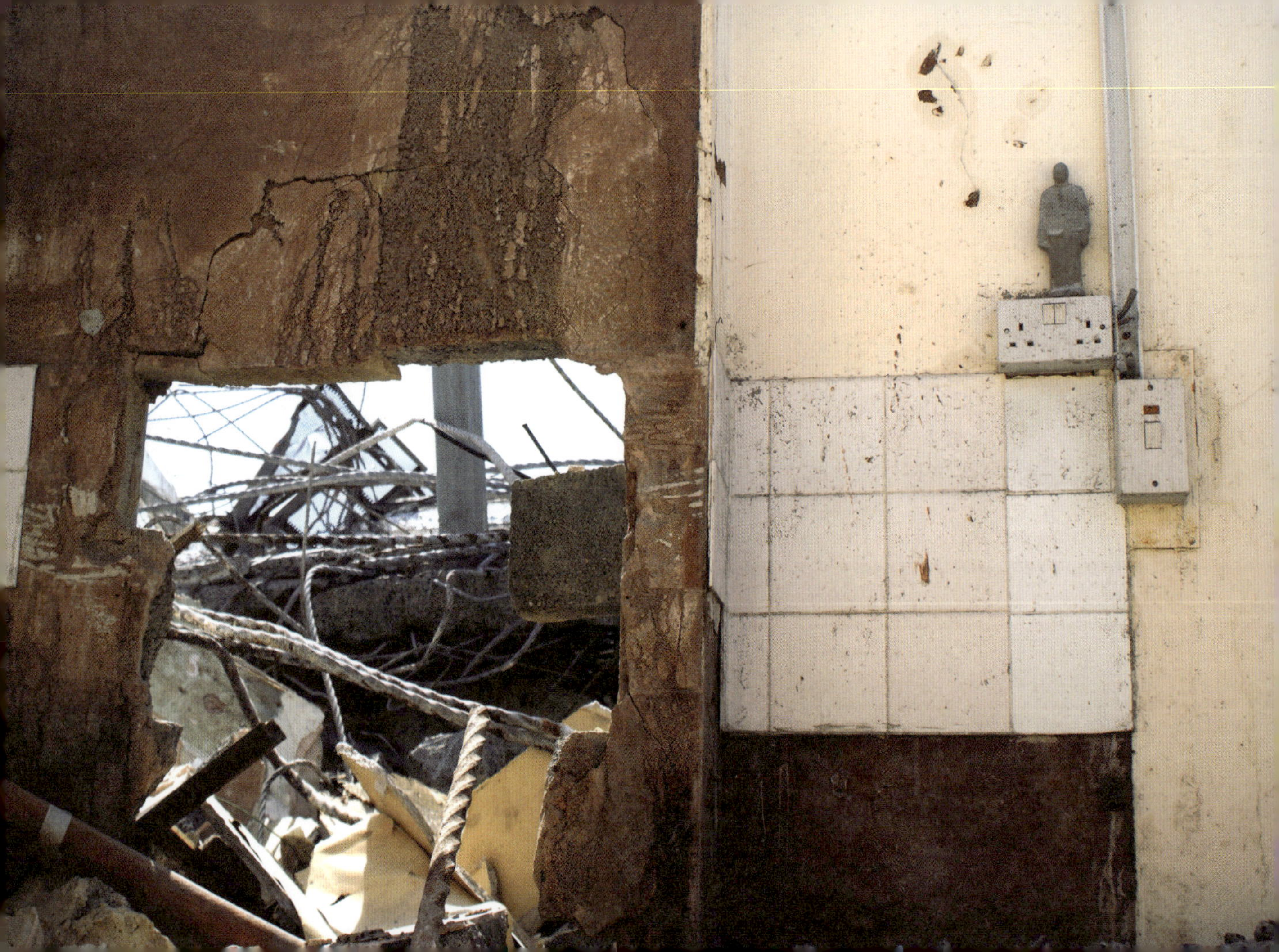

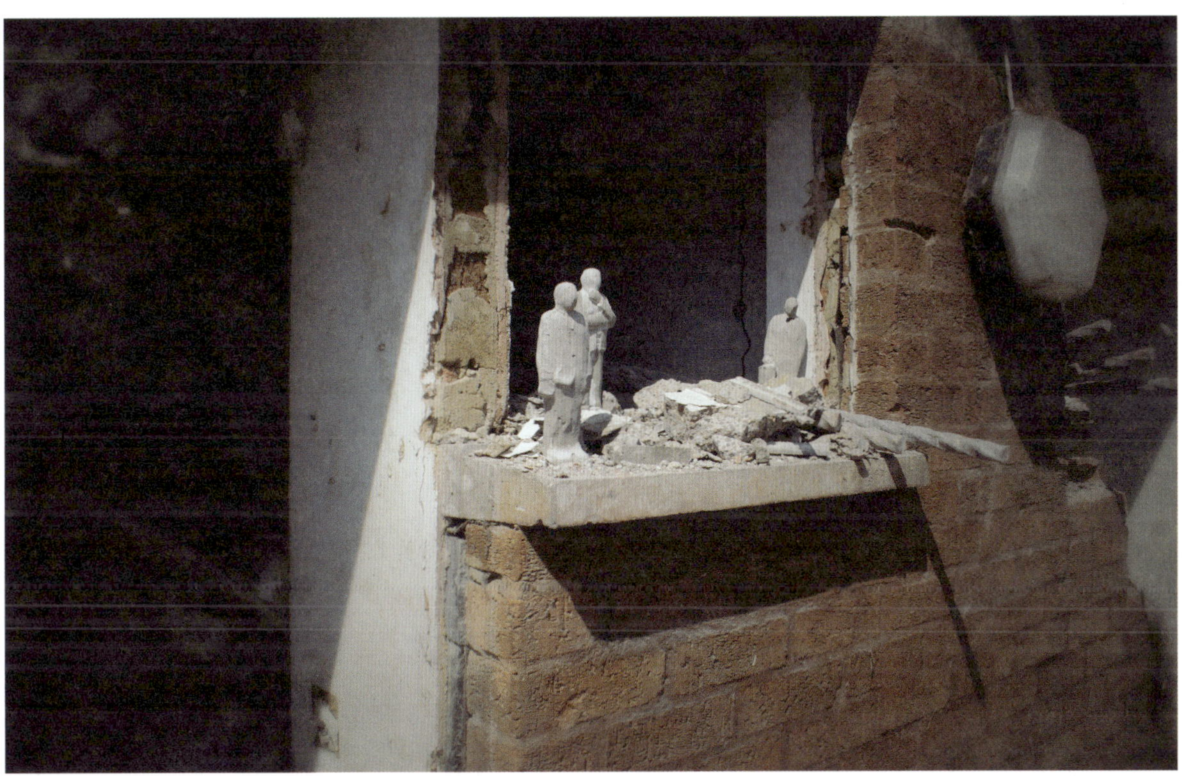

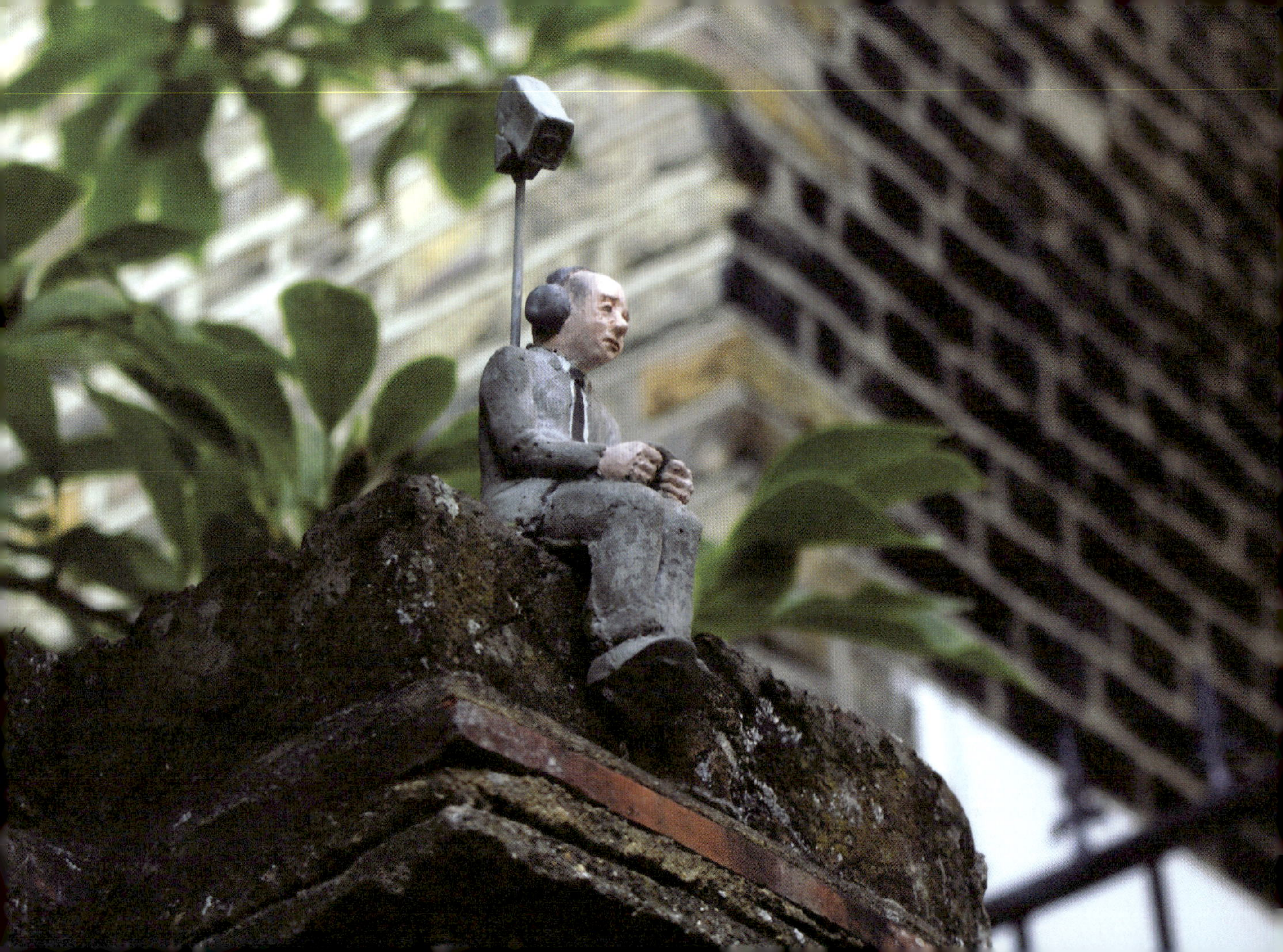

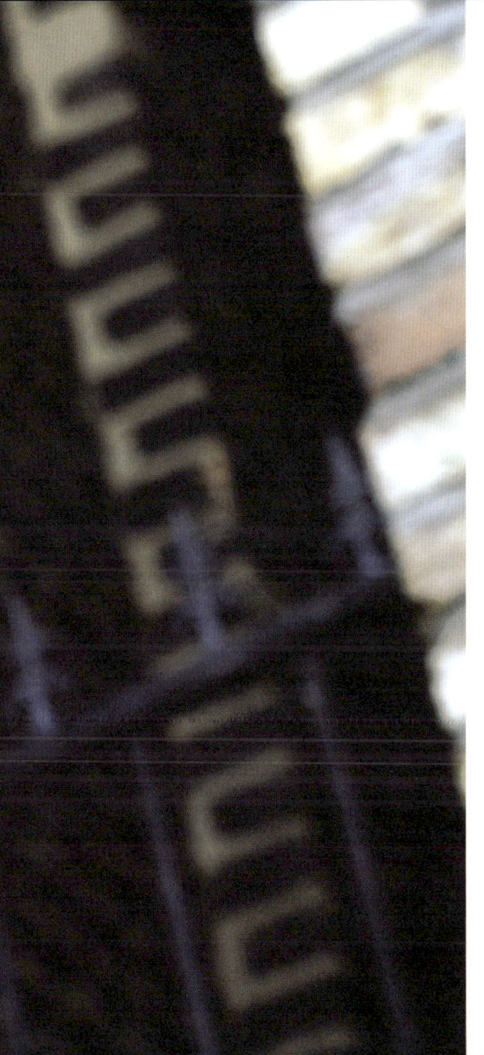

CCTV AUTOMATA
LONDON
2010

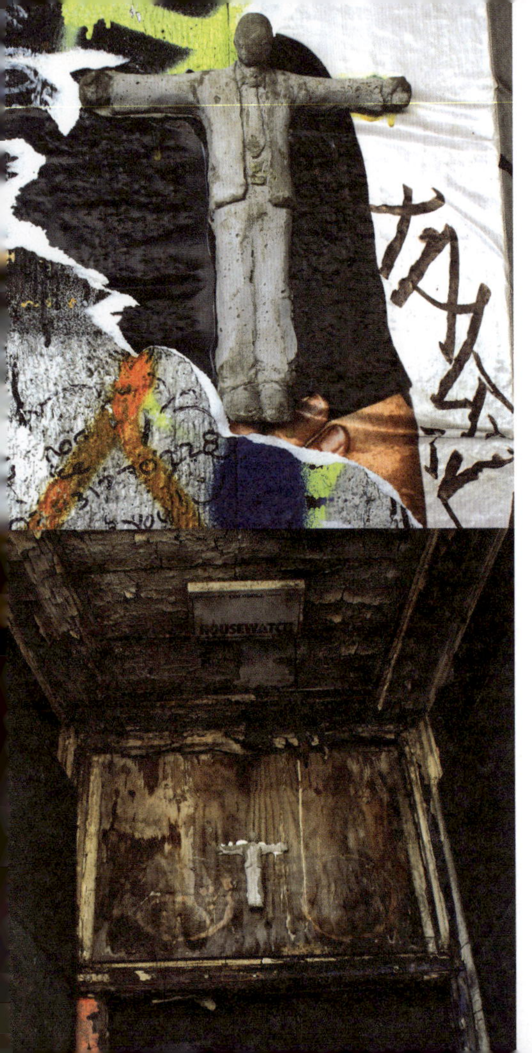

CAPITALISM
LONDON
2009

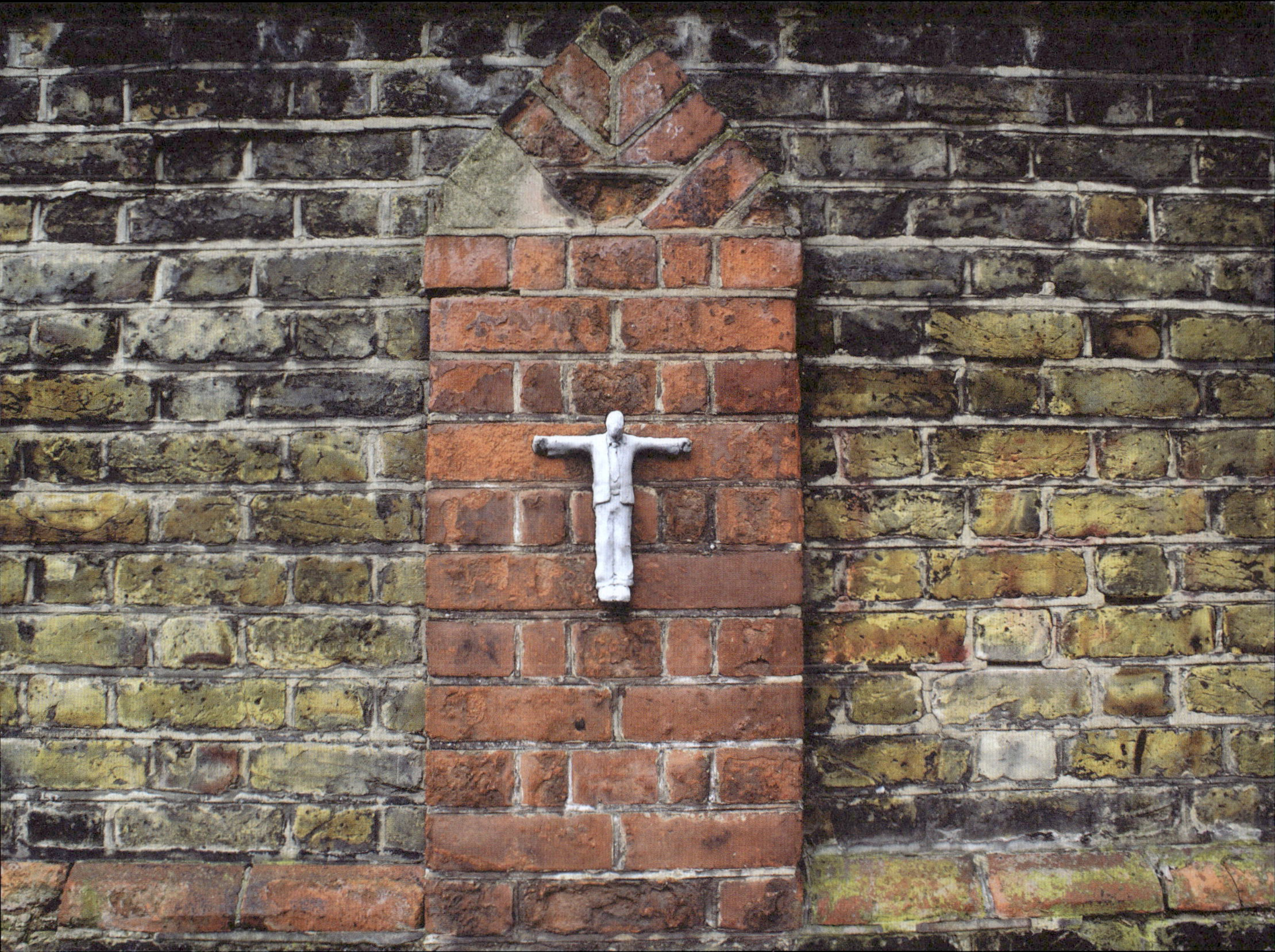

FOLLOW THE LEADER
LONDON
2009

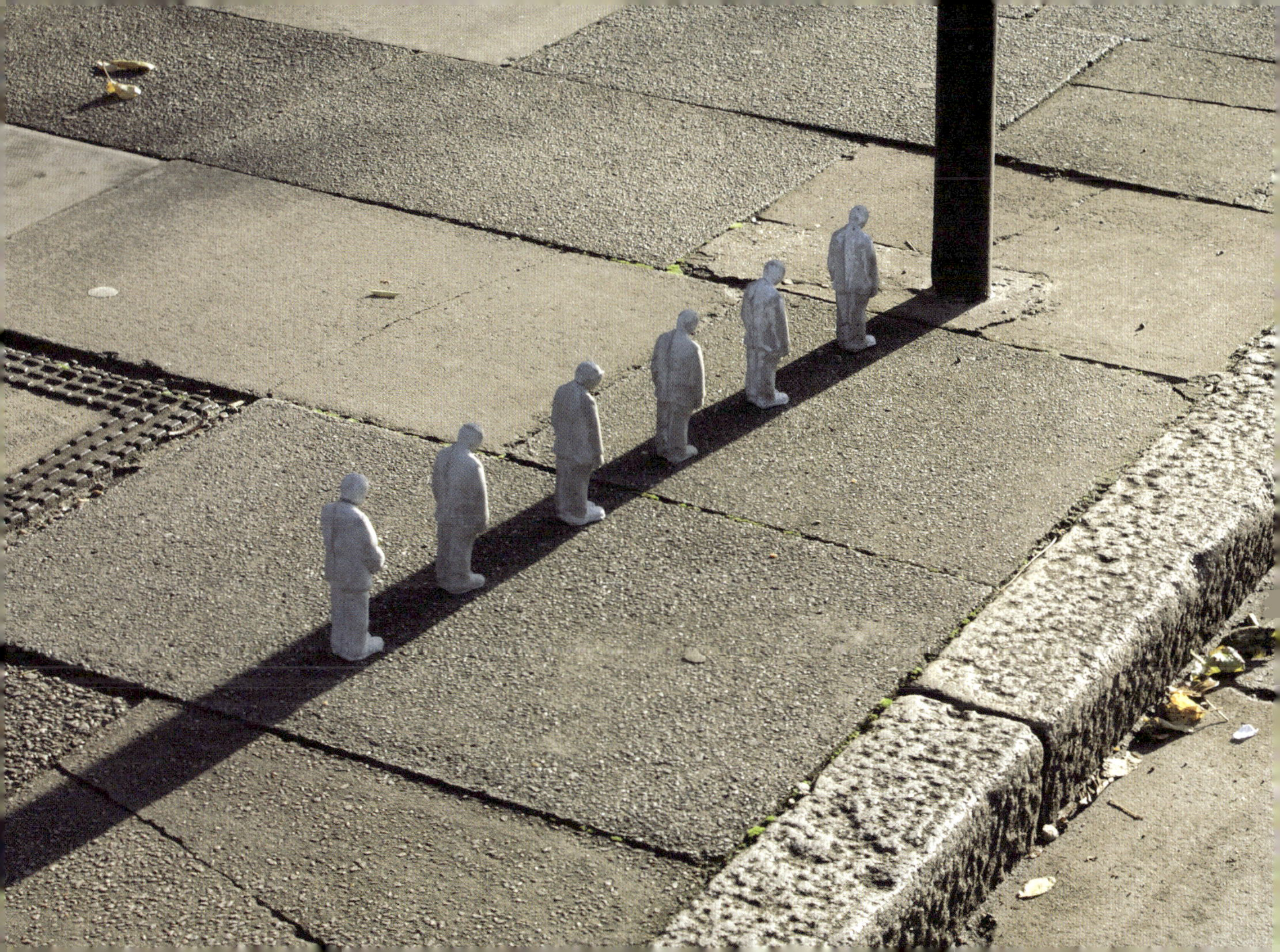

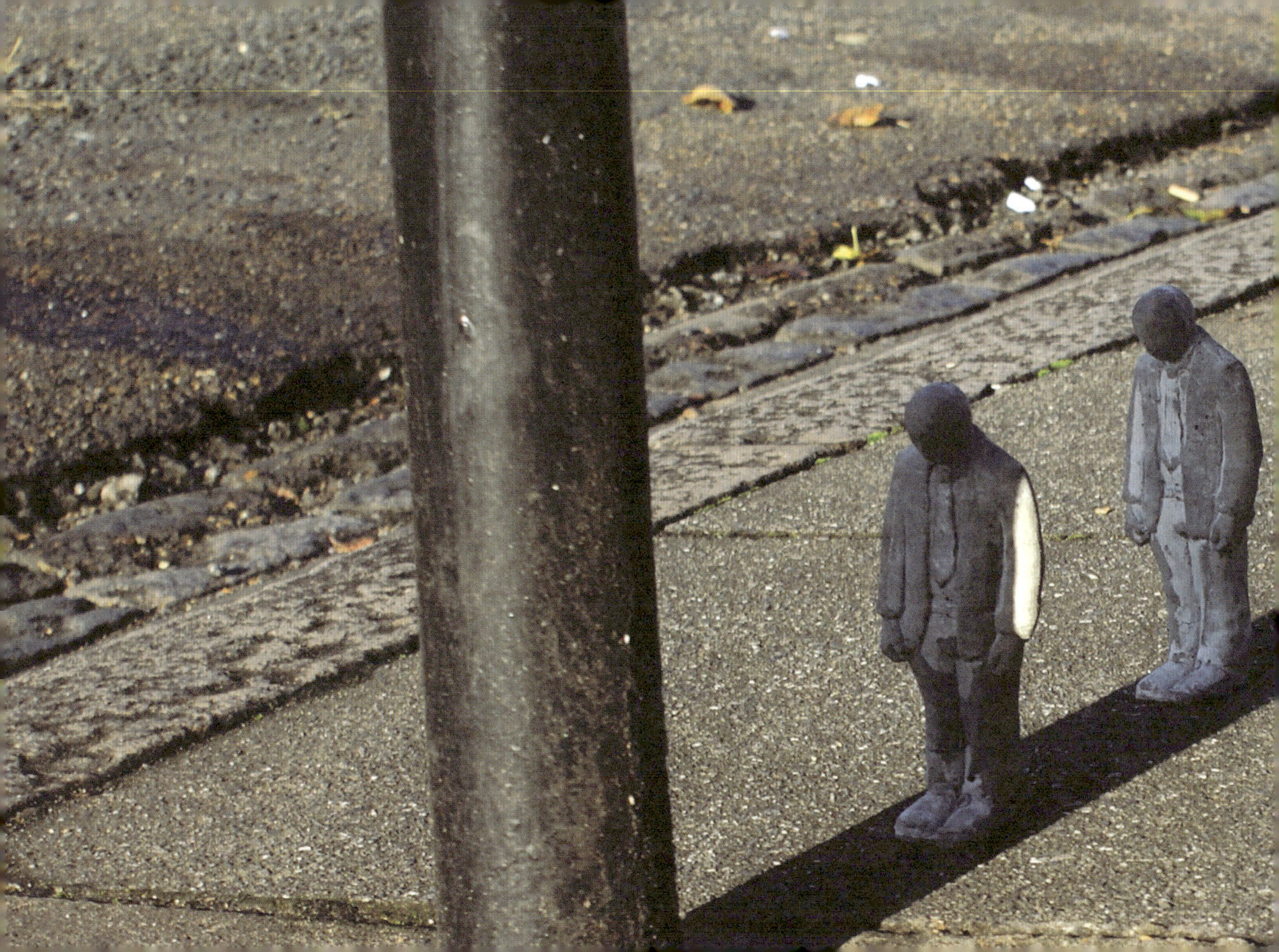

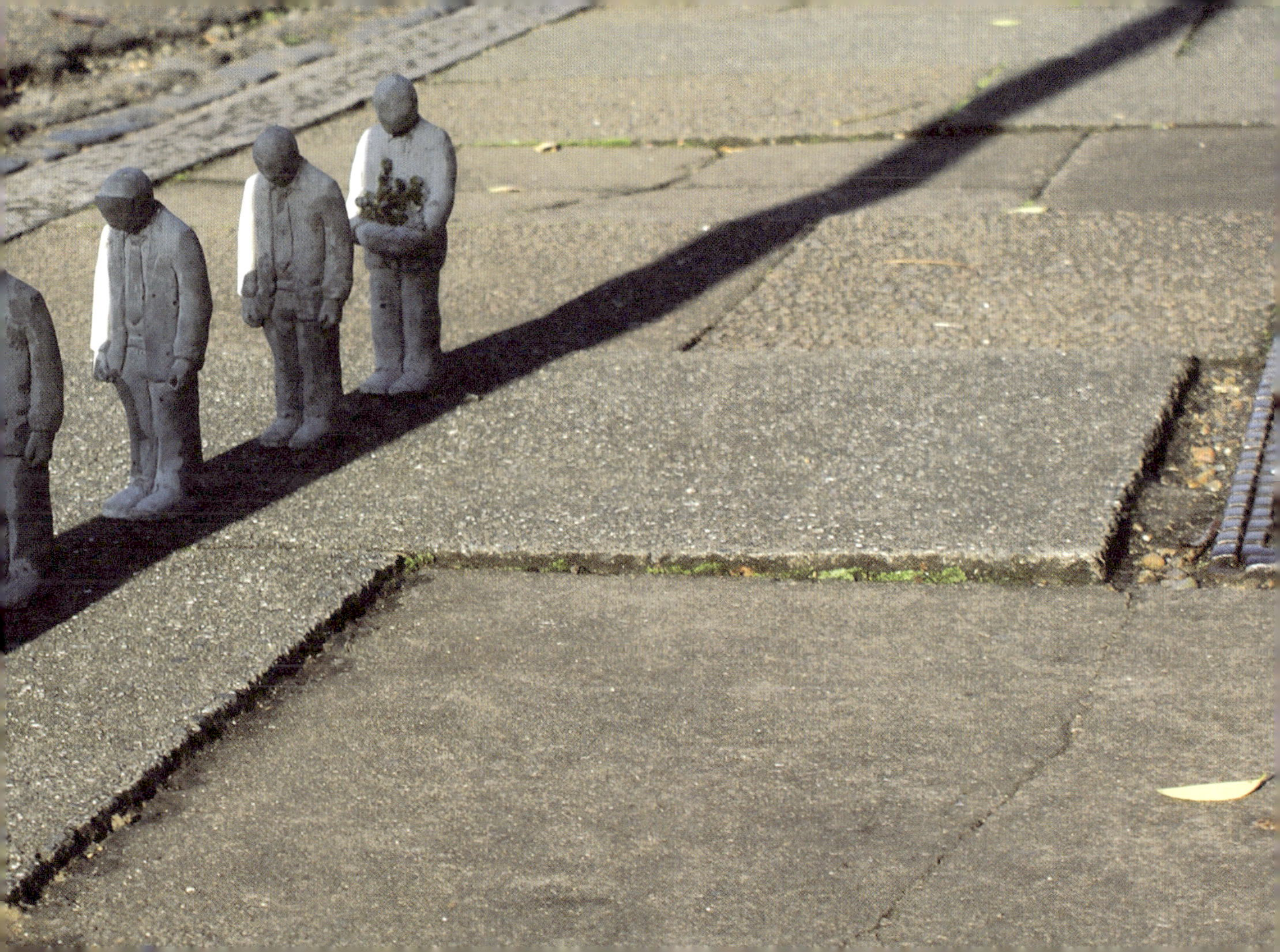

REMEMBRANCES FROM NATURE
LONDON
2009

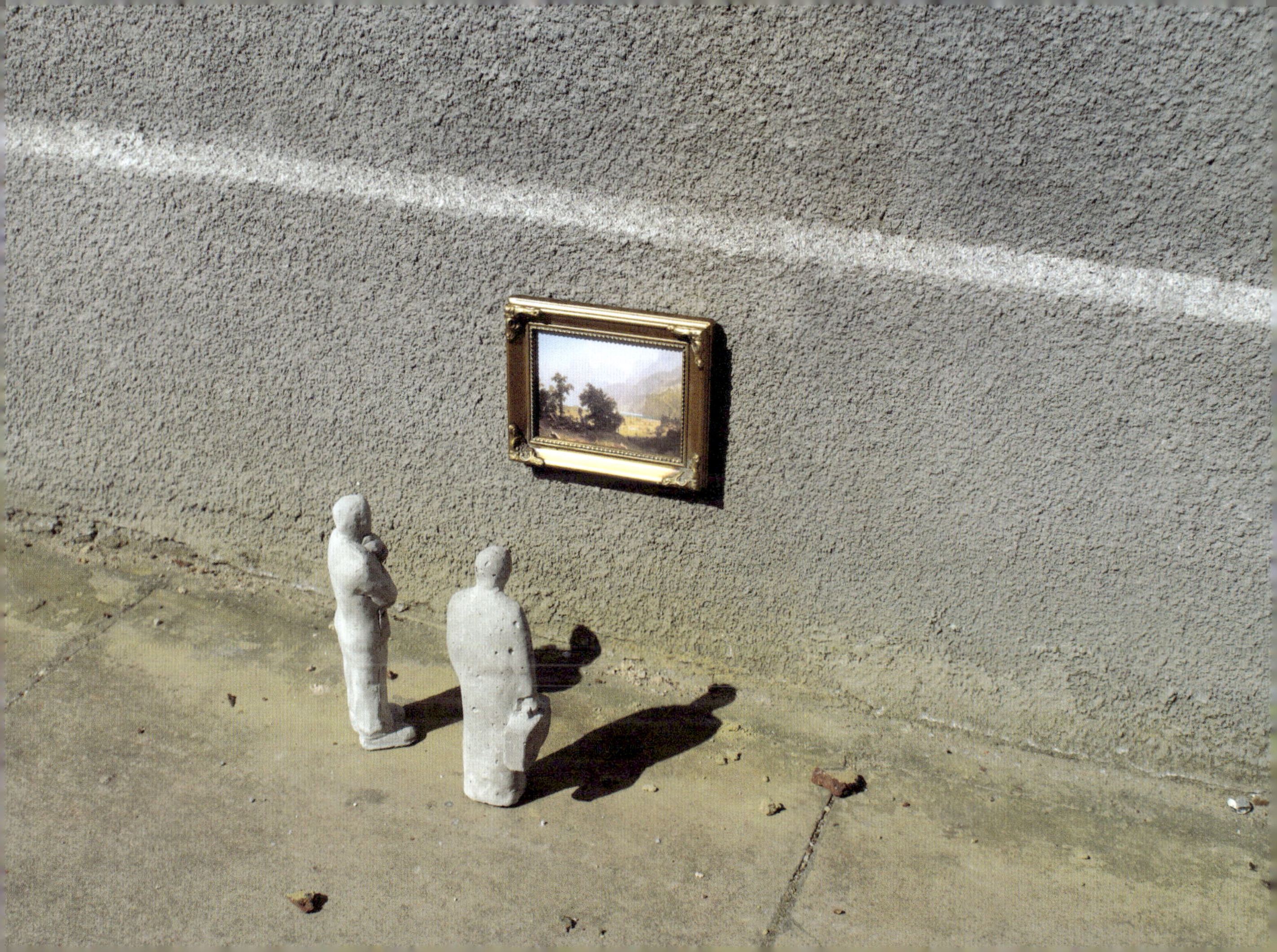

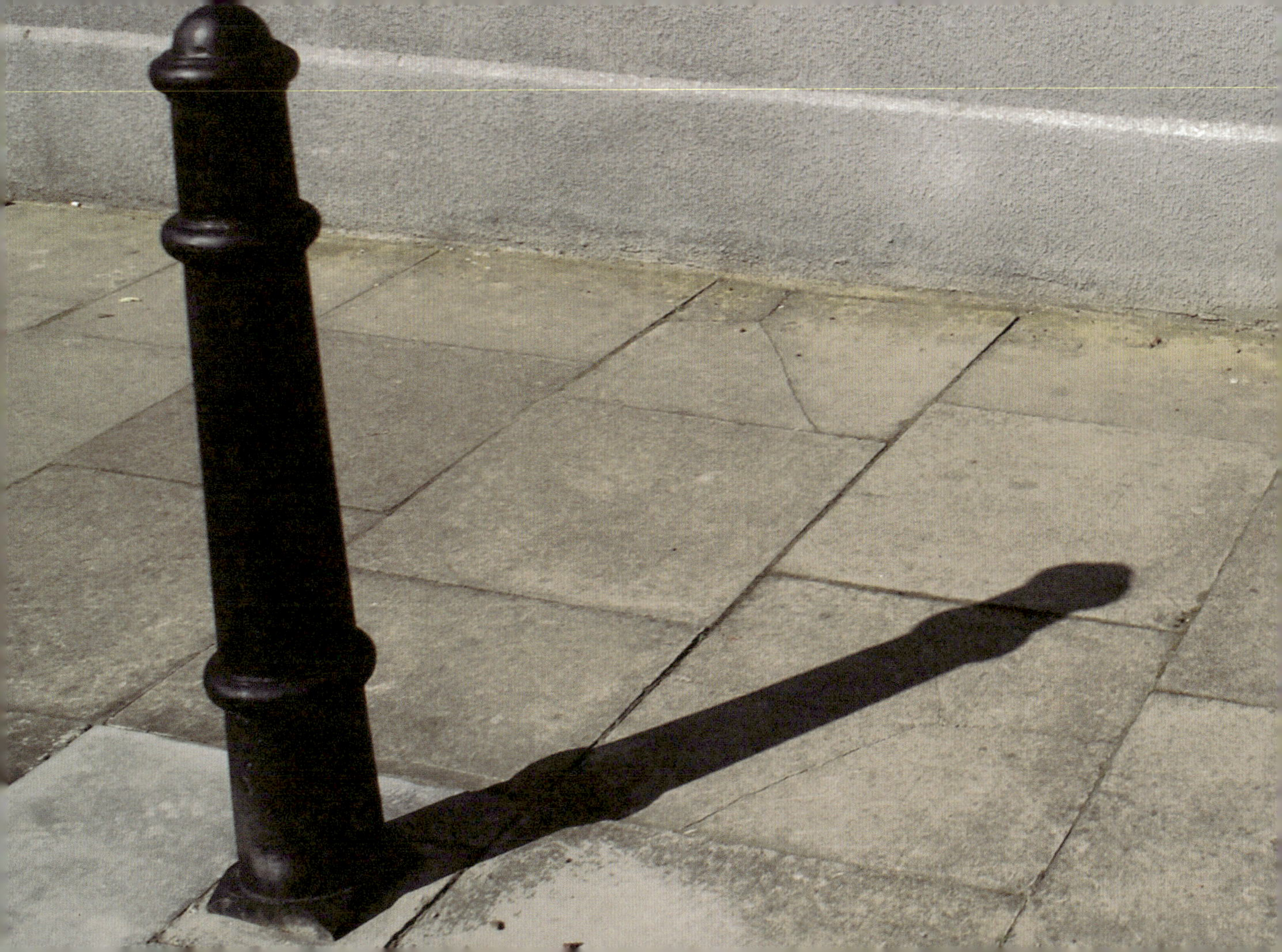

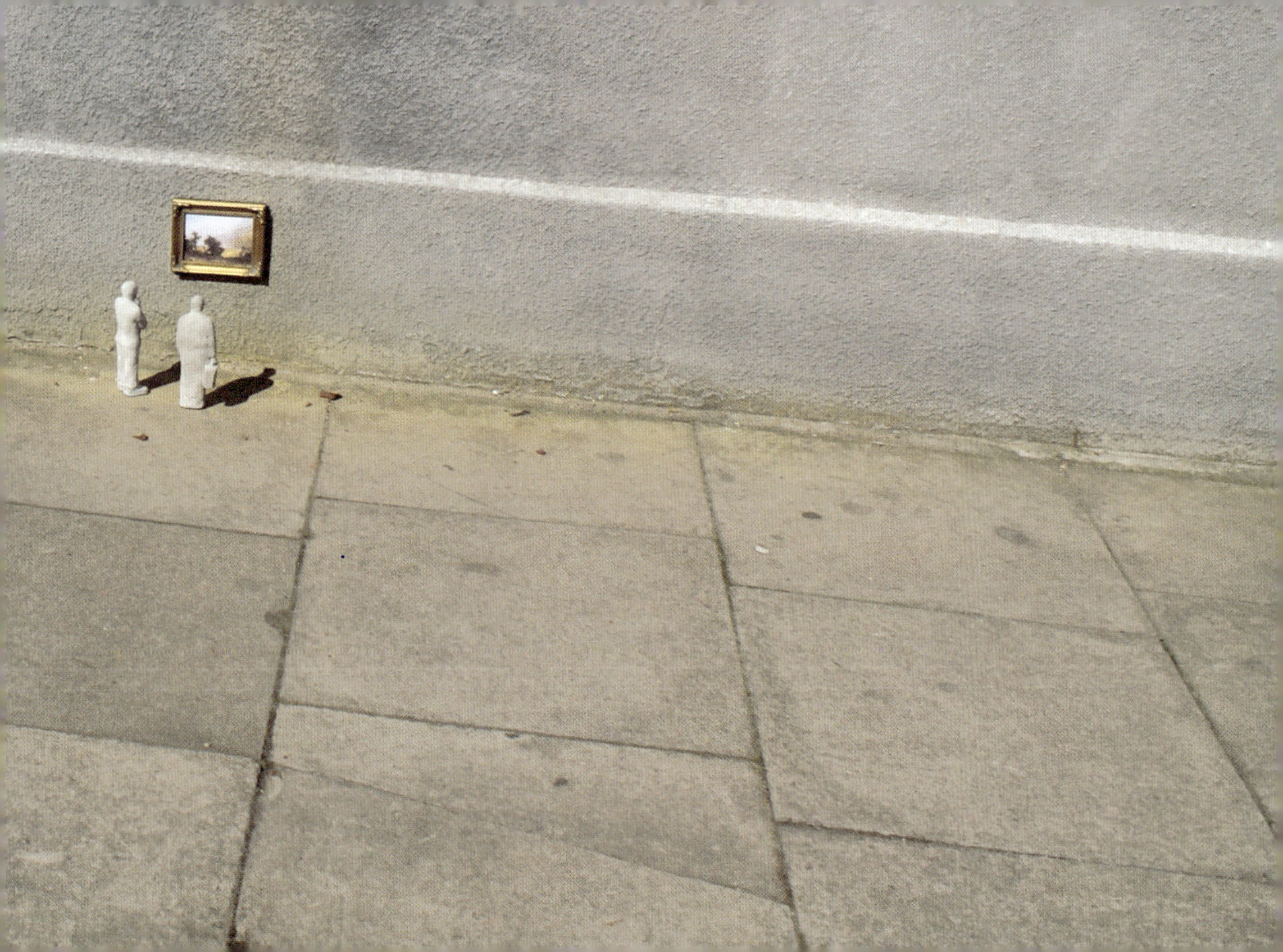

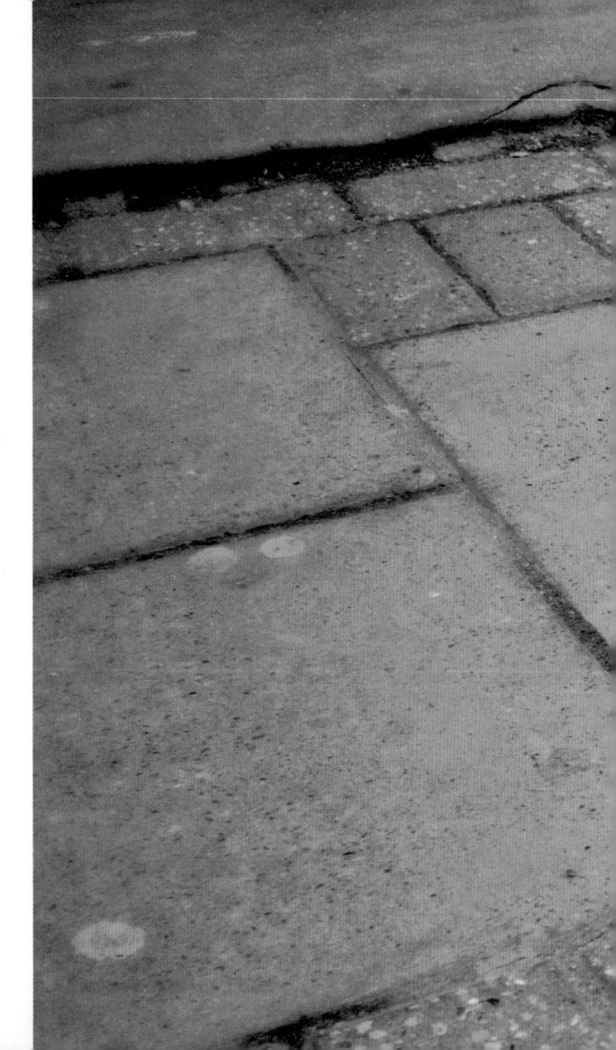

FOREST ROAD
LONDON
2009

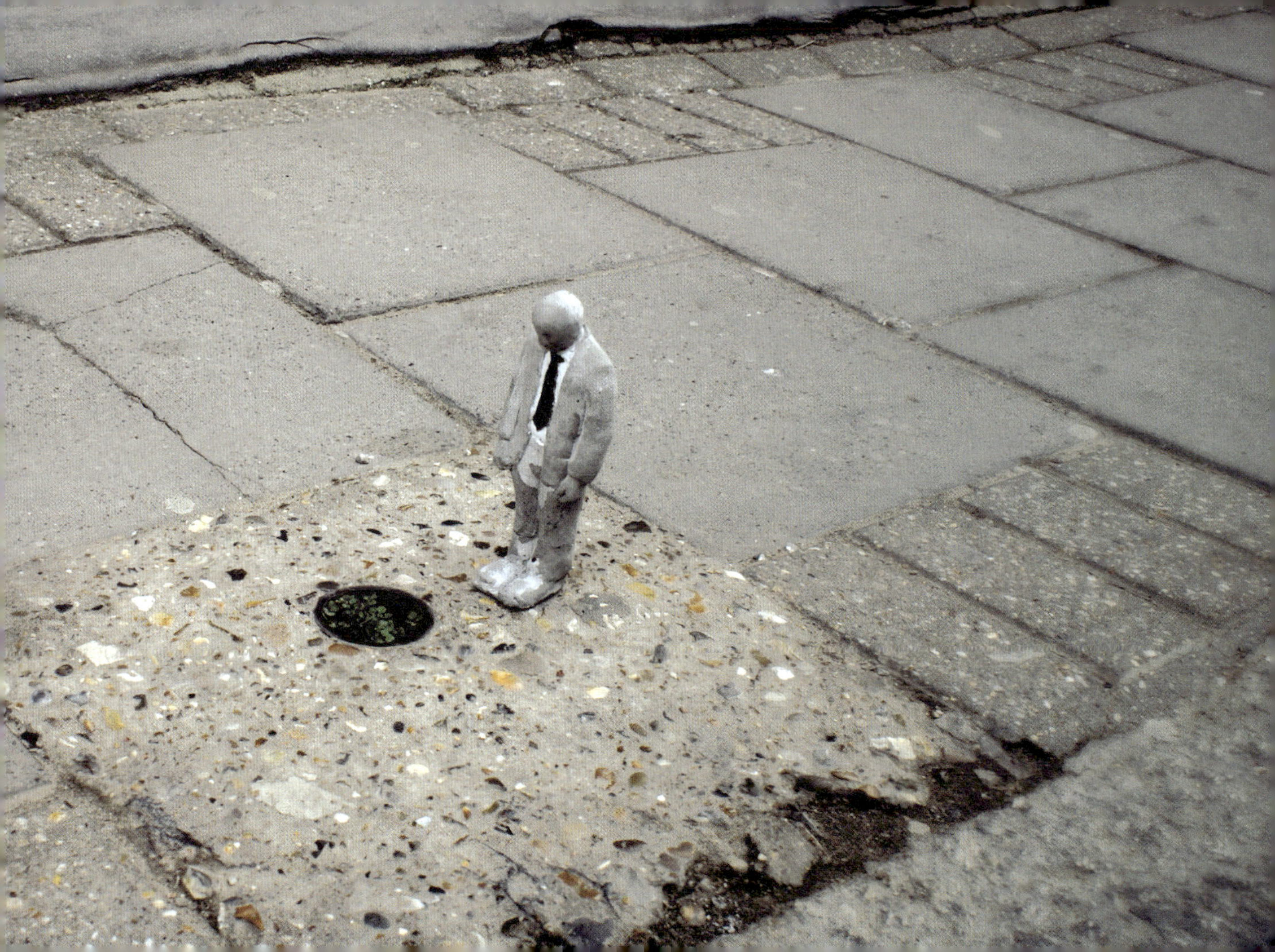

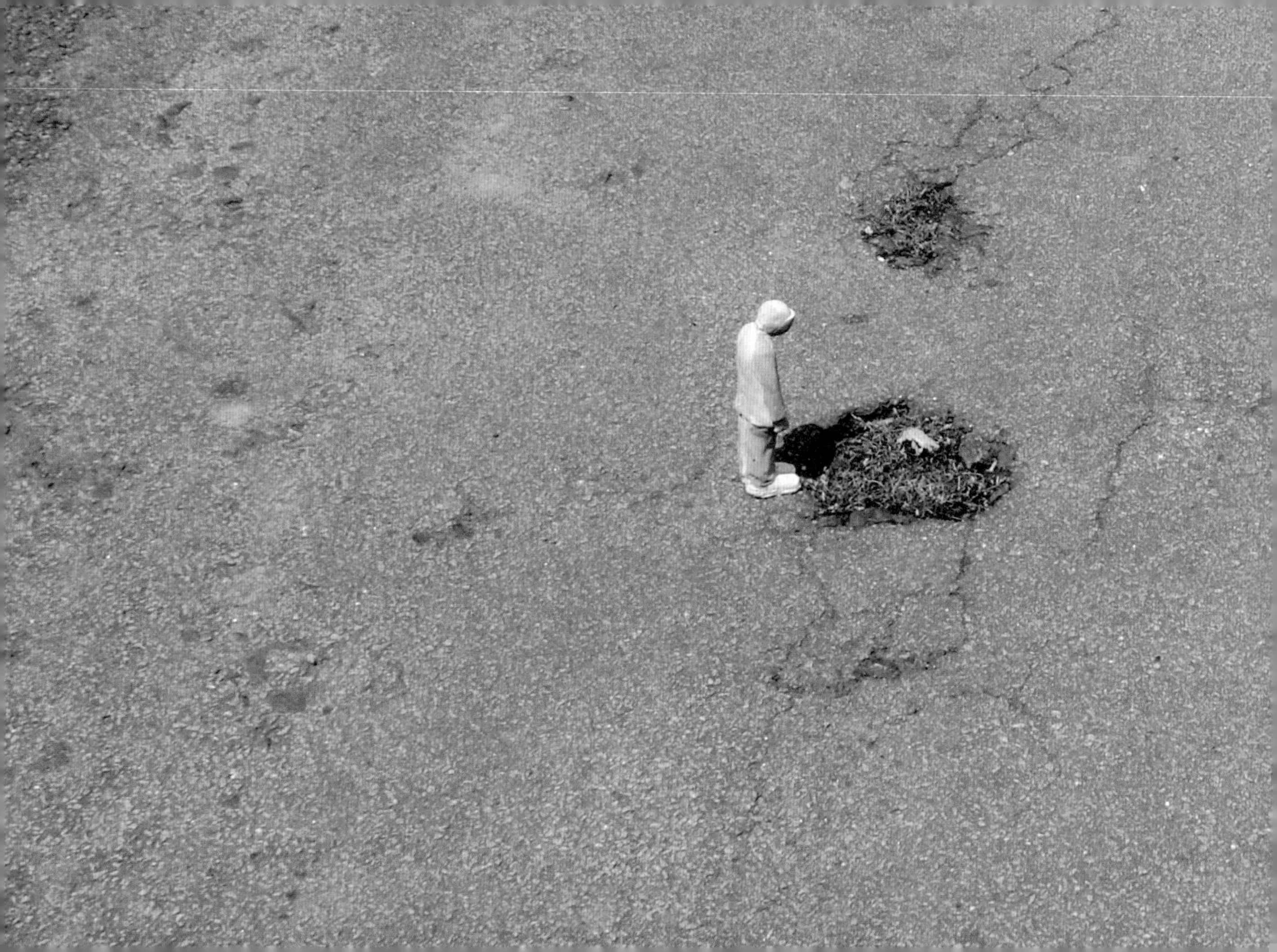

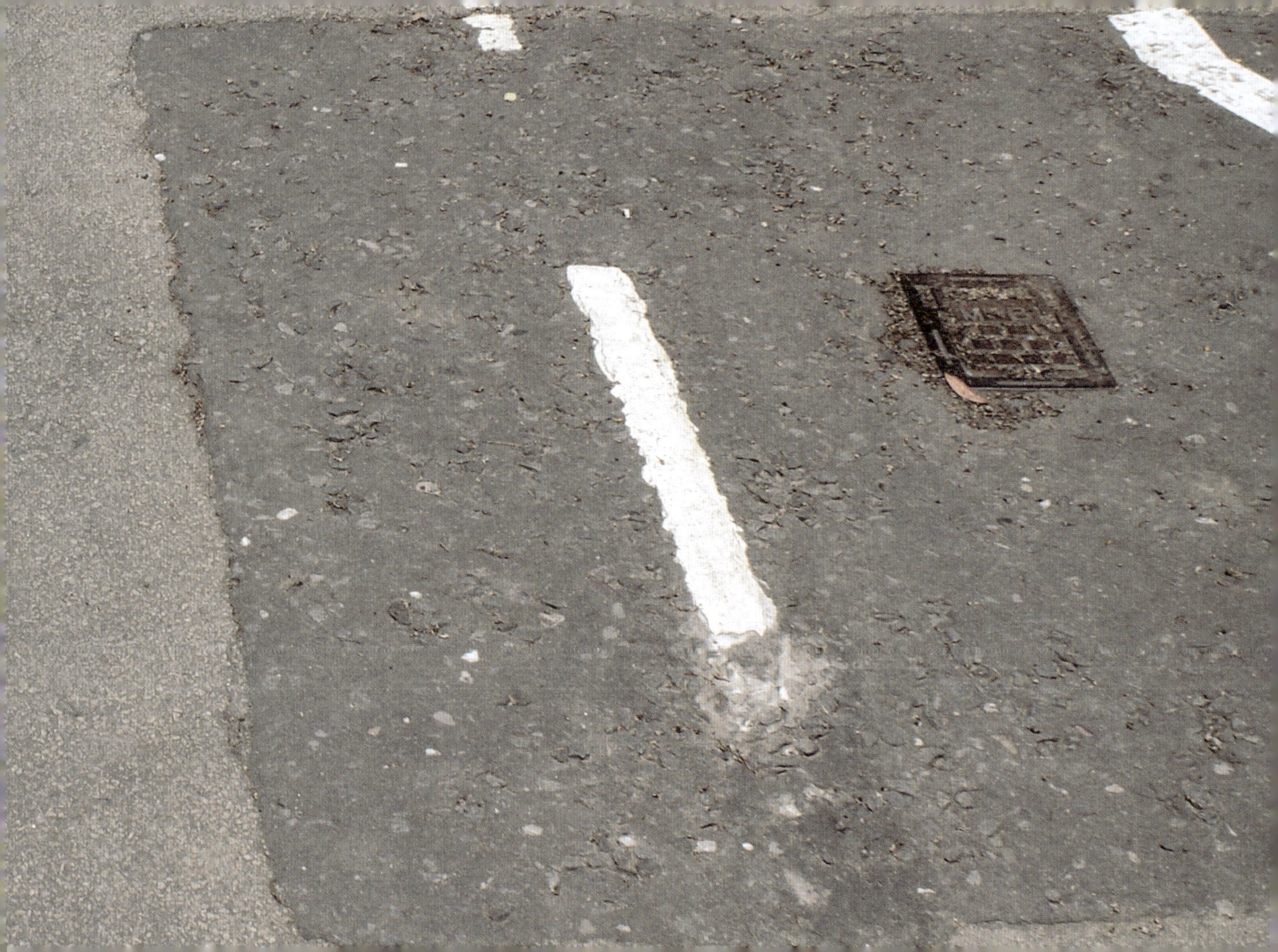

WHEN WE USE THE TREES AS A PEDESTAL
LONDON
2009

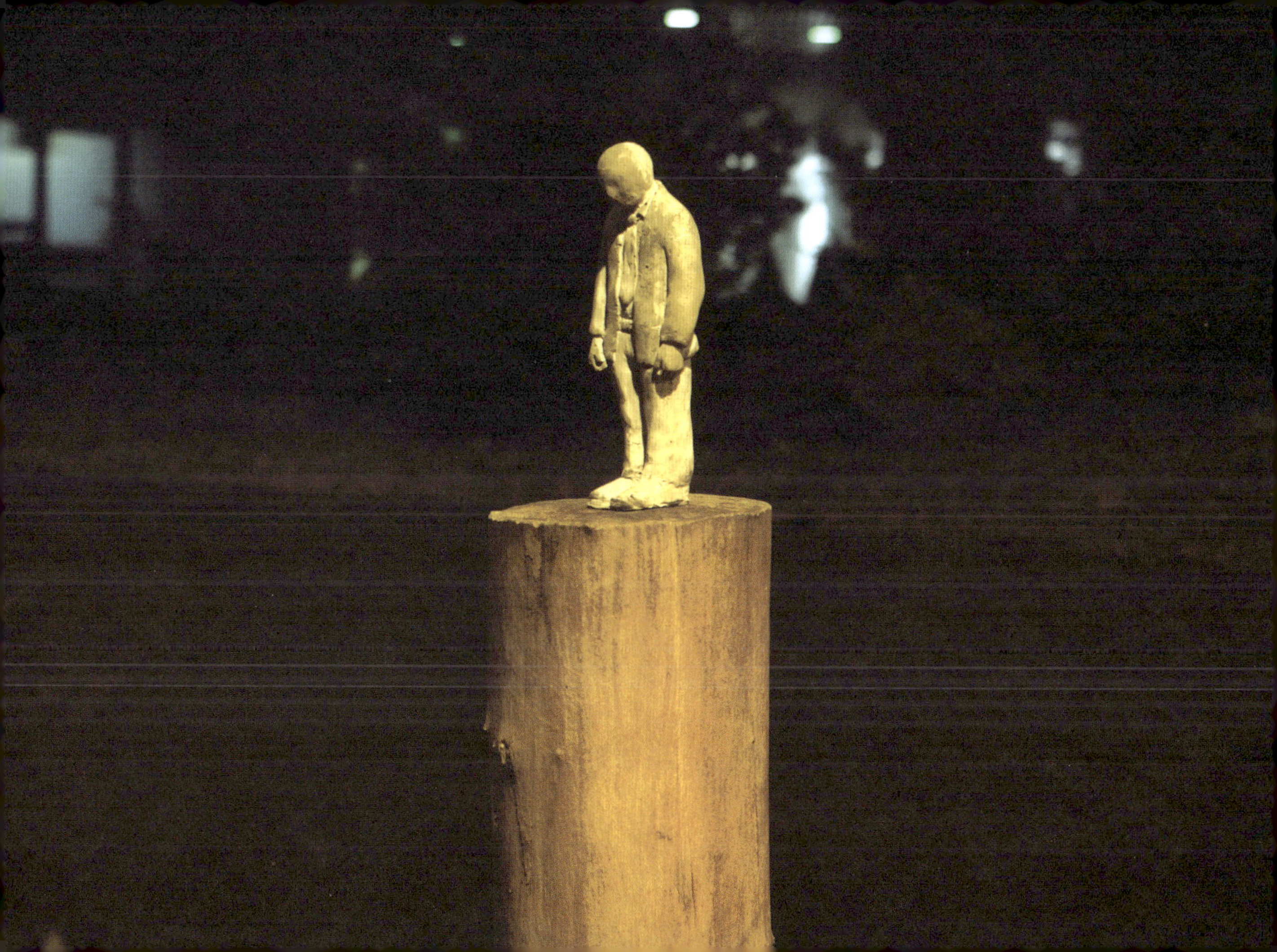

FUNERAL FOR A CONCRETE SCULPTURE
LONDON
2010

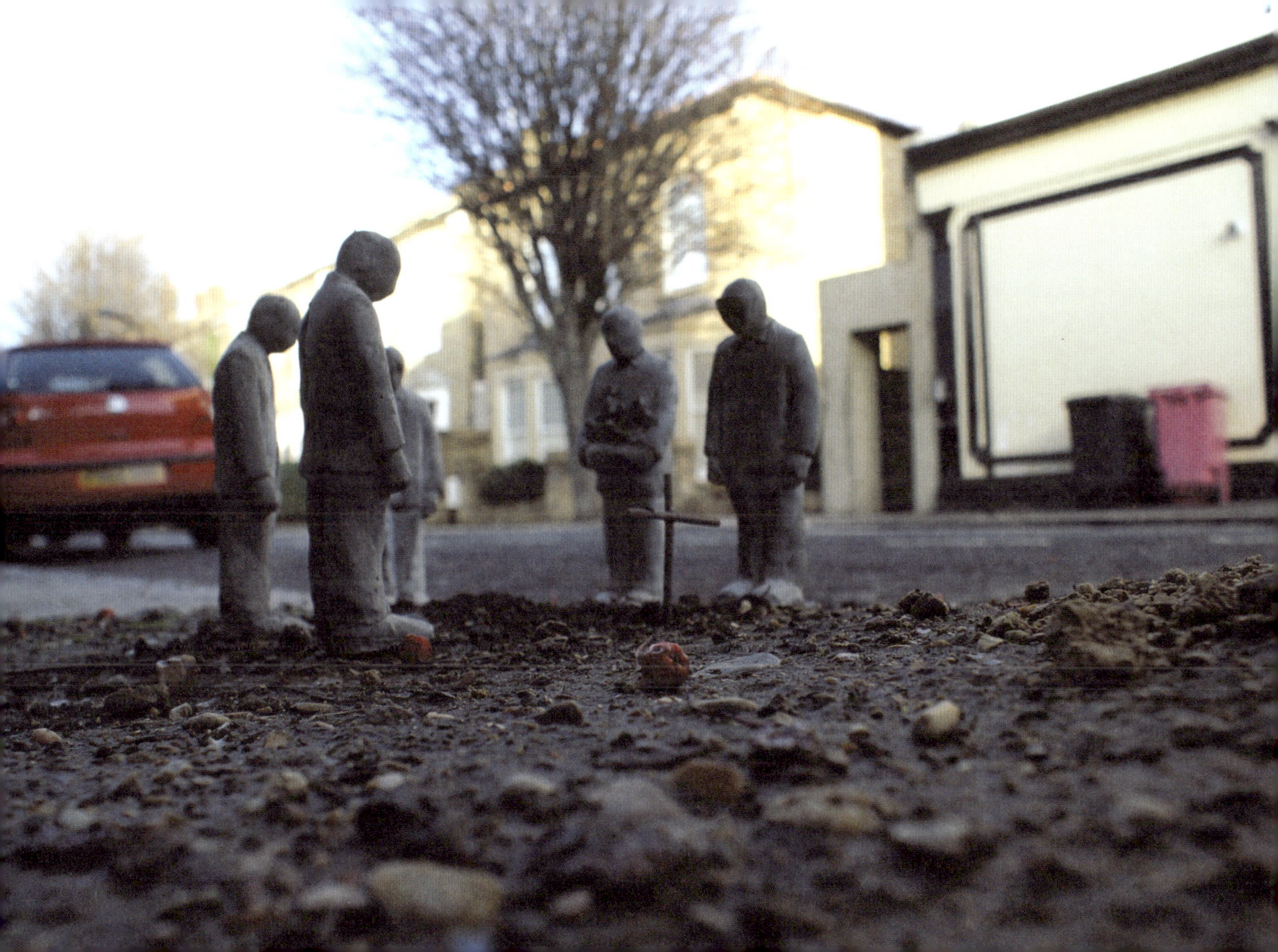

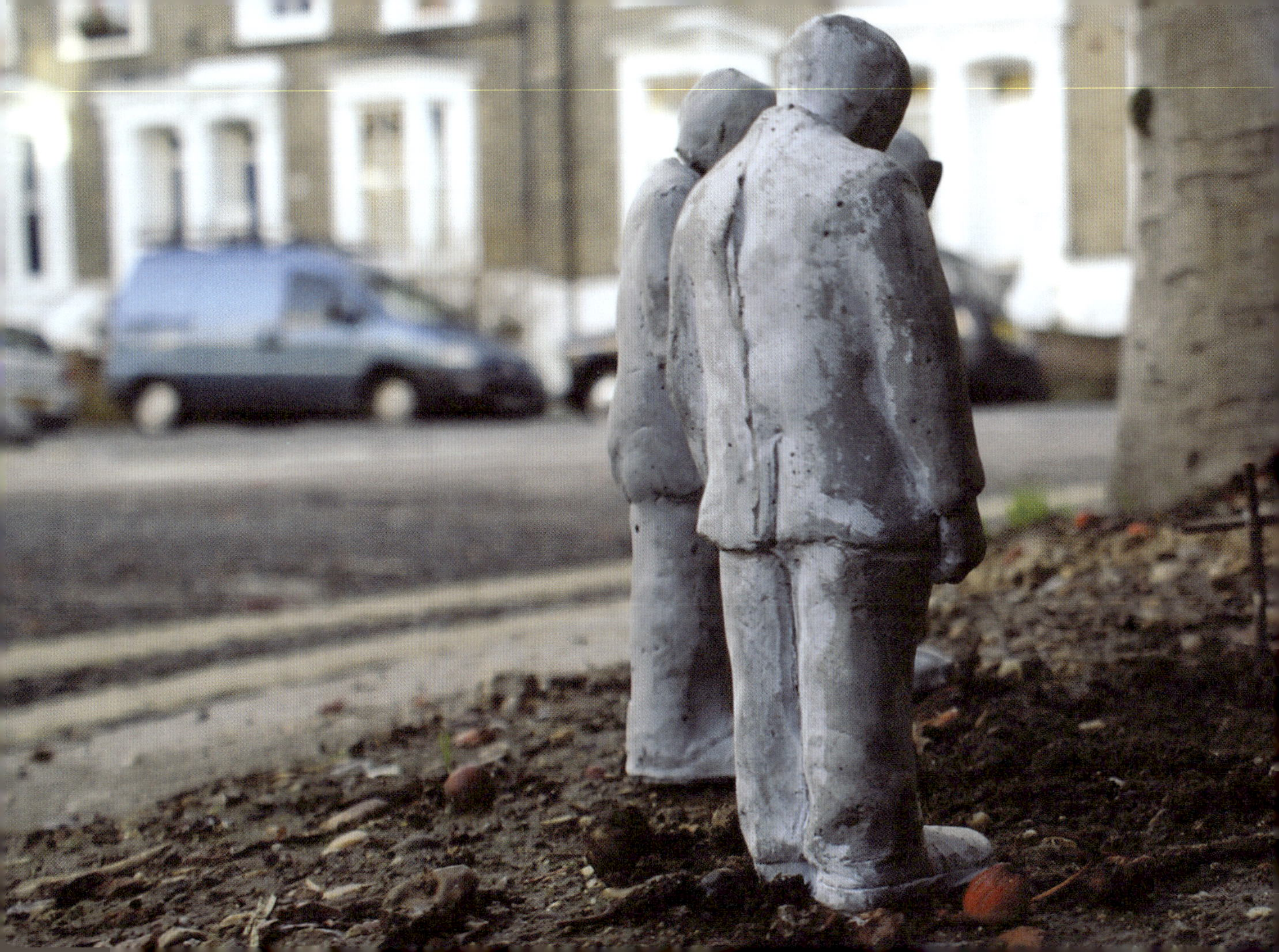

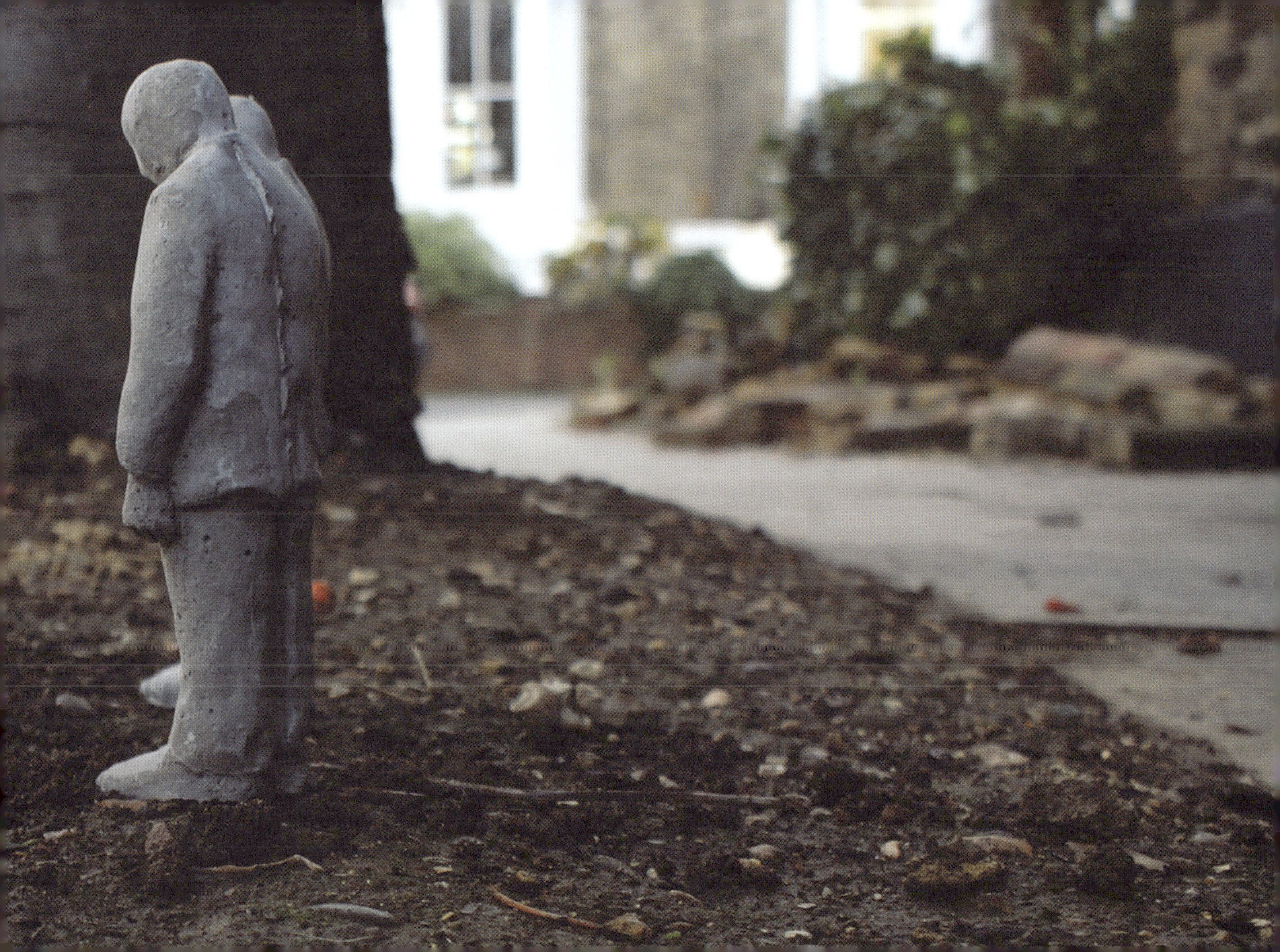

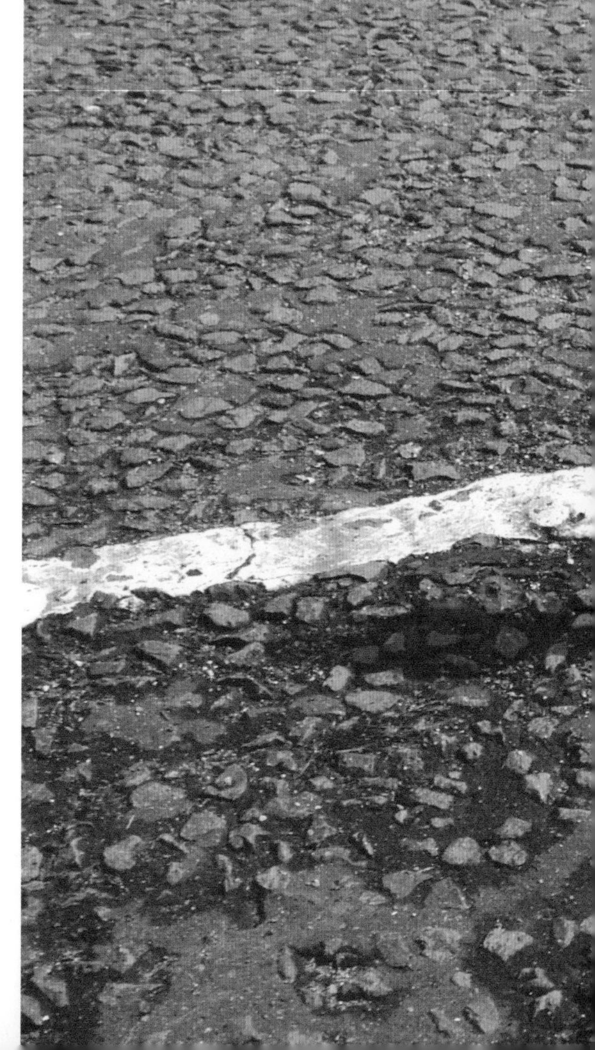

?
LONDON
2010

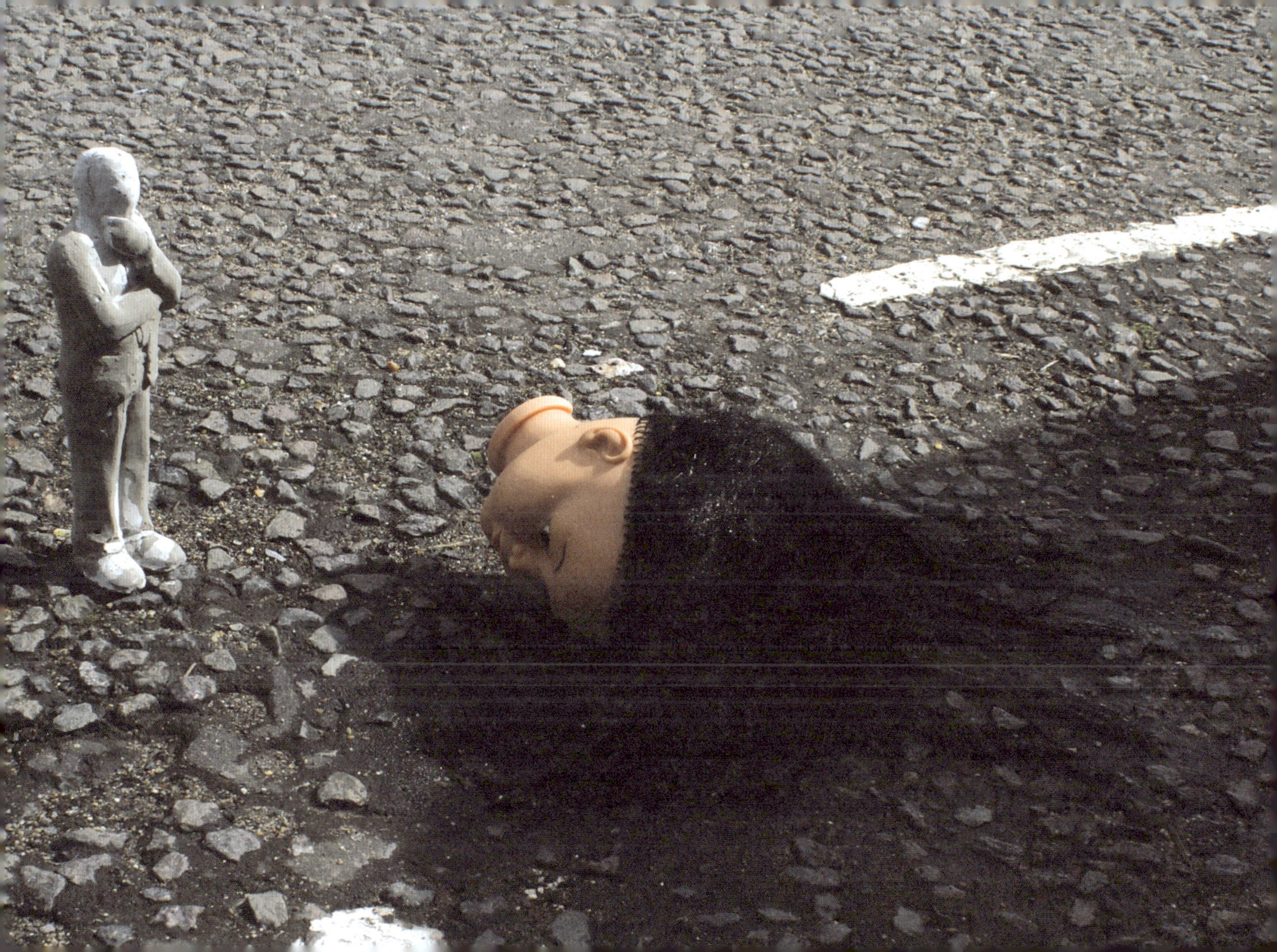

HIKIKOMORI
LONDON
2009

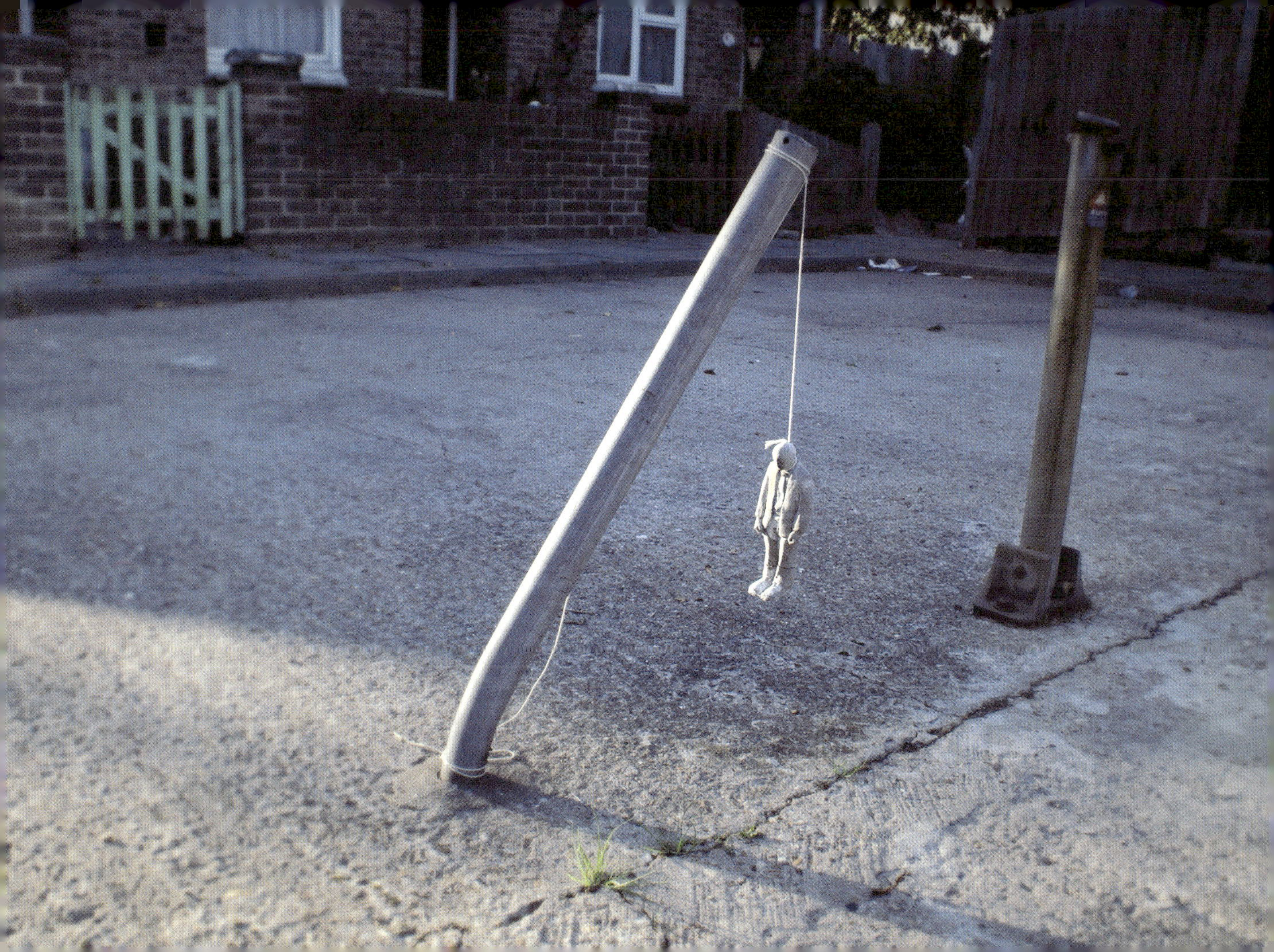

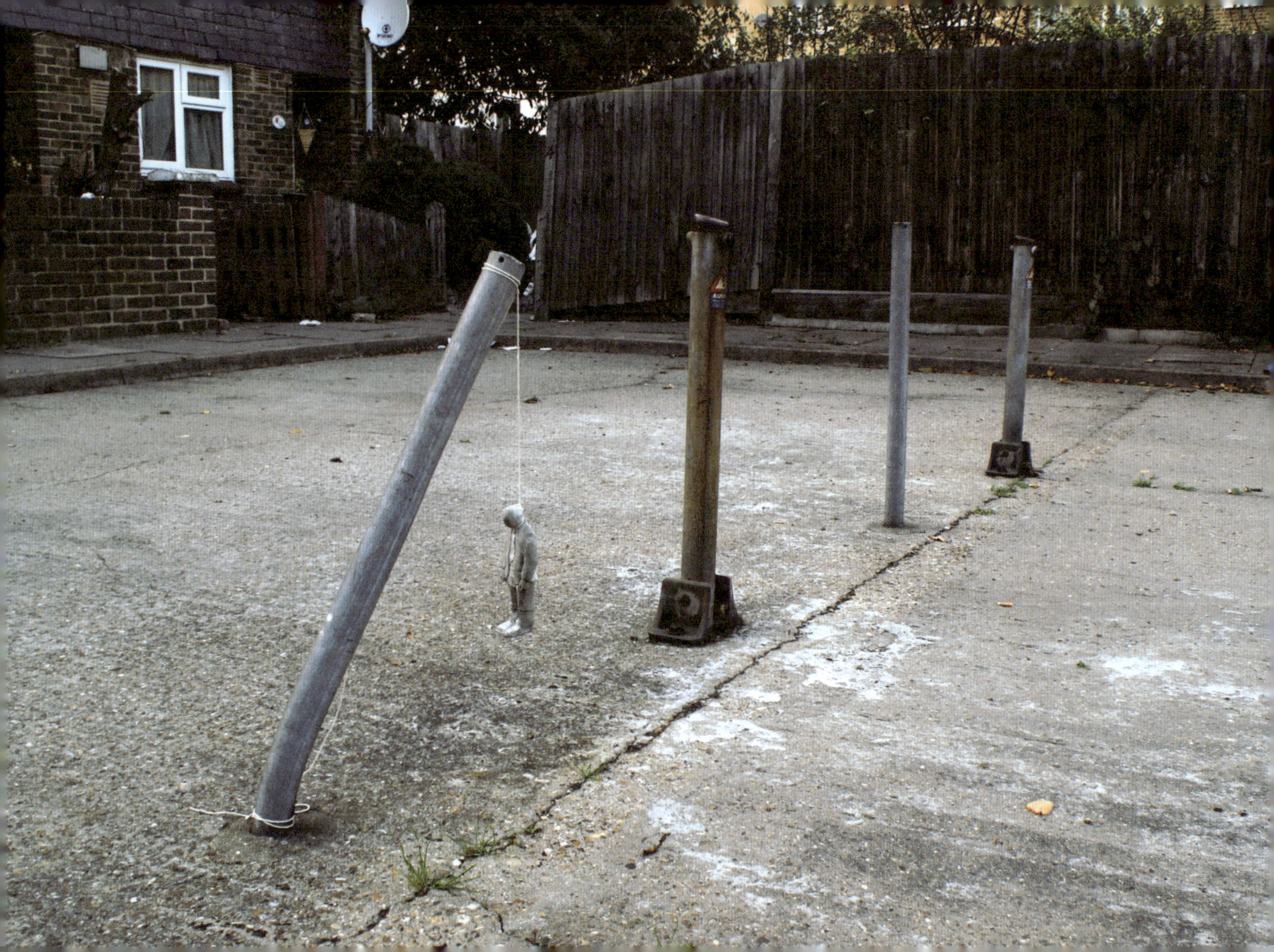

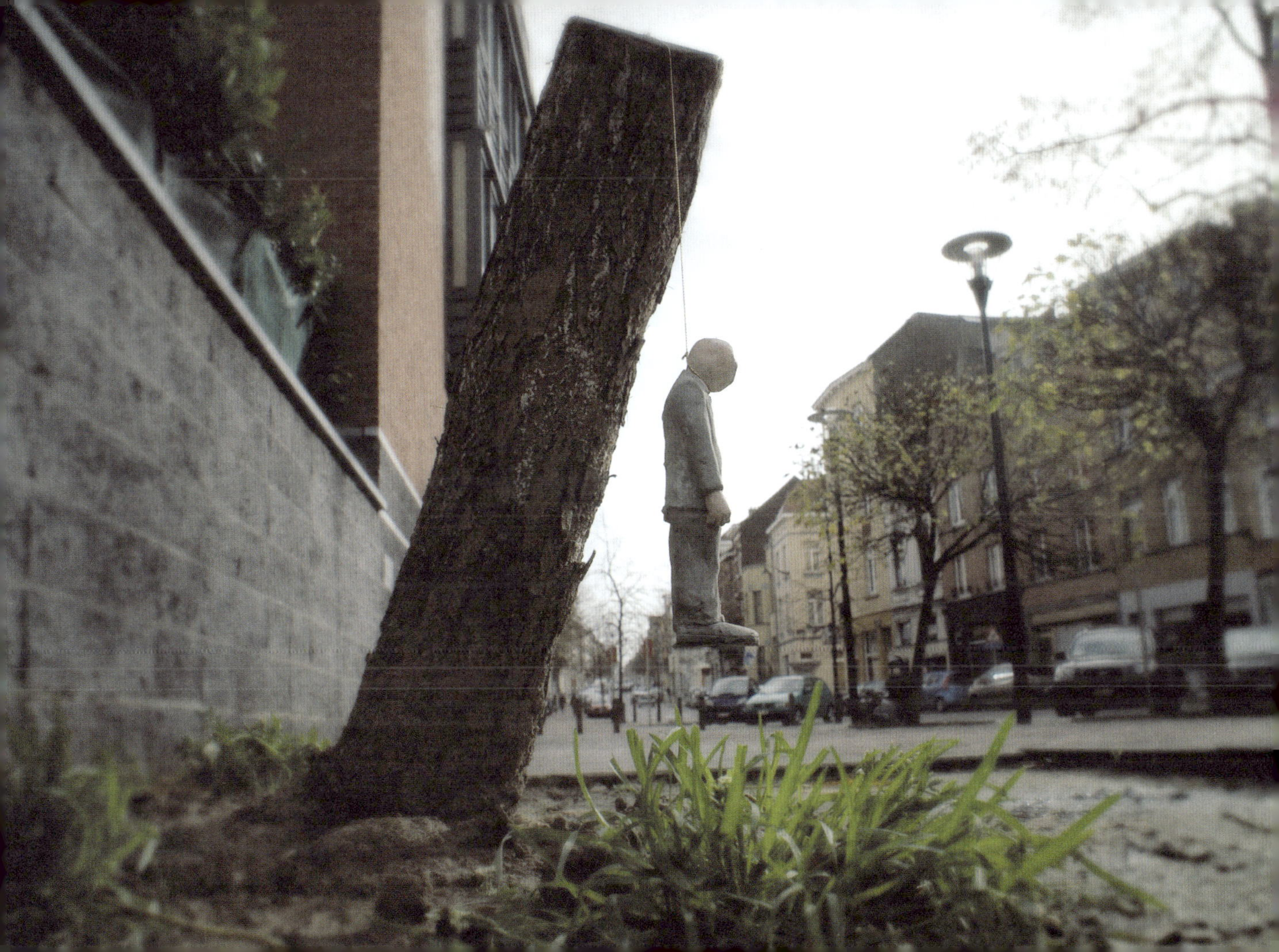

HOLE
LONDON
2010

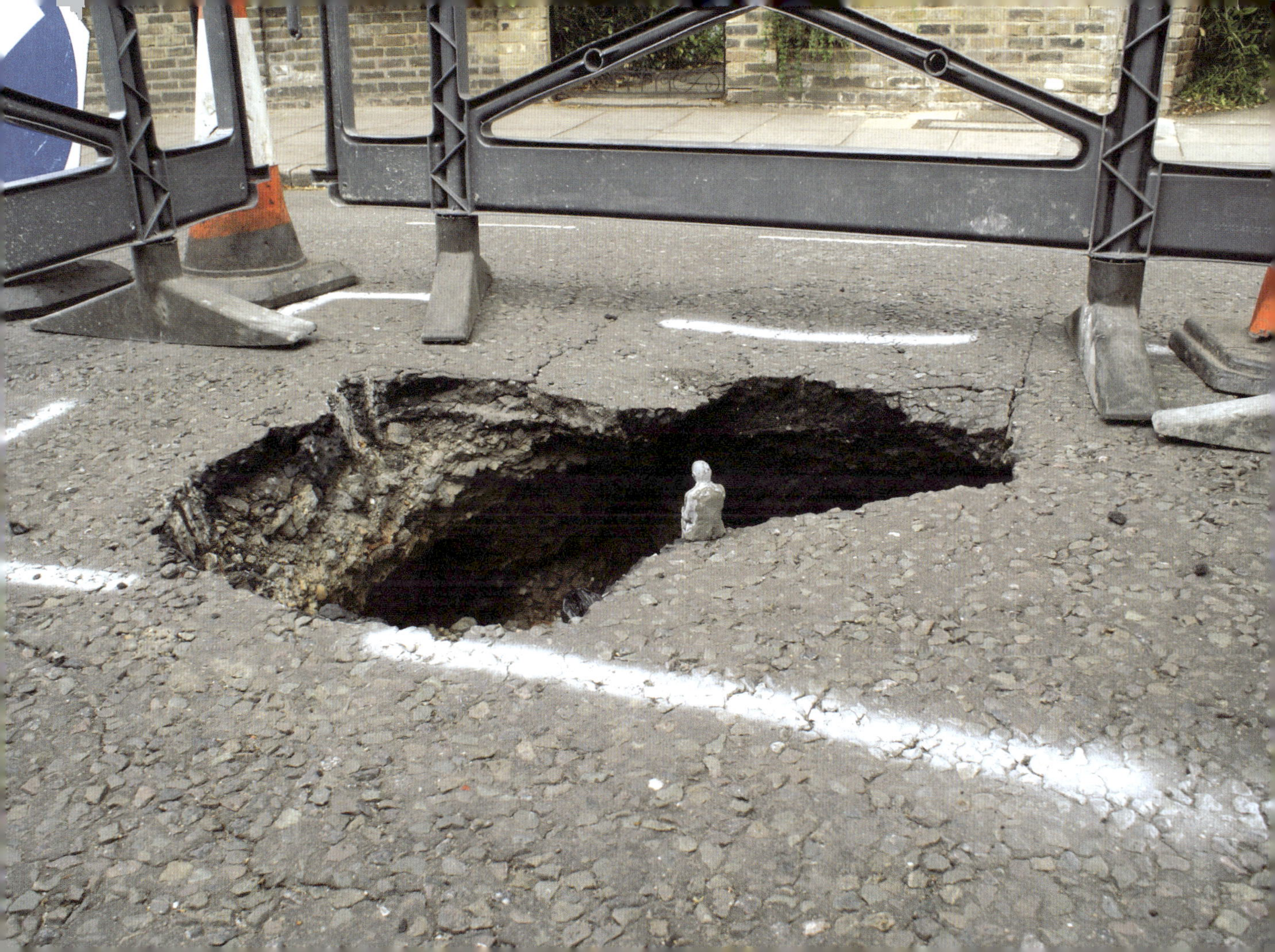

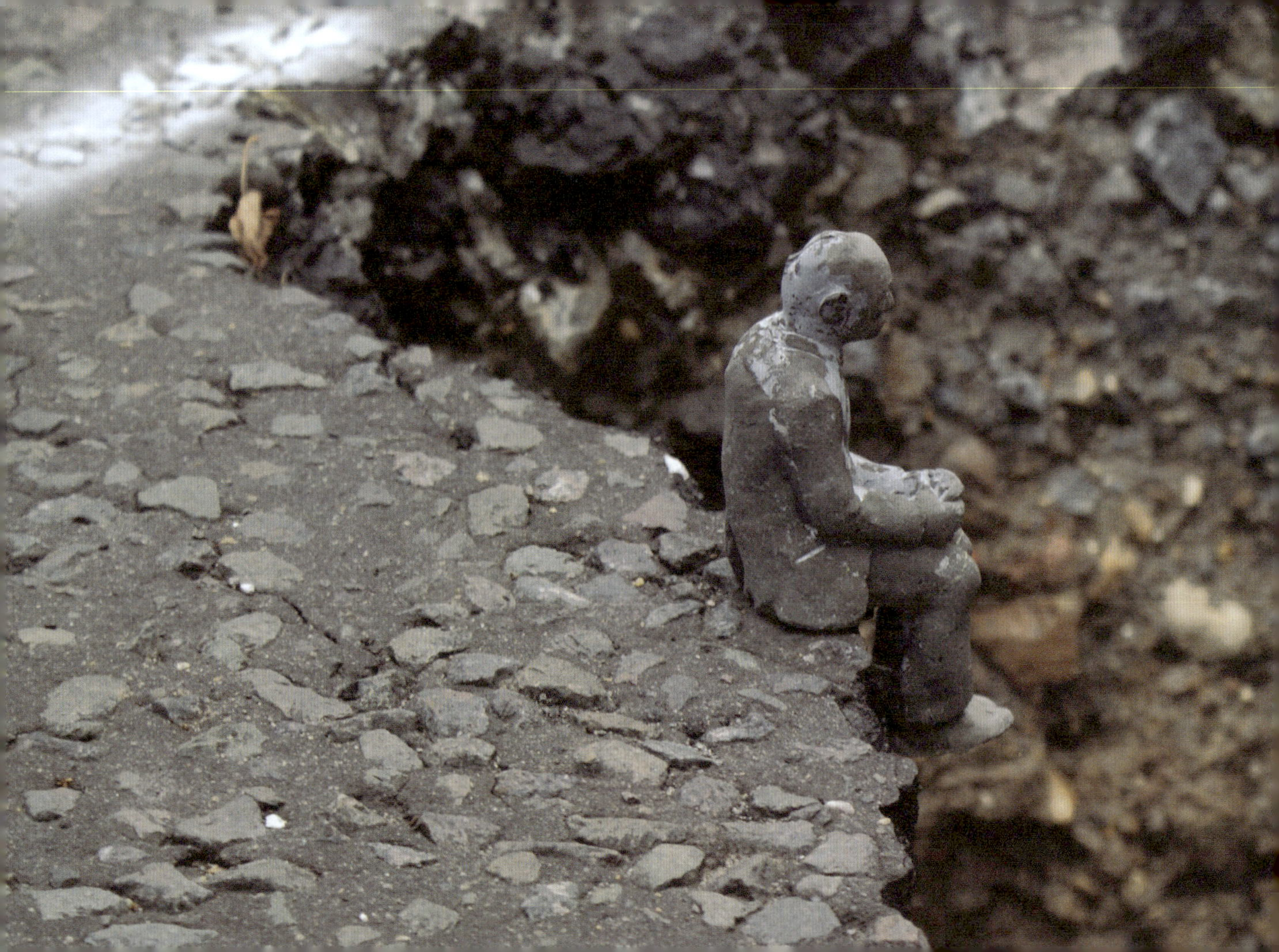

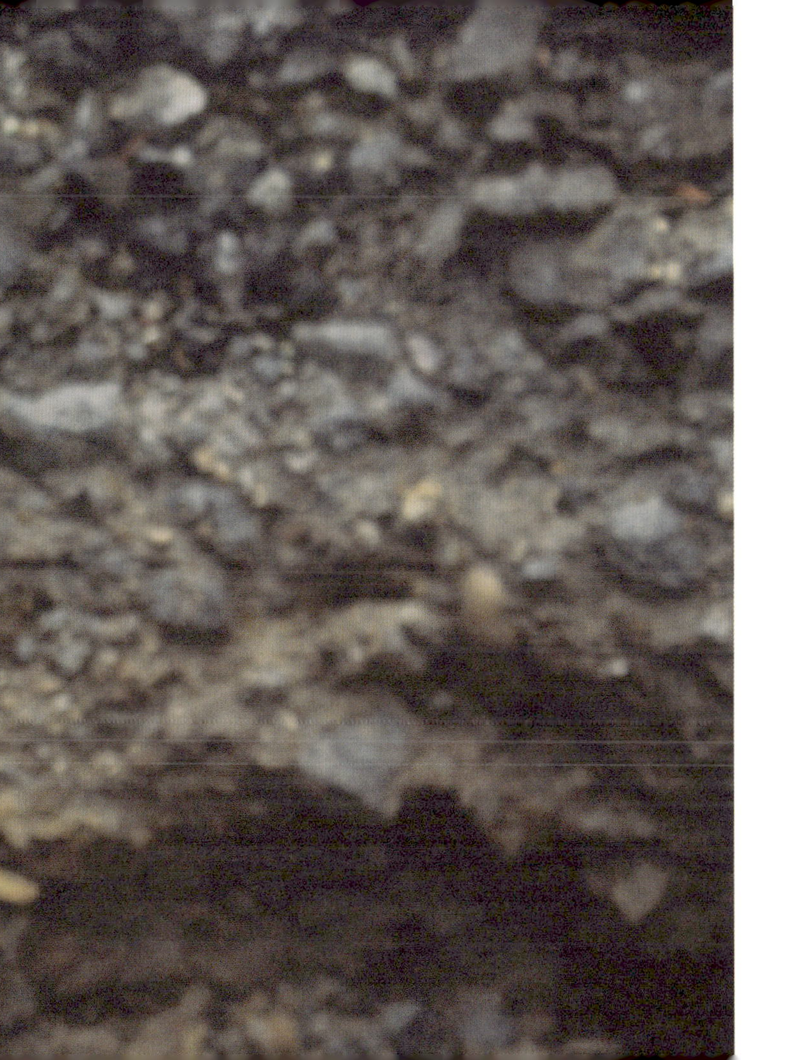

HOME
LONDON
2010

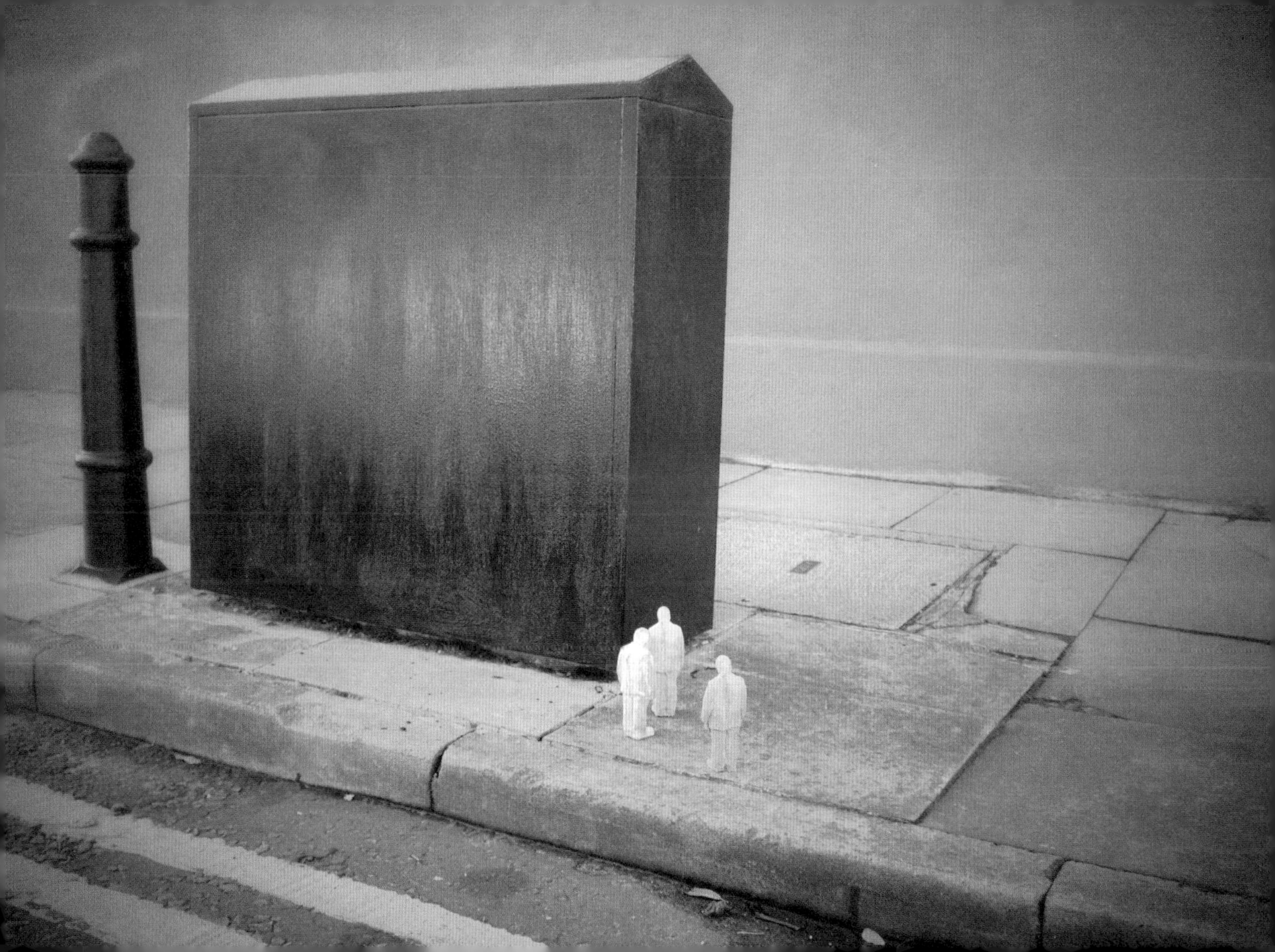

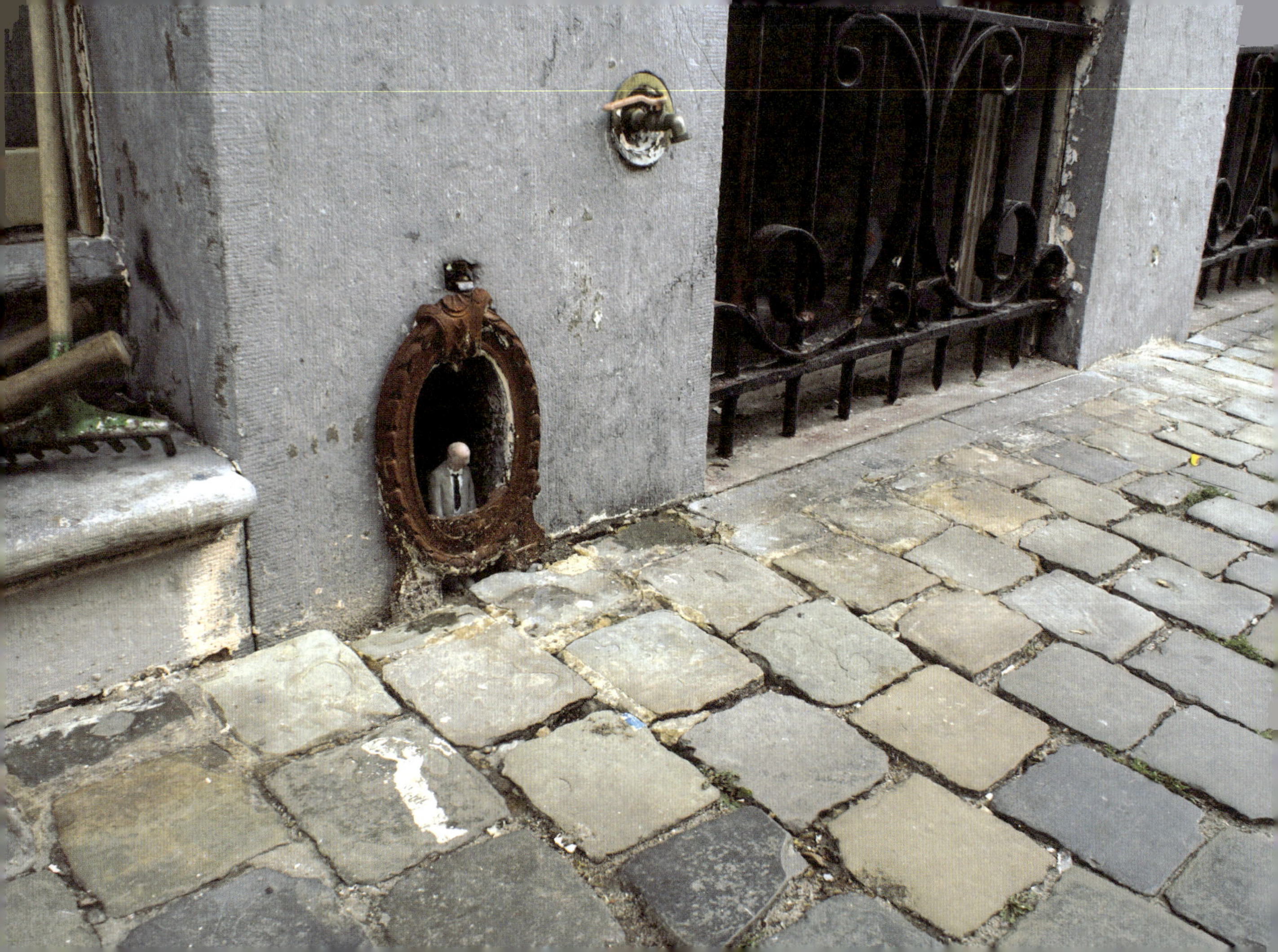

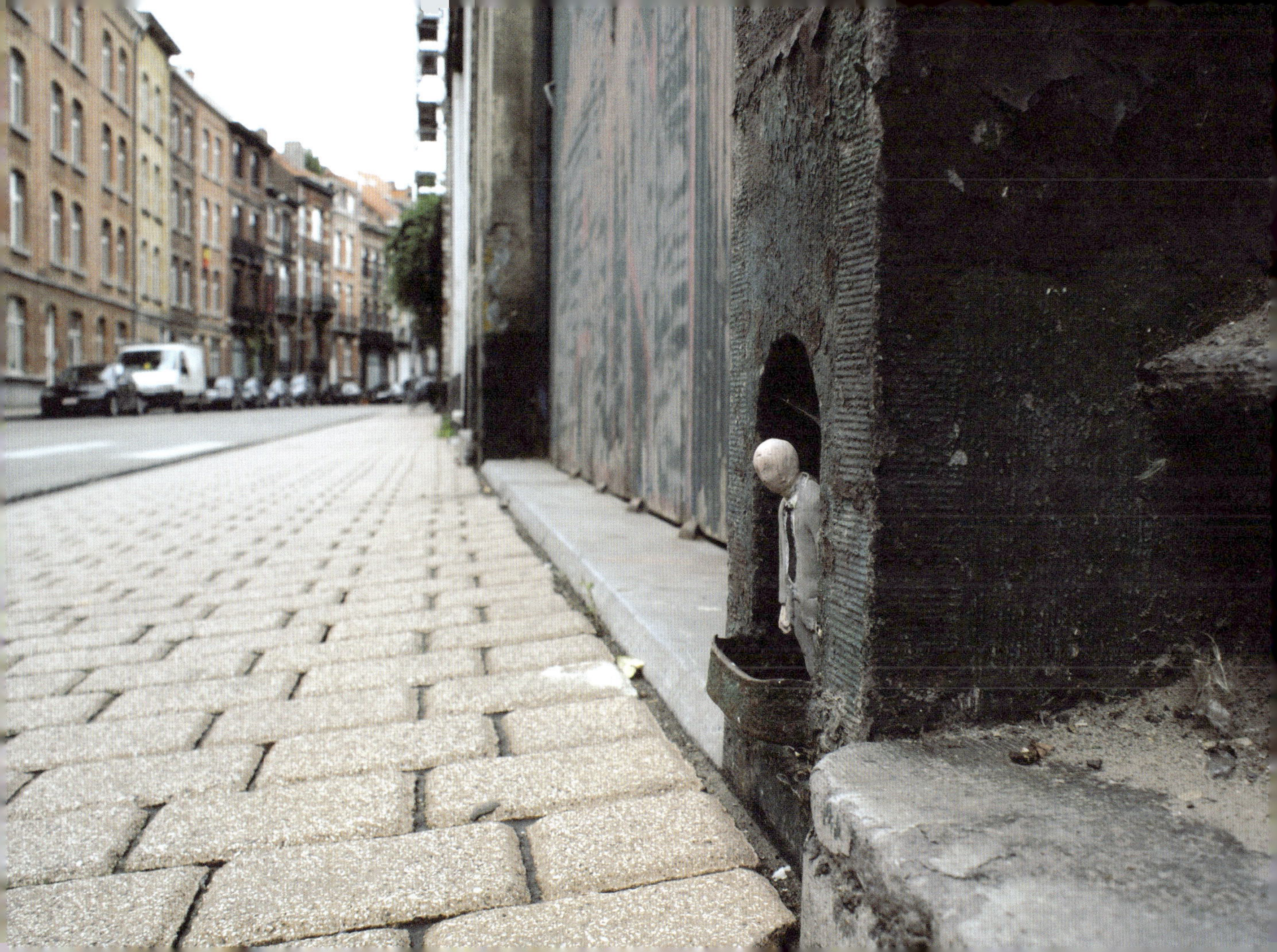

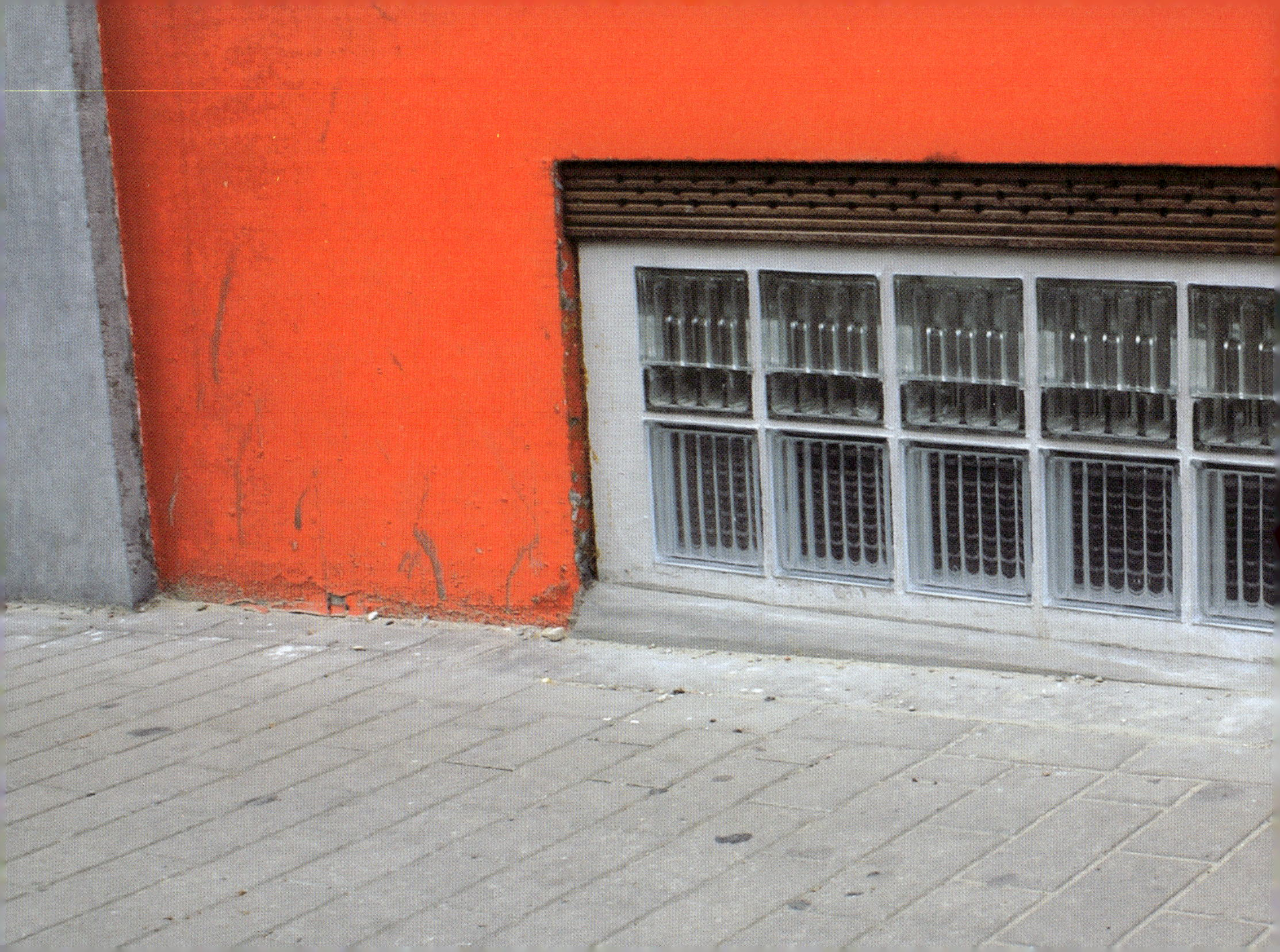

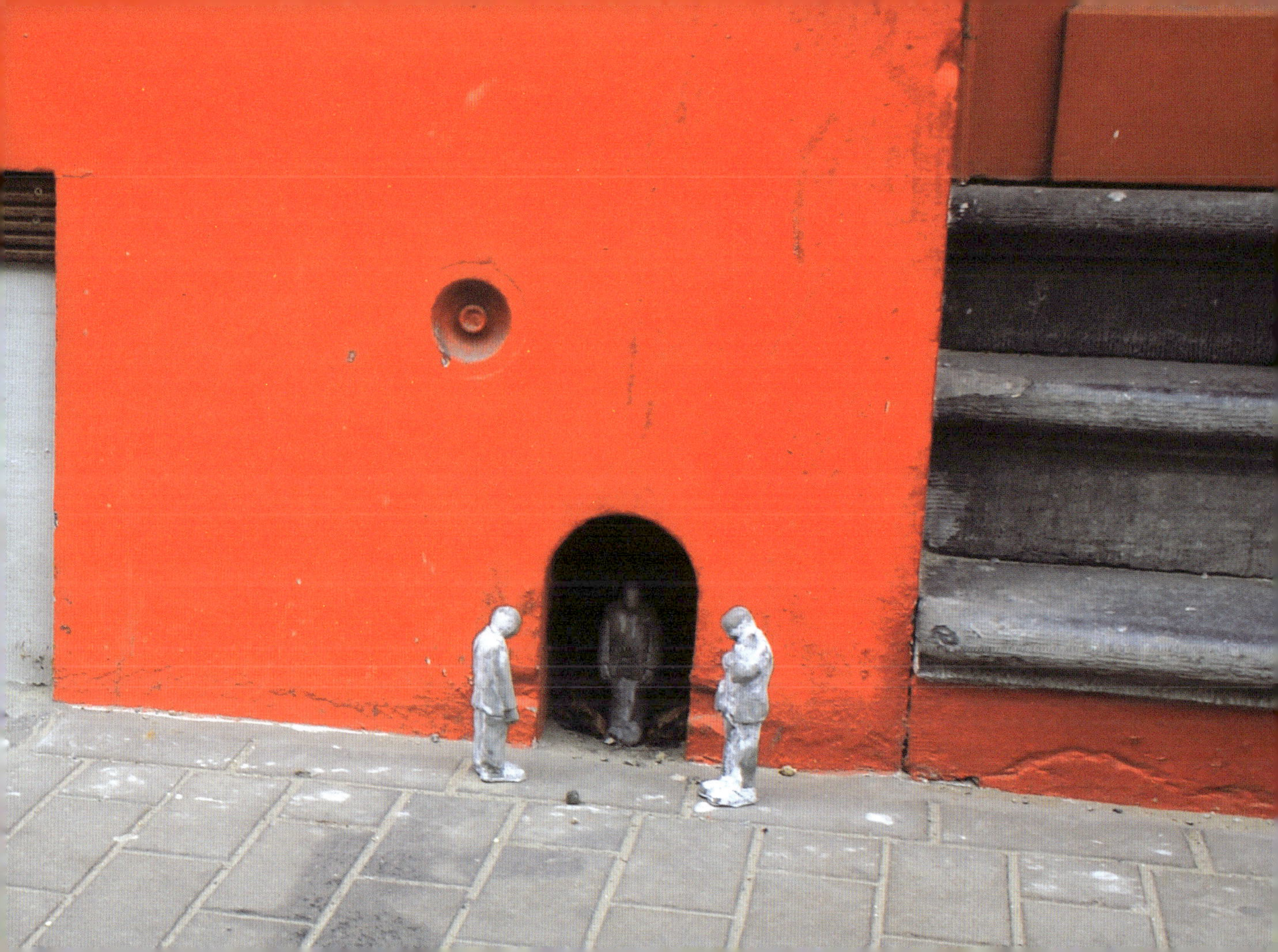

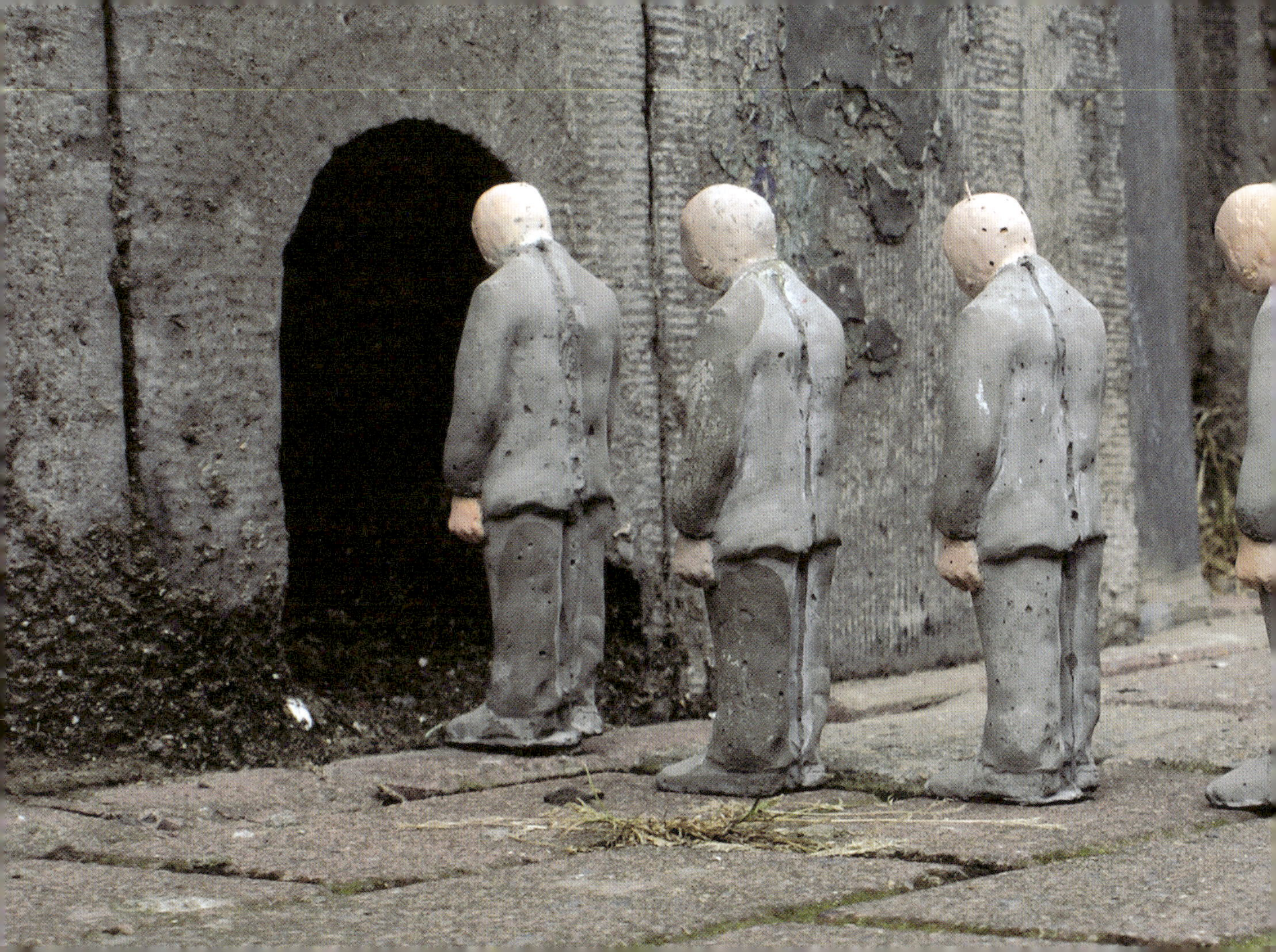

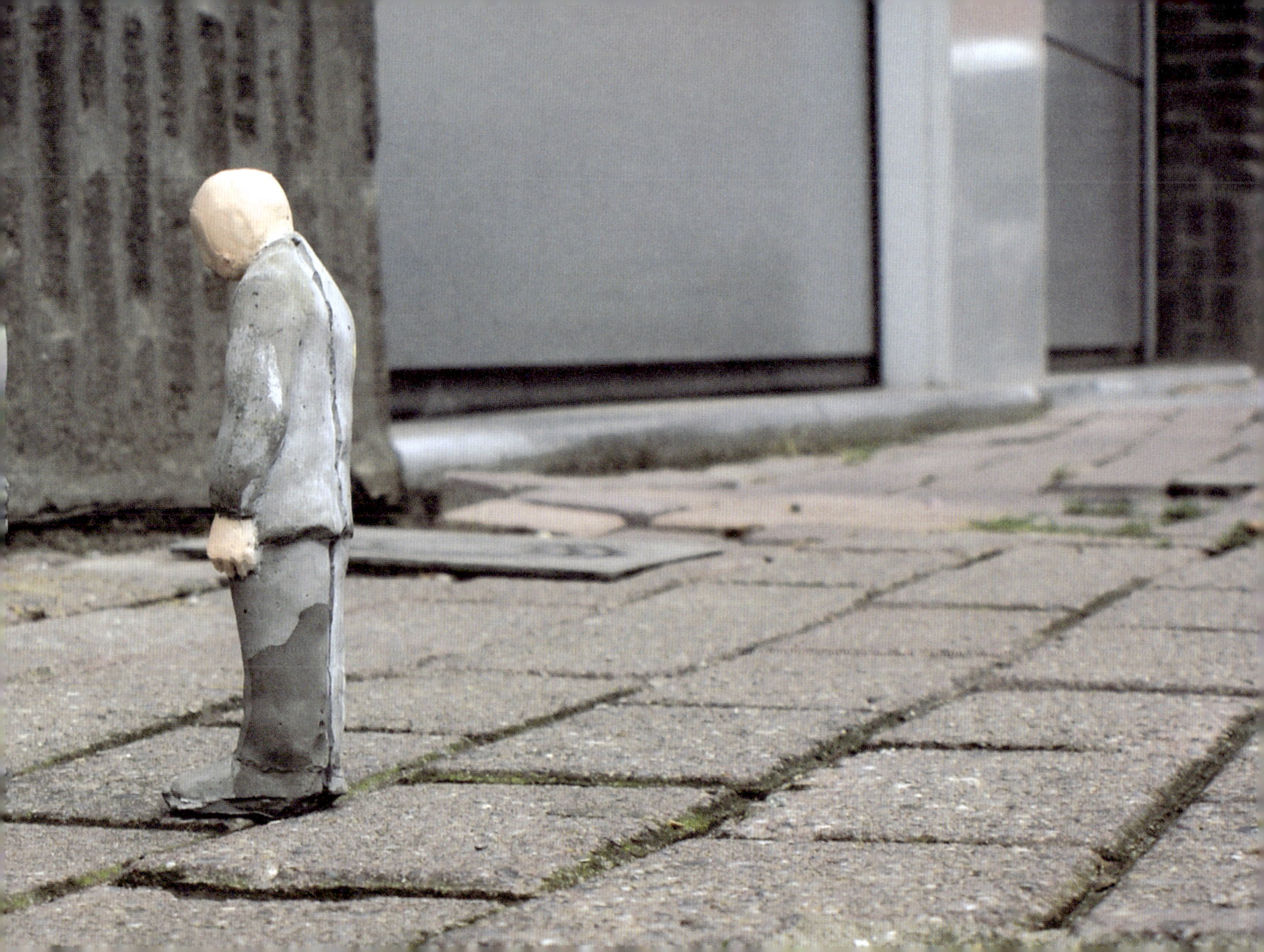

WINTER
BRUSSELS
2010

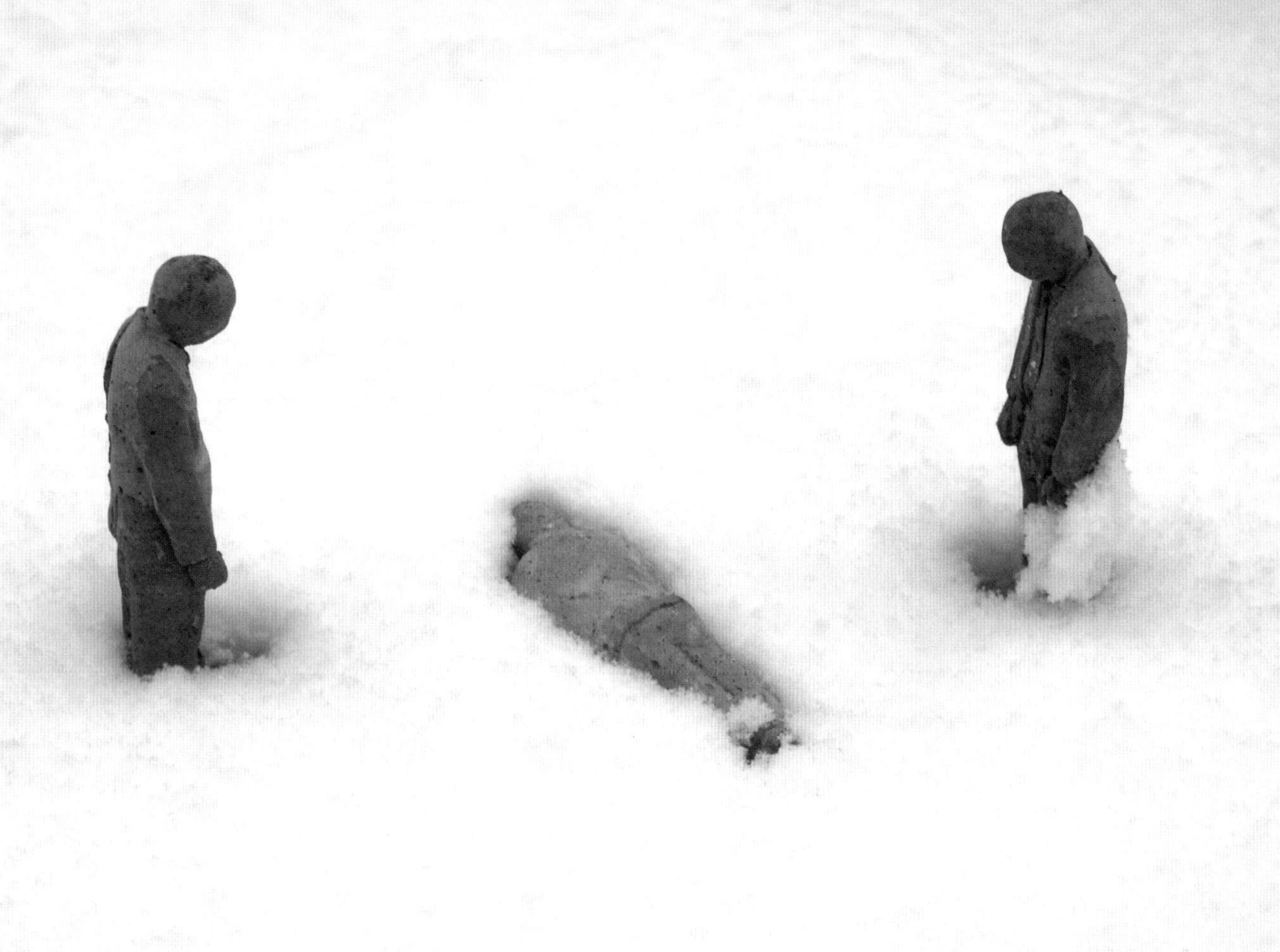

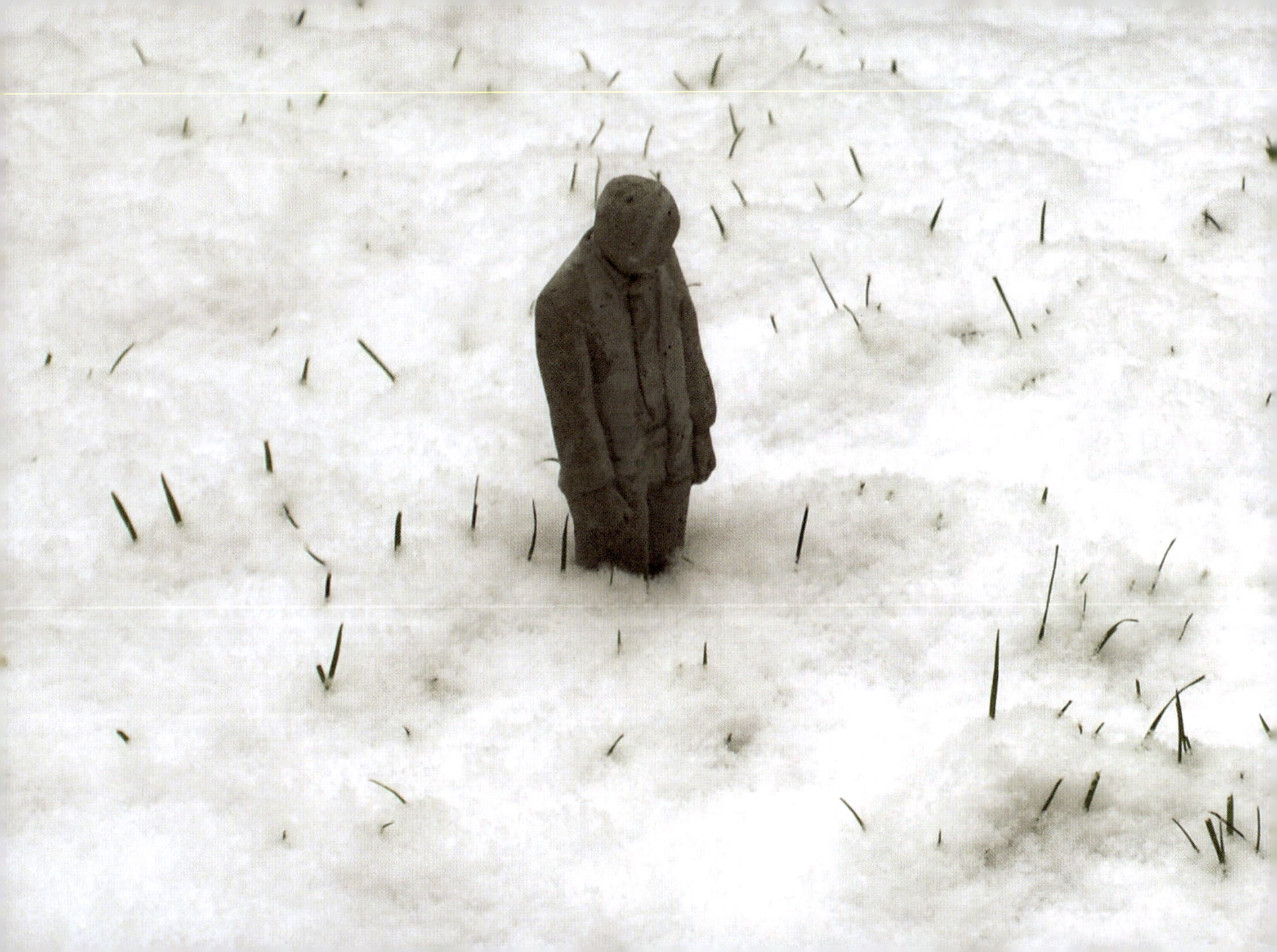

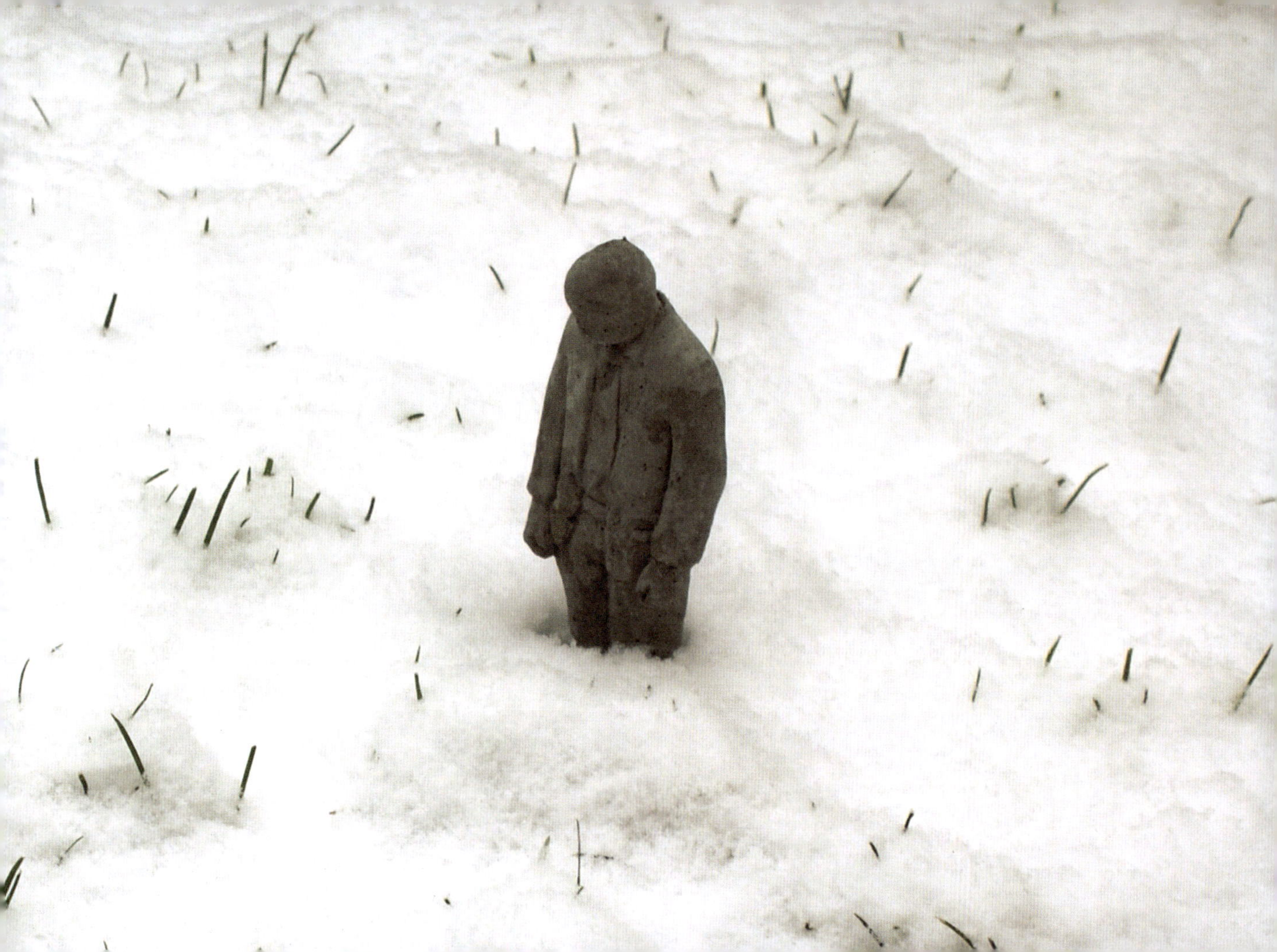

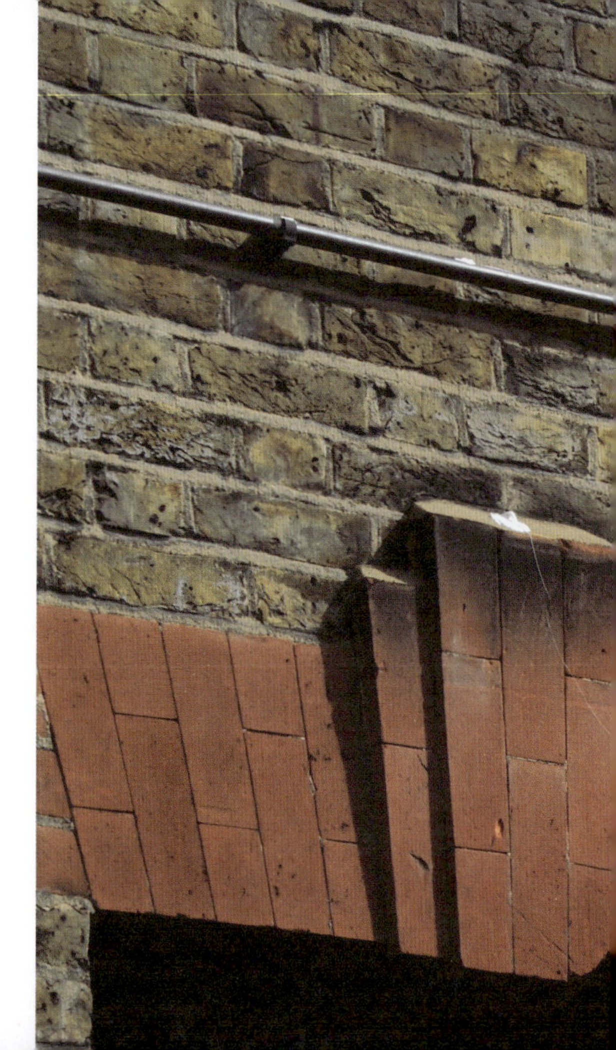

SLEEPWALKER TRAPPED
LONDON
2010

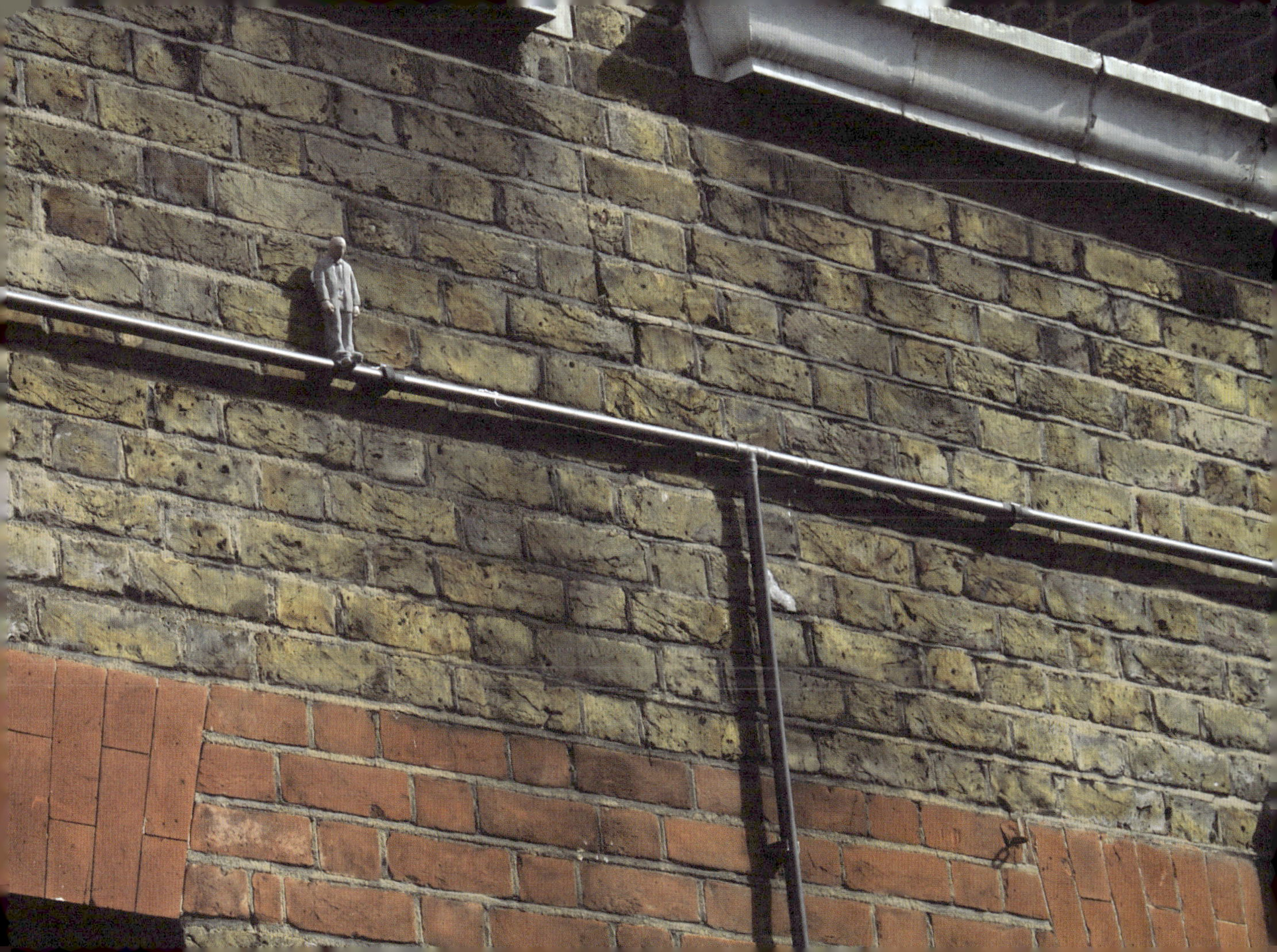

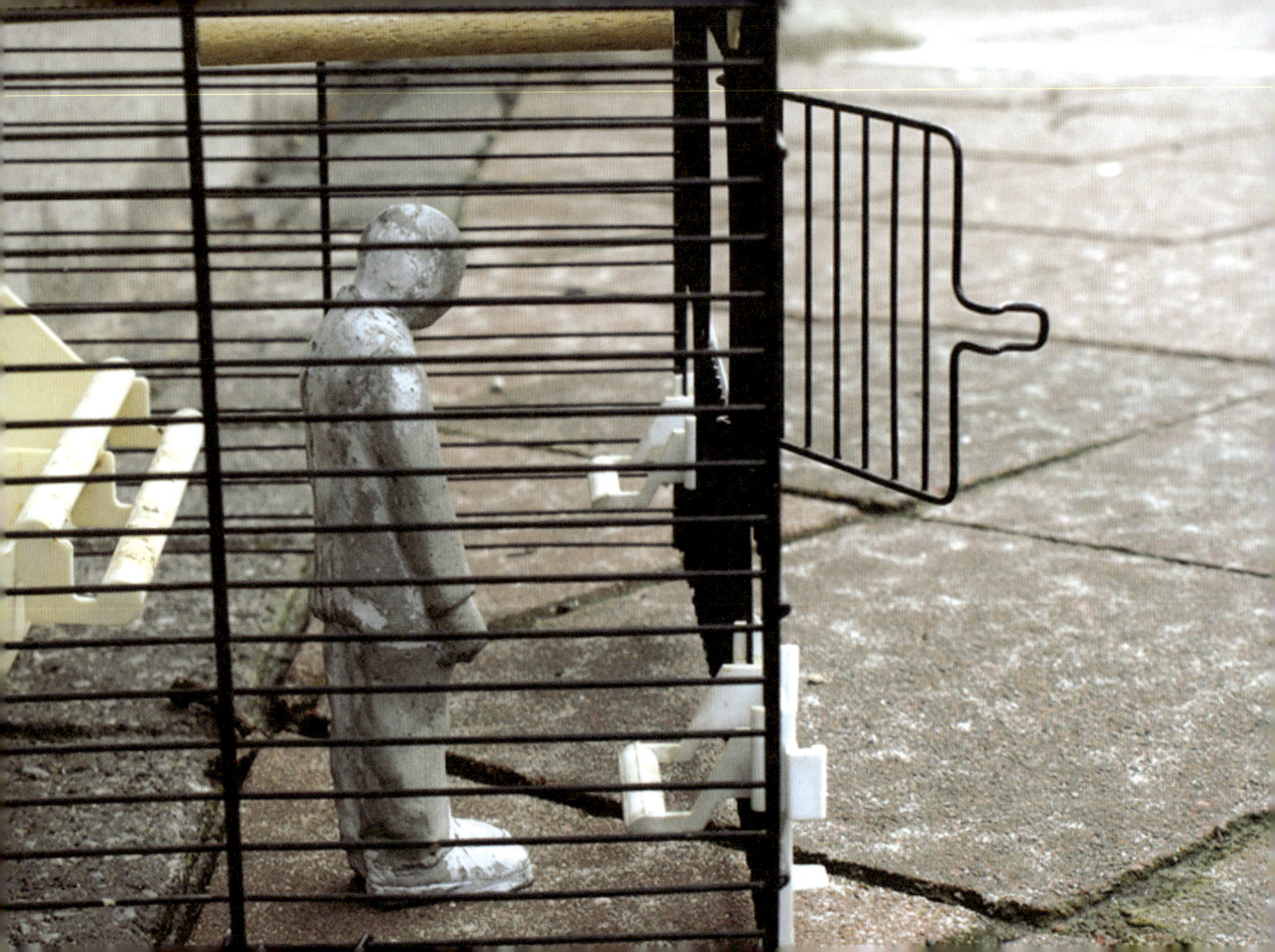

WHEN YOU SEE THE CAGE
BRUSSELS
2010

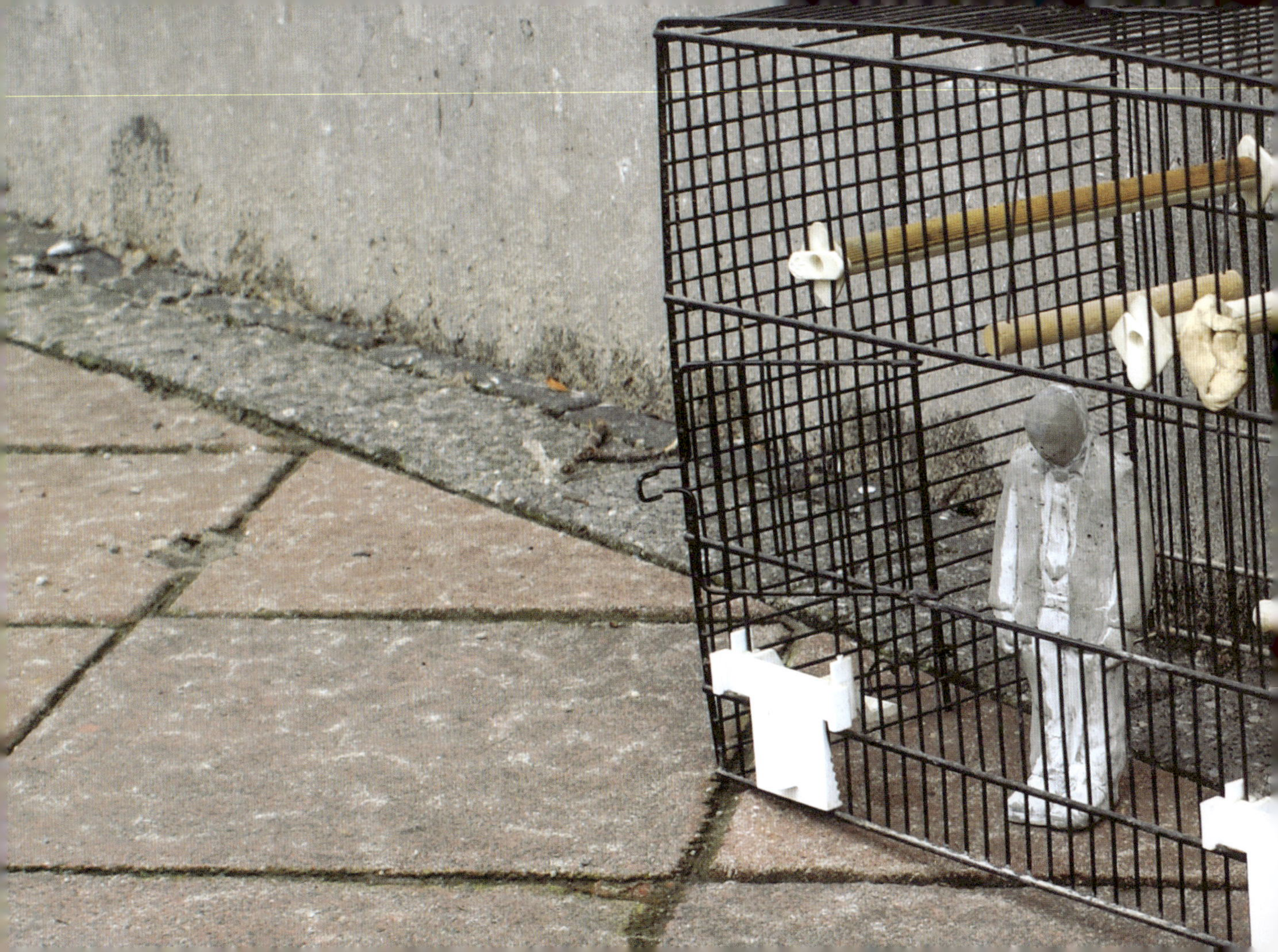

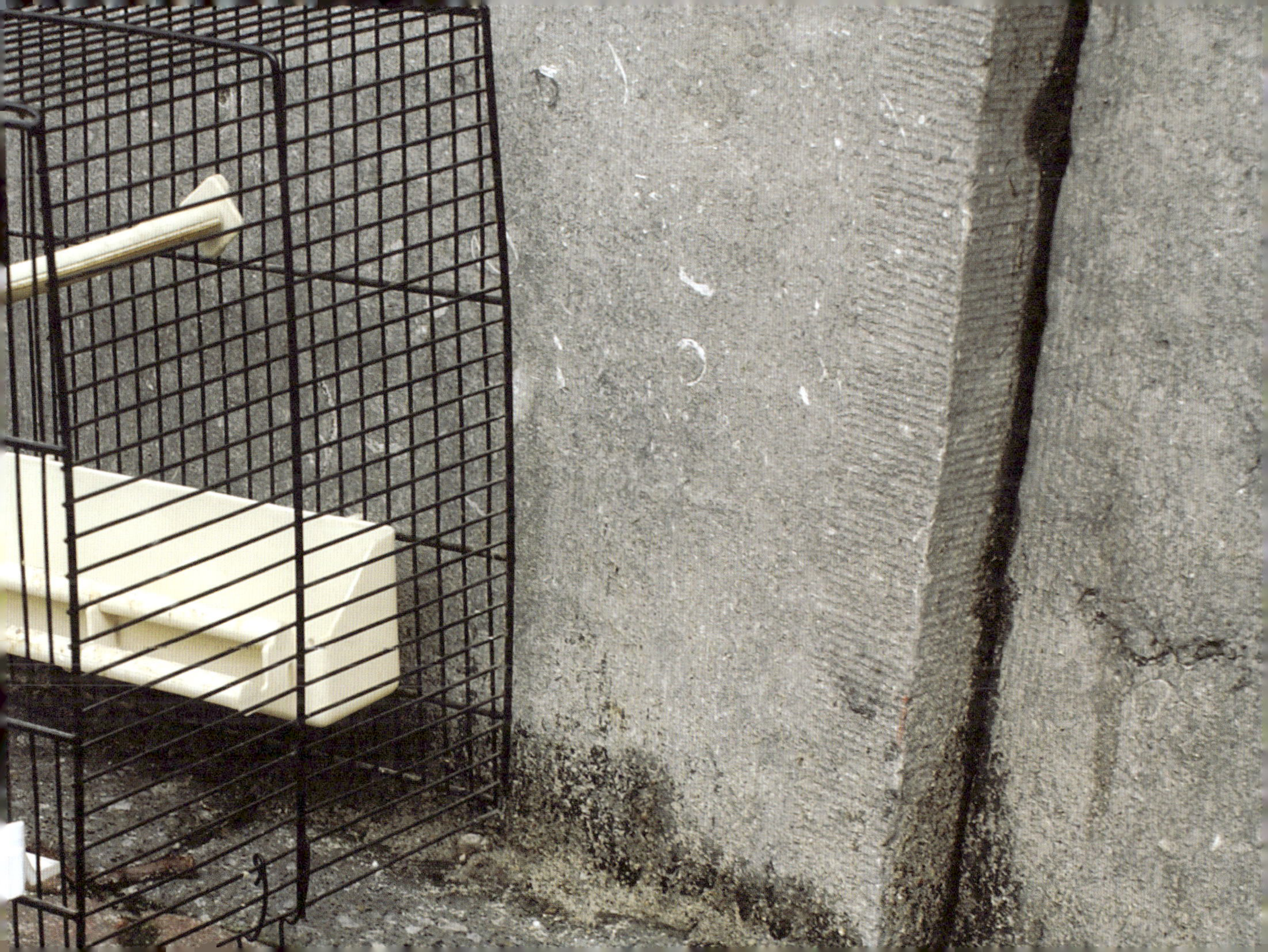

LOOKING FOR A NEW THRONE
LONDON
2010

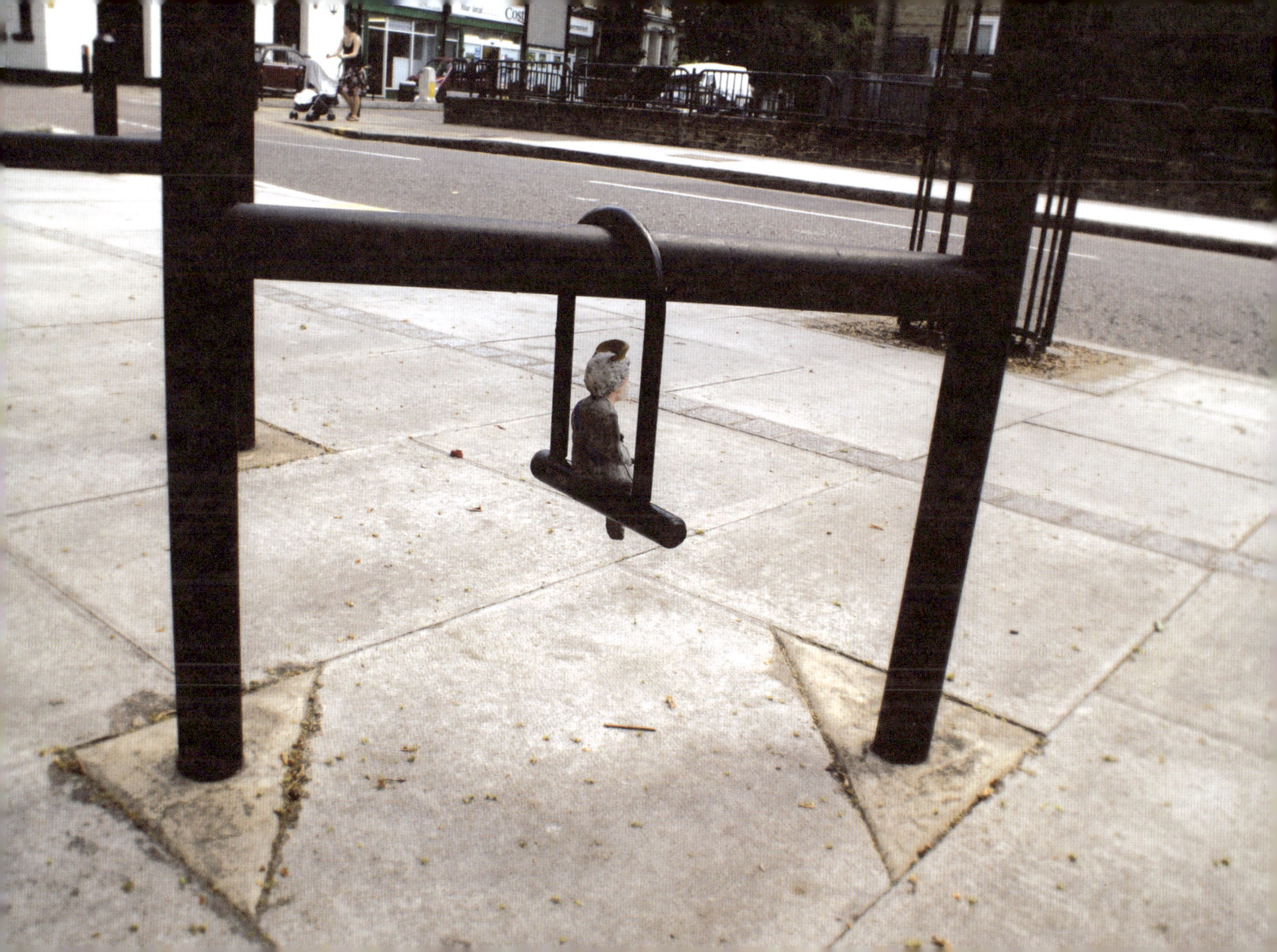

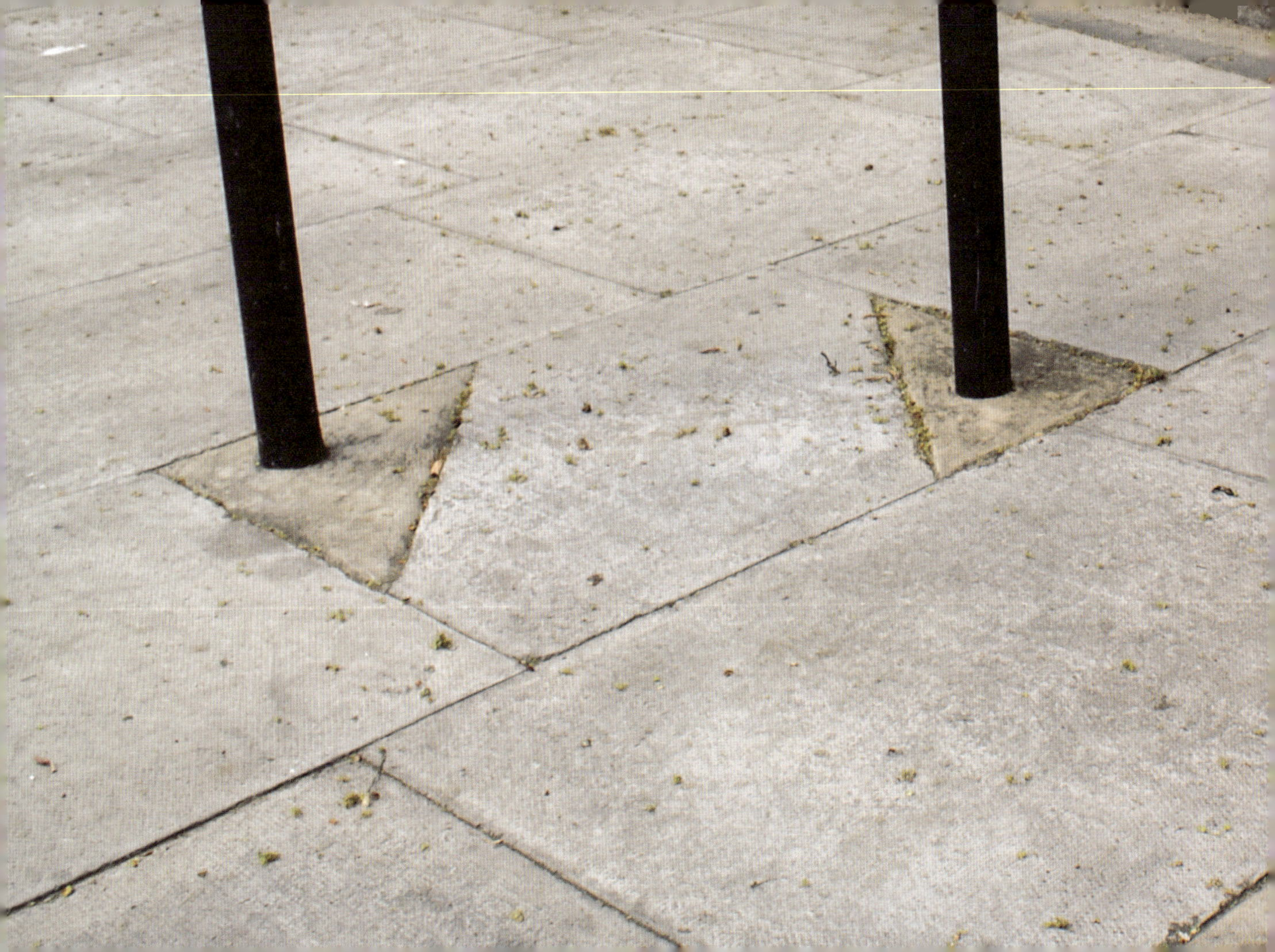

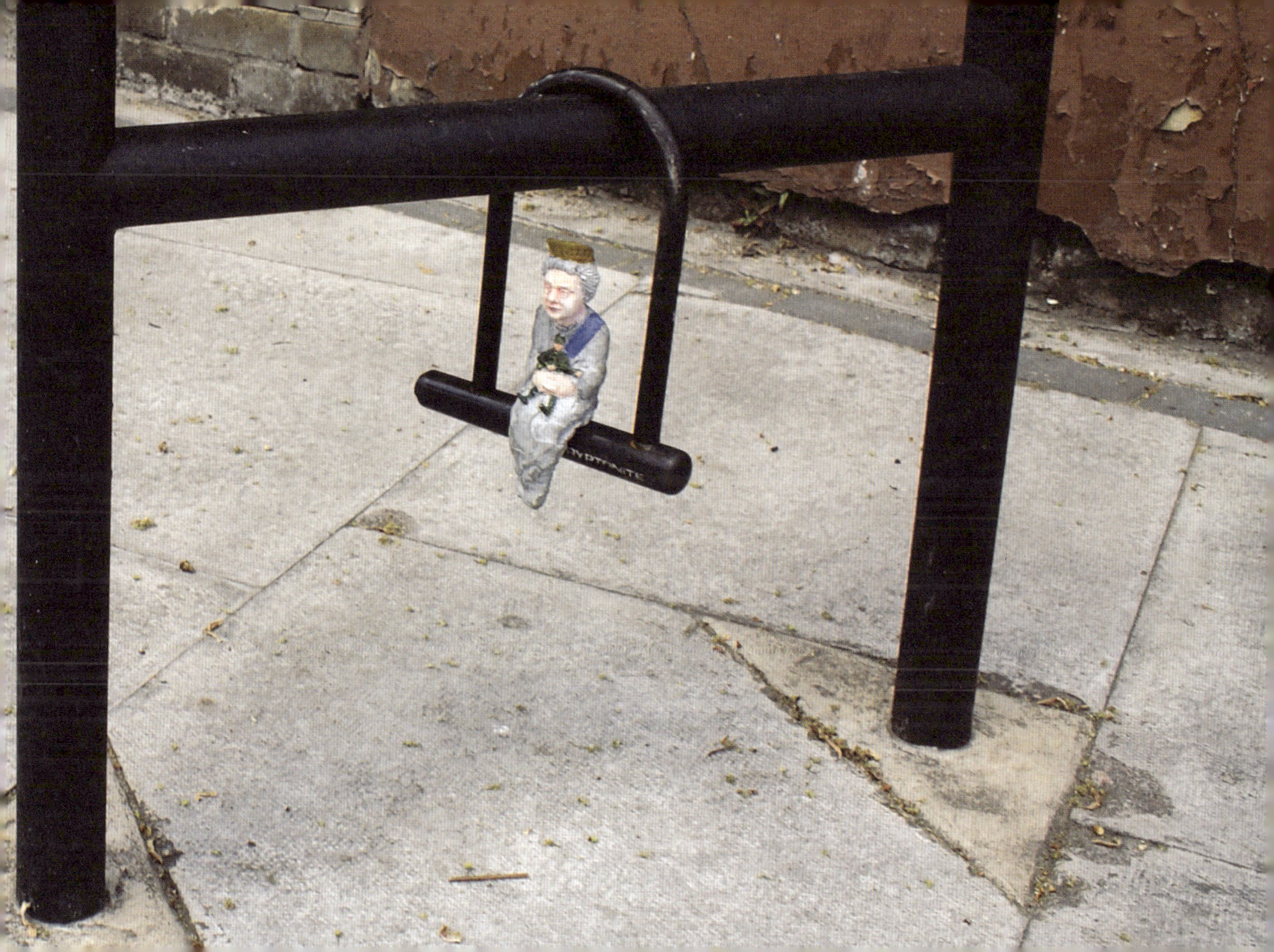
KRYPTONITE

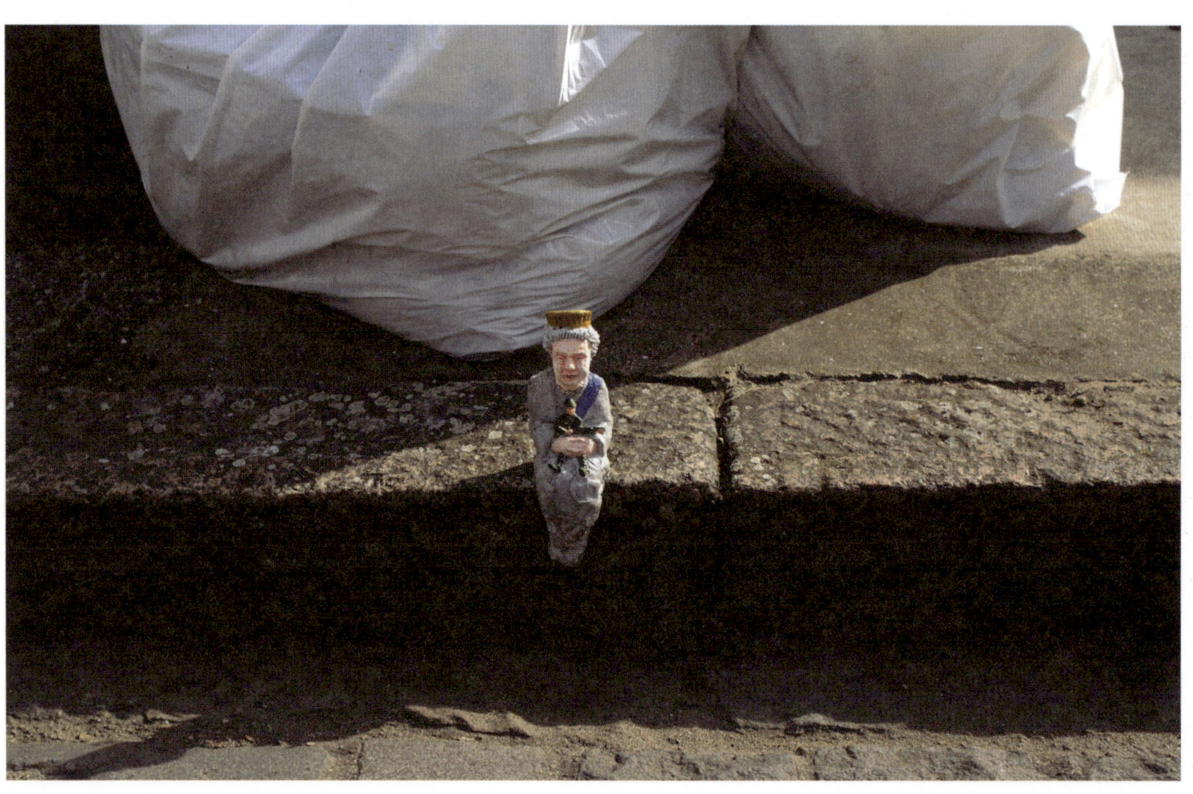

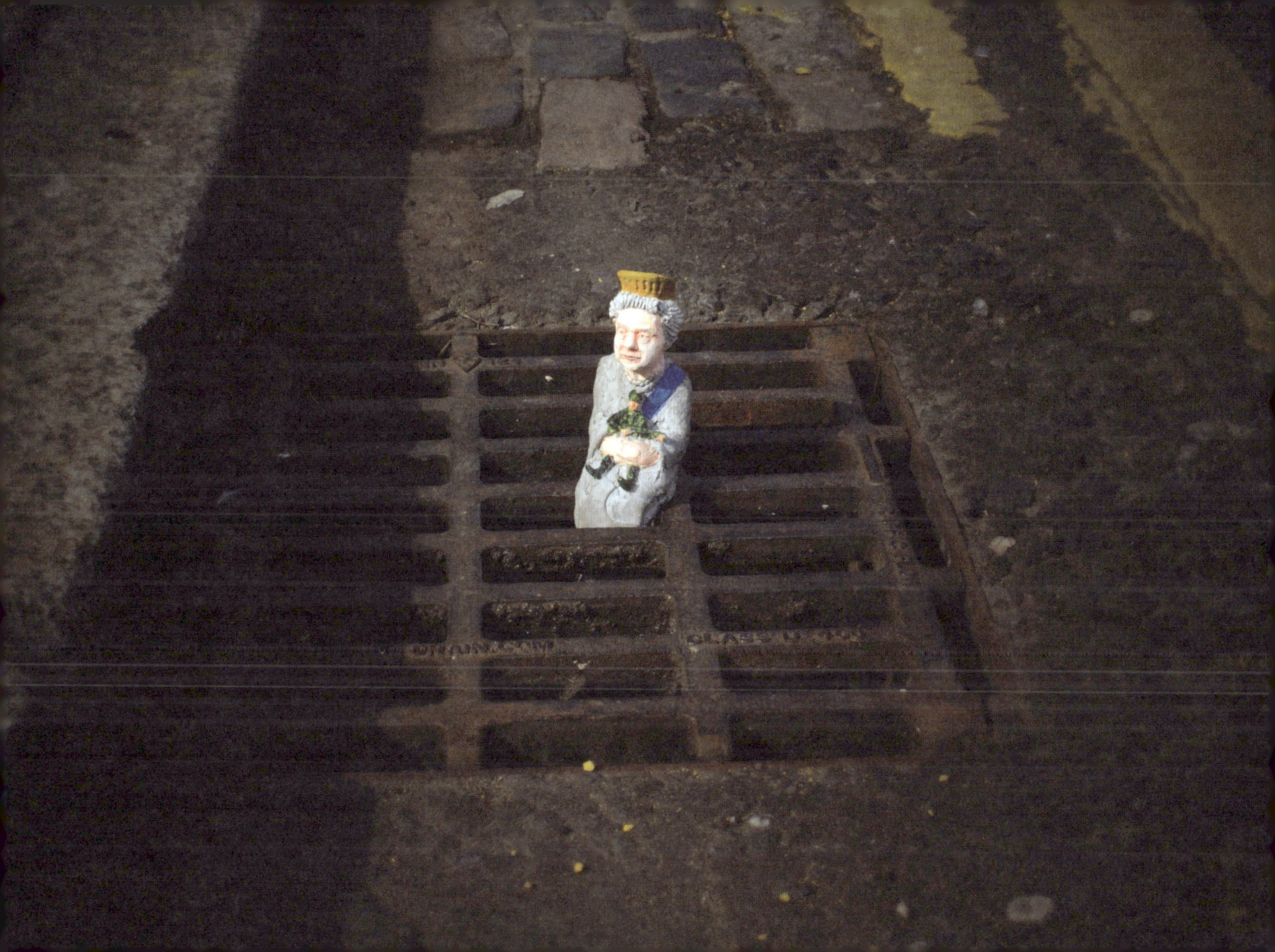

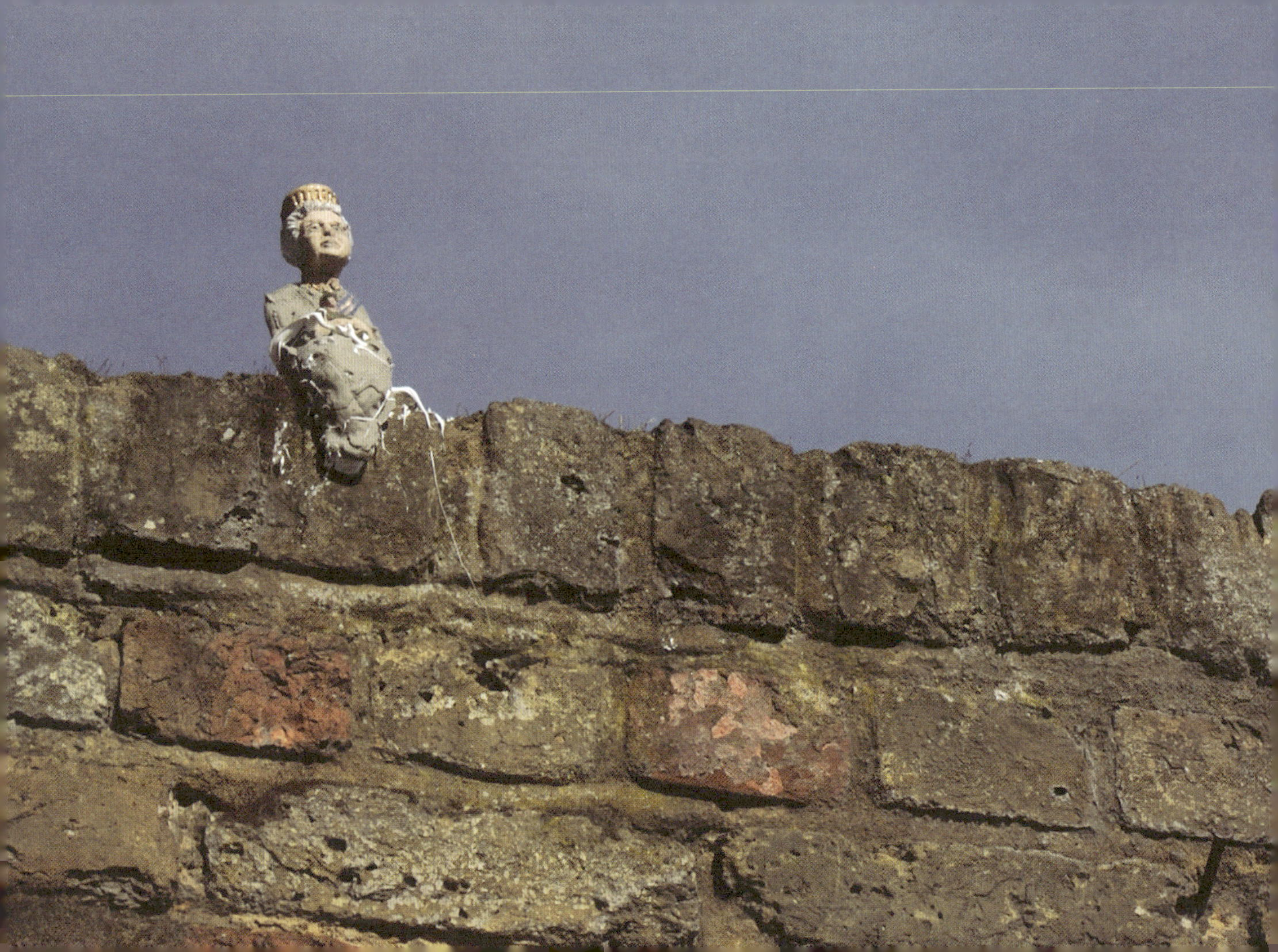

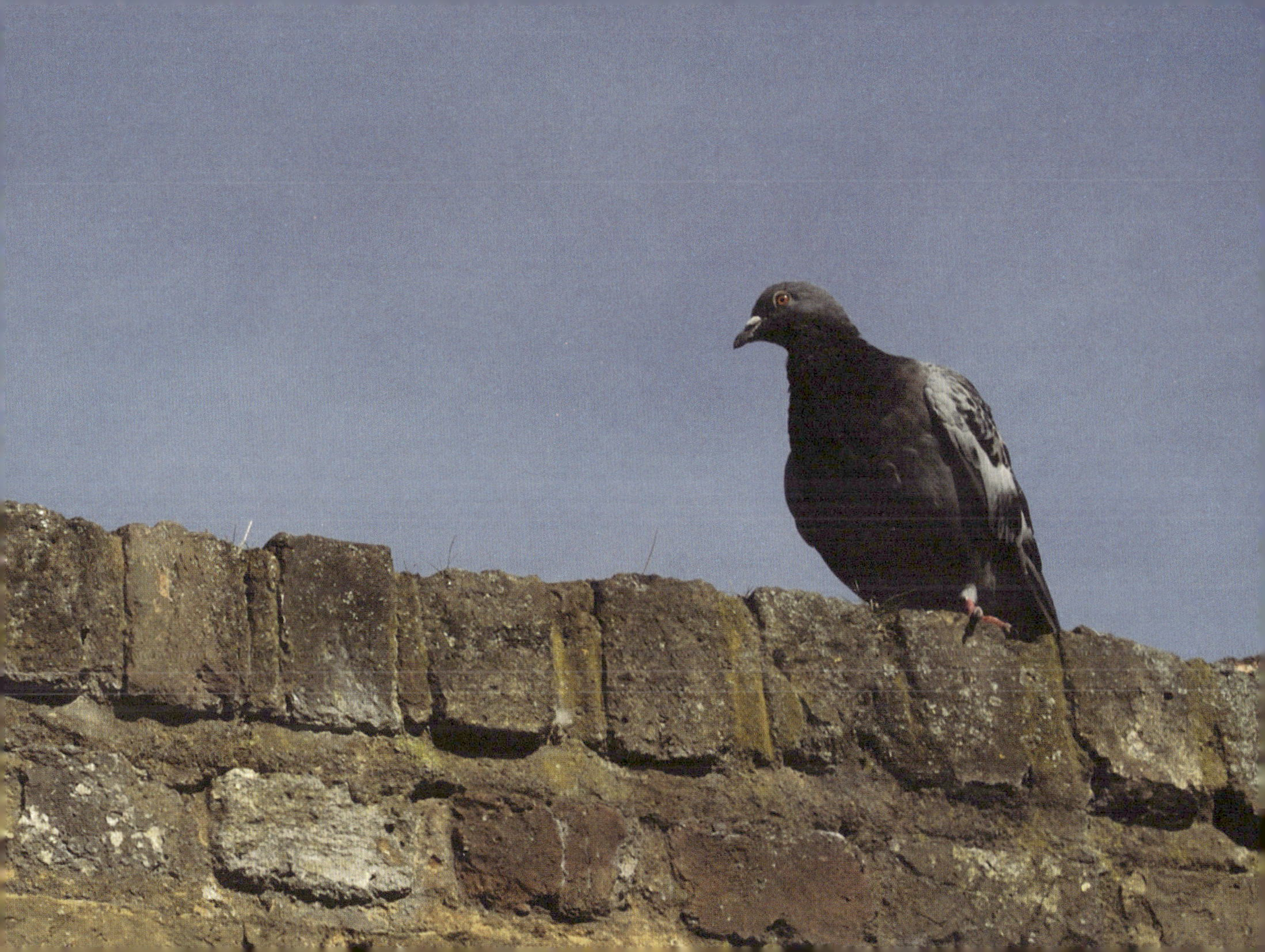

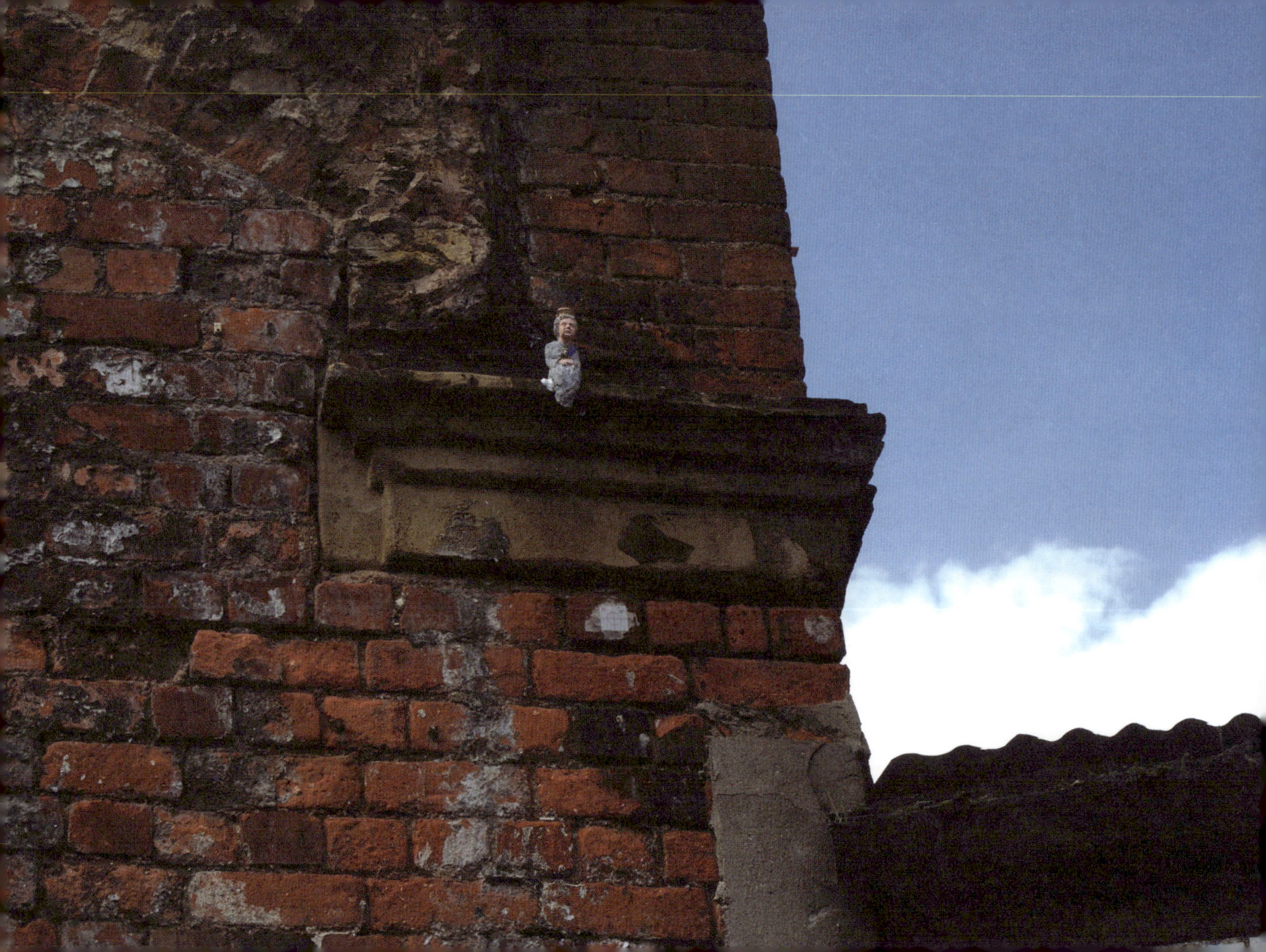

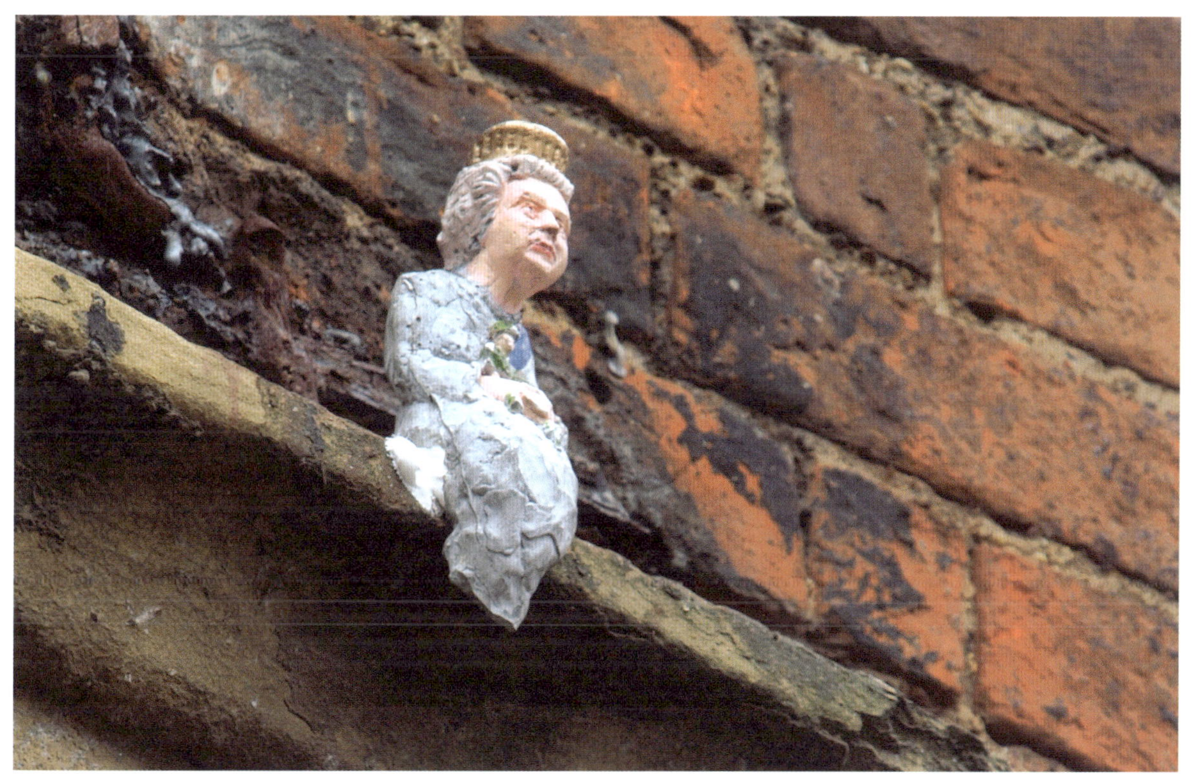

Photo by Claude Crommelin

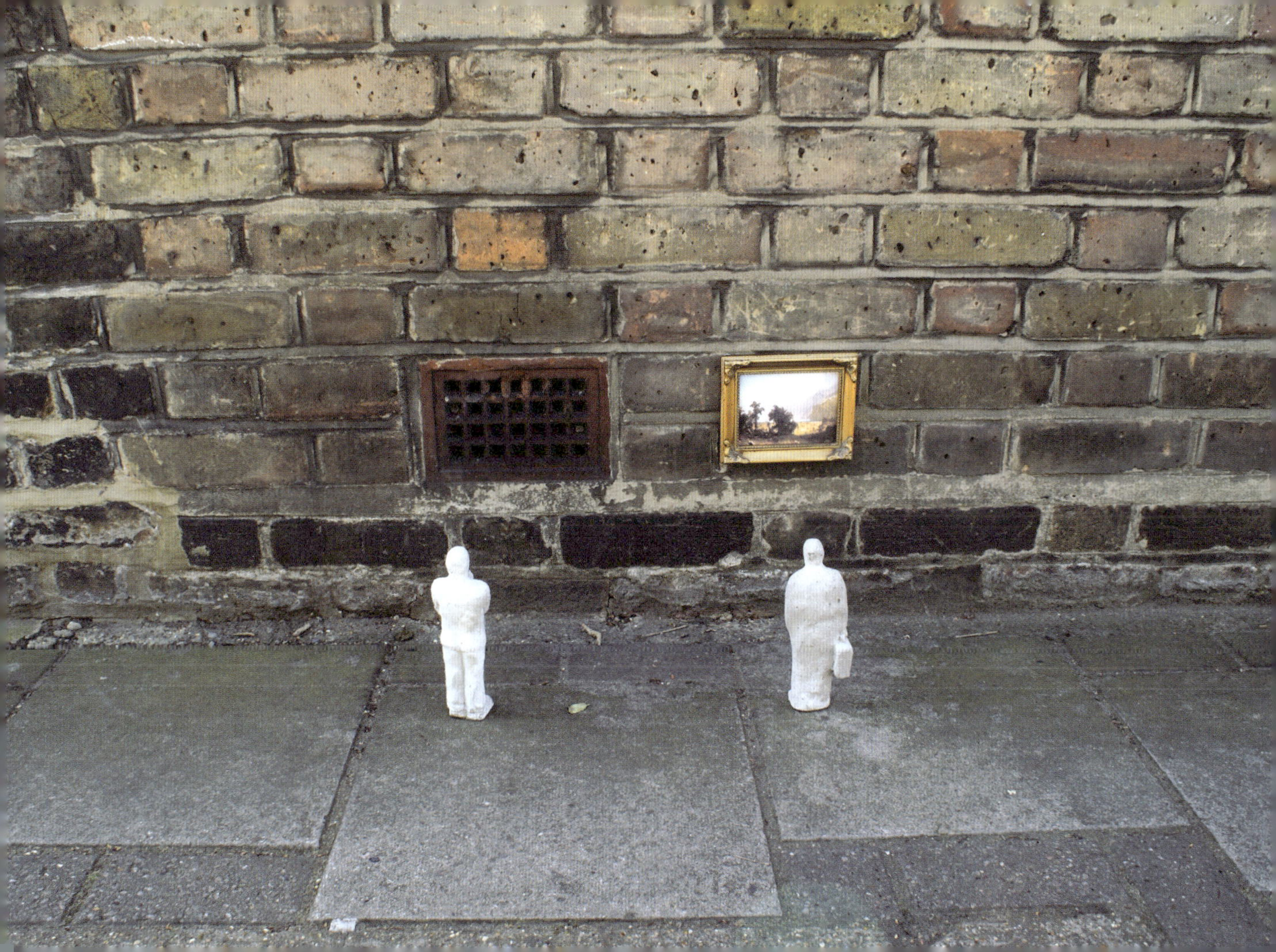

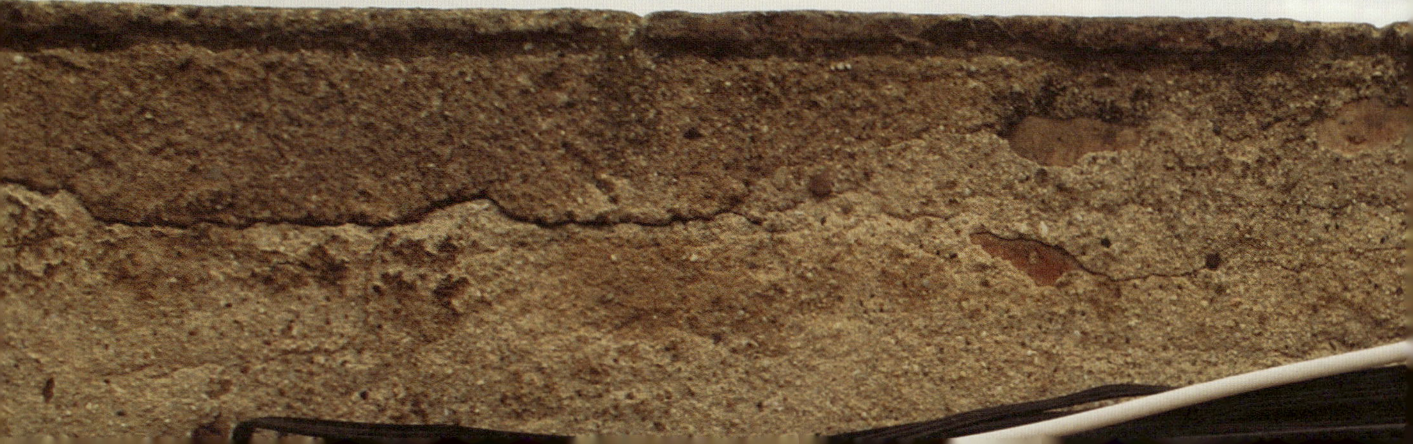
INHABITING THE STREETS

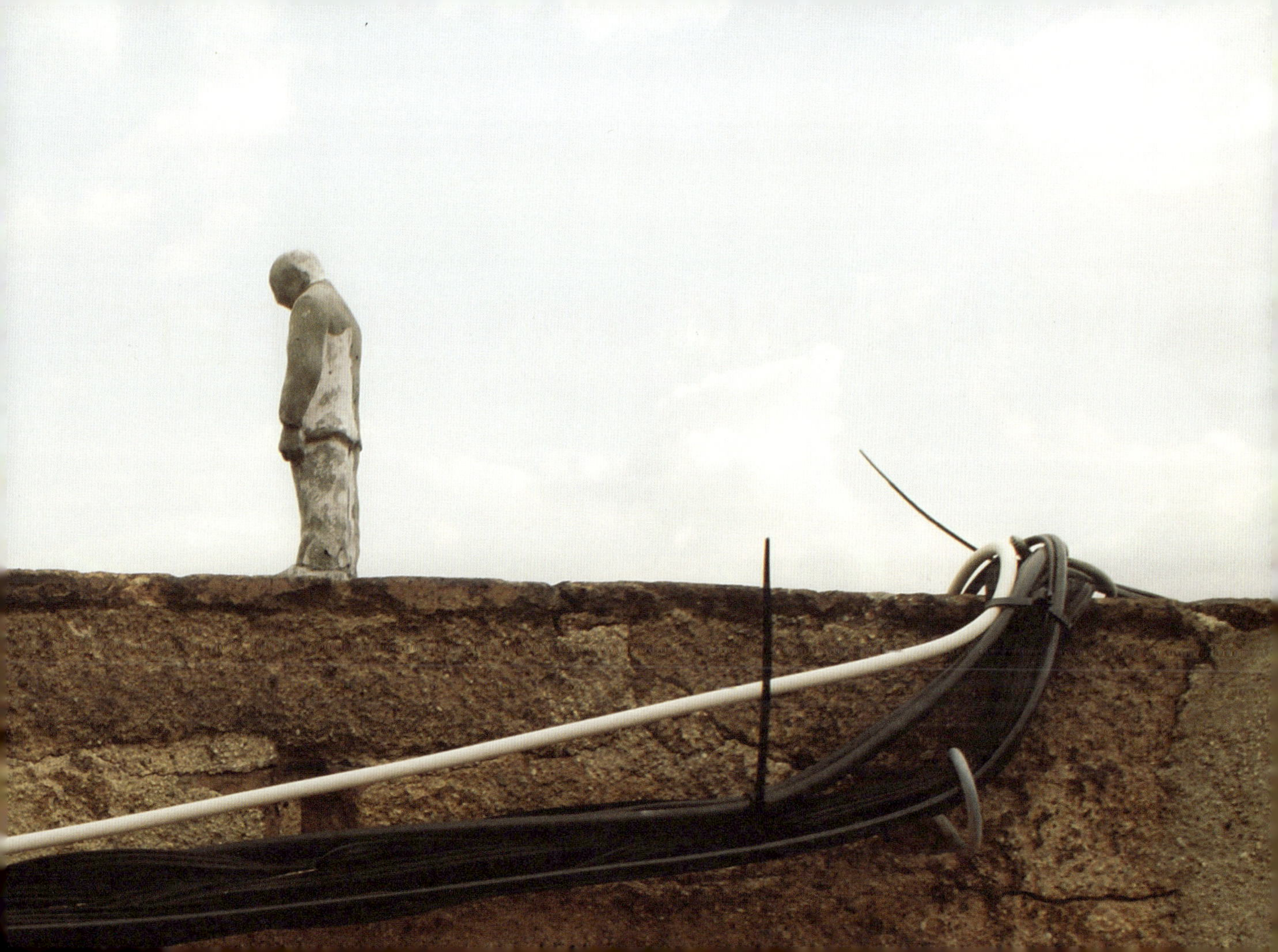

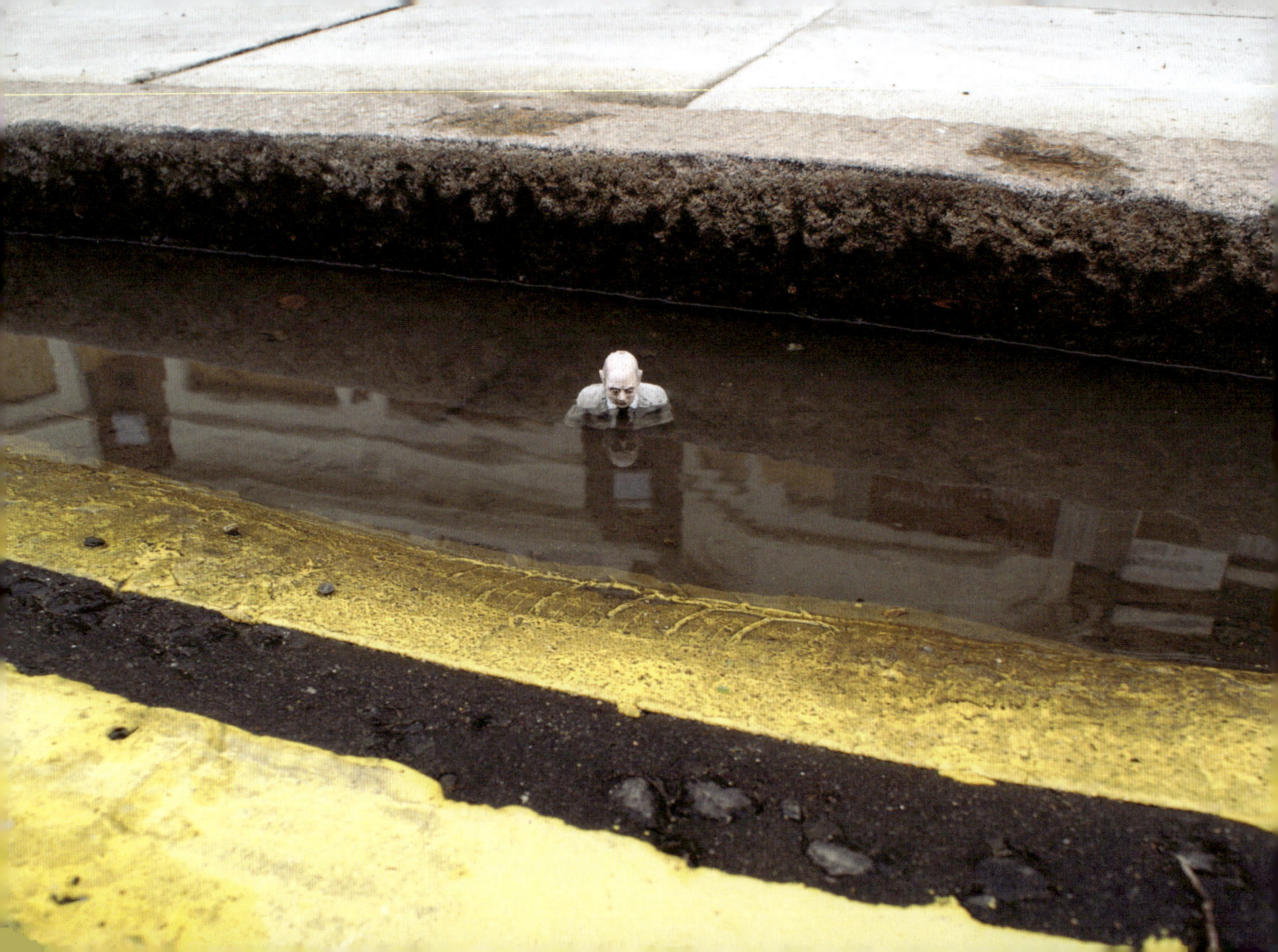

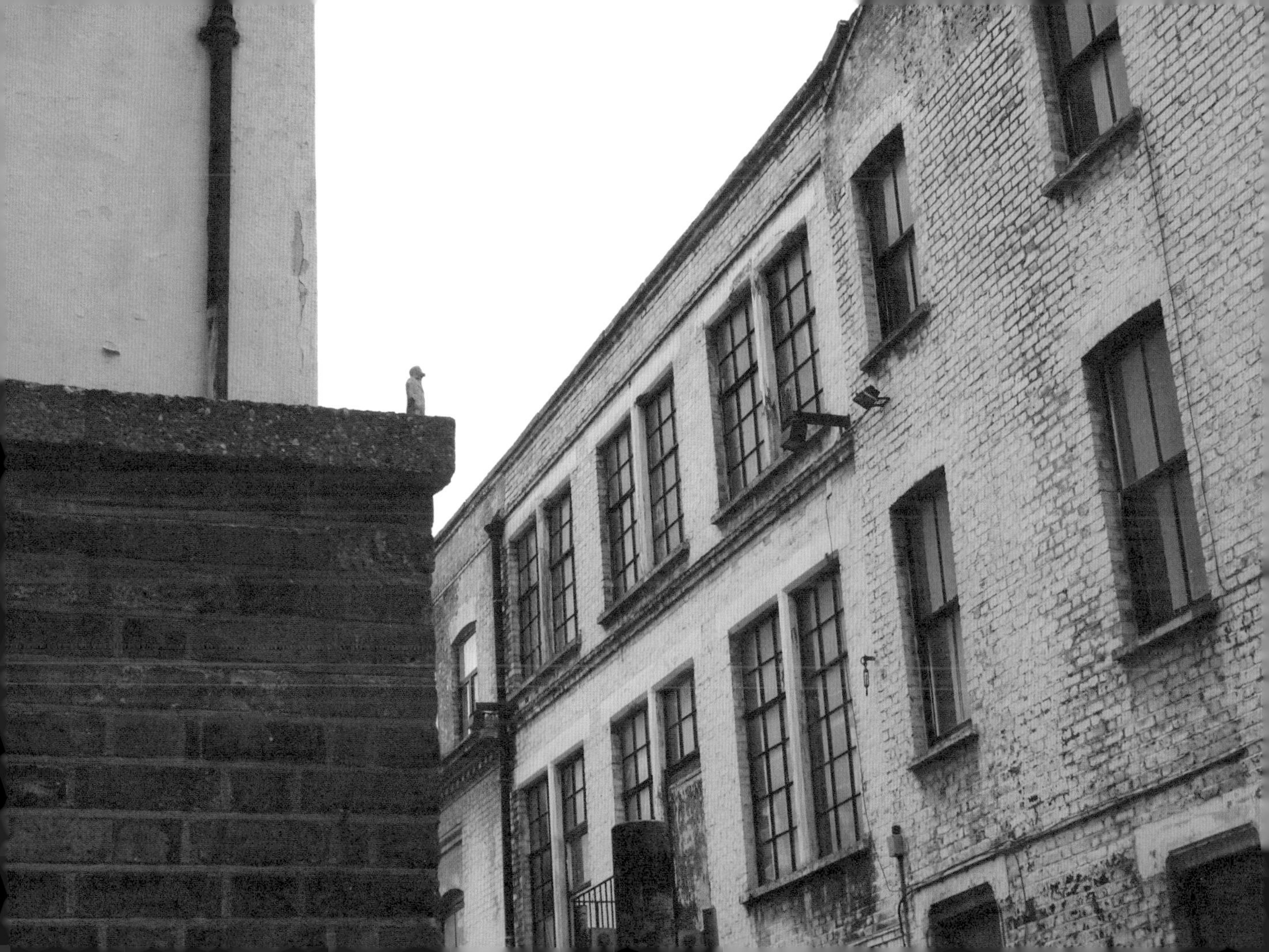

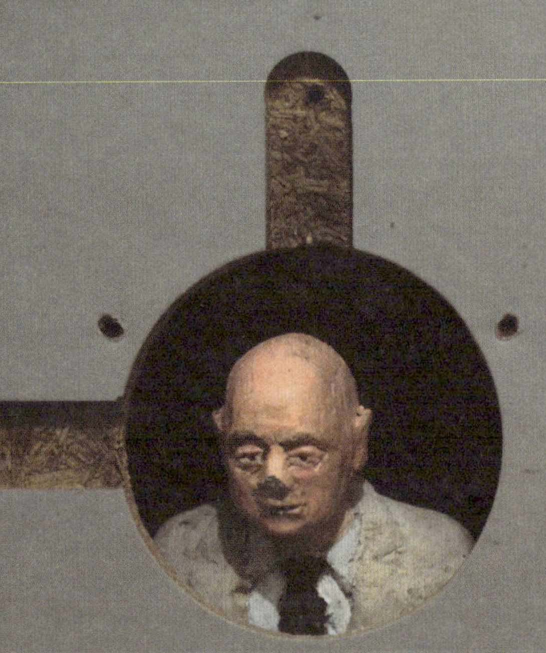
SPEAKER SYSTEM
MODEL No. CP-S5
IMPEDANCE 4 OHMS
MAX.POWER 20 WATTS
SANSUI ELECTRIC CO.,LTD.
MADE IN JAPAN
CAUTION WITH HIGH TEMPERATURES
DO NOT LEAVE THIS UNIT IN DIRECT SUN
-LIGHT, NEAR A HEATING APPLIANCE OR

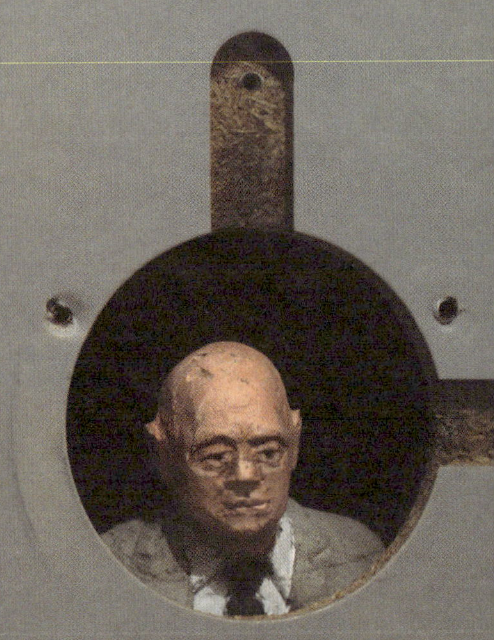
07873300
SPEAKER SYSTEM
MODEL No. CP-S5
IMPEDANCE 4 OHMS
MAX.POWER 20 WATTS
SANSUI ELECTRIC CO.,LTD.
MADE IN JAPAN
CAUTION WITH HIGH TEMPERATURES
DO NOT LEAVE THIS UNIT IN DIRECT SUN
-LIGHT, NEAR A HEATING APPLIANCE OR

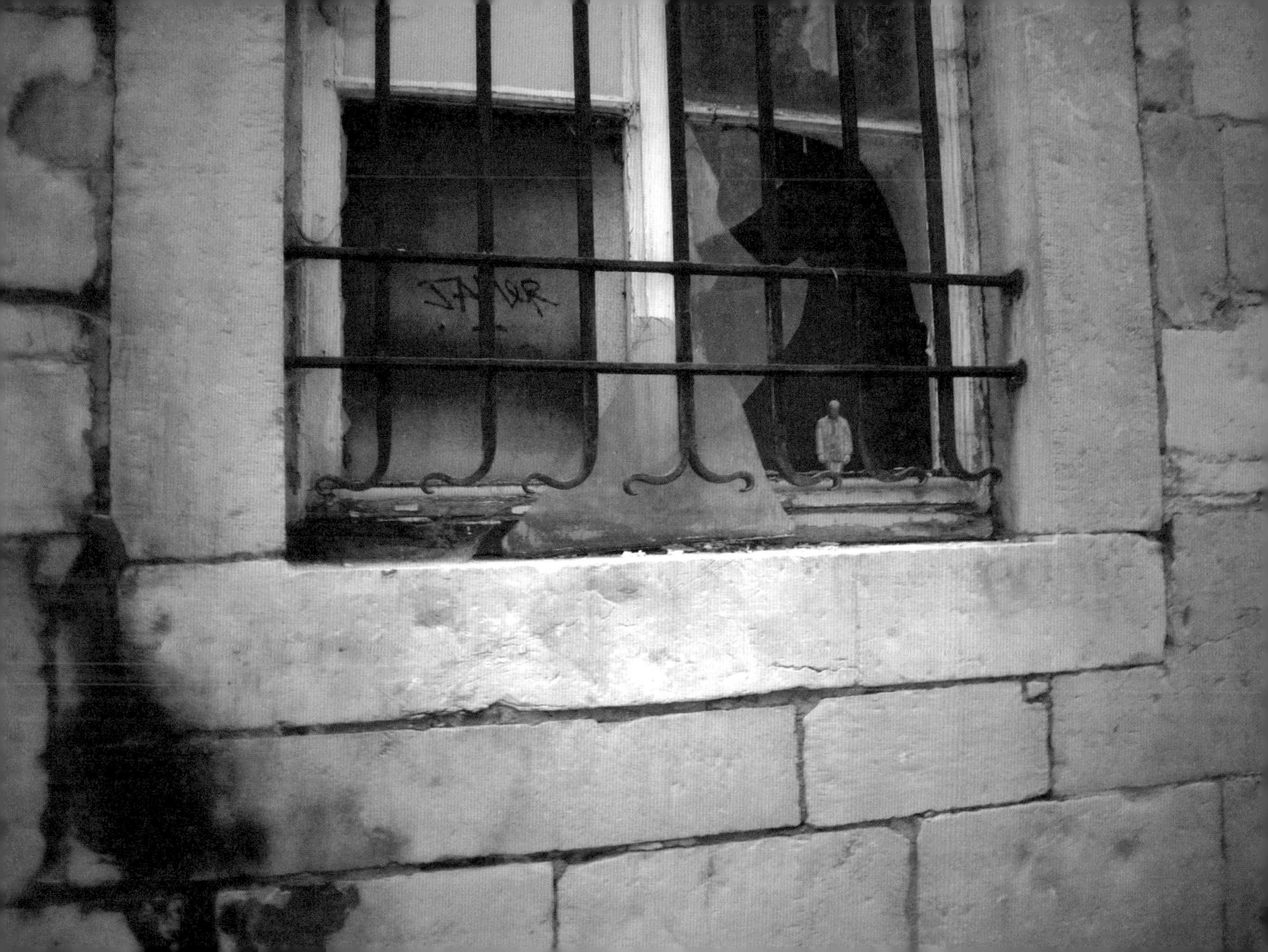

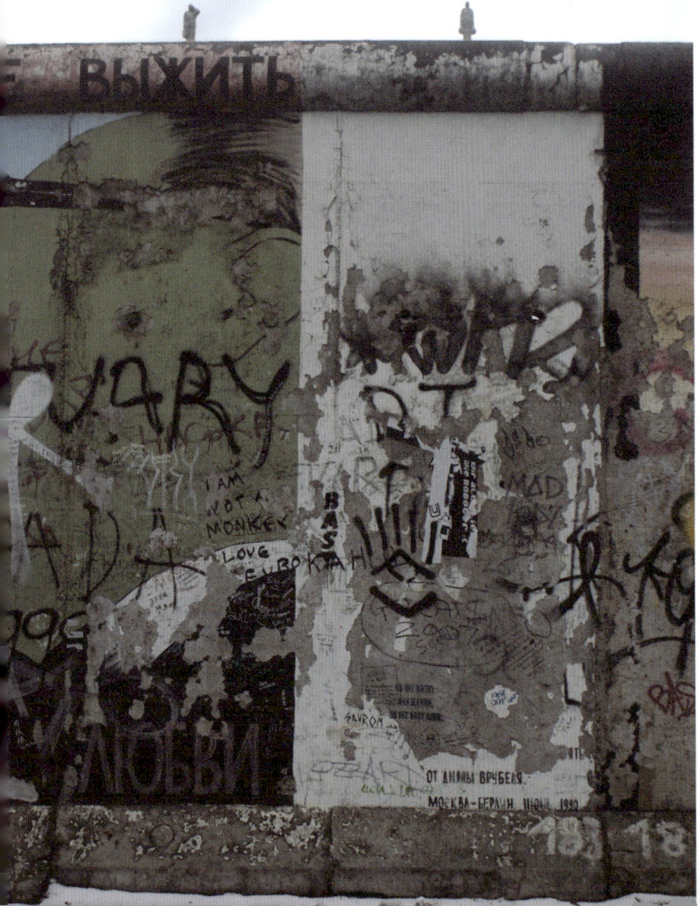

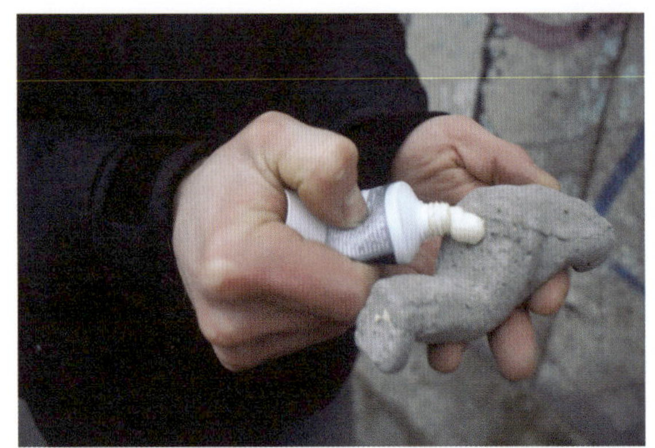

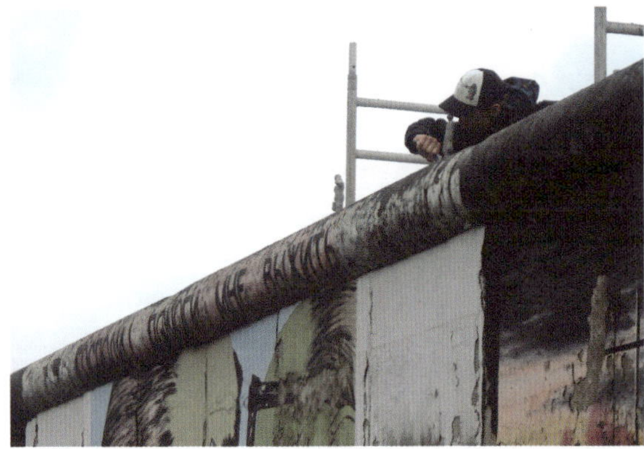

with Marco
Berlin, Germany

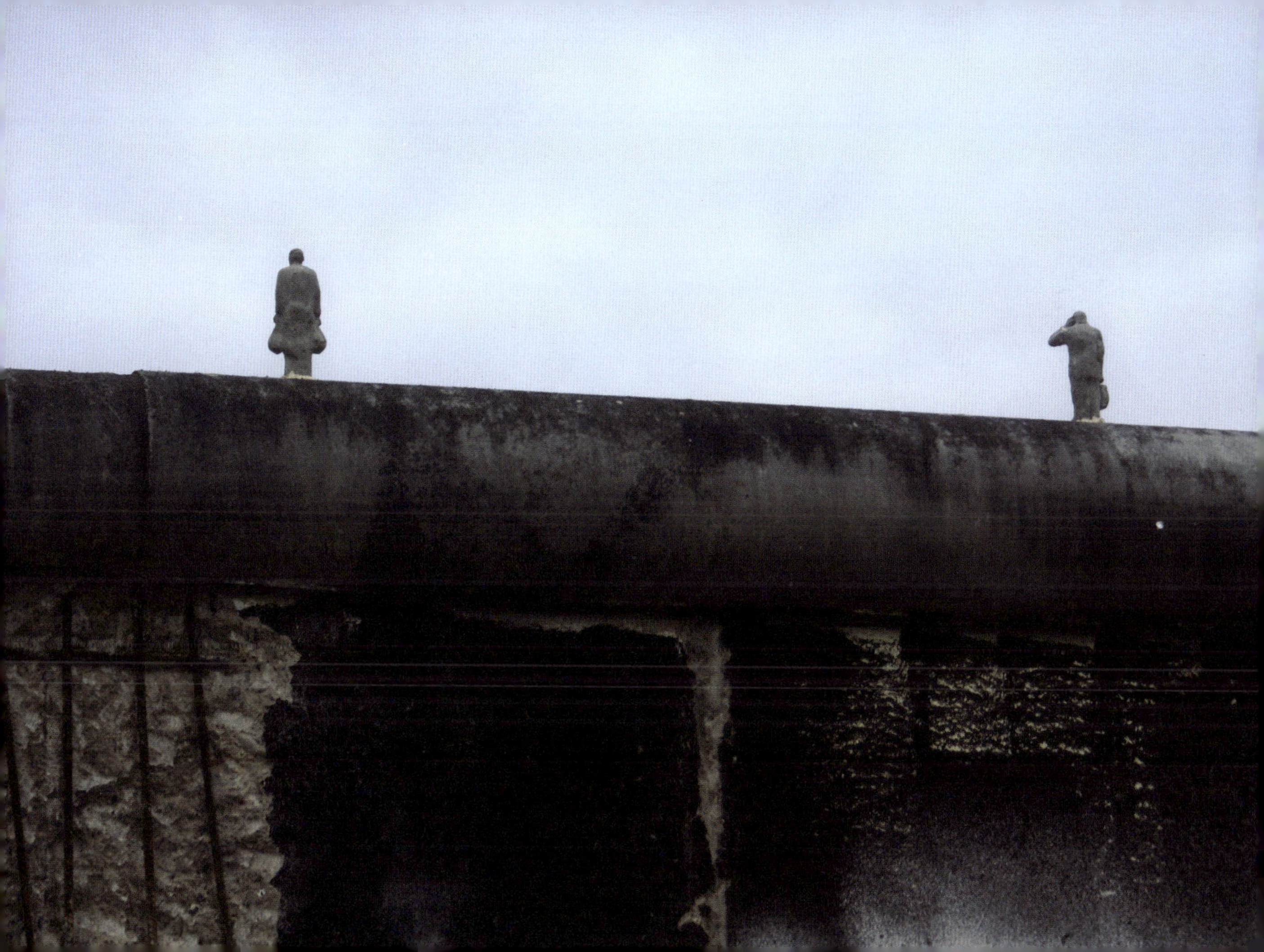

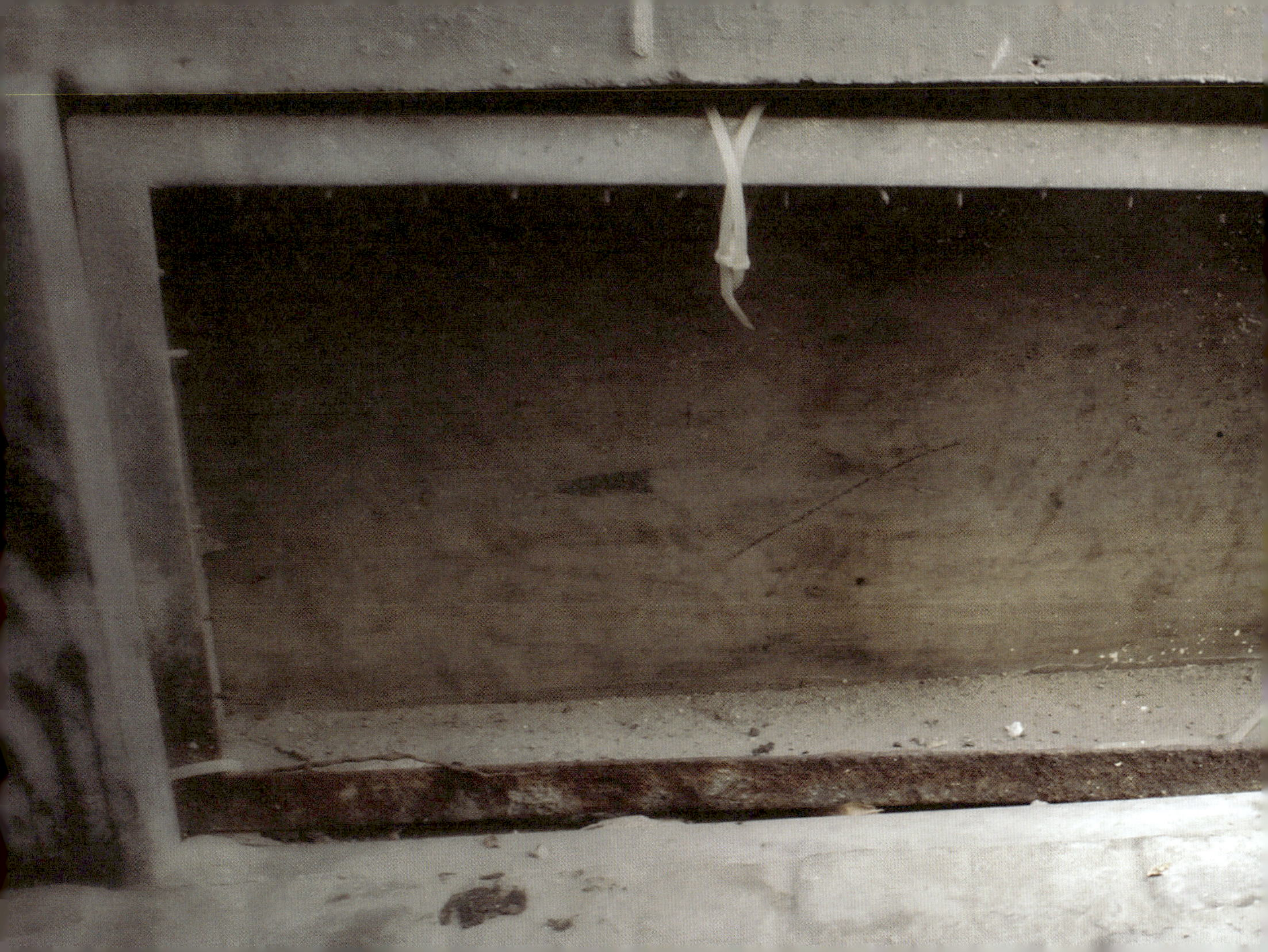

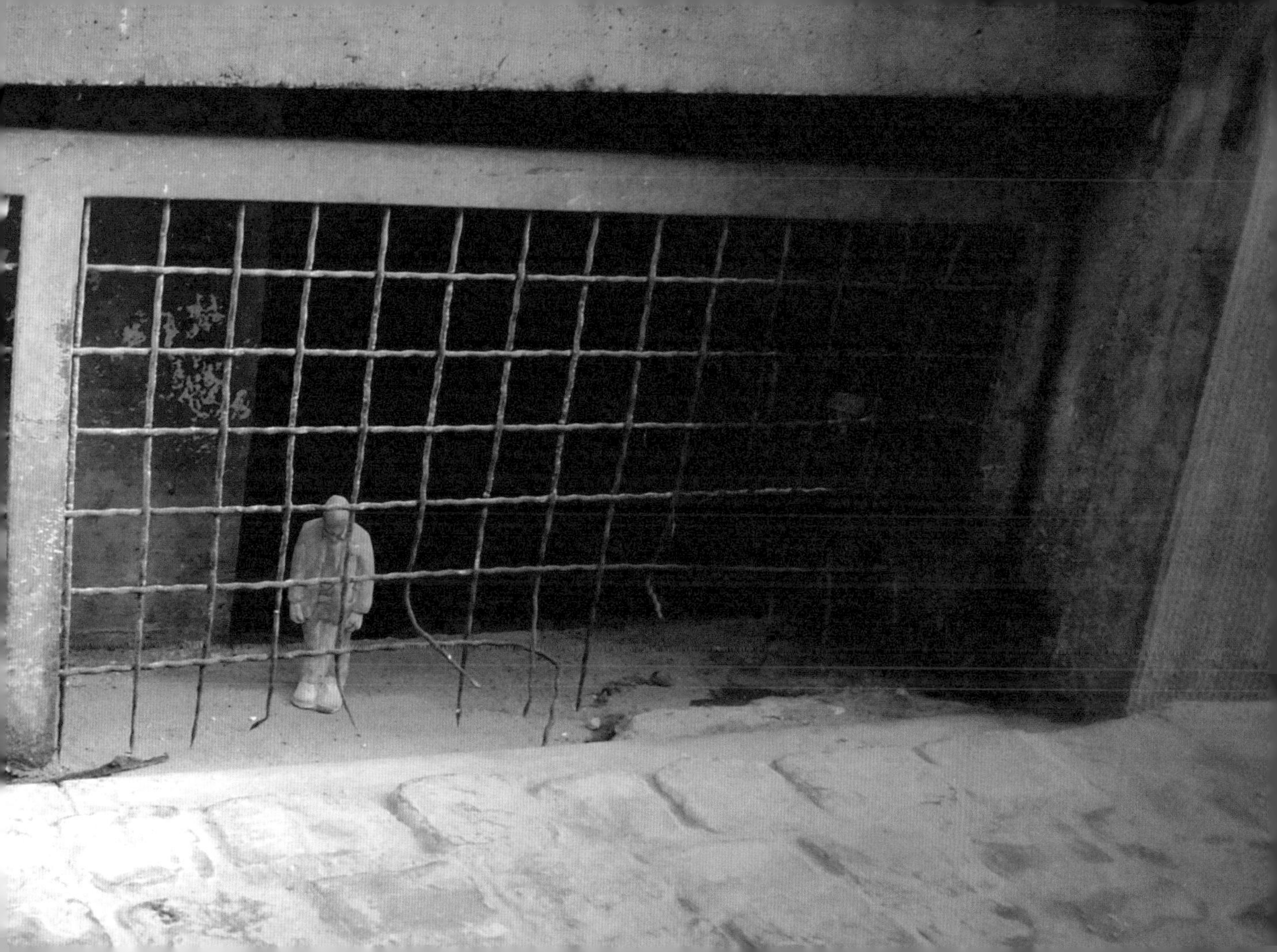

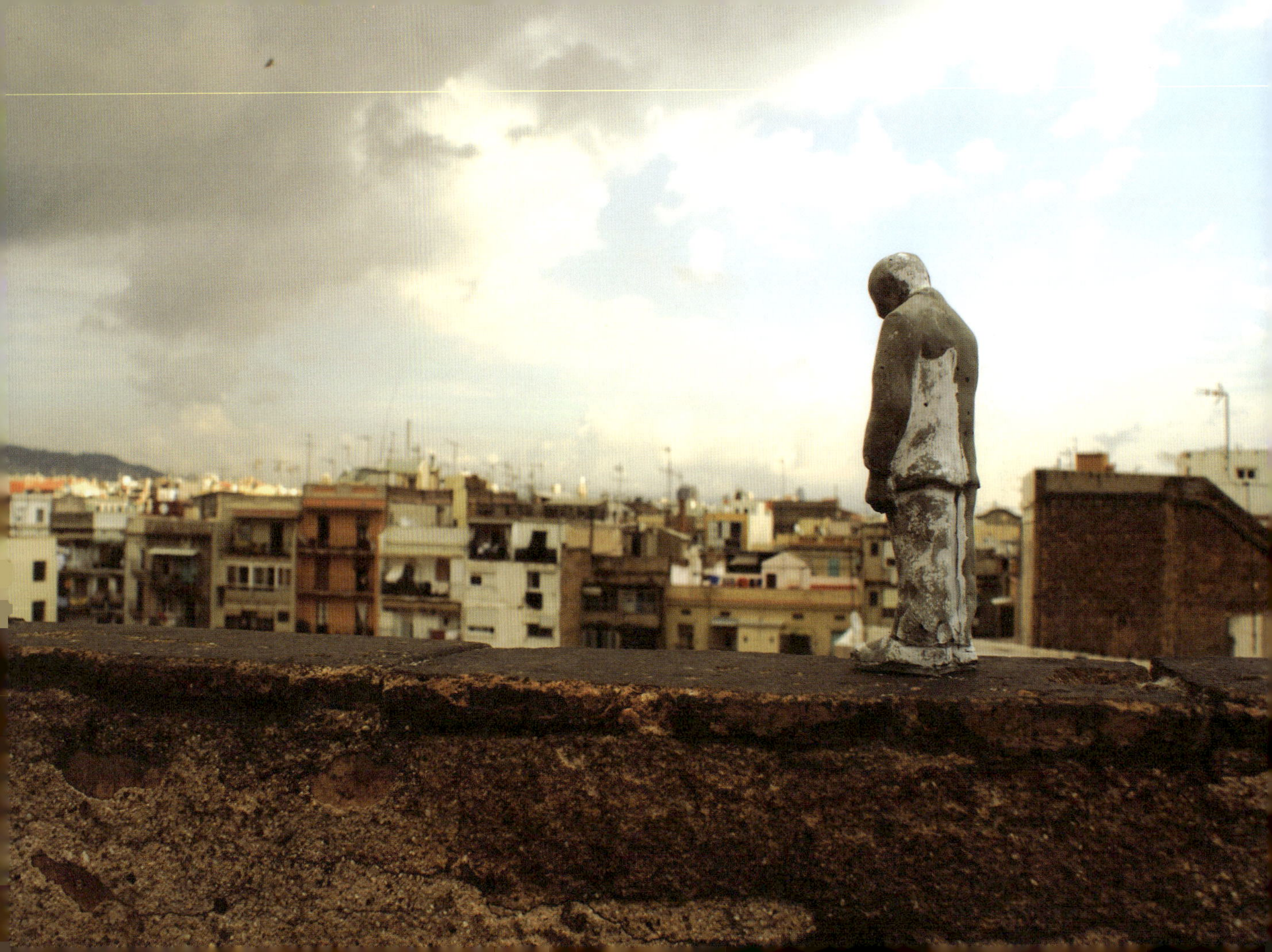

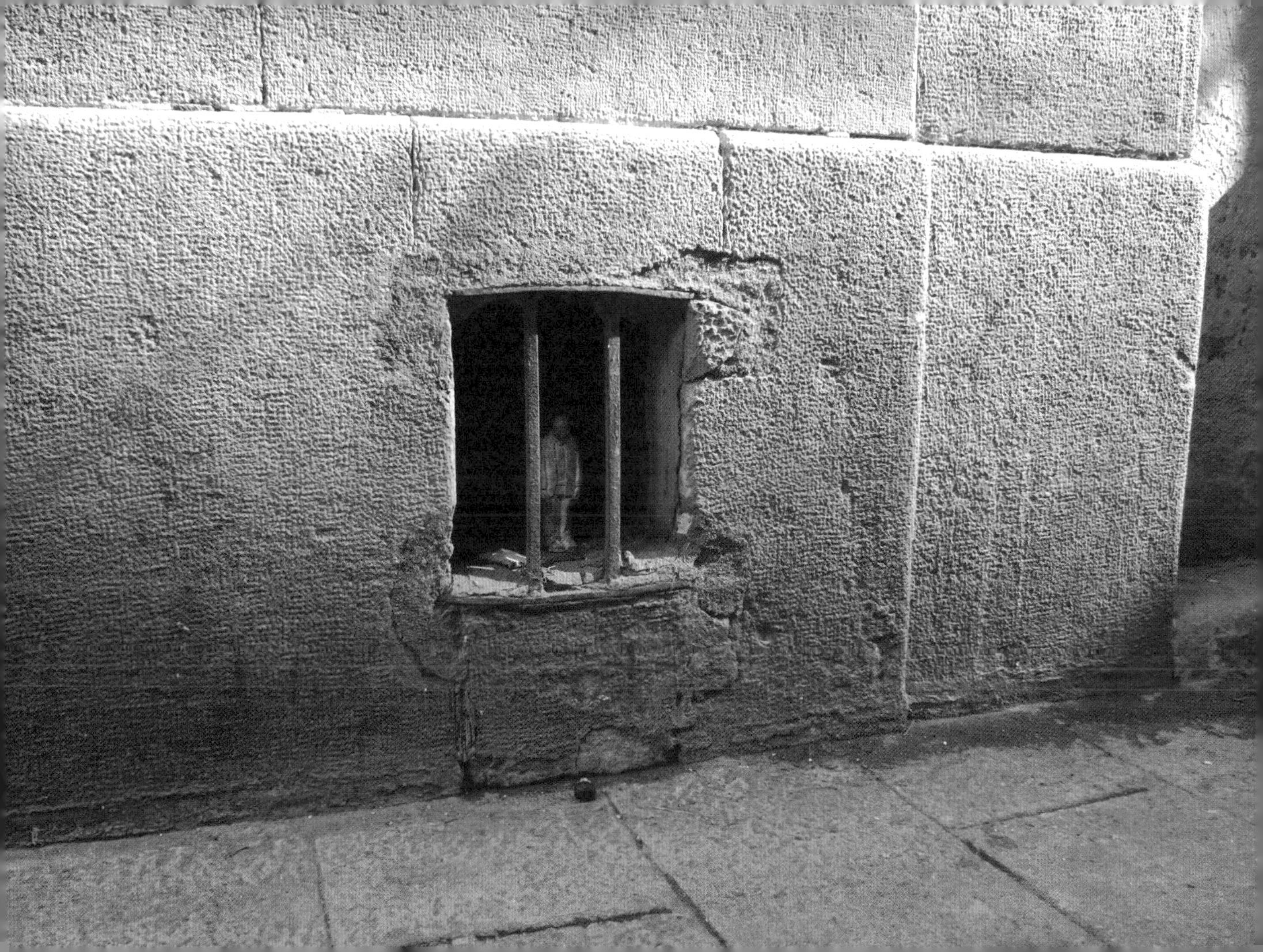

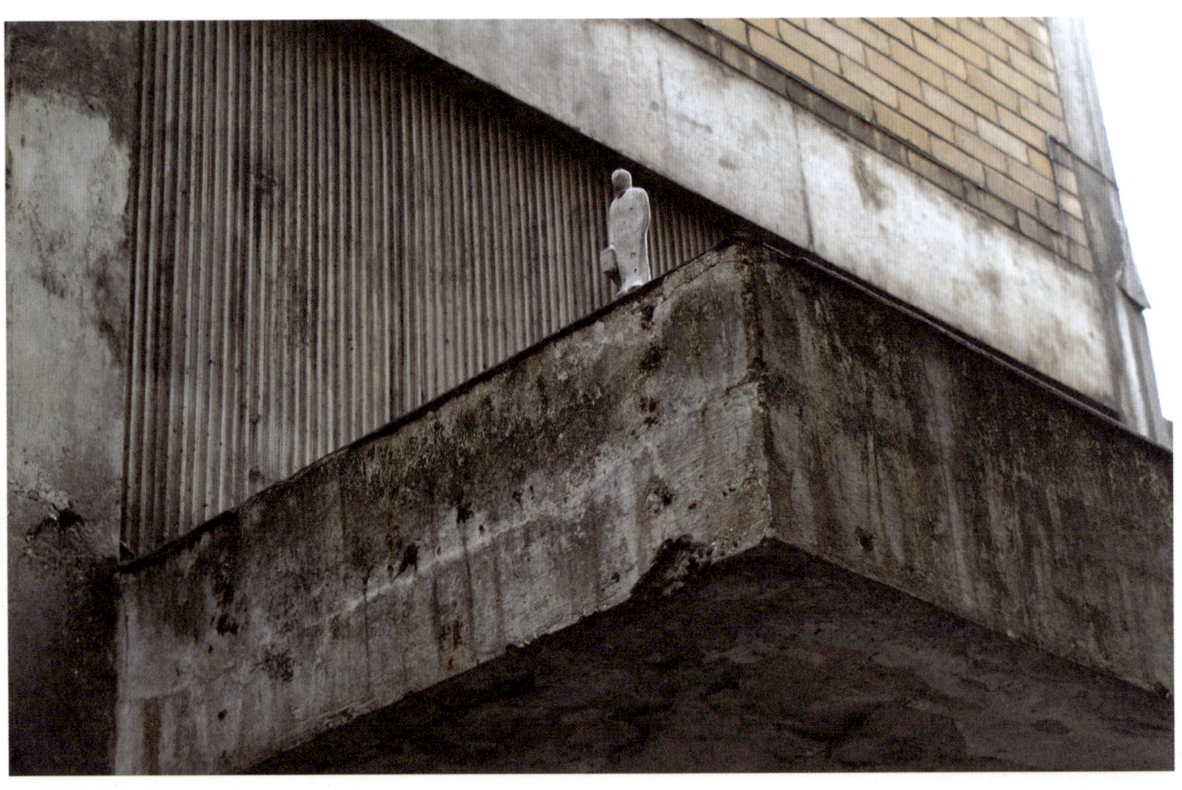

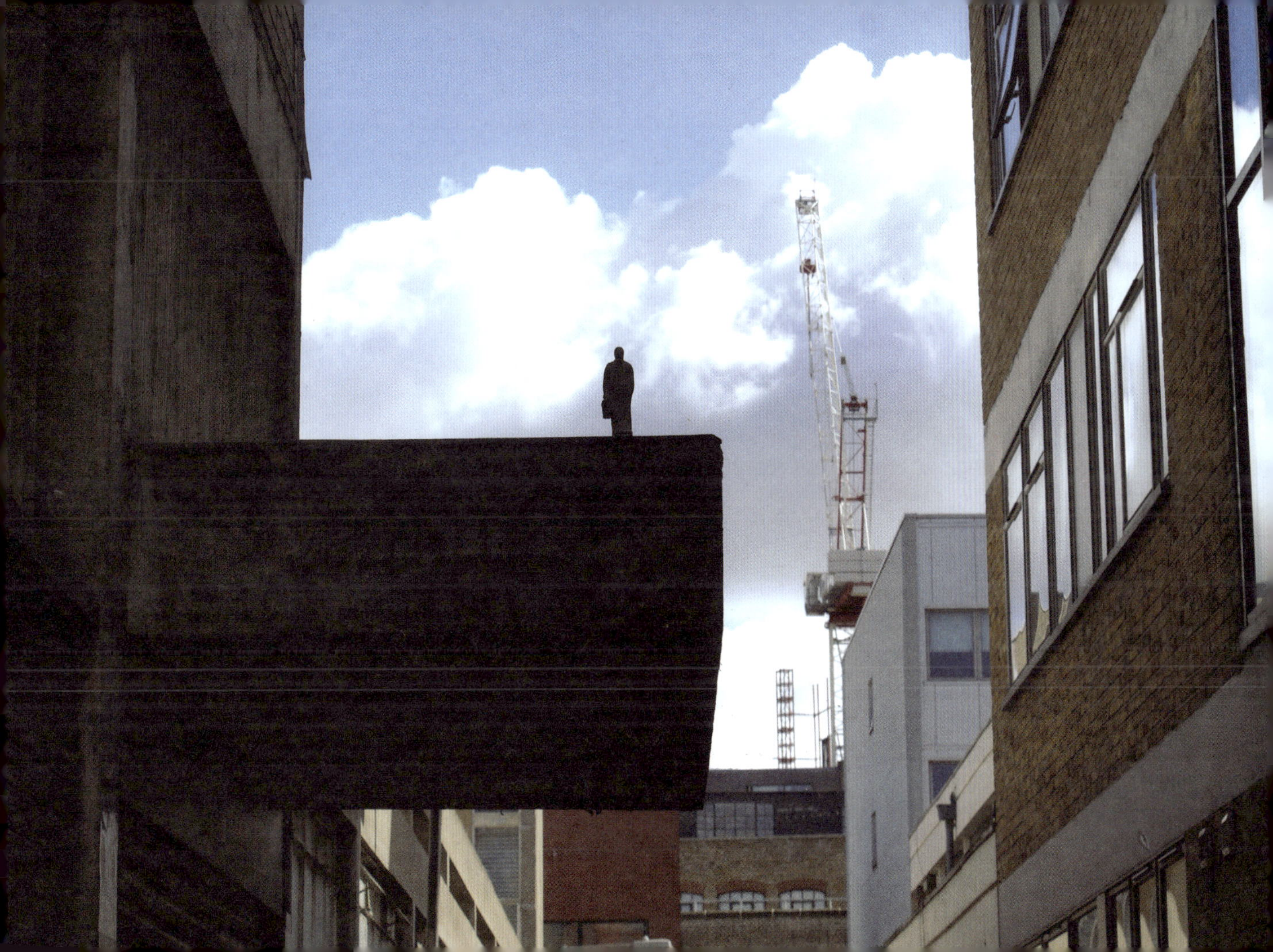

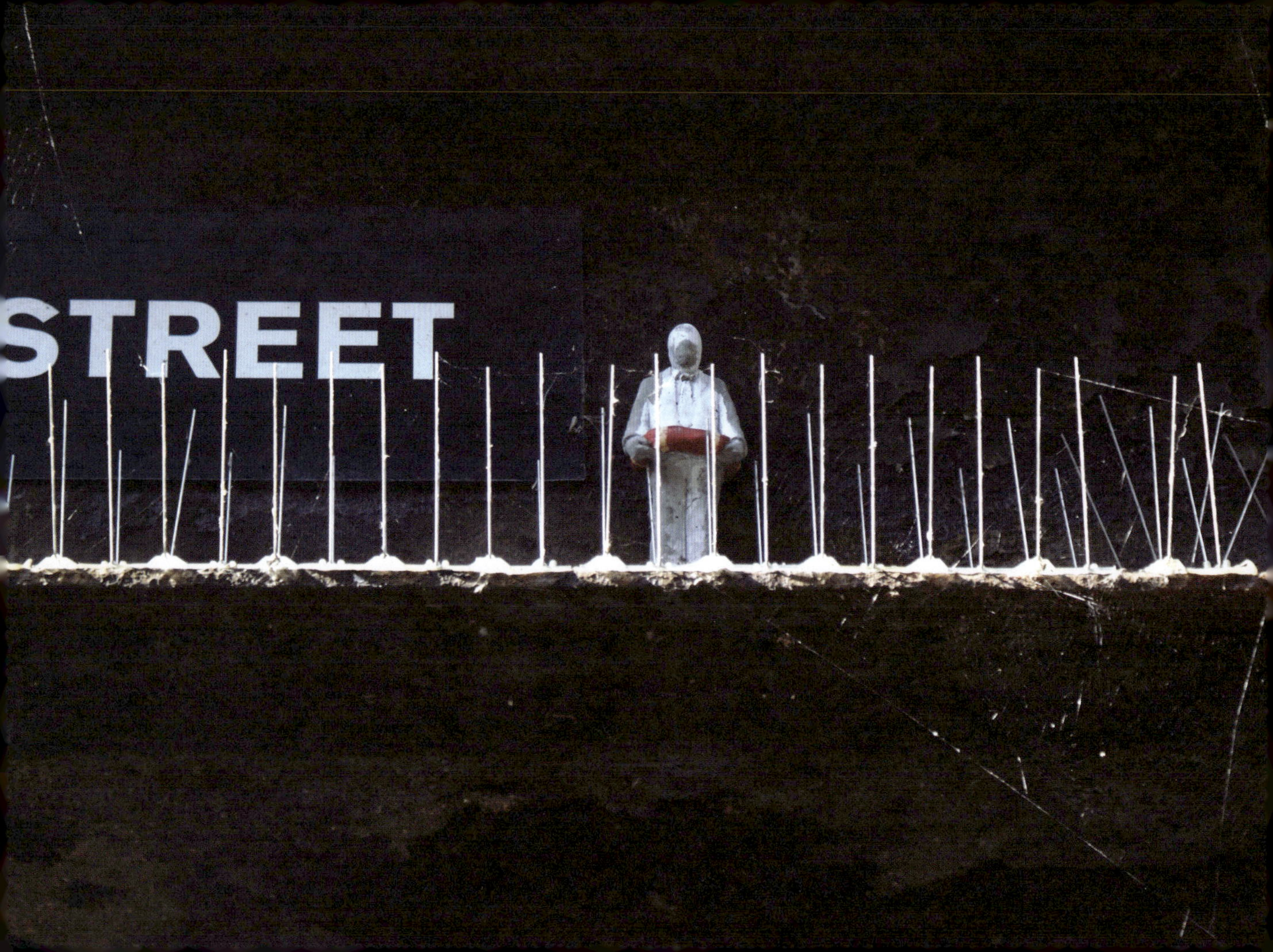

STREET

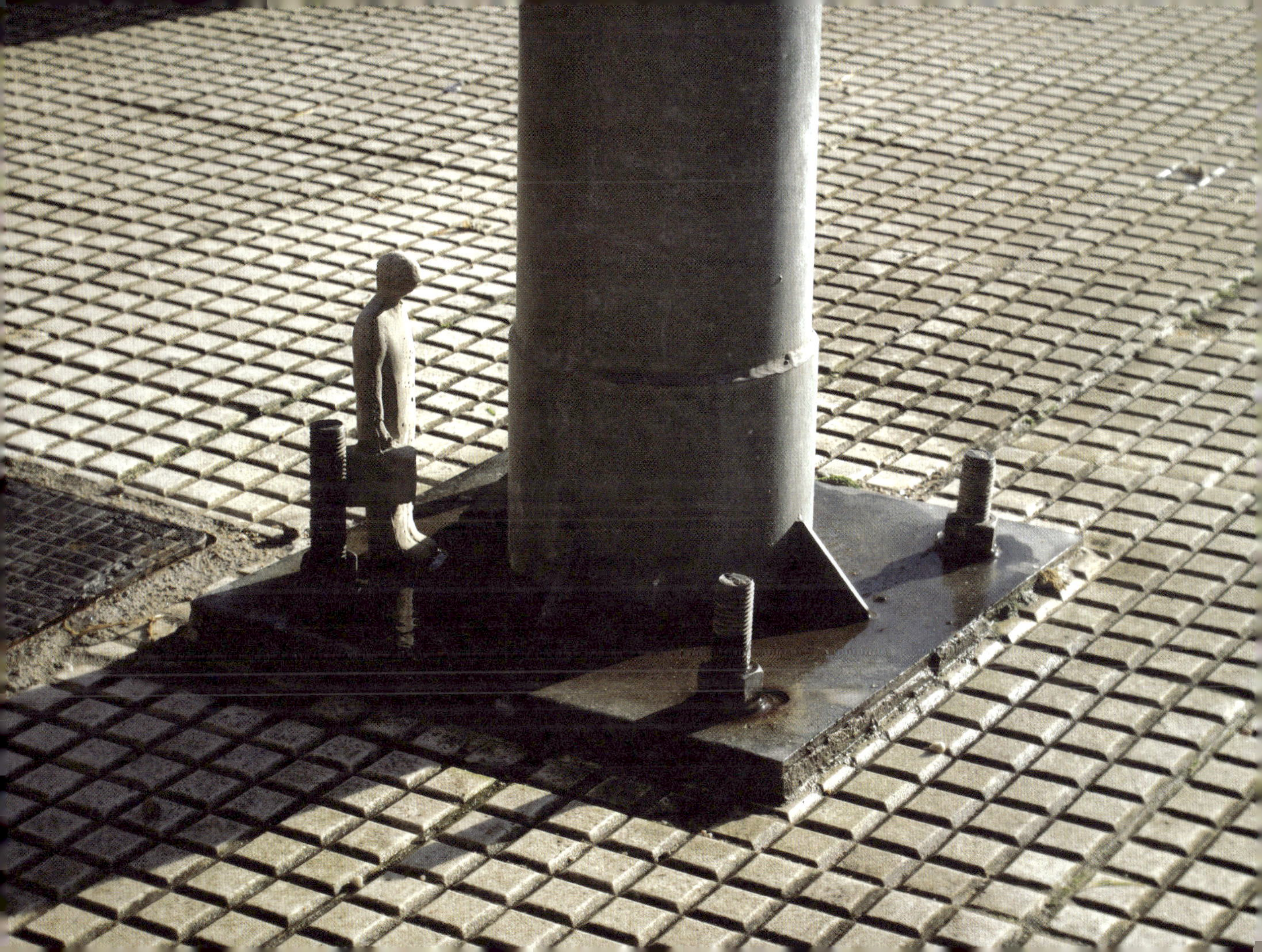

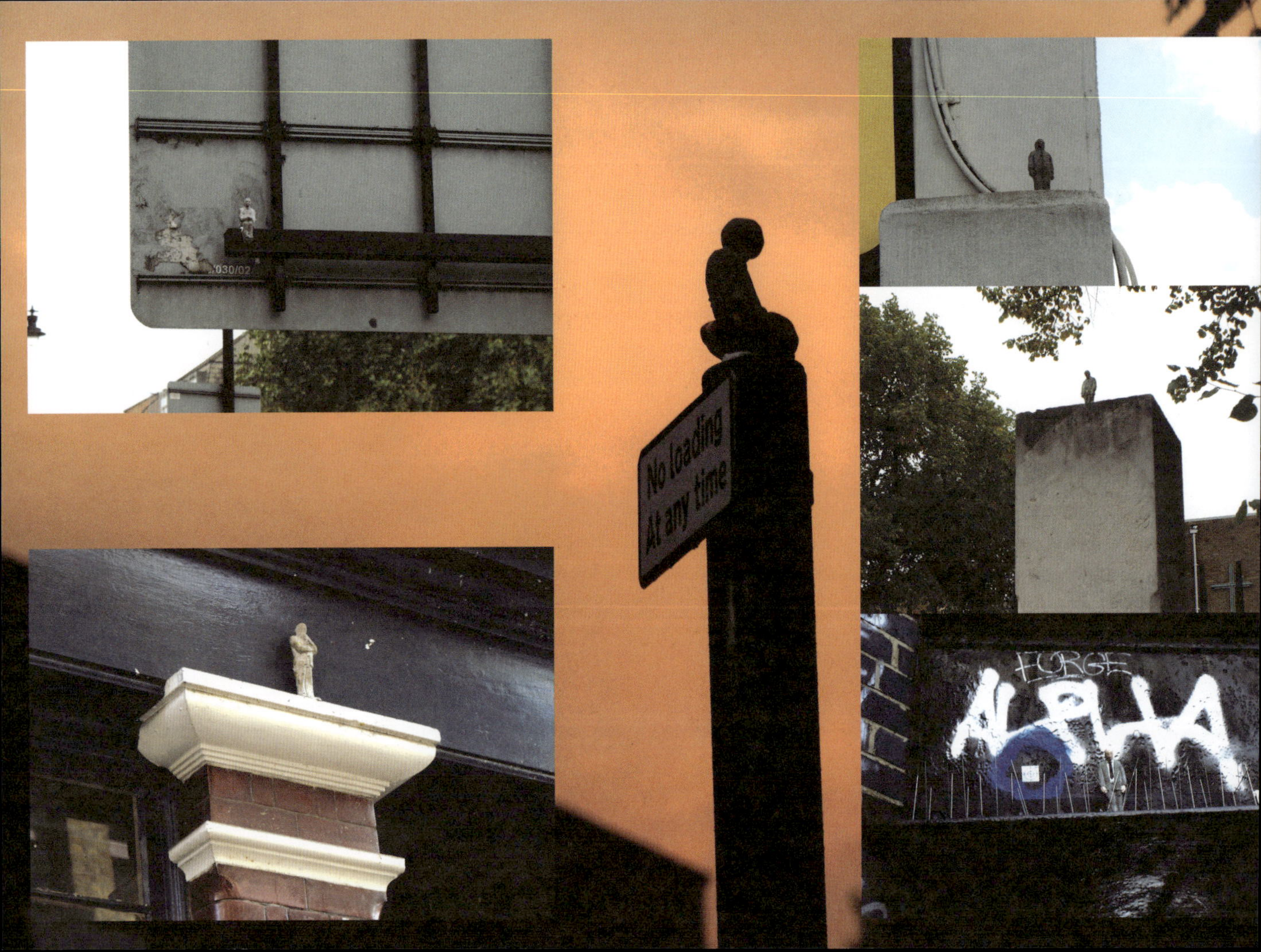
No loading
At any time
FORGE
ALPHA

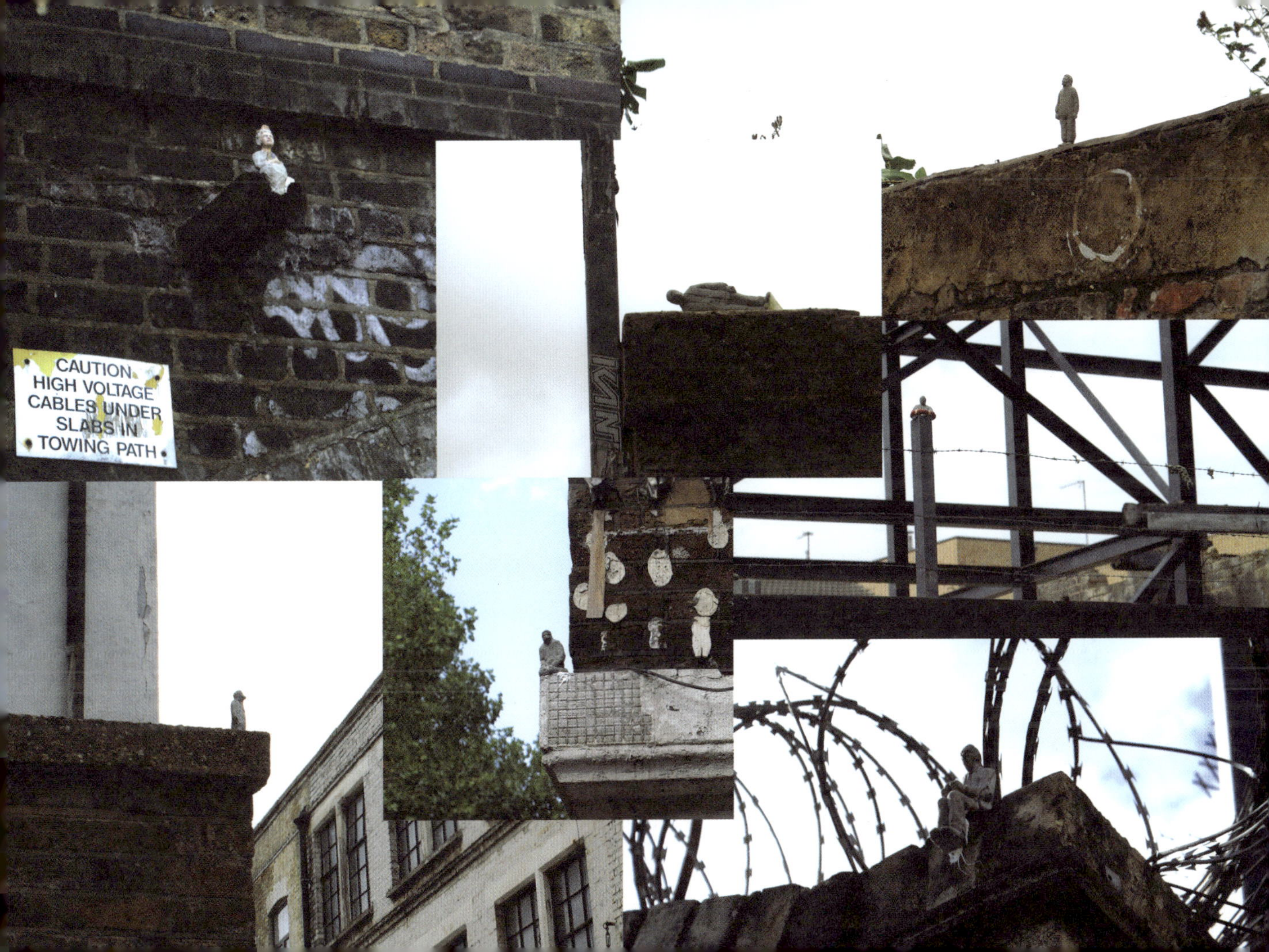
CAUTION
HIGH VOLTAGE
CABLES UNDER
SLABS IN
TOWING PATH

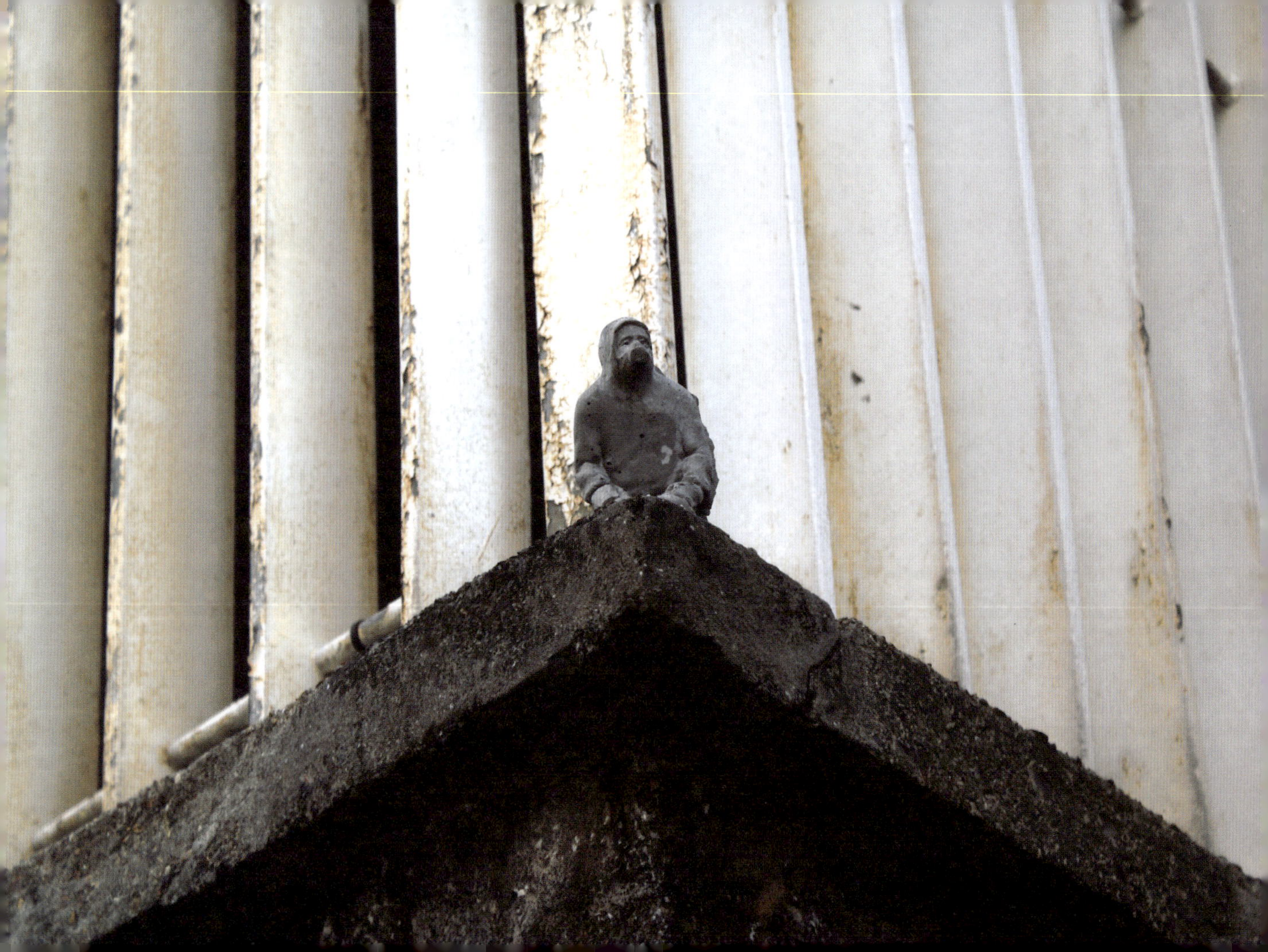

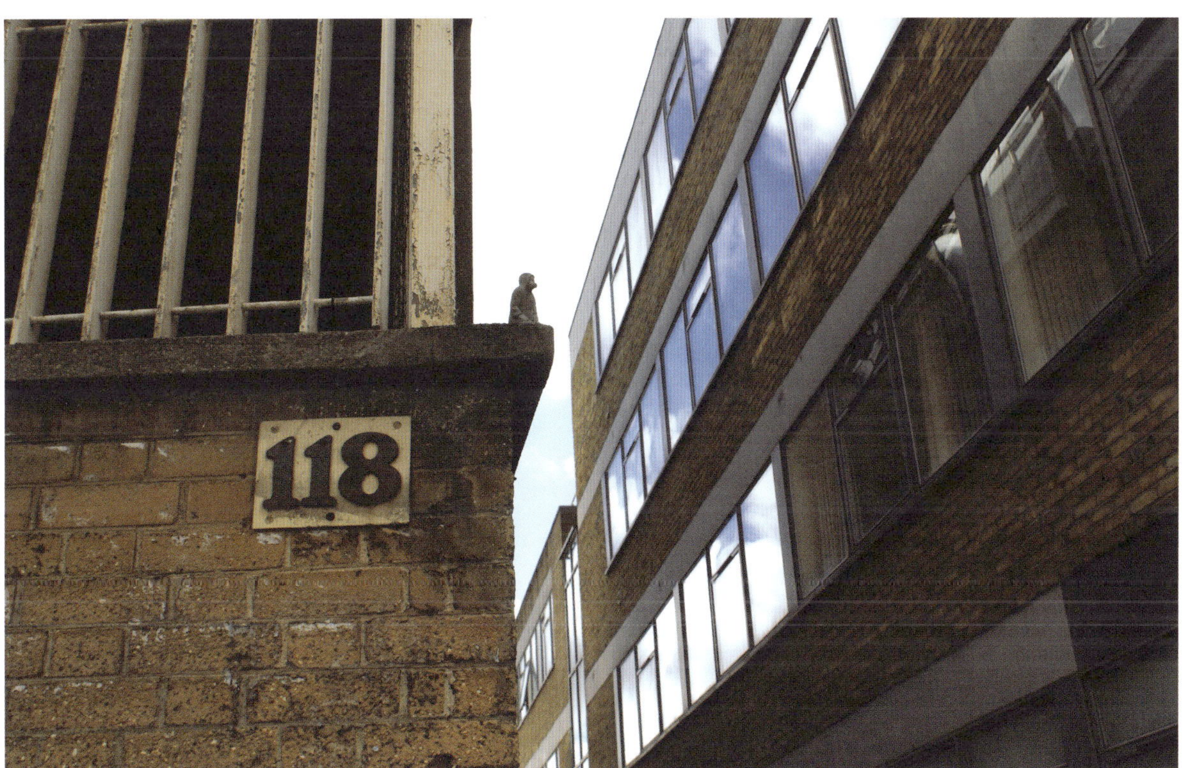

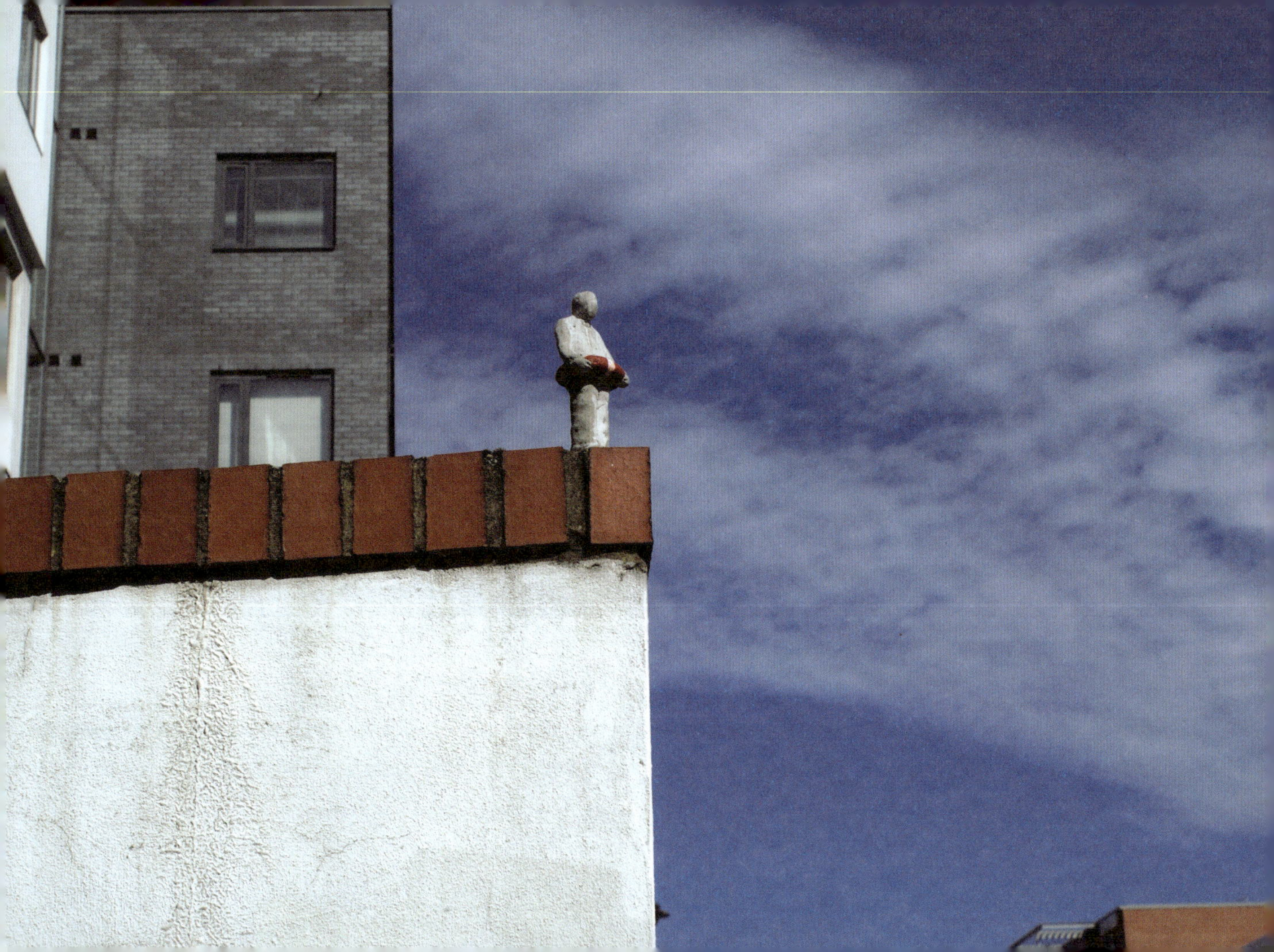

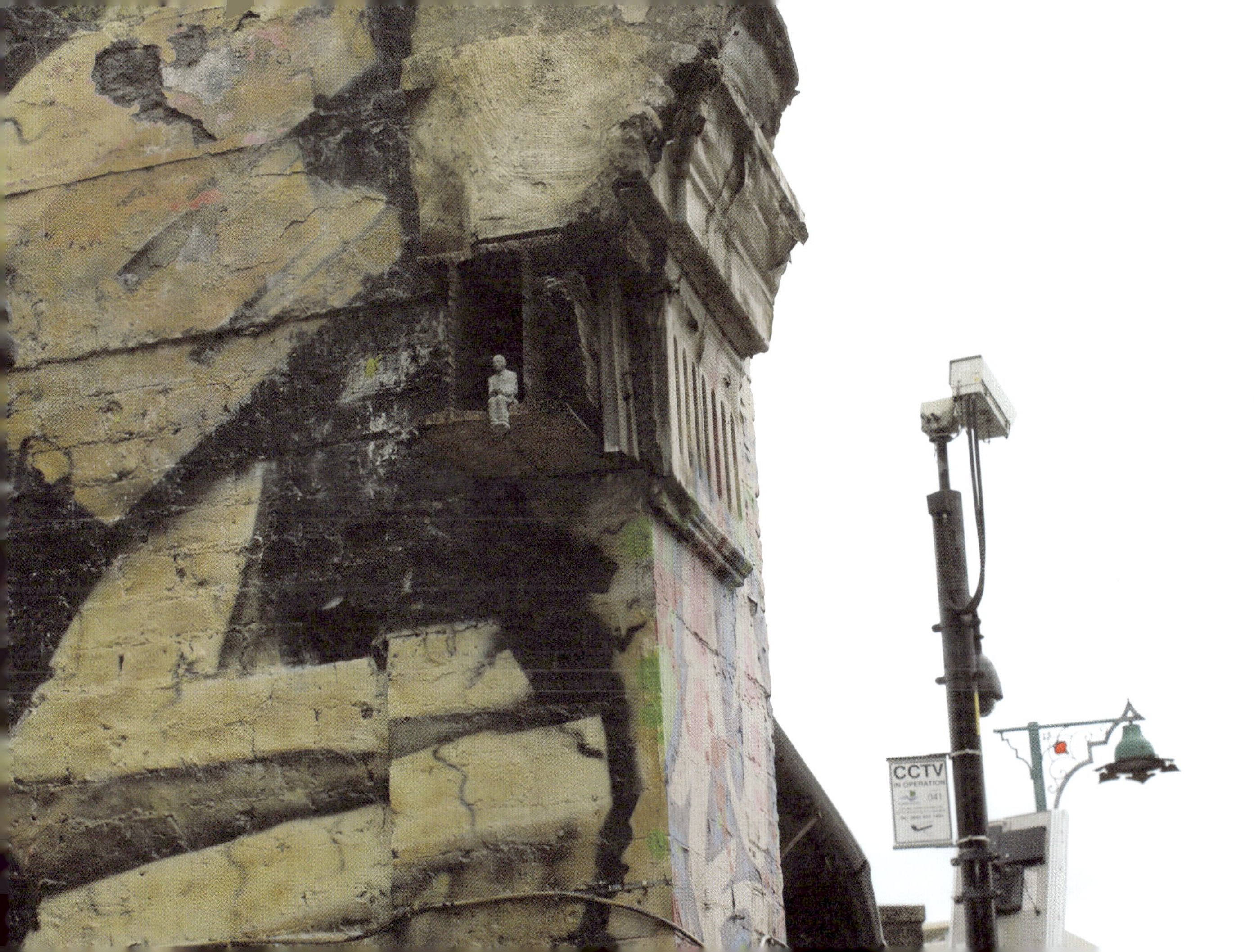

CCTV
IN OPERATION
041

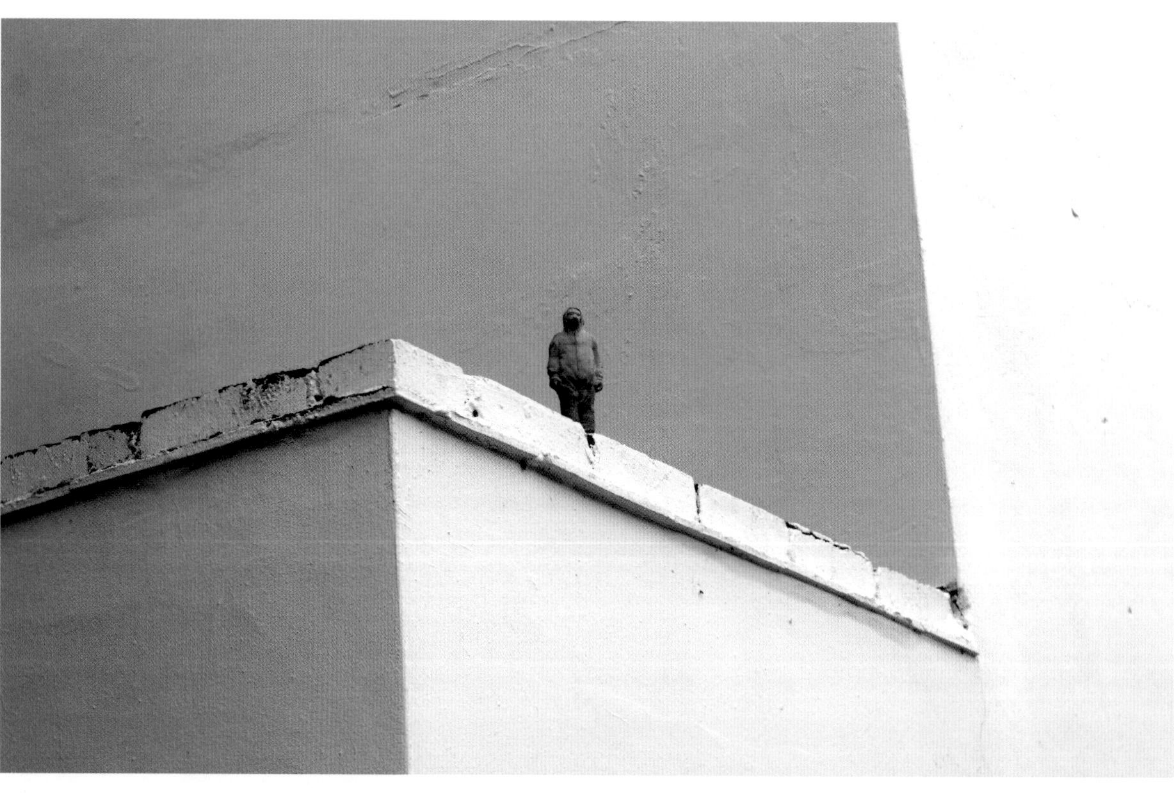

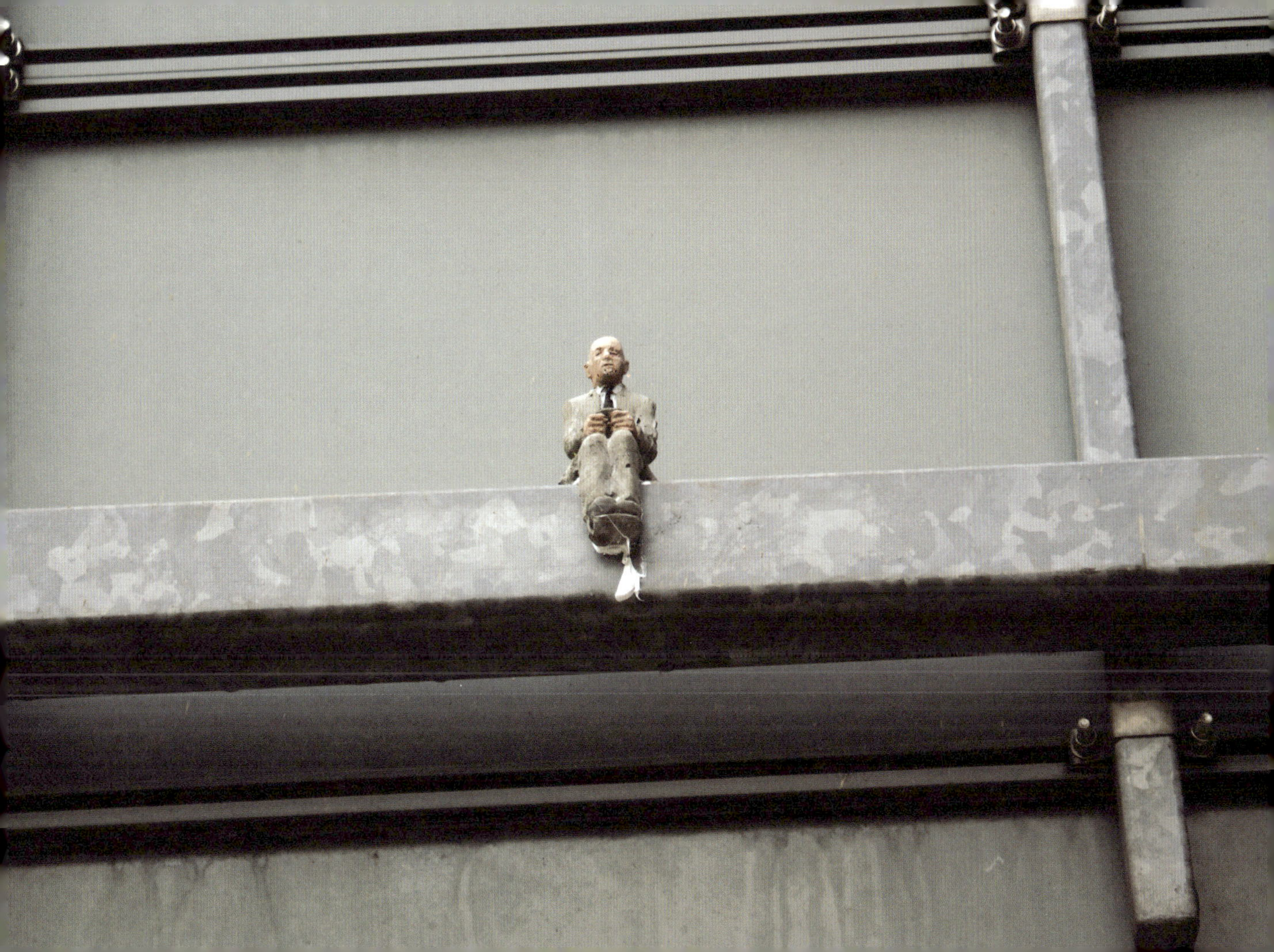

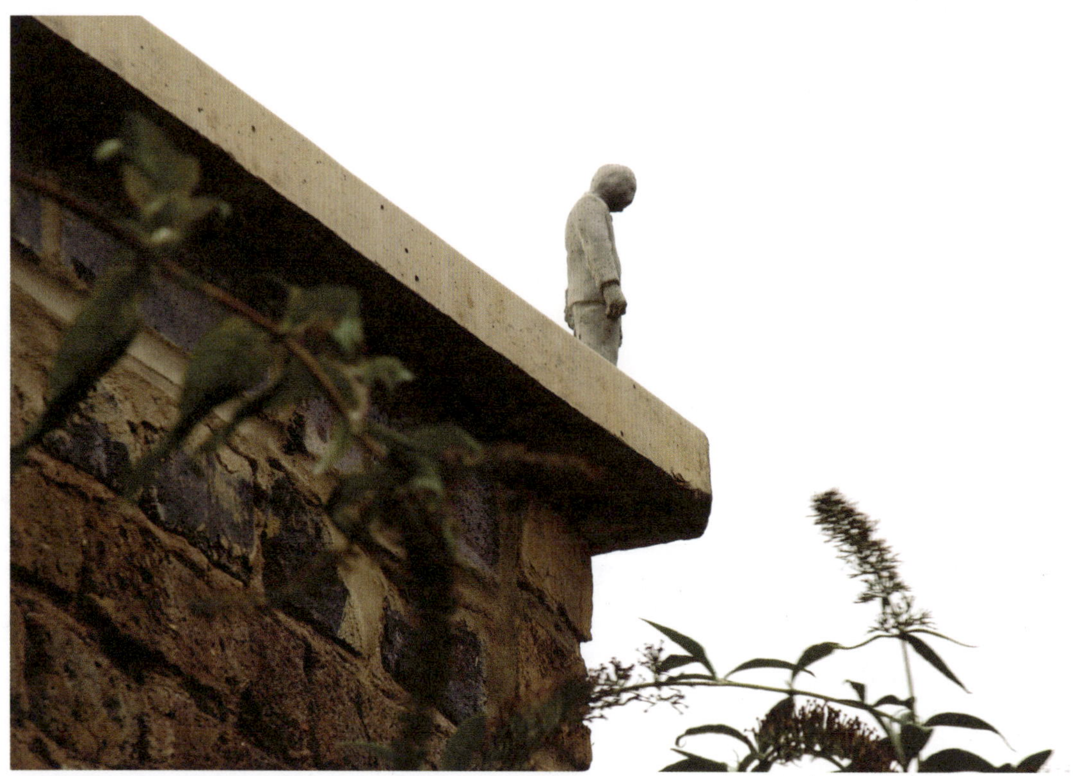

Photo by Claude Crommelin

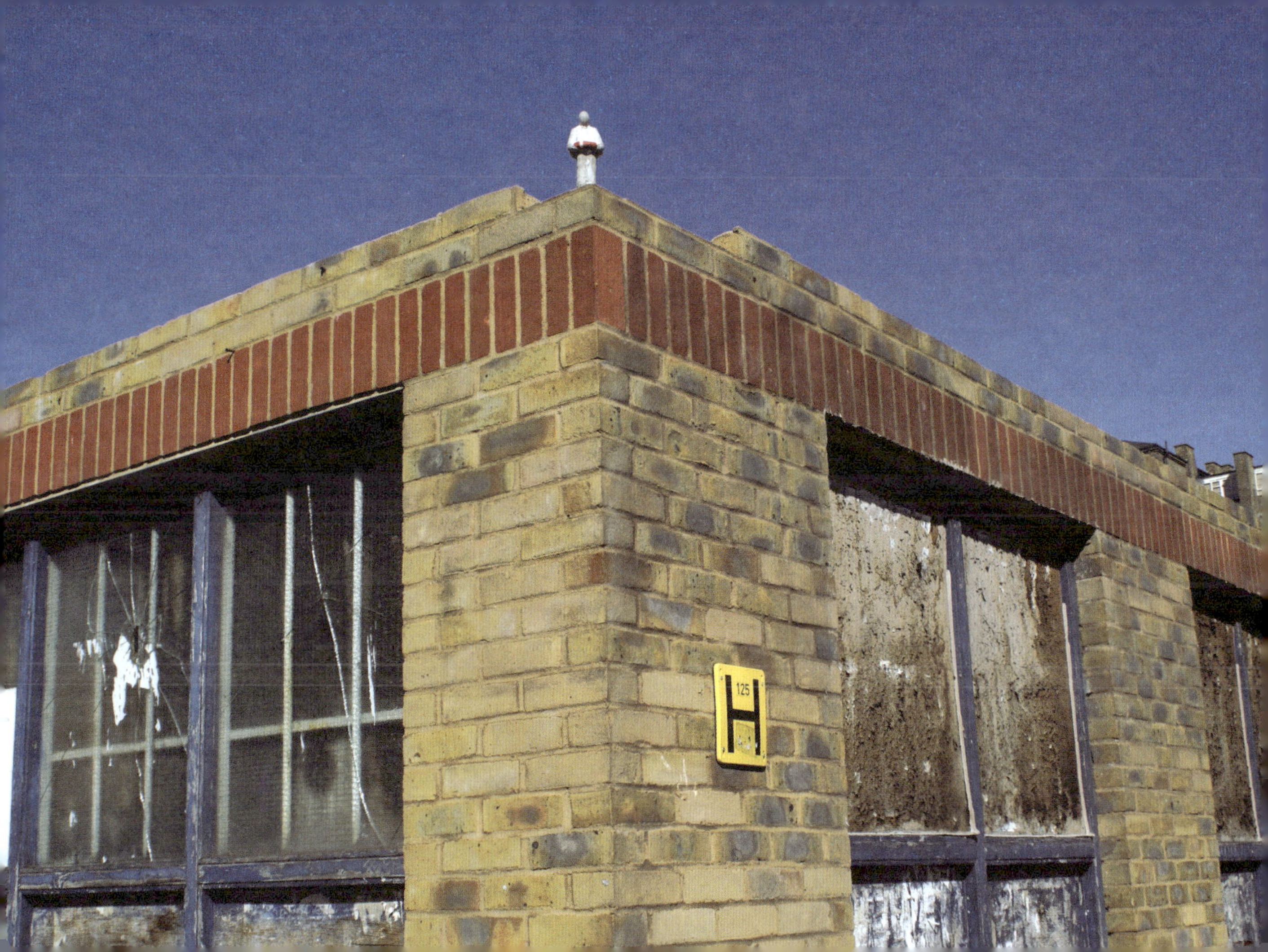
125
H

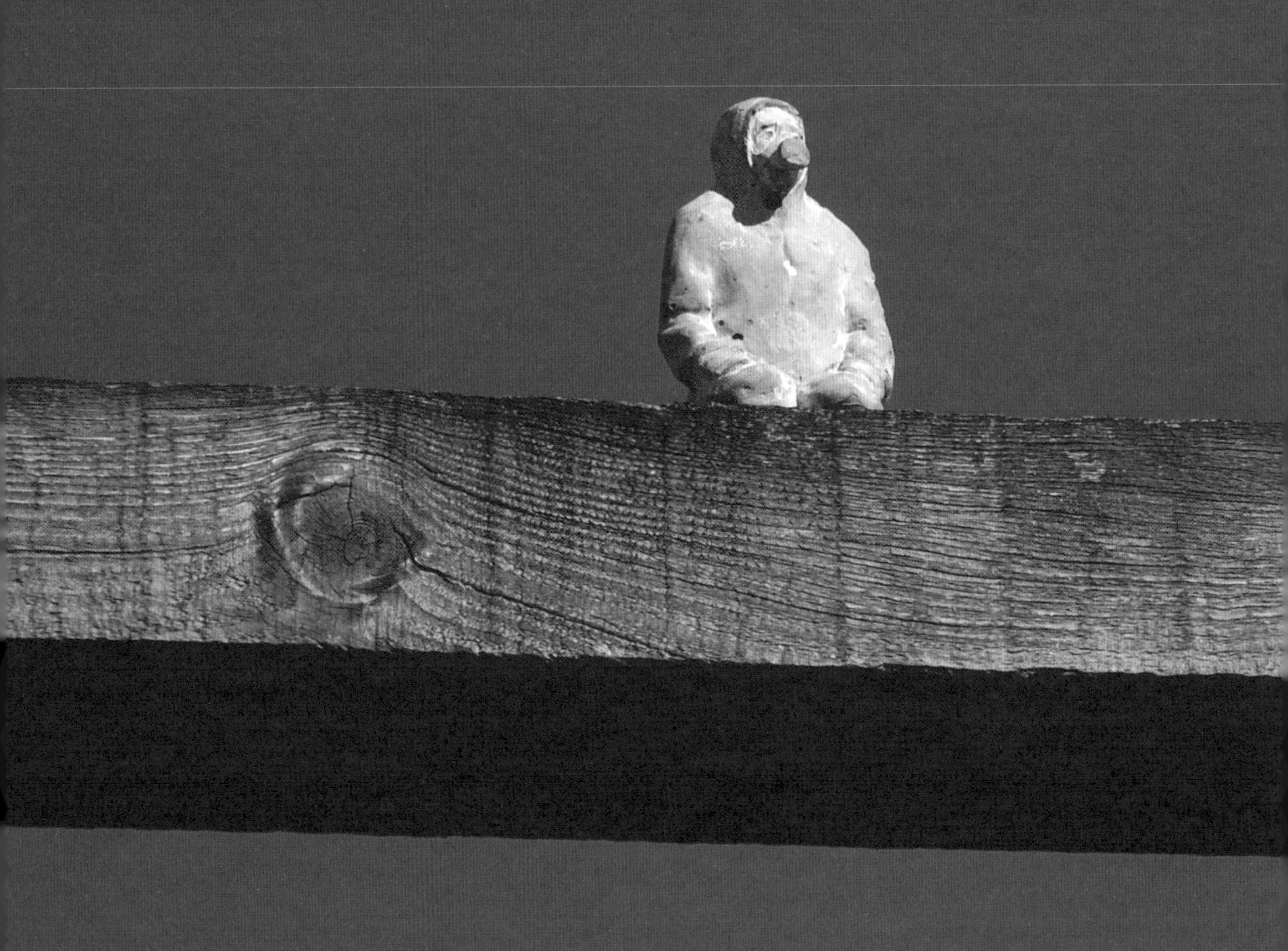

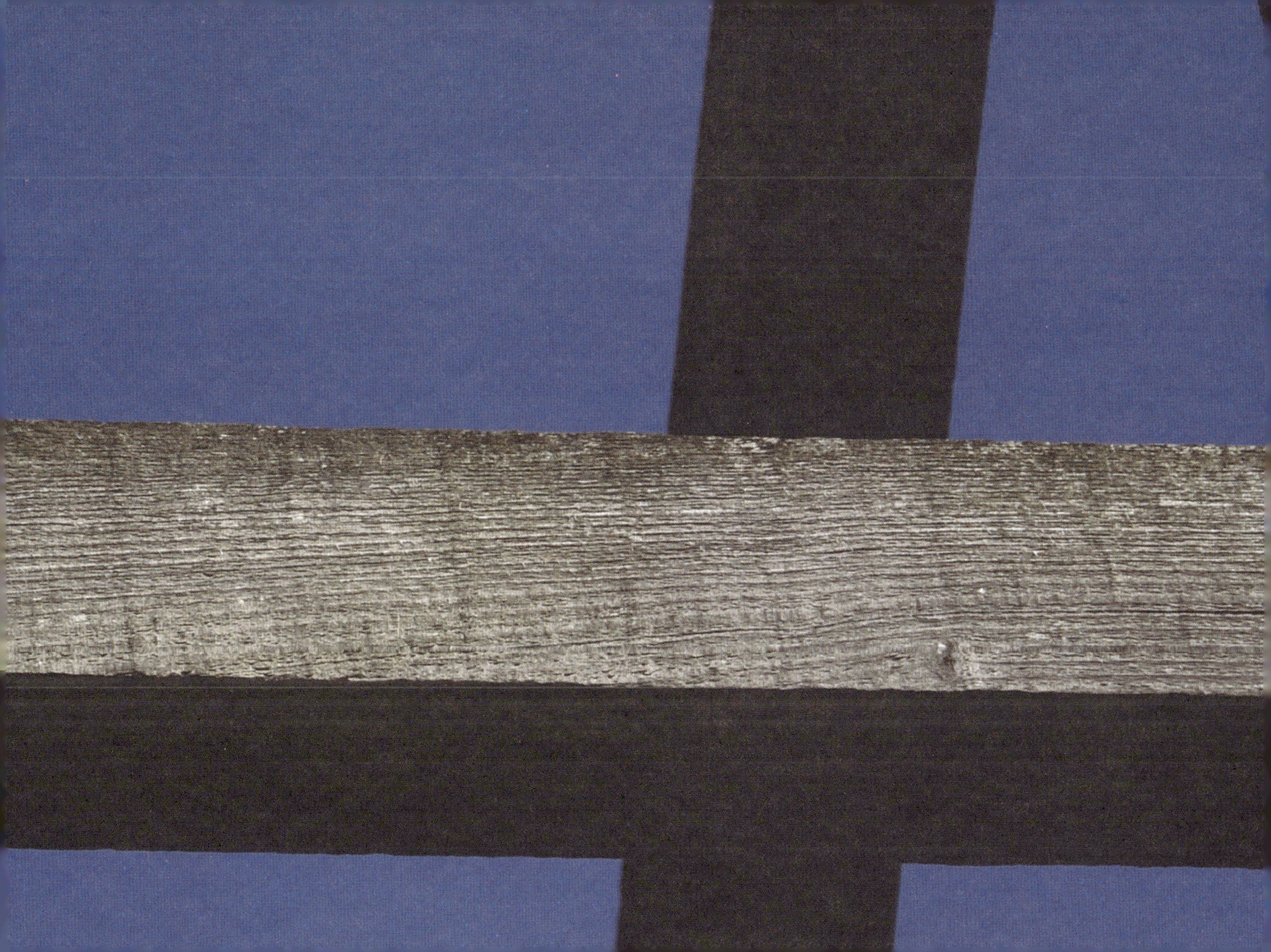

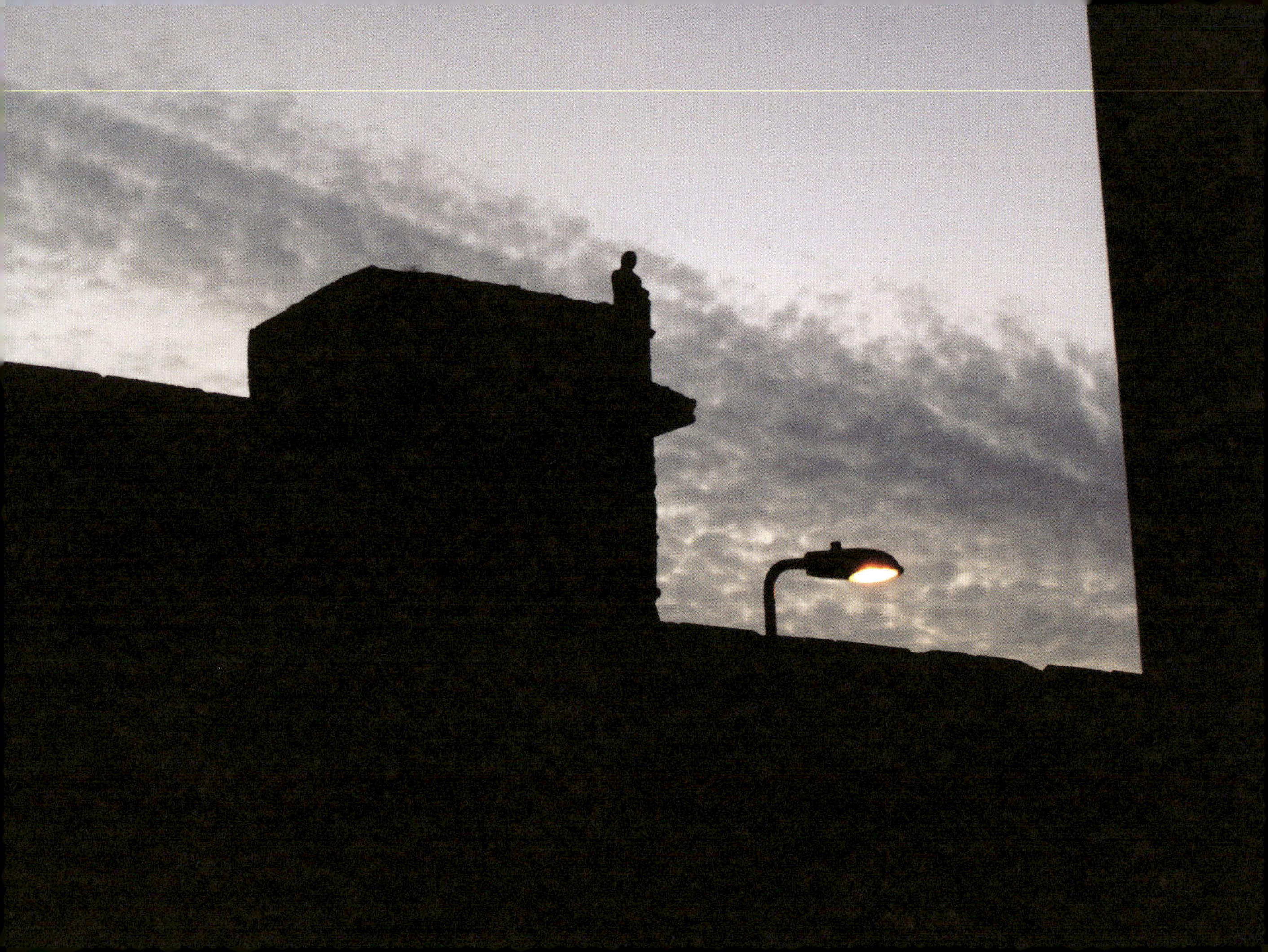

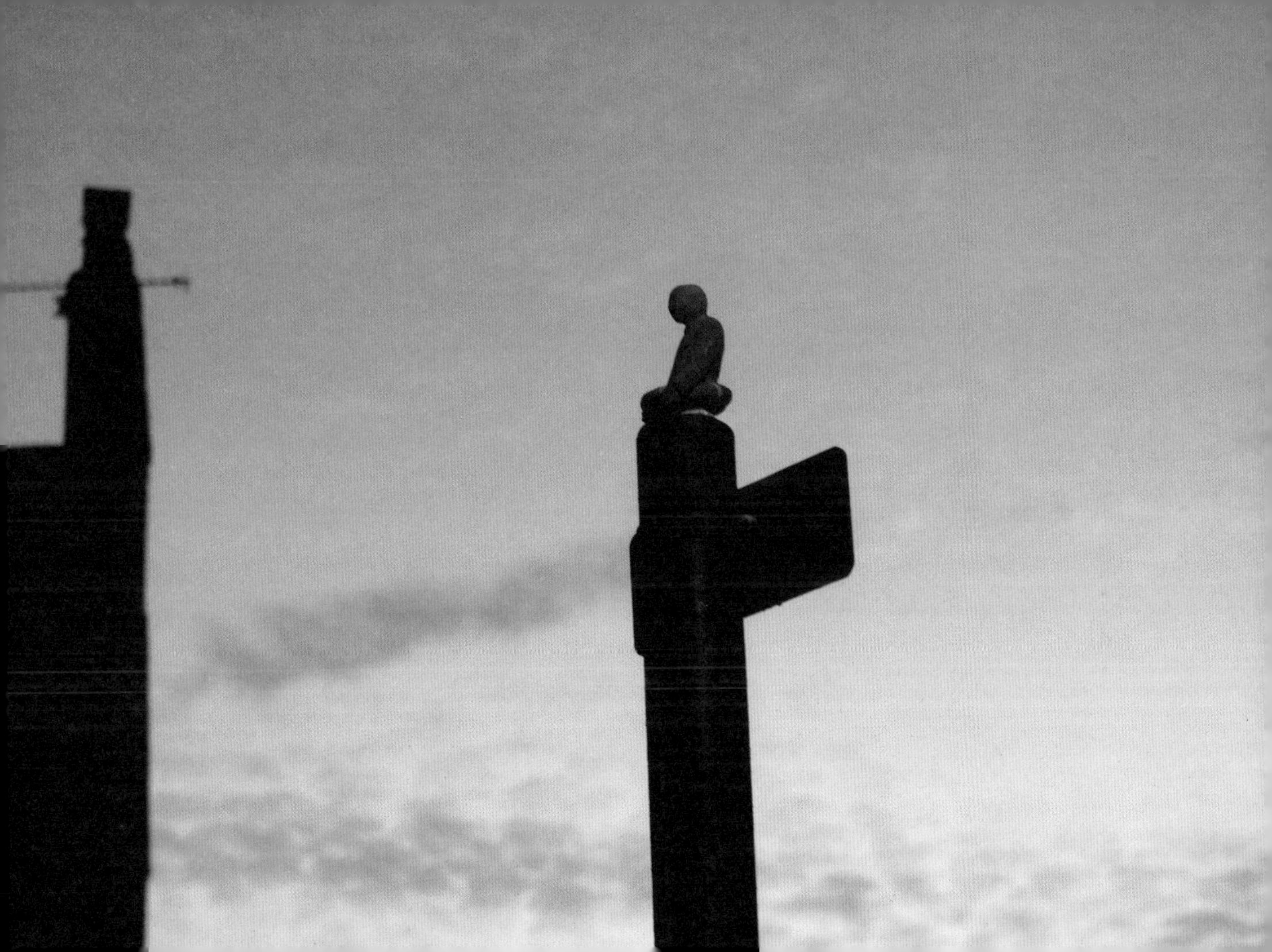

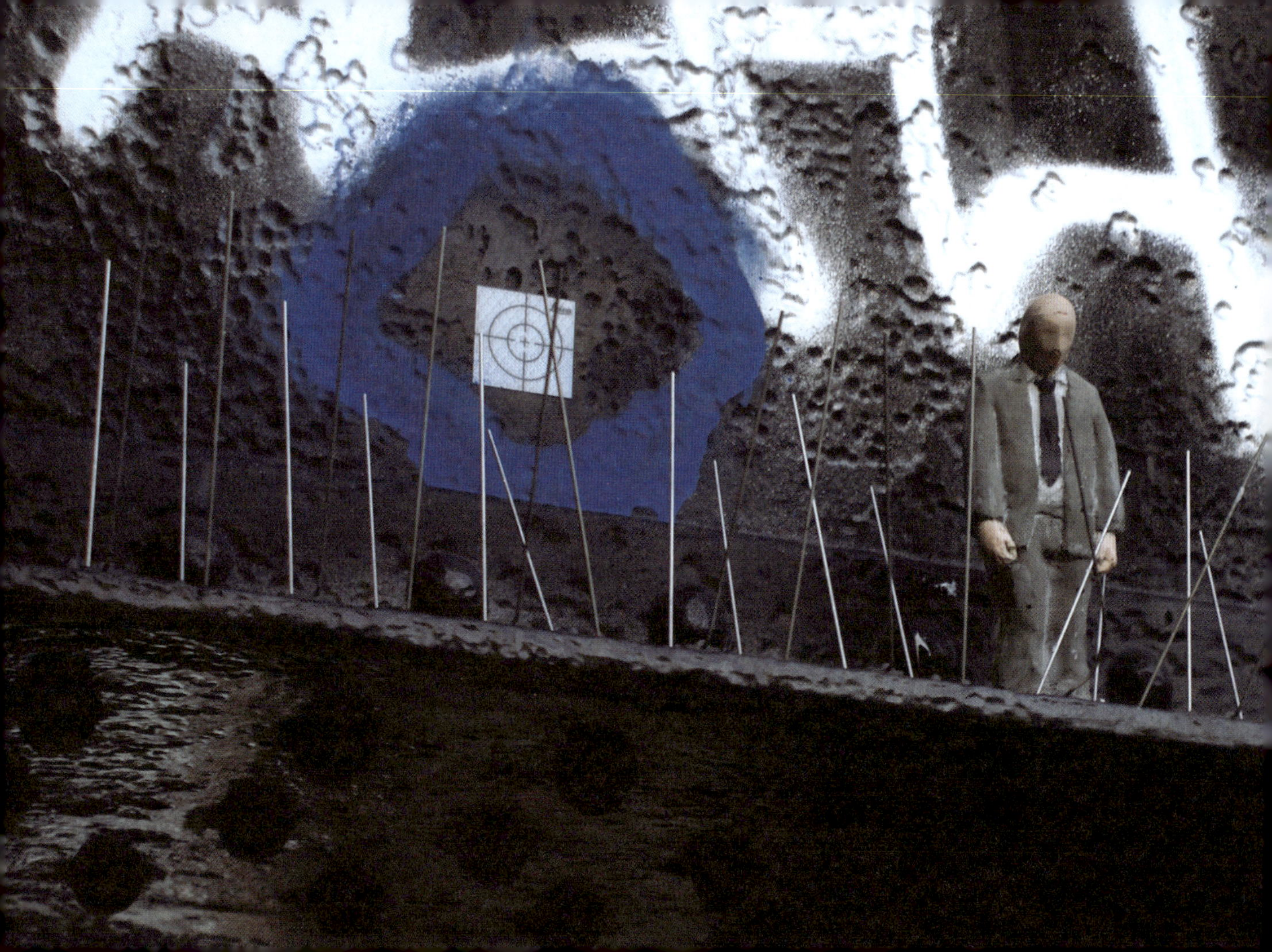

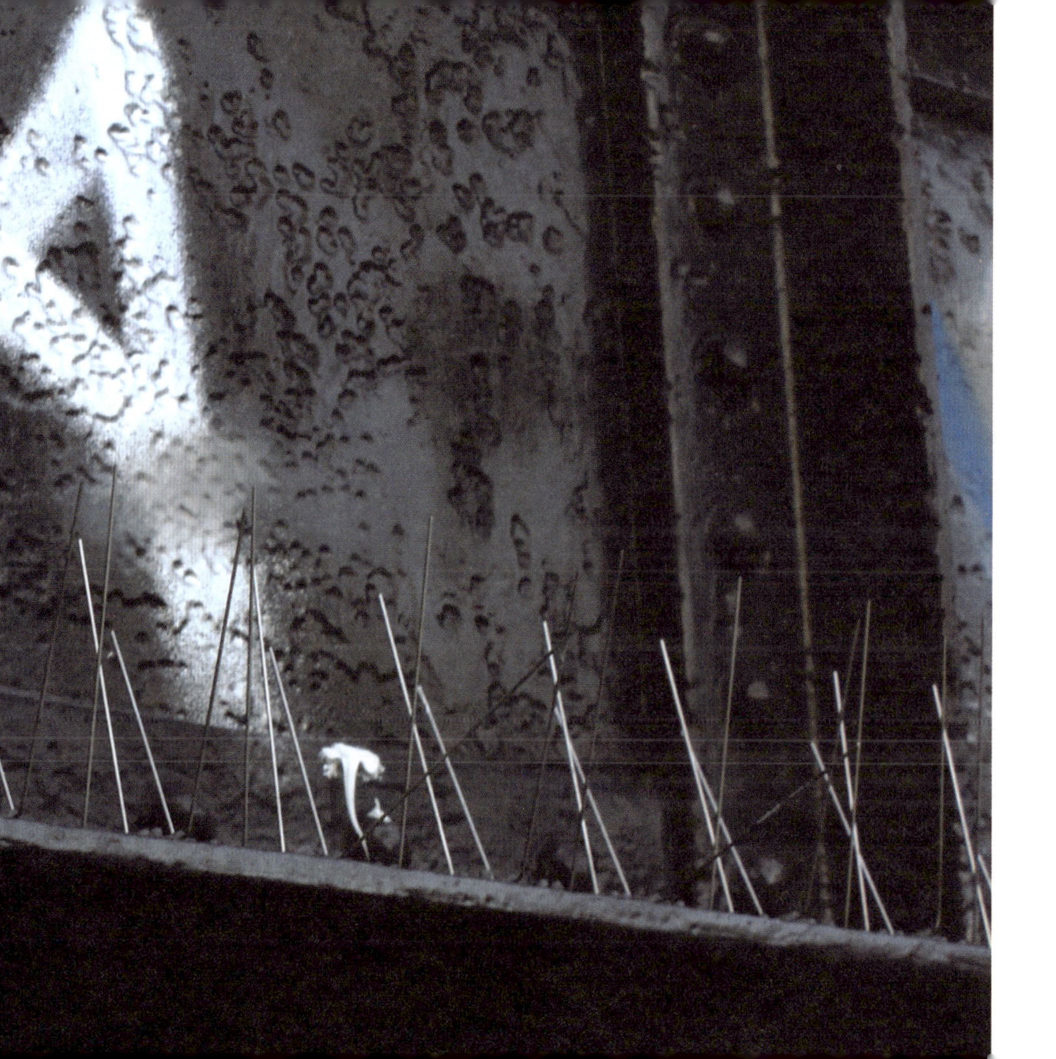

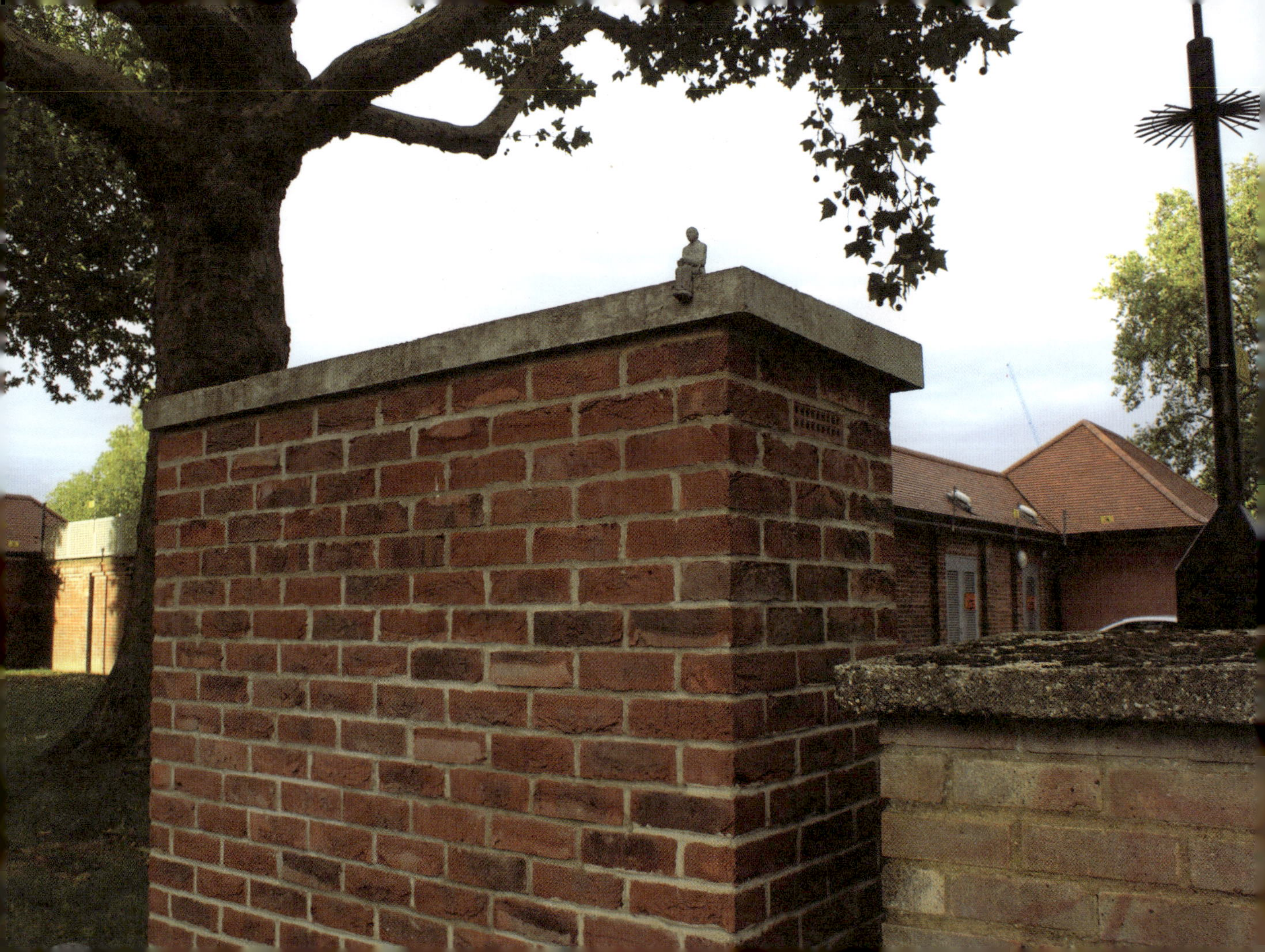

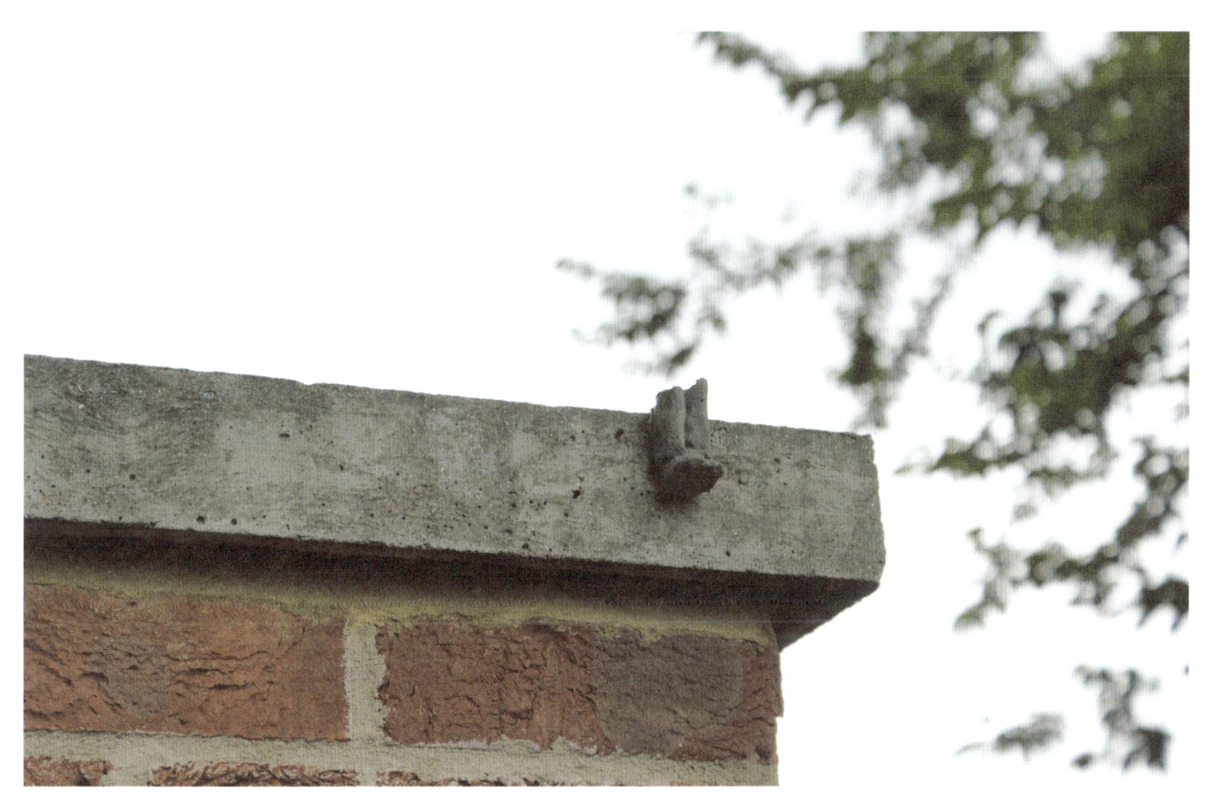

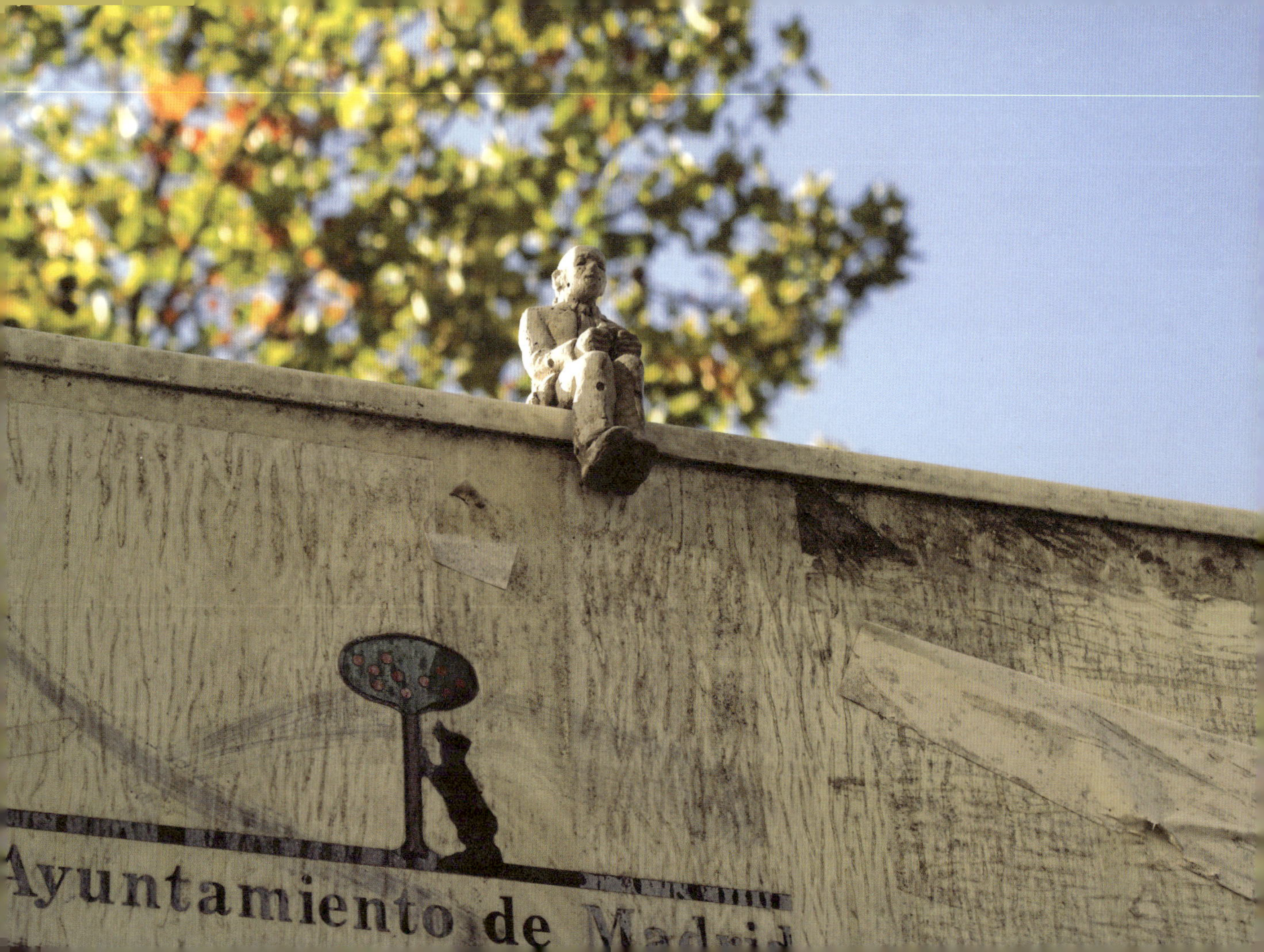

Ayuntamiento de Madrid

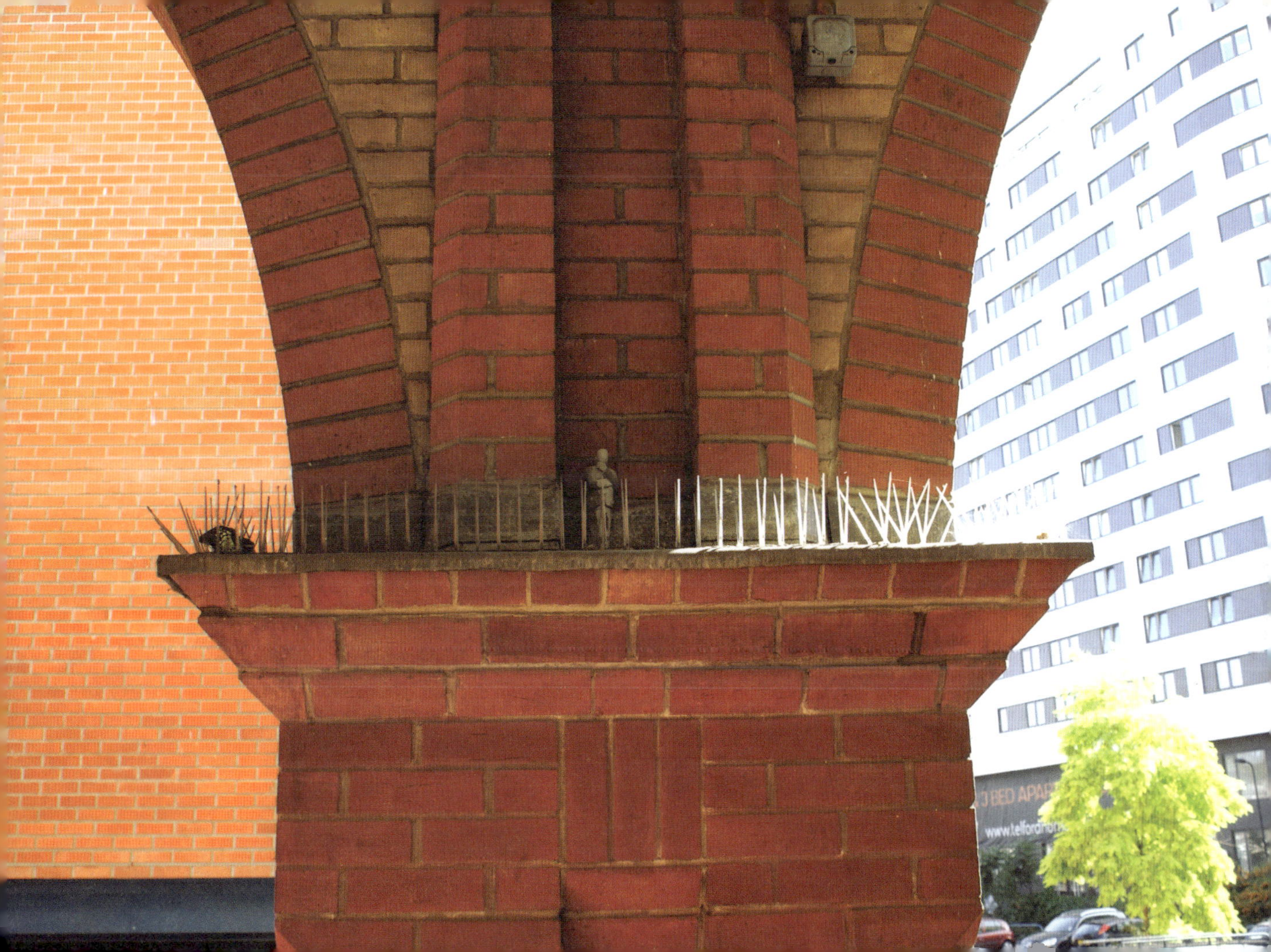

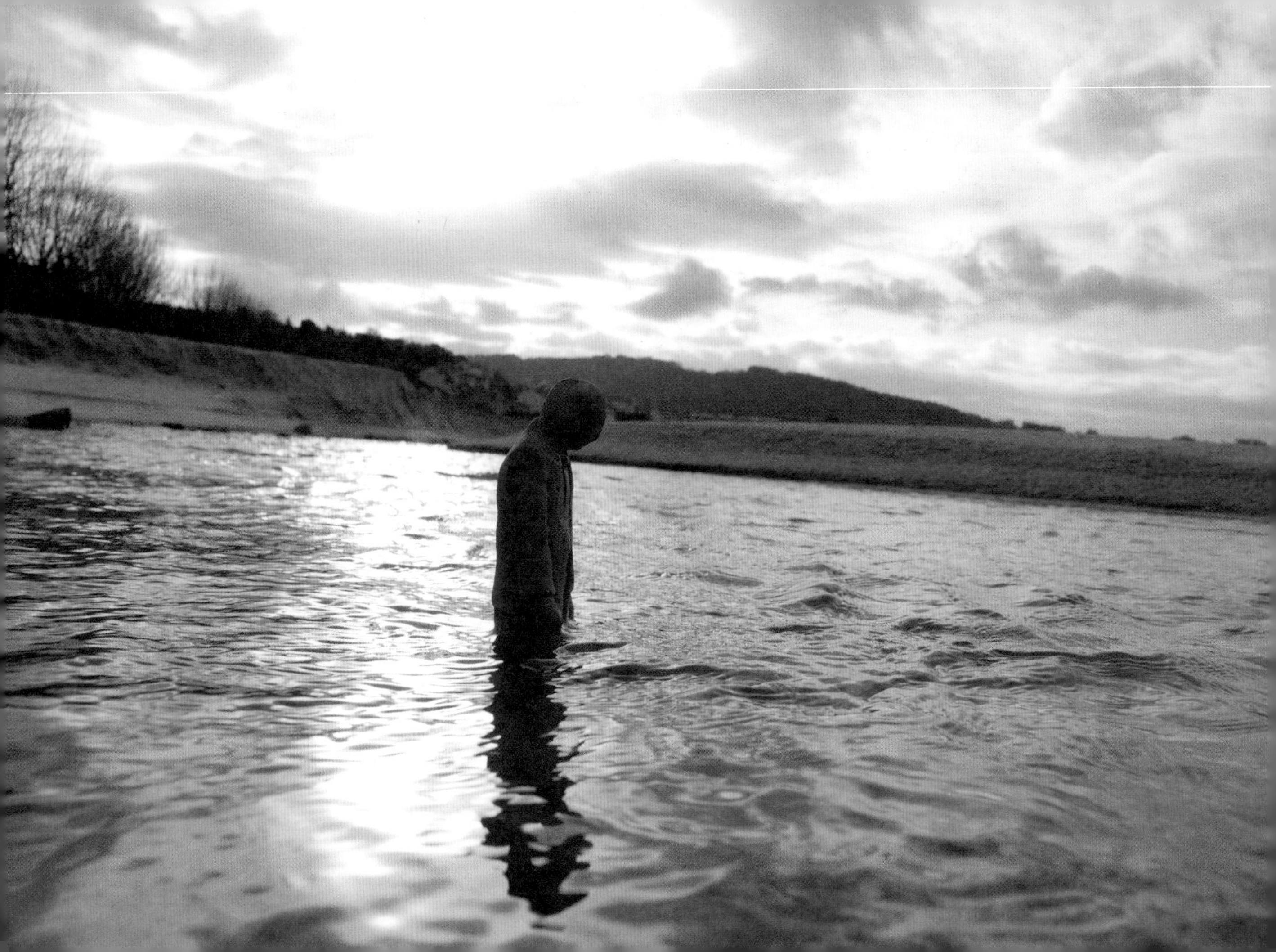

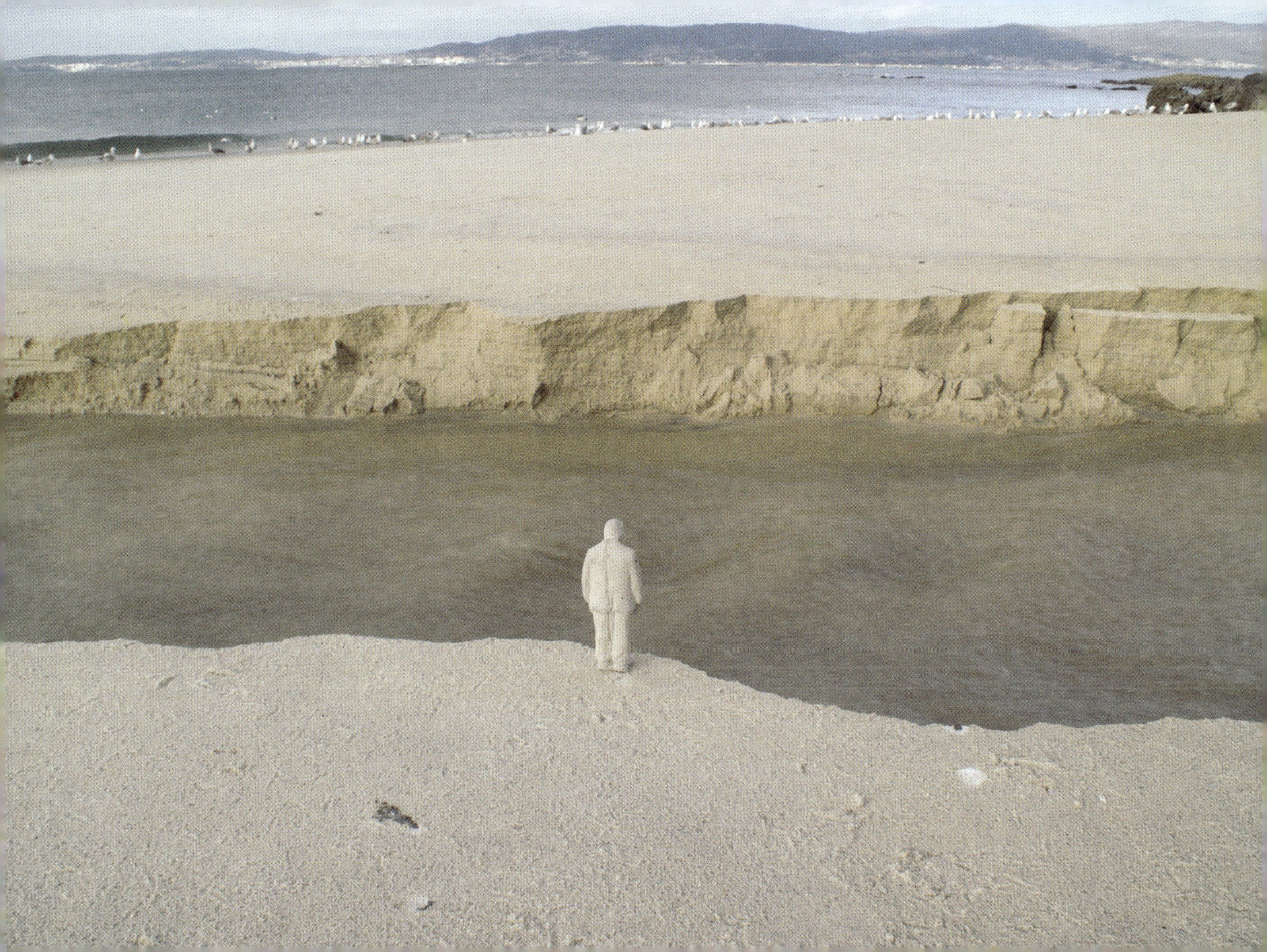

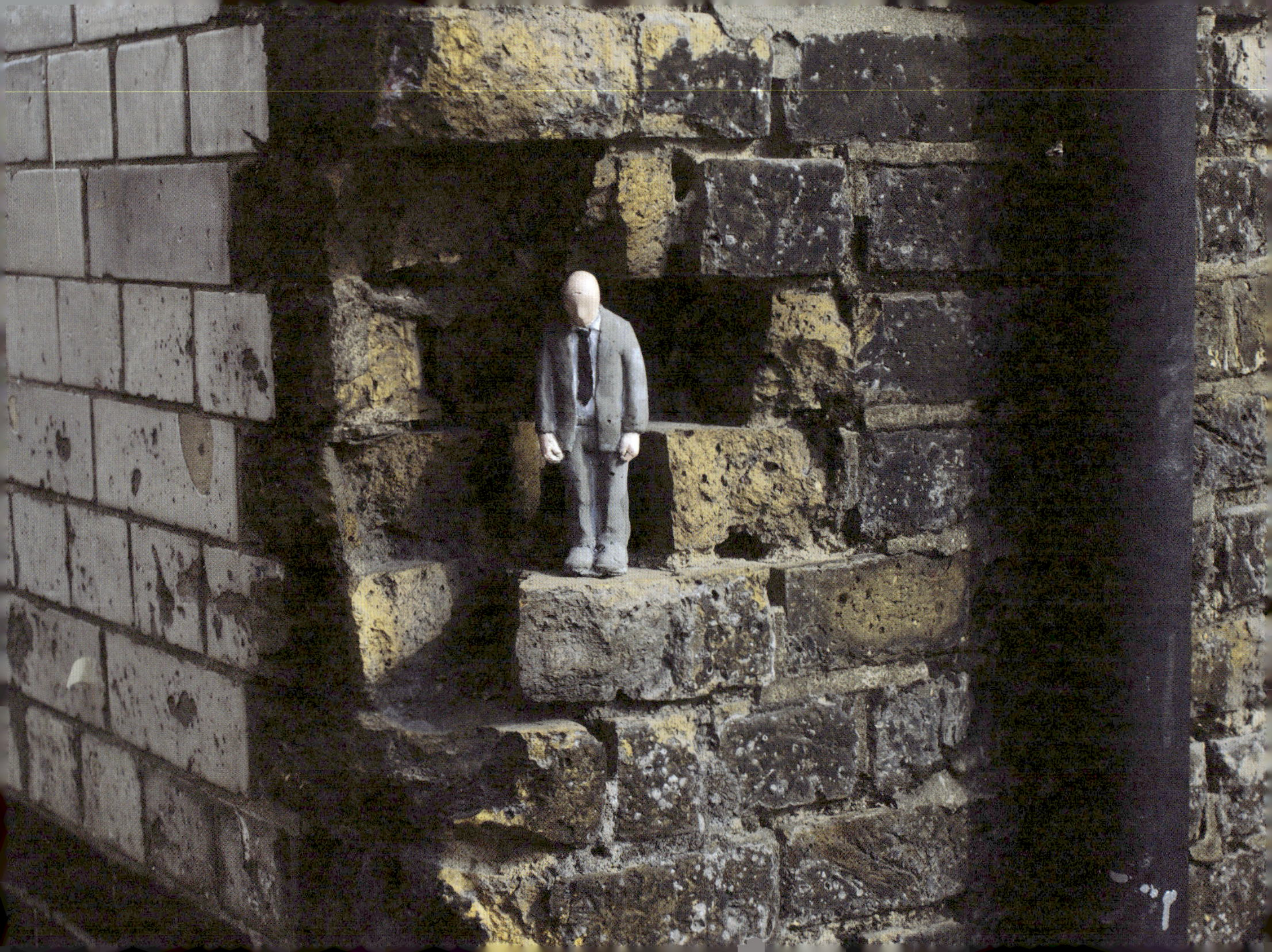

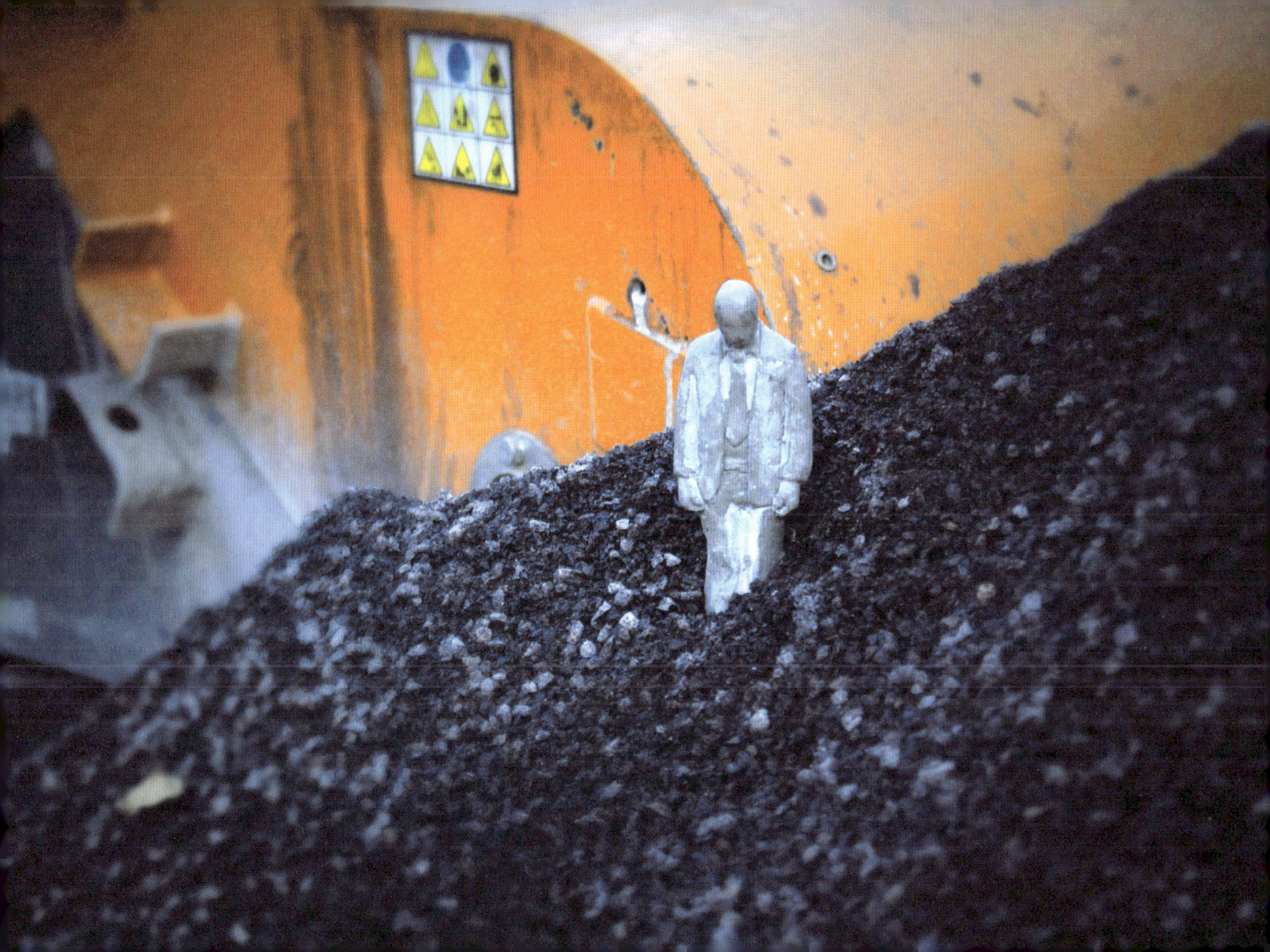

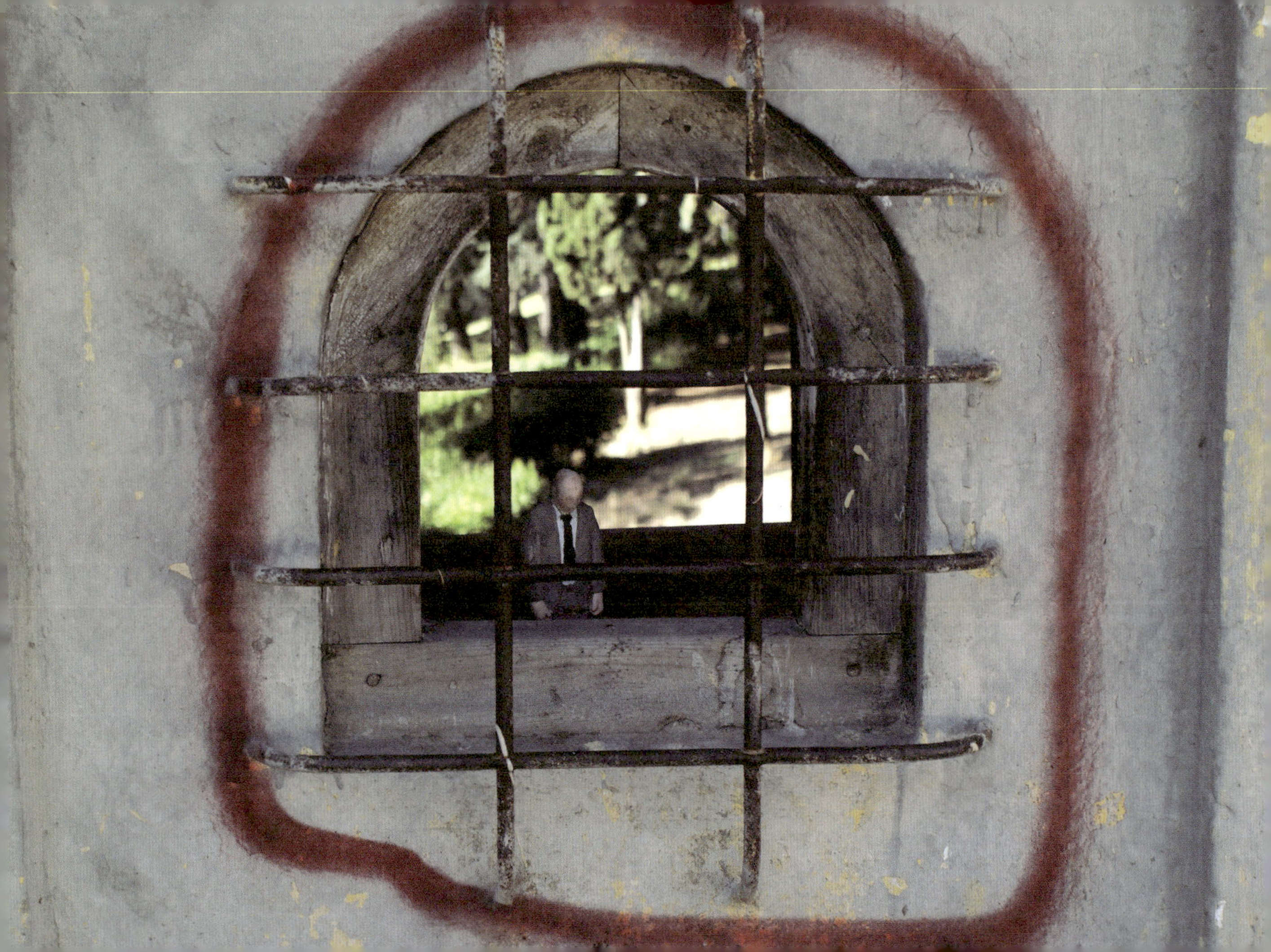

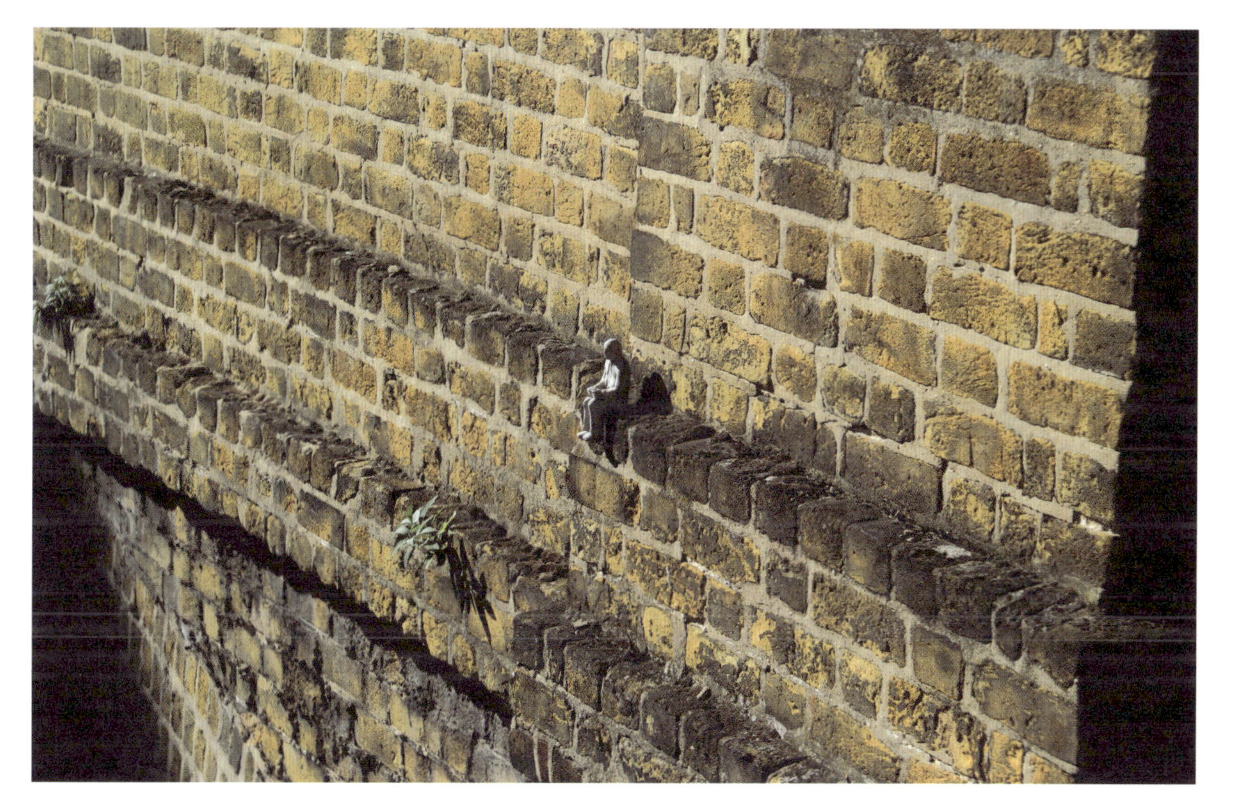

Isaac Cordal, Cement Eclipses - Concrete Avatars

Isaac Cordal works with big ideas on a small scale. His cement vignettes disrupt the cold monologue of the cityscape with interruptions of human empathy, articulated in the very language of the city itself. The lexicon of concrete, telling ambiguous short stories about the people of flesh and blood that created and in turn are created by the city.

This is melancholy work, but with a twinge of humour. Cordal places 30cm high figurines molded in cement at random locations in the city, each one engaged in a scene from some unknown play and yet each scene familiar to everyone. Cordal's figurines are 'everymen' or 'everywomen' dwarfed and vulnerable in the hard grey landscape of the contemporary city.

Their humanity is somehow emphasised and made stronger by their facelessness, their capacity to evoke emotional responses from the viewer enhanced by their visual neutrality. We don´t see the conventional tags and markers of urban identity, the hair style or the trainers, the colour of their skin. Their identity is stripped down to that which is common to all: the struggle to live a meaningful life in an urban monolith that dwarfs the concerns of individual identity and gives us nightmares of being ants or worse yet, batteries powering the senseless machines of our own making al la "The Matrix".

Maybe the concrete figures of Cordal's work are there to commemorate the physical spaces which once were the cornerstones of our social life? While our physical bodies are enfeebled and trapped at desks, lit by the ghostly light of TIT screens and held firmly in place by the sea of data that transfixes us like cats staring at birds through a window, outside the artist is shuffling about with his hood up, paying a reverential and quietly symbolic tribute to the world that once was, the world of the physical body in space.

Perhaps these grey men and women are simulacra (ghosts) showing us what has become of our physical selves now we are almost, but not quite, divorced from them. They are the children lost in the custody battle between our incandescently beautiful digital selves and the dull, fleshy body that tenaciously hangs on to us, crumpled into a chair with a complaining spine and a ceaseless cycle of needs to interrupt our second lives with.

Nevertheless, it is the simple open endedness of the little narratives that you will find in these images that endures. The artist invites you to interpret each scene and involve yourself in the story which instantly makes you a part of the work. When you discover them, they change you, or perhaps better said – they make you aware of changes that are already taking place within us all.

Of course that doesn´t mean you can't laugh. When the Buddha transcended the physical realm he was laughing. He's still laughing now.

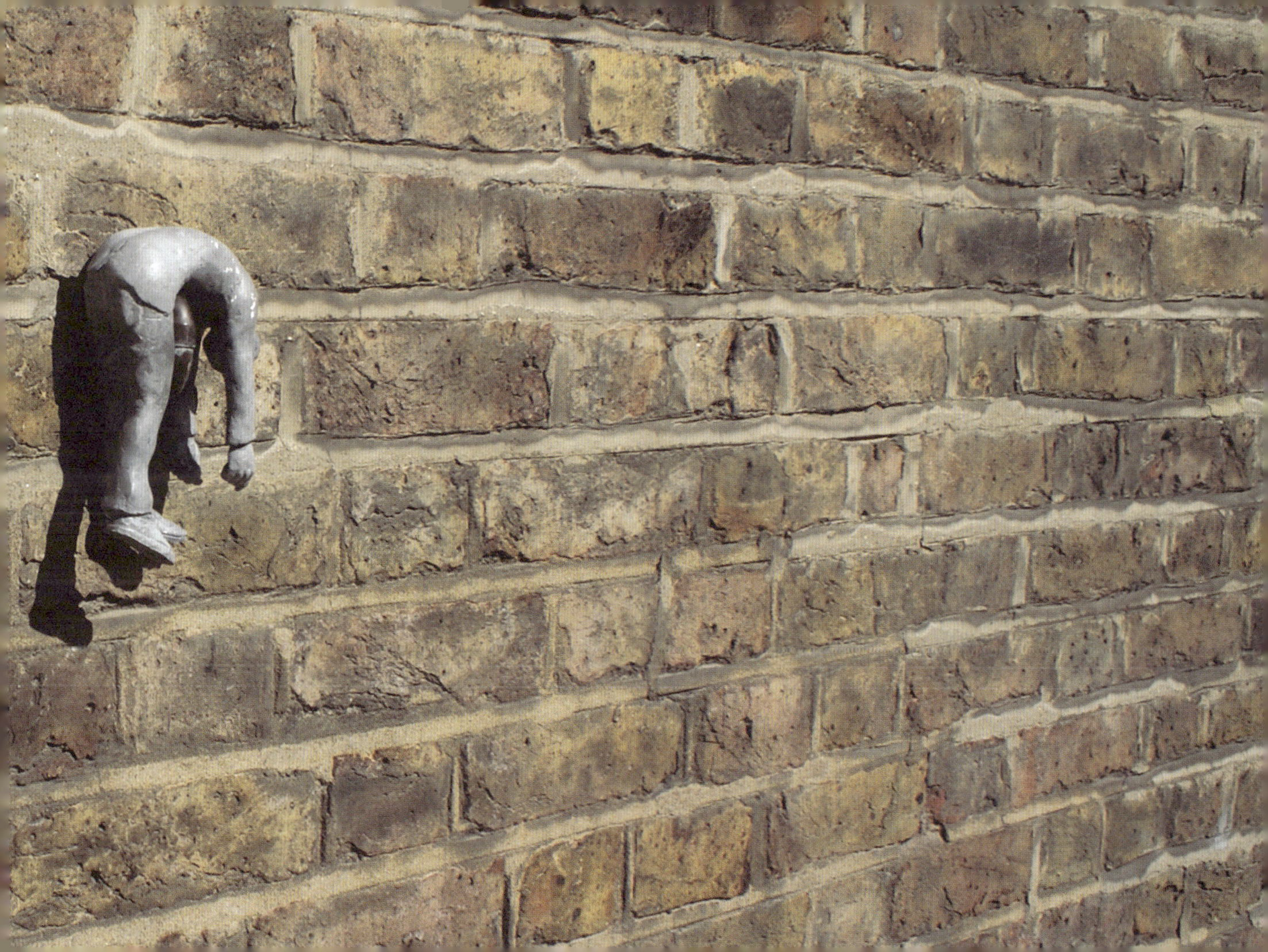

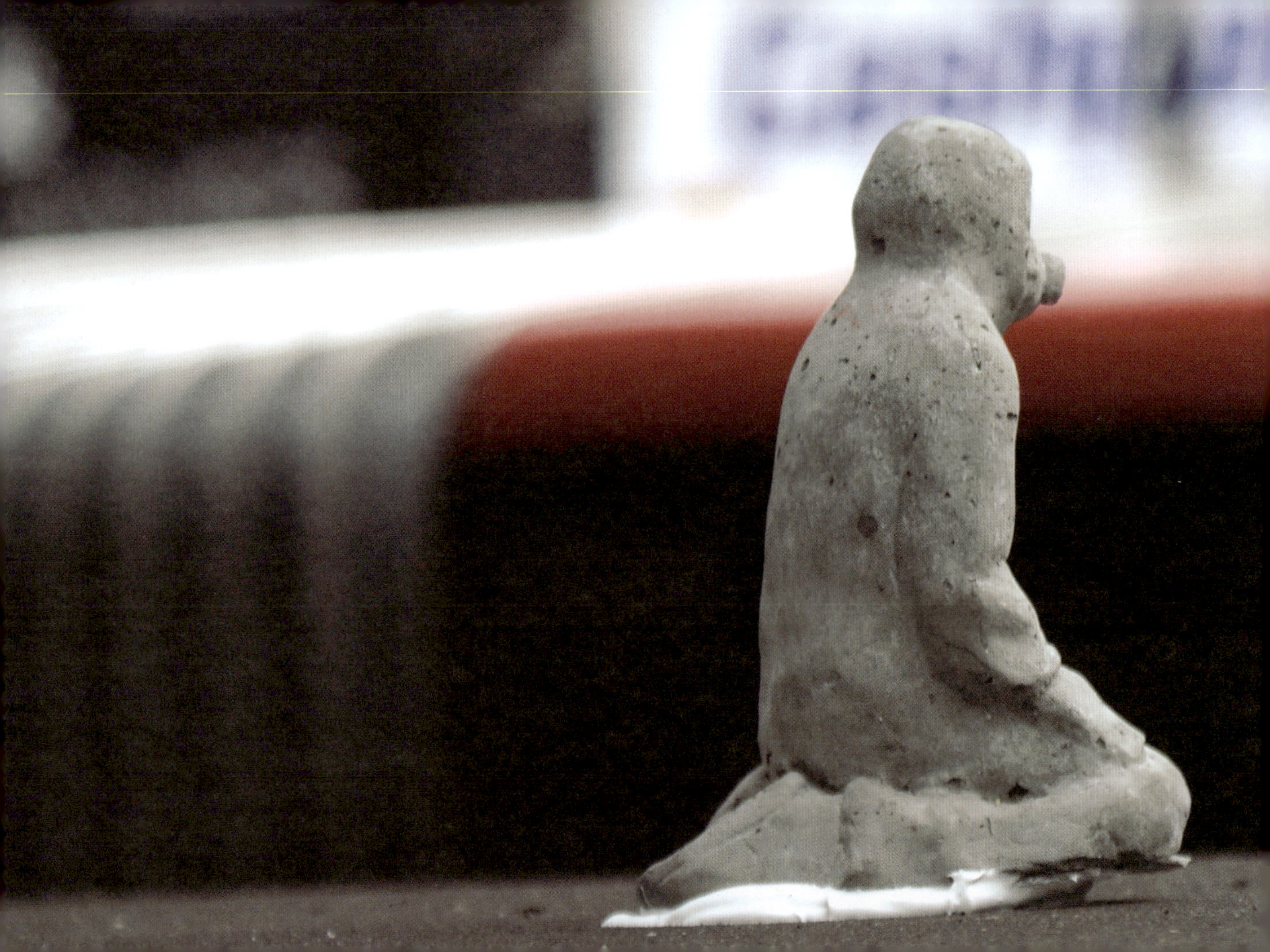

BUS STOPS LDN

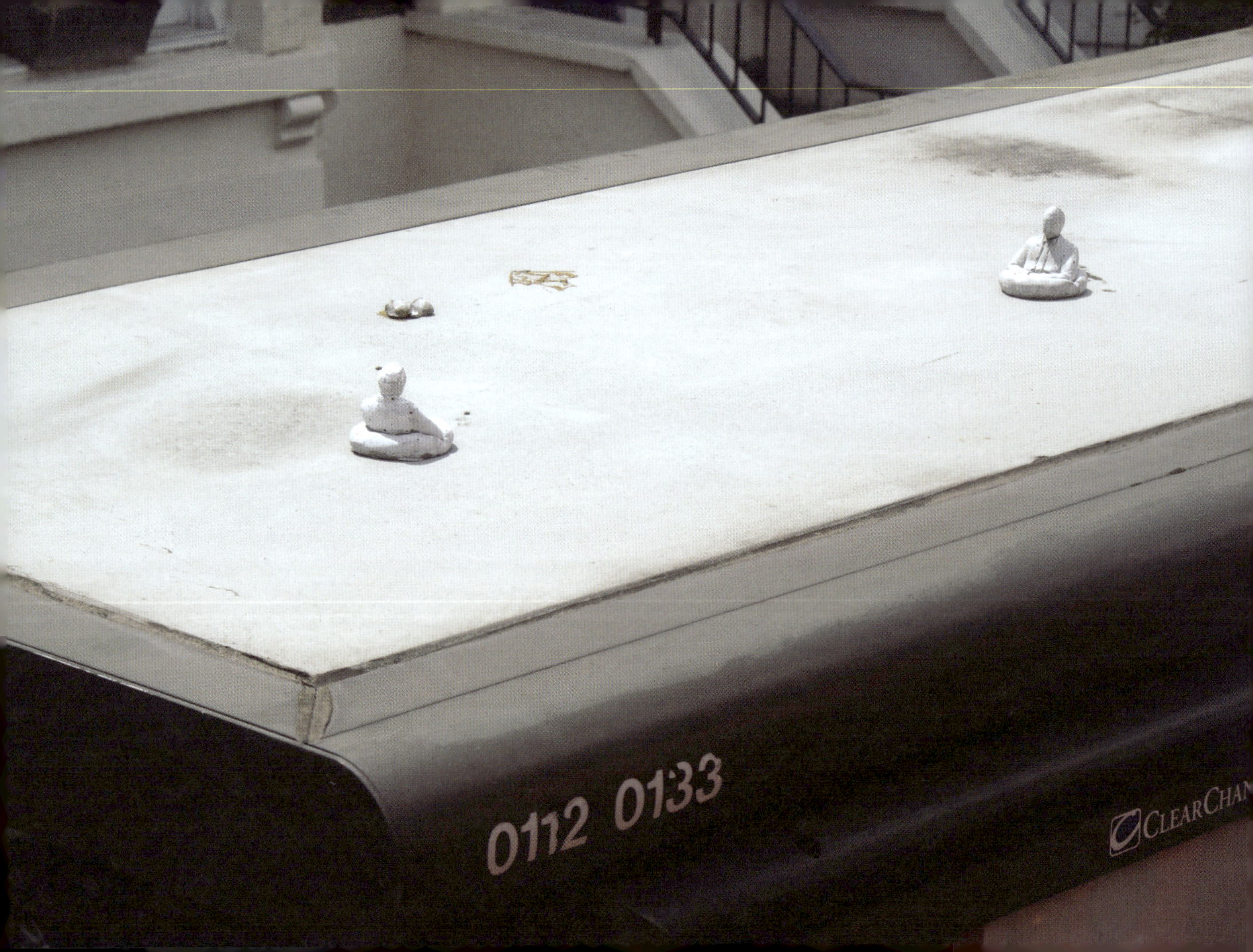

0112 0133
ClearChannel

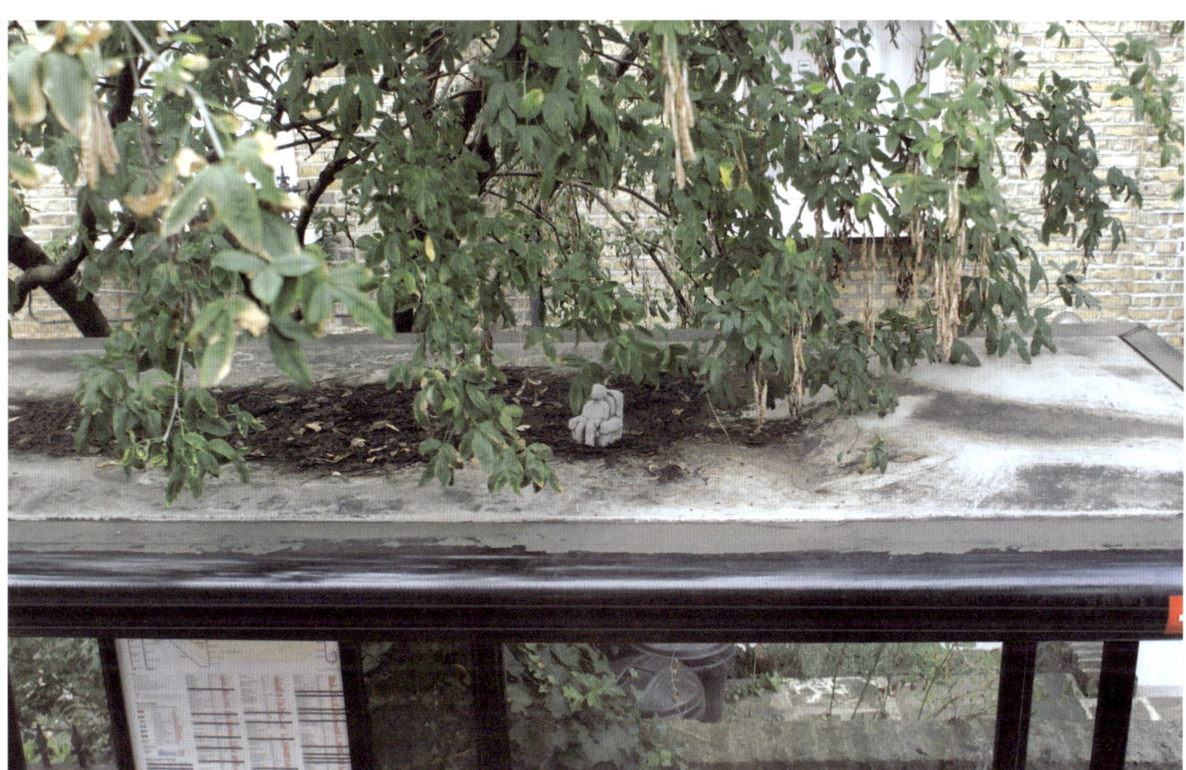

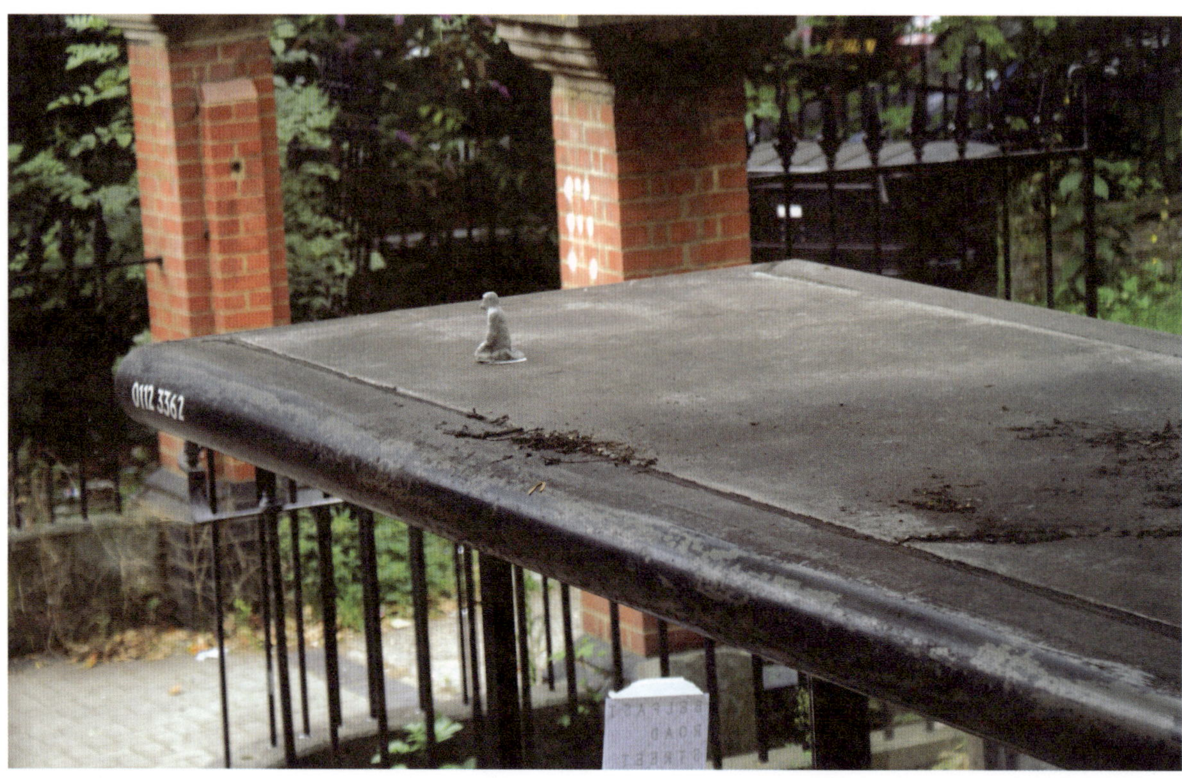

0112 3362

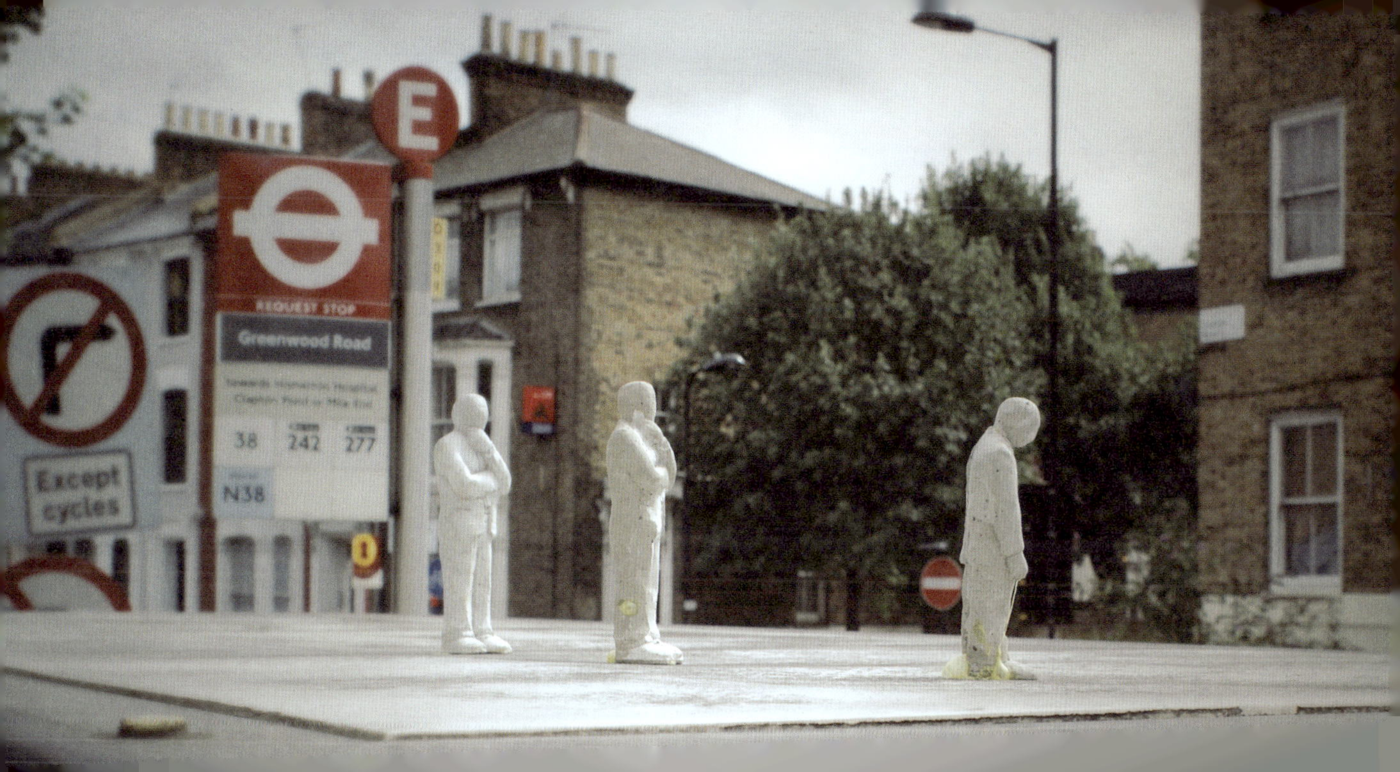
E
REQUEST STOP
Greenwood Road
38 242 277
N38
Except cycles

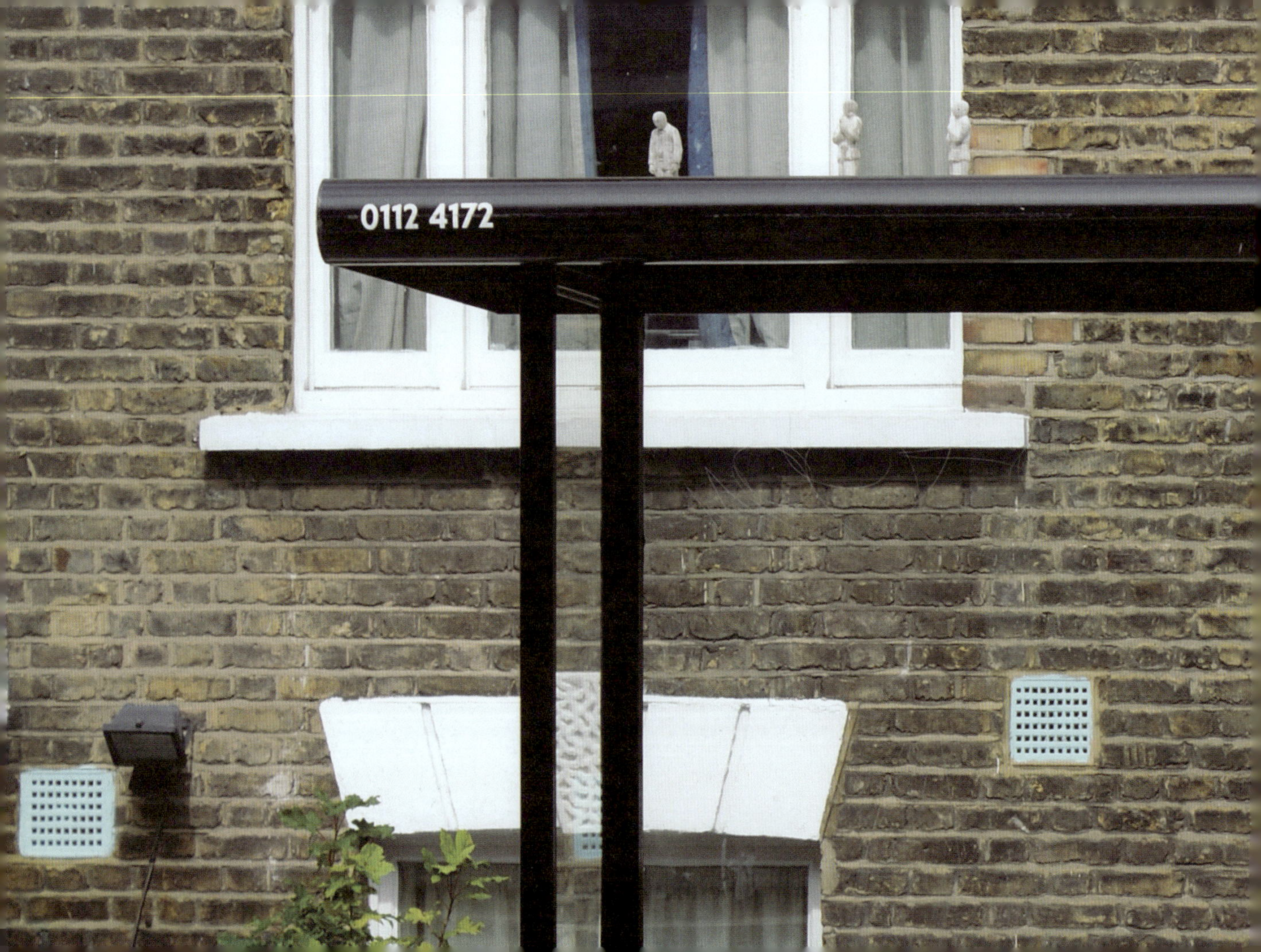
0112 4172

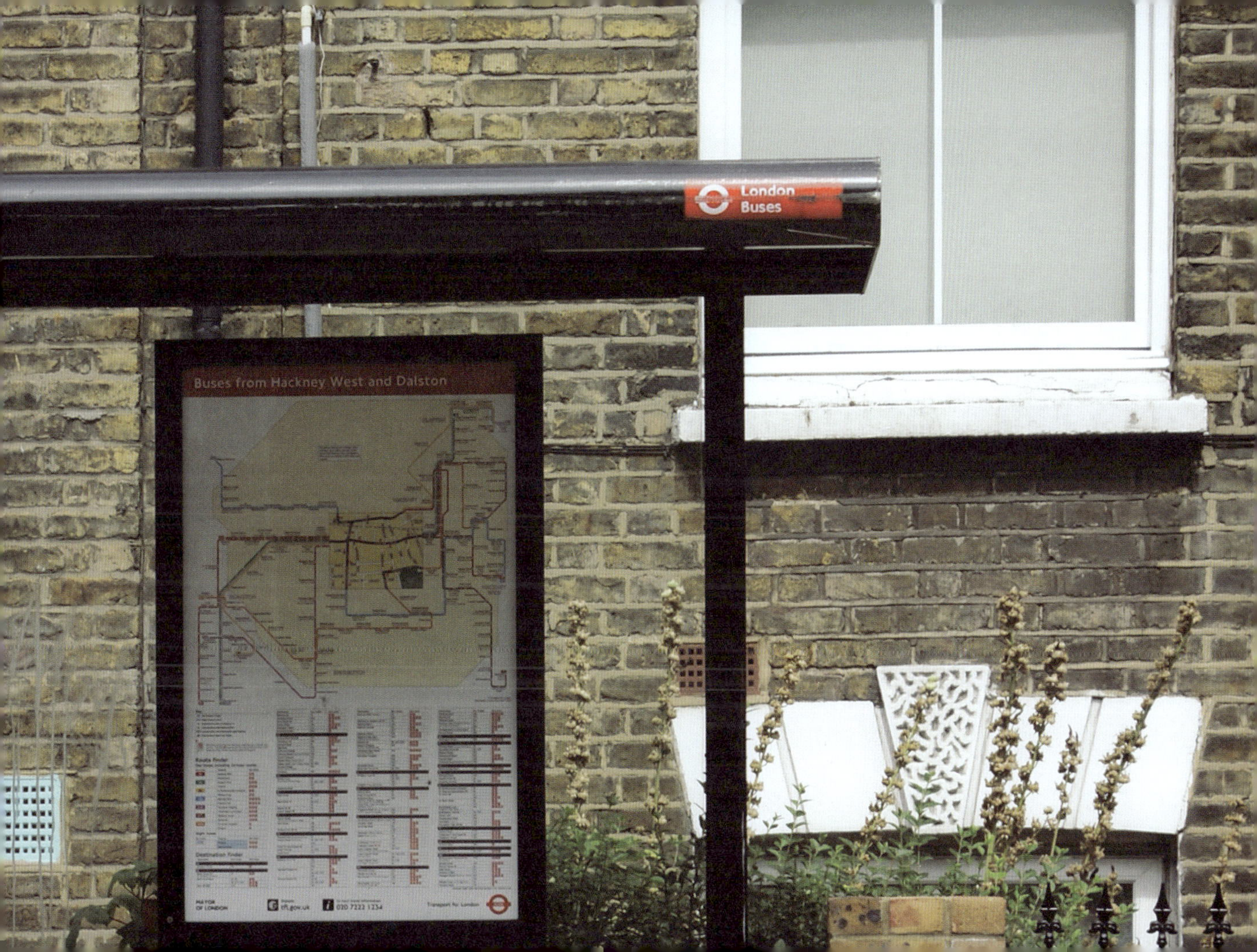
London
Buses
Buses from Hackney West and Dalston

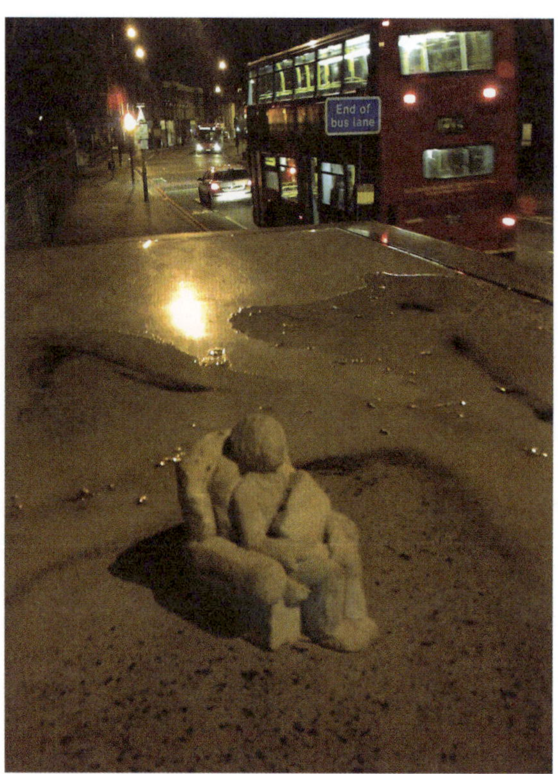

Photo by Zai Tang with a mobile phone

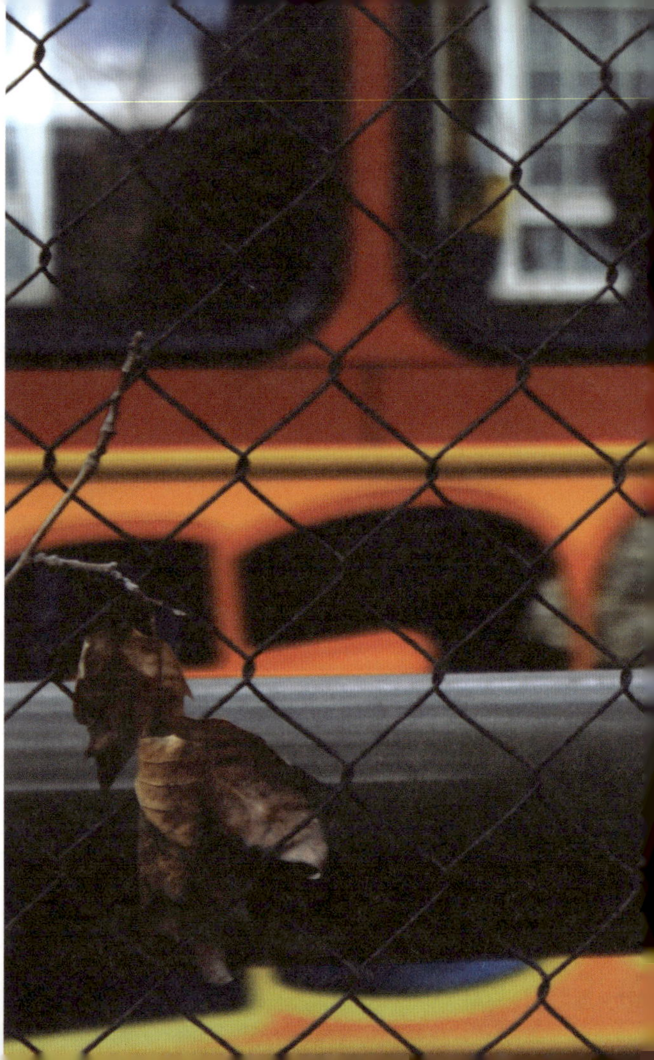

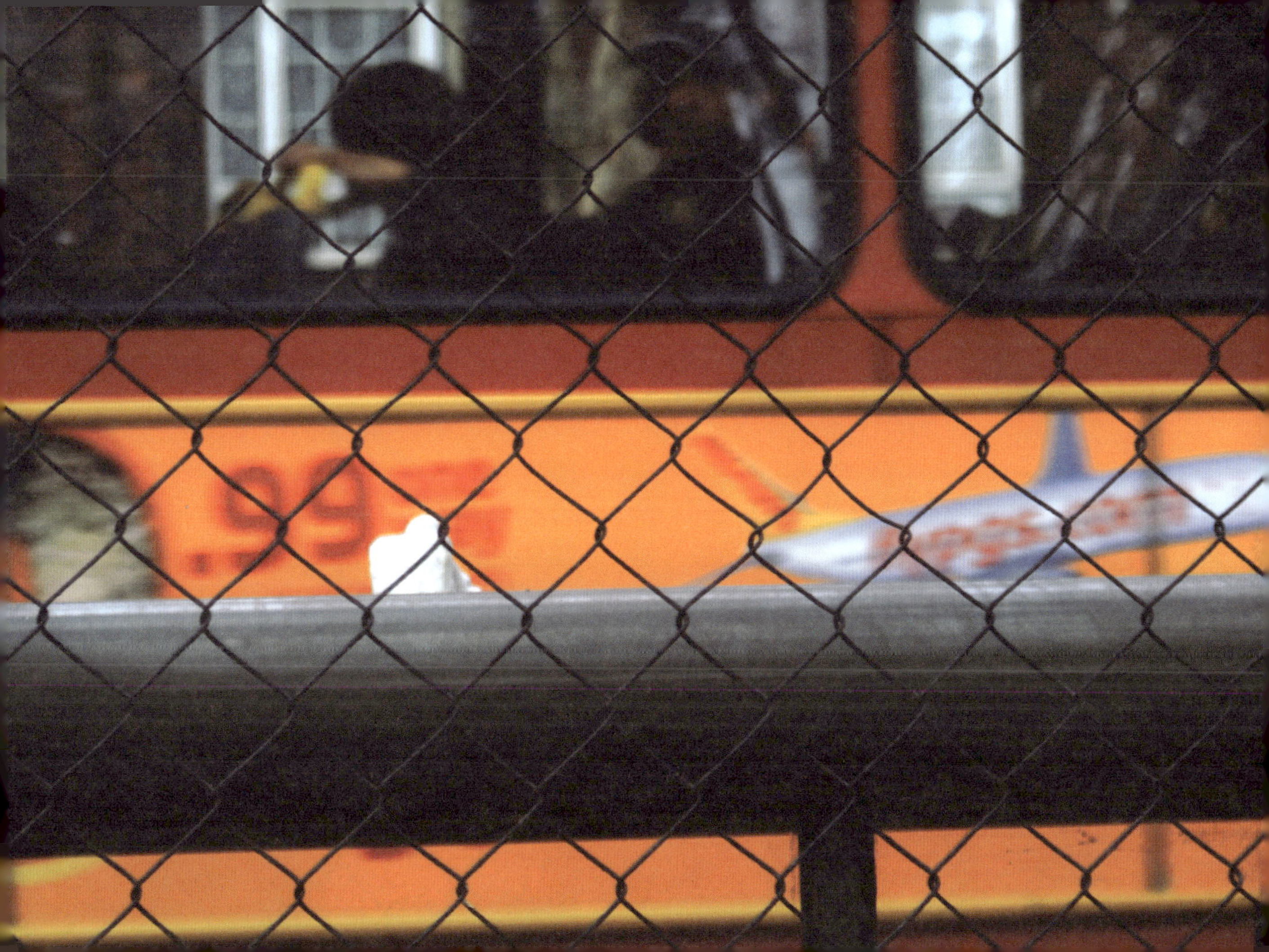

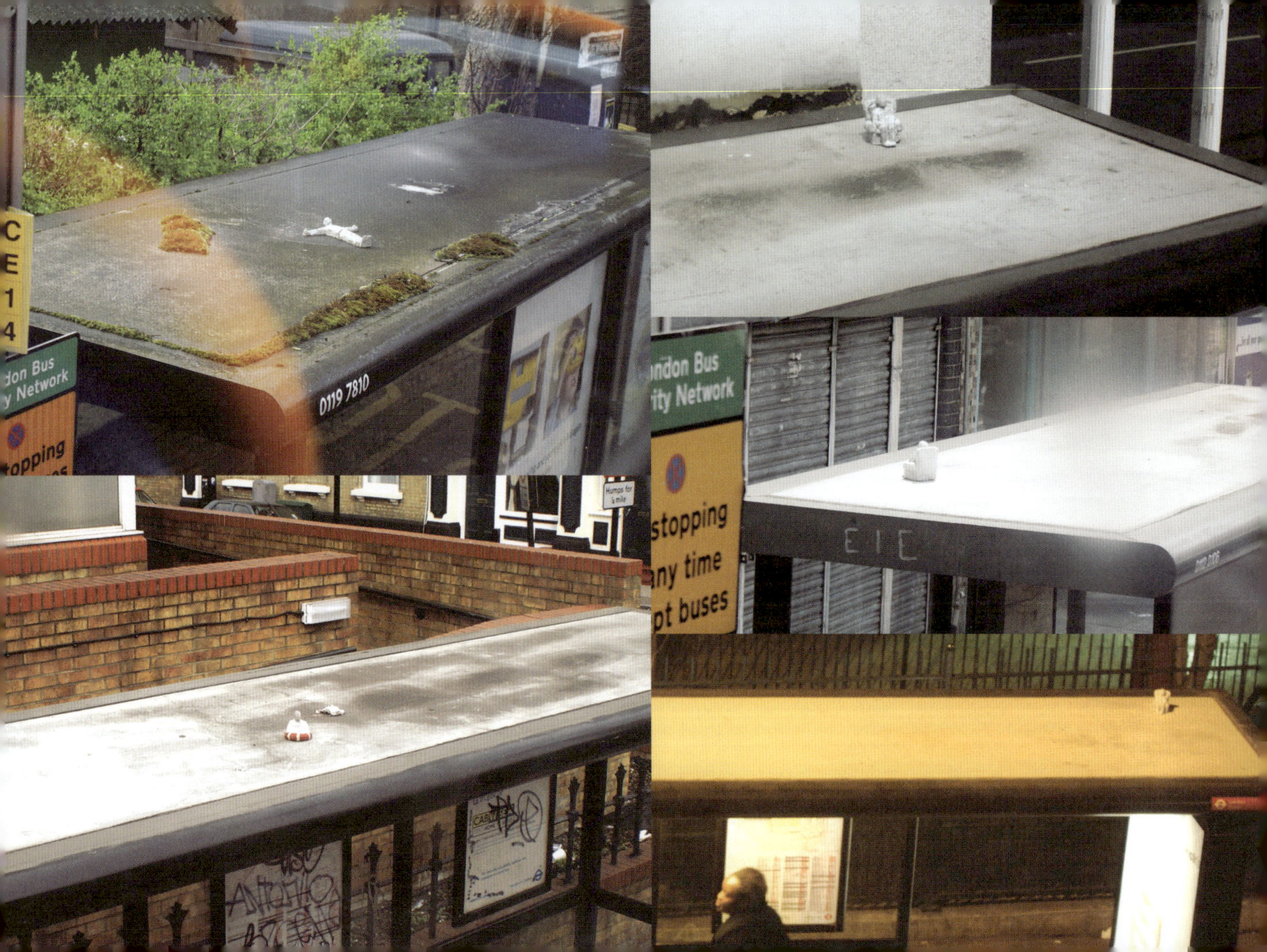
CE14
don Bus
y Network
topping
0119 7810
London Bus
rity Network
stopping
any time
pt buses
Humps for
¼ mile

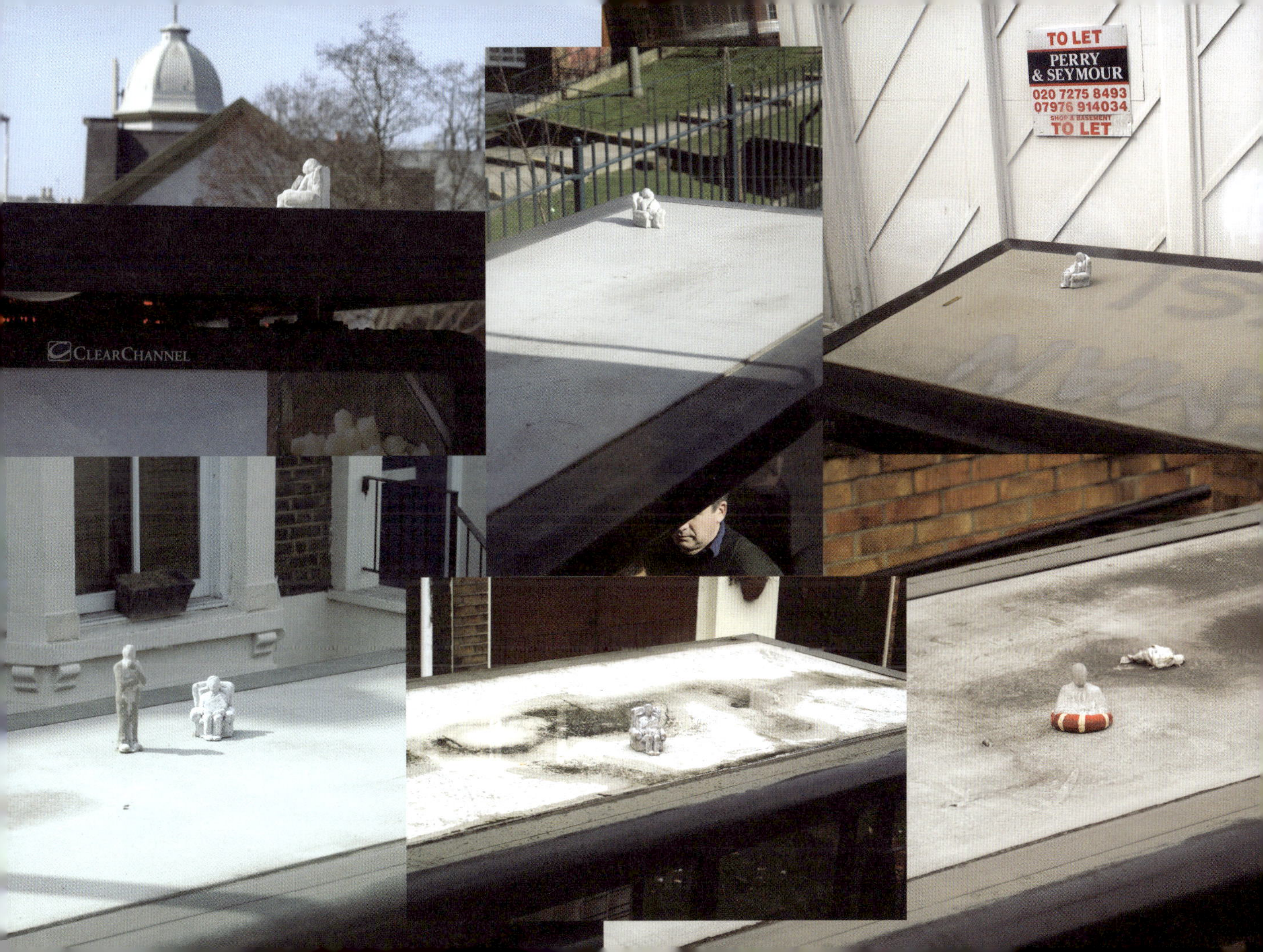

ClearChannel
TO LET
PERRY
& SEYMOUR
020 7275 8493
07976 914034
SHOP & BASEMENT
TO LET

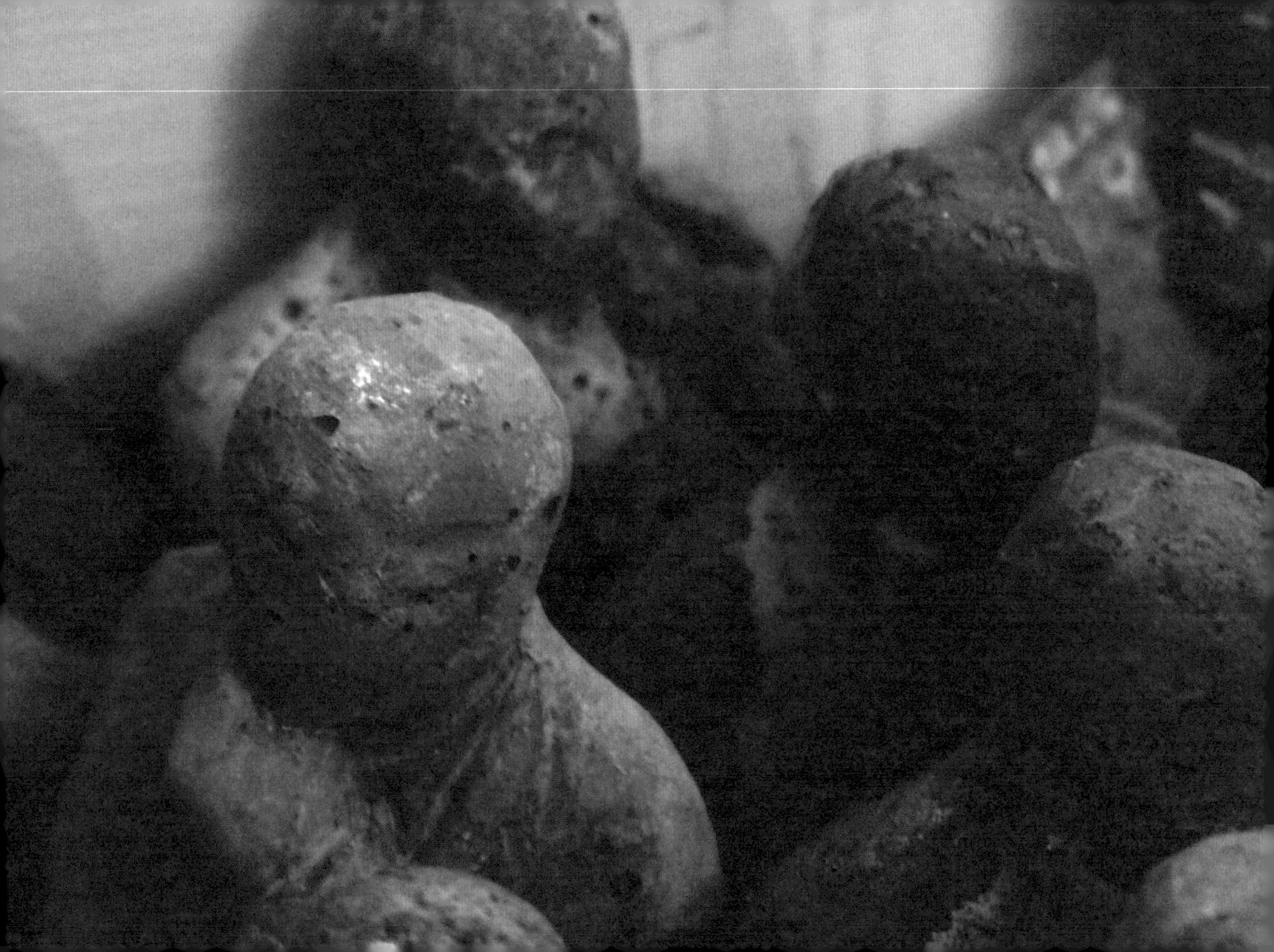

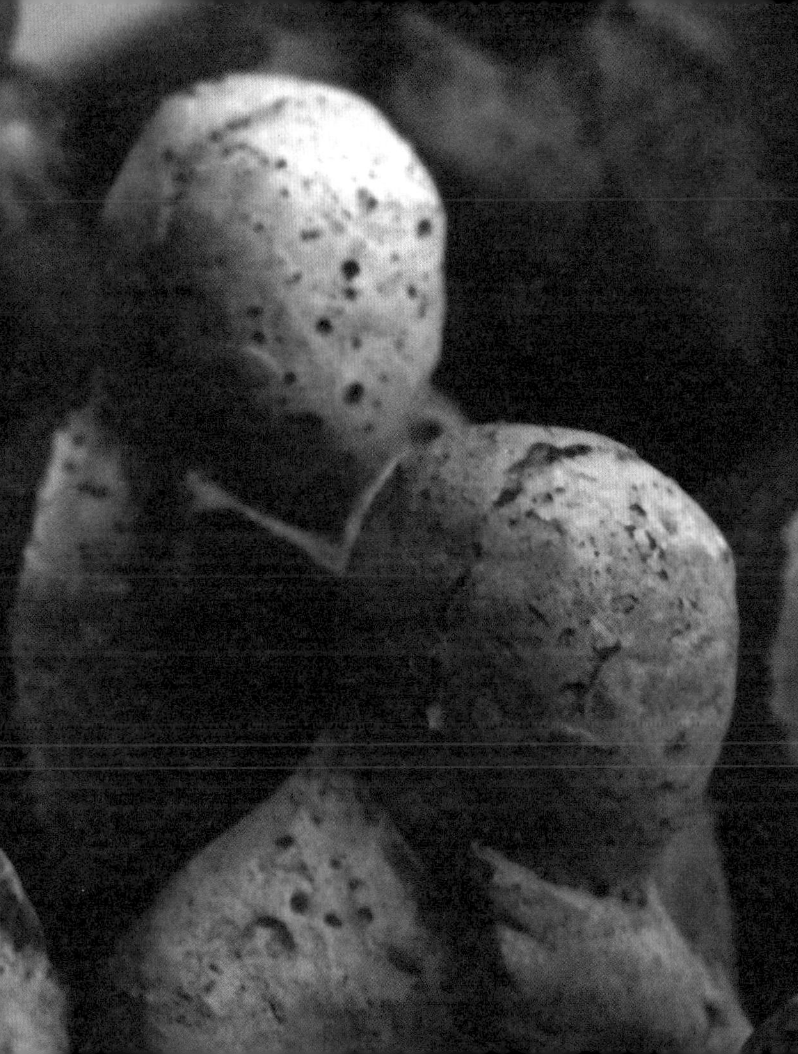

CREDITS

Thanks and hello to Gary Shove, Simon Ball, Esperanza Muñoz Torrero, Zai Thang, Marcos Juncal, Vanesa Díaz Otero, Valérie Mouton, Marco Farr and Estela Buján, Claude Crommelin, Sebastian Buck (Unurth), Pablo Casas, Rita Parente, Jorge Cortés, Iria and Bart, Tamara and Josue, Maria and Rudi, Rafa and Loli, Jan and Yoo Jae, Dean and Theresa, Rupert and Nathan, Joe and Catriona, Berio Molina, Chiu Longina and Hermi Basalo, Cris Lores, Ivan and Jose (Dismal), Esther Quintás, Edu and Marijana, Genetic Moo, Antía Sánchez, all in Alg-a.org, all in Atelier 210, Galería JM, Fundación Pedro Barrié de la Maza, Escola de Canteiros, Manuel Rial, Miguel Espada, Maureen Kinnear, all blogs and zines who wrote about Cement Eclipses, all my friends and family.

This book is dedicated to the memory of Javier and Marcos Barros.

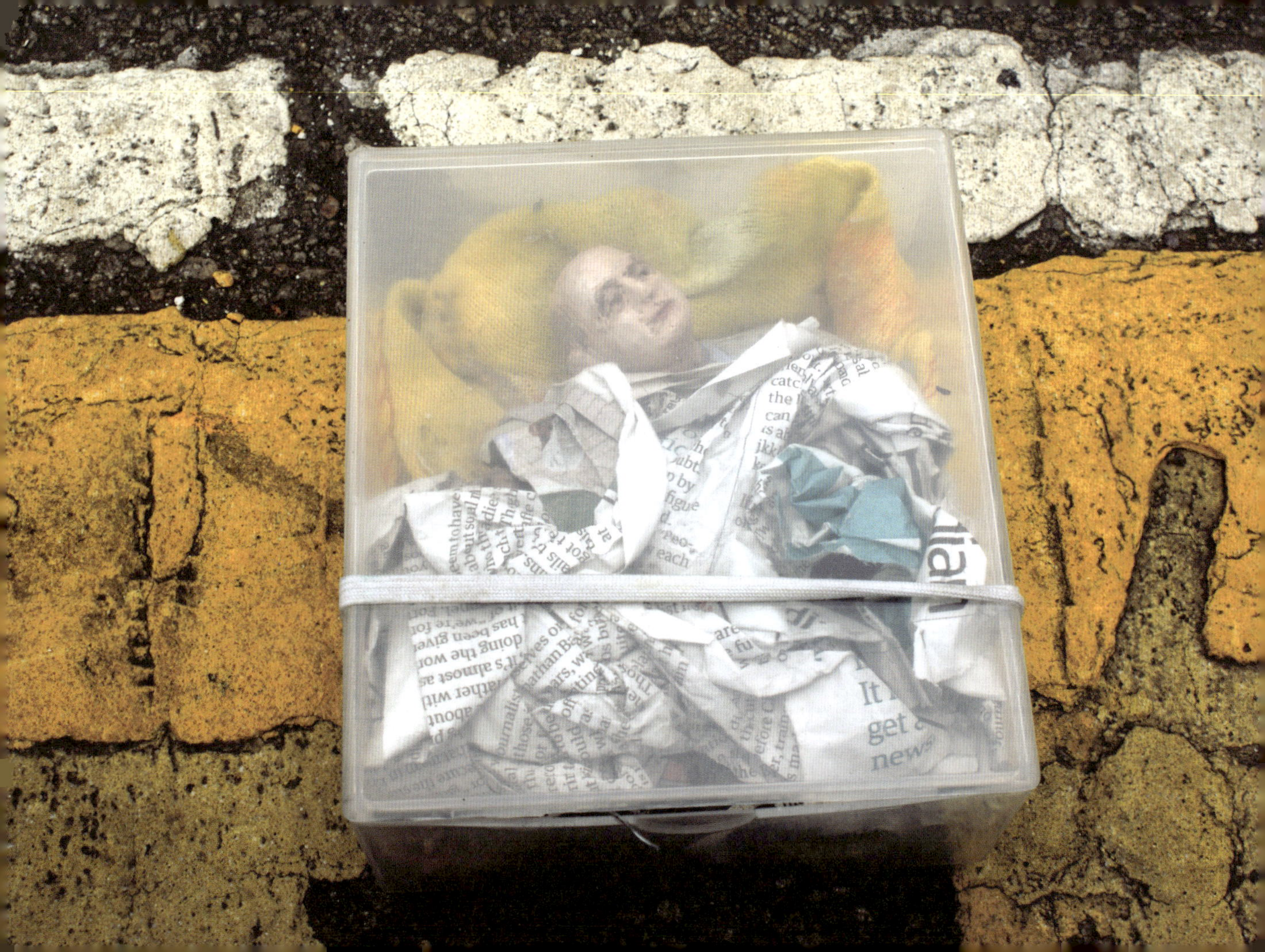